D1241378

REBELS RISING

Rebels Rising

Cities and the American Revolution

Benjamin L. Carp

OXFORD

UNIVERSITY PRESS

2007

OXFORD

UNIVERSITY PRESS

Oxford University Press, Inc., publishes works that further
Oxford University's objective of excellence
in research, scholarship, and education.

Oxford   New York
Auckland   Cape Town   Dar es Salaam   Hong Kong   Karachi
Kuala Lumpur   Madrid   Melbourne   Mexico City   Nairobi
New Delhi   Shanghai   Taipei   Toronto

With offices in
Argentina   Austria   Brazil   Chile   Czech Republic   France   Greece
Guatemala   Hungary   Italy   Japan   Poland   Portugal   Singapore
South Korea   Switzerland   Thailand   Turkey   Ukraine   Vietnam

Published by Oxford University Press, Inc.
198 Madison Avenue, New York, New York 10016

www.oup.com

Oxford is a registered trademark of Oxford University Press

Library of Congress Cataloging-in-Publication Data
Carp, Benjamin L.
Rebels rising : cities and the American Revolution / Benjamin L. Carp.
p. cm.
Includes bibliographical references and index.
ISBN 978-0-19-530402-2
1. United States—History—Revolution, 1775–1783—Social aspects. 2. Cities
and towns—United States—History—18th century. 3. City and town life—United
States—History—18th century. 4. United States—Social conditions—To 1865.
5. United States—History, Local. 6. Political participation—United States—
History—18th century. 7. United States—Politics and government—
1775–1783. I. Title.
E209.C33 2007
973.3'1091732—dc22   2007001802

9 8 7 6 5 4 3 2 1

Printed in the United States of America
on acid-free paper

For Peter Onuf
and for Robert and Jane Carp
Three cherished teachers

ACKNOWLEDGMENTS

I owe debts to many people for their various contributions to my work on this manuscript. First and foremost, I would like to dedicate this book to my adviser, Professor Peter S. Onuf. I arrived at the University of Virginia with Joanne Freeman's assurance that Professor Onuf was the greatest mentor on earth. In the ensuing years, he embodied the truth of her assertion with his insights, wit, candor, encouragement, and careful criticism. I can never thank him enough. I am also deeply indebted to the other members of my dissertation committee, Professors Gary W. Gallagher, Maurie D. McInnis, and the late Stephen Innes. All three were influential in myriad ways, as teachers and critics. Susan Ferber of Oxford University Press took an early interest in this project, and I have been grateful for her continued enthusiasm.

I have appreciated the contributions of the scholars and friends who commented on earlier versions of this manuscript. David Waldstreicher, Jane Kamensky, and a particularly heroic William A. Pencak each read through entire drafts, and their sharp comments helped me to improve the manuscript at crucial moments. Jon Butler and Louis Nelson also gave extensive assistance during the writing process. Elaine Forman Crane, S. Max Edelson, Eliga H. Gould, Derek S. Hoff, Joshua Kavaloski, Jason M. Opal, Joseph S. Tiedemann, Dell Upton, and Douglas L. Winiarski read earlier drafts of individual chapters and provided useful suggestions. I am also grateful to participants at various conferences where I presented chapters and at the lively seminars hosted by the McNeil Center for Early American Studies and the Omohundro Institute for Early American History and Culture.

Faculty members and graduate student colleagues in the Department of History at Virginia offered insightful critiques, especially participants in Ronald G. Dimberg's dissertation seminar, Edward L. Ayers's Southern seminar, and Michael F. Holt's thesis seminar. Members of the Early

American Seminar, under the auspices of Peter Onuf and Andrew Jackson O'Shaughnessy of the International Center for Jefferson Studies, bore with me patiently over the course of several chapters. Thanks to all of them for their helpful comments, especially those in and around my cohort: Laurie Hochstetler, Charles F. Irons, Johann N. Neem, Robert G. Parkinson, Katherine A. Pierce, Leonard J. Sadosky, and Brian Schoen.

I have twice benefited from the financial support of the Woodrow Wilson National Fellowship Foundation as a recipient of the Andrew W. Mellon Fellowship in Humanistic Studies (1998) and the Charlotte W. Newcombe Doctoral Dissertation Fellowship (2003). The University of Virginia offered a variety of forms of support, including a President's Fellowship. The Leverhulme Trust and the University of Edinburgh funded a research fellowship in 2005, and I used part of the time for the completion of this manuscript. I owe them a great deal of gratitude, and my fondness for the American historians at Edinburgh abides—thanks to Francis D. Cogliano, Alan F. Day, Owen Dudley Edwards, Rhodri Jeffreys-Jones, Robert Mason, and Mark Newman. Herbert Sloan and Eric Foner enabled me to conduct research at Columbia University during the fellowship year. Funding from Tufts University helped me to apply the finishing touches to the manuscript. The Department of History at Tufts has extended a warm welcome, and I am deeply grateful.

I have also received generous support from the following grants: the Massachusetts Society of the Cincinnati Fellowship from the Massachusetts Historical Society; the Price Visiting Research Fellowship from the William L. Clements Library; the Winterthur Fellowship from the Winterthur Museum, Garden and Library; the Kate B. and Hall J. Peterson Fellowship from the American Antiquarian Society; the W. M. Keck Foundation and Fletcher Jones Foundation Fellowship from the Huntington Library; the Barbara S. Mosbacher Fellowship from the John Carter Brown Library; the Gilder Lehrman Fellowship in American History for research at the New-York Historical Society; the American Society for Eighteenth Century Studies Fellowship for research at the Library Company of Philadelphia and the Historical Society of Pennsylvania; and the Andrew W. Mellon Foundation Library Resident Fellowship from the American Philosophical Society Library.

I am profoundly grateful for the research assistance I received from the staffs of each of the preceding libraries. In addition, I would like to thank the staffs at the Boston Public Library, the British Library, the Columbia University libraries, the Houghton Library at Harvard University, the Library of Congress, the Museum of the City of New York, the New York County Clerk's Office, the New York Genealogical and Biographical Society, the New York Public Library, the Newport Historical Society, the Public Record Office, the Rhode Island Historical Society, the South Carolina Historical Society, the South Carolina Room of the Charleston County Public Library, and Tisch Library at Tufts University. I would especially like to thank the staffs of Alderman Library, Clemons Library, Fiske Kimball Fine Arts Library, and the Albert and Shirley Small Special Collections Library at the University of Virginia, as well as the staff of the George Washington Papers. They have facilitated my research in countless ways. Thanks also to the institutions who provided image reproductions, and especially to Bronwyn Low and Aimee Saunders for their able assistance. I could not have finished this without them.

In my travels I have had the privilege of meeting and corresponding with a number of scholars who took the time to offer advice or references. These include Rohit T. Aggarwala, Jonathan M. Beagle, John L. Bell, George A. Billias, Patricia U. Bonomi, Carl P. Borick, Gretchen Buggeln, John E. Crowley, Stephen C. Bullock, Kenneth Cohen, Richard Drayton, Dan Finamore, Paul A. Gilje, Jack P. Greene, Sally Hadden, Kevin R. Hardwick, Paul D. Halliday, Tim Harris, Emma Hart, Ellen Hartigan-O'Connor, Bernard L. Herman, Benjamin J. Hinerfeld, Michael J. Jarvis, Joseph F. Kett, Albrecht Koschnik, Jesse Lemisch, Michelle Craig McDonald, Allan Megill, Matthew Mulcahy, Simon P. Newman, Marcus Rediker, Kym S. Rice, Thomas N. Rightmyer, Seth Rockman, Sophia A. Rosenfeld, John W. Shy, Christopher Sleeper, Barbara Clark Smith, Holly Snyder, Harry S. Stout, Jose Torre, Thomas M. Truxes, and Alfred F. Young. They deserve recognition for helping the wheels of scholarship turn.

I will conclude by honoring the memory of Itzolin Garcia, Stephen Innes, and Ann and Herman Rothblatt, who each brightened my world. Thanks also to the friends and family members whose kindnesses helped bring this manuscript about in a variety of ways: Anna Baker, George Boudreau, Herb and Selma Carp, Jay Dixit, Eliot and Tyra Duhan, Elizabeth Dunn, Joel Hafvenstein, Amy Kuras, Jessica Leshnower, Jonathan Marr, Damon May, Carlos Mena, Steve Mooney, Janice and Ken Negin, Daniel Negin, Adam Raviv, Jennifer and Derek Roth Gordon, Rachel Rothblatt, Richard Rothblatt, Robert and Sharon Rothblatt, Jeffrey Shih, Jill and Brian Sowell, Juliet and Bram Spector, and Clifton Stubblefield. I must also thank a remarkable run of wonderful teachers, from Hewlett-Woodmere Public Schools through Yale University to the University of Virginia. Finally, I offer my everlasting love and thanks to my brothers, Brian and David, and my parents, Robert and Jane, who make it all possible. This book is also dedicated to my parents, who are still my greatest teachers.

CONTENTS

REBELS RISING

INTRODUCTION

Political Mobilization in the Urban Landscape

In the cities of eighteenth-century America, any two people might know one another. The populations of the largest colonial cities numbered in the tens of thousands, not millions, and the inhabitants lived in compact, concentrated settlements clustered at the tips of islands or peninsulas. Houses were low to the ground and crowded together—their close proximity characterized them as much as anything else.[1] The people of these cities also felt much closer to the rivers and harbors—their main avenues of transportation and trade—that flowed beside them. When they craned their necks, the highest things they saw were ships' masts and church steeples, along with the occasional tower atop a public building.

City dwellers jostled one another in the streets, dodging pigs and reckless wagons. They haggled with one another in the shops and in the marketplace, hauled goods from ships' holds to warehouses and back again, saw the law handed down in the assemblies and courthouses, and prayed in places of worship. On occasion, large crowds might gather for a parade or celebration, or a riot or a hanging. The cities of British America, like other cities around the world, were shared places where people came together.

If one looks more closely at the ways people moved through the cities, however, this sense of community begins to crumble. For some, the city represented boundless opportunities. A wealthy merchant or lawyer could saunter forth from his mansion and find comfortable seating in a number of locations—in the carriage he rode around town, in the pew he owned at church, in the upscale tavern where he met to debate philosophy, or perhaps even in the Assembly where he helped make decisions for the rest of the colony. A gentleman such as this could also find comfort at the local mercantile exchange, library, playhouse, or pleasure garden. A middle-class retailer or artisan would not usually have access to such luxury.

He might own a shop or a marketplace stall, and attend periodic meetings of the local Freemasons or fire company. If he accumulated enough wealth, he might strive to own a pew or a substantial dwelling. For others, the city was divided up into walls, locked doors, and restricted areas. A laboring person might wake up in a rented room of a modest dwelling, go to work at the docks or a cobbler's shop, knock back a dram of rum at a seedy grogshop, and perhaps find solace praying in the galleries of a wooden church on Sundays. When such people fell behind in payments or stole for sustenance, a workhouse or prison would limit their movements even more.

Women of any class never held seats of legislative or judicial power, and belonged to no tavern associations, but they still maintained a vigorous presence as buyers and sellers in the marketplace, patrons of fashion and culture, mistresses of the household, workers in and out of the home, and communicants at church. A black slave, or even a free black person, was more limited in the places where he or she could go, especially after dark—nevertheless, blacks saw much of the city as they used the side entrances of white-owned properties, gathered in illegal taverns known as "disorderly houses," met for religious worship (often relegated to the worst seating in churches), worked or traded around the city, and slept in garrets and outbuildings.

James Hamilton, a governor of Pennsylvania, once claimed that "he formerly knew every person white & black men women, & children, in the City of Philadelphia, by name," though by 1775 this was no longer the case.[2] Whether they were neighbors or strangers, city people interacted in meaningful ways. They met in back rooms and plotted political tactics. They cornered each other in taverns and debated the issues of the day. They heard politically charged sermons, and their prayers took on political significance. They confronted one other on the wharves and in the streets. The authorities placed restrictions on liberty and ordered executions, while masters had the power to grant freedom or send slaves out of town and away from their families. Even people's consumer choices came under scrutiny.[3]

Because they had such tight concentrations of people (see appendix 1) and such a pluralistic mixture of inhabitants and newcomers, the largest cities offered fertile ground for political consciousness, political persuasion, and political action. After 1763, Americans noticed that the British Empire was enforcing commercial regulations, enacting new taxes, challenging the power of provincial assemblies, limiting westward expansion, and establishing firmer secular and ecclesiastical authority over the colonies. As a result, American dissatisfaction with the empire erupted during the 1760s and 1770s, and Americans began to see the imperial government as an oppressor rather than a protector. Connected economically and politically, city dwellers had always depended on one another for their livelihoods. Now American city dwellers found that they depended on one another for their independence as well. The cities' panoply of interdependent groups would need to work together to mobilize against the mother country.

The residents of the cities drew upon their turbulent history of charged political action, and they were the first to voice their discontent. In the cities, merchants began meeting to discuss the repercussions of new laws, printers fired off provocative pamphlets and newspaper articles, and protesters took to the streets. During the dozen years before the Declaration of Independence, city dwellers developed a political awareness of imperial proportions and organized to perform a series of political acts: mass meetings, petition signings, tea protests, boycotts, bonfires, and riots.[4] Together with their rural neighbors, they formed coalitions in defense of their rights and interests. Through this process, Americans began to imagine themselves as an independent national community. Ultimately, many of them rebelled against Parliament and the Crown; yet the coalitions that organized for rebellion were also shaky. The electric political atmosphere gave city dwellers the opportunity not just to unite but also to negotiate their differences.

This heightened political awareness and the collaborative political action it inspired were most evident in the prerevolutionary cities. An exploration of political mobilization is crucial for understanding the key developments of the late colonial period and the nature of the colonists' resistance to Great Britain. *Mobilization* represents the difference between reading a fiery pamphlet and acting on it—the difference between a peaceful, orderly, obedient city and a city filled with active, organized groups attending tense meetings or engaging in violent acts. By focusing on some of the most cataclysmic events of the eighteenth century as they unfolded in the most dynamic places in Anglo-America, I argue in *Rebels Rising* that city dwellers coalesced into civic communities, defined the boundaries of their community, and contended with the challenges inherent in social and political change. Revolutionary mobilization contained within it new challenges to local authority, as well as the broader challenge to imperial authority. These various forms of urban mobilization during this period helped make the Revolution possible.[5]

Traditional studies of political mobilization during the Revolutionary era focus on rebellious action within colonial institutions and new, "extralegal" structures, such as the Sons of Liberty, committees of correspondence, or crowds.[6] This book builds on these works by examining the ways in which city dwellers persuaded one another and cooperated with one another in a variety of everyday settings. The participants in revolutionary political mobilization required resolutions to questions of home rule and independence, as well as the questions of democratization and social change. Americans would not settle such contentious issues in just a pamphlet, in an assembly, in a meeting, or in a riot; they would have to search for answers by negotiating on many fronts at once. The cities were crucial for the successful mobilization of a broad Patriot coalition; at the same time, the cities presented a complex and unpredictable setting for the formation of alliances.

Historians have noted instances of revolutionary mobilization in small towns, where life was simpler, where people knew their leaders and had long-standing relationships with one another. While rural villages and towns (where most Americans lived) were small enough to embody their residents' will, this was much more difficult in cities, where populations, politics, and alignments shifted constantly.[7] The cities therefore provide the best laboratories for observing and understanding the nature of political mobilization during the American Revolution. The inhabitants of the American cities were more directly connected with the empire than other colonists, so for them the stakes were higher during the imperial crisis.

Only five cities in the thirteen rebellious colonies had more than 9,000 people by 1775, and each was the most important economic, political, and social hub in its province. These were Boston, Massachusetts; Newport, Rhode Island; New York, New York; Philadelphia, Pennsylvania; and Charleston, South Carolina.[8] During the eighteenth century, these cities had grown from small towns to flourishing commercial centers in just a few generations. The rapid progress of the cities was remarkable— Philadelphia had become the largest city in British America in less than a century. The cities owed their growth partly to physical advantages that encouraged trade: deep harbors, access to rivers, and robust hinterlands. They had developed specialized economic functions and crafts, and each had multiple taverns, public buildings, houses of worship, sophisticated entertainment, and intellectual opportunities. Their populations displayed a wide array of religious beliefs (and degrees of religious belief), ethnic and racial backgrounds, and social gradations. Urban associations and intercity alliances generated social capital that enabled the American cities to meet economic and political challenges such as war, depression, debt, taxation, and imperial unrest.[9]

While they had grown into vibrant, exciting metropolises in their own right, the American provincial cities were also part of a larger British imperial system. London remained the metropolis for every subject of the British Empire. Americans took their social and cultural cues from London, the pound sterling remained the ultimate source of specie, Parliament had the power to overturn their laws, and the colonists swore all oaths to the king. The American cities had a distinctive role as way stations of the British Empire, and they would also become the hubs of the revolutionary movement. Their role in the empire is crucial, therefore, for understanding the actions of city dwellers in the eighteenth century.

The cities were primarily important to the empire as centers of trade.[10] Here it becomes difficult to generalize about the cities, since each meant different things to the British Empire, and each was subject to competition, slumps, and other economic factors. The American export trade relied upon the cities: Boston built ships for trade and exported fish, potash, and whale oil; New York and Philadelphia sent wheat, flour, beef, and pork to the Caribbean and elsewhere; Newport was a key nexus for the trade of molasses, rum, and slaves; and Charleston exported rice and indigo to Great Britain. Of course, the rural countryside was crucial to the production of agricultural products, but the cities were the hubs of trade and transport. Not all of America's valuable exports needed cities—tobacco trading, for instance, was largely concentrated in Britain and had no American entrepôt of its own.

The largest cities' mills, tanneries, distilleries, and sugar refineries also helped process goods, while urban artisans produced goods for regional markets. In the realm of finance, underwriters and brokers allowed for more efficient deployment of capital. At the same time, transatlantic merchants in the American cities relied on credit from London or Liverpool, or were sometimes employees of British firms. In times of economic contraction, these credit relationships left the cities particularly vulnerable. If British merchants decided to call in their debts, such a decision could send waves of financial hardship through the cities, from American merchants down to the customers who were in turn indebted to them.

All of the cities also played a vital role in importing goods. Tea, textiles, wine, ceramics, glassware, metalware, and hundreds of other commodities washed ashore for urban consumption, for reexport to other towns, and for sale to the countryside. Though precise measurement is difficult, cities no doubt took in a disproportionate share of consumer goods. Each city teemed with wealthy customers engaging in a conspicuous, competitive display of consumption that reached downward toward the middle classes. The cities also keenly felt one of the great economic grievances of the pre-revolutionary decades—competition from British exporters who undersold American merchants. Under the Navigation Acts, some "enumerated" commodities could travel only between the colonies and England, while other goods freely traveled among American cities as part of the coastal trade, or to other parts of the world. At the same time, smugglers operated within shadowy commercial networks, bringing sugar from foreign ports or delivering tea to the various inlets and coves along the American coasts. Finally, the cities were significant places of exchange for the trade in laborers, indentured and enslaved as well as free.[11]

Political power concentrated in the largest cities. Boston, New York, Philadelphia, and Charleston were not only the largest population centers in their respective colonies but also the seats of the governor, supreme judiciary, and legislature for these colonies. Some colonies, such as Rhode Island and New Jersey, had multiple (even competing) centers of government. In other colonies, such as Virginia and Maryland, other cities dwarfed the political power centers in size and economic importance. The inhabitants of commercial and administrative centers like Boston and Charleston came face to face with the constant reminder that they belonged to an empire that governed them. Royally appointed governors, as well as customs officials from the Treasury, became familiar figures in these cities. Many city dwellers had close political connections to the British Empire, and substantial groups of them supported the king and Parliament during the imperial crisis. It would take a great deal of political mobilization for the city dwellers to decide to cut themselves loose from the empire.

These cities commanded spheres of cultural and economic influence that reached beyond colonial boundaries to take in entire slices of the Atlantic coast.[12] They pulled the empire together as centers of communication and transportation. As entrepôts for transatlantic shipping and coastal trade, as postal distribution points and travel hubs, their taverns and exchanges were conduits for written and oral communication of ideas, news, goods, and cultures from every direction of the compass. Boston, New York, Philadelphia, and Charleston all had multiple printers, who digested and distributed news from around the world to city dwellers and to the countryside. Religious denominations took advantage of cities, too—influential ministers often used large and wealthy urban congregations as a base of operations, and cities provided convenient places for Presbyterian Synods, Quaker Yearly Meetings, colleges, revival meetings, and the dissemination of printed sermons and tracts. Communities of faith also tapped these religious networks to exchange information, establish trade connections, facilitate migration, raise money, and advocate their shared interests. Other social and cultural networks, from the horse-racing circuit to the American Philosophical Society, engendered a shared language and identity, while also bringing people together for recreational pursuits, scientific inquiry, and the arts. Unsurprisingly, the seventeenth-century founders of the American settlements had believed that establishing cities would ensure that the colonies remained civilized.[13]

The colonial cities' military value was mixed. Military recruiters often found sailors (sometimes forcibly, a practice known as impressment) and soldiers in American cities. All the cities built fortifications (though they often neglected their upkeep), and in times of war or colonial unrest, Boston's Castle William or New York's Fort George might serve as barracks for British redcoats or headquarters for important military commanders. A stronghold overlooking the mouth of the Delaware or Hudson river, or guarding Massachusetts or Narragansett bay, or glowering southward and westward from the Carolina coast, provided the British Empire with some strategic advantage. Nevertheless, the British military presence was always stronger in the port towns of the Caribbean and the areas that became Canada. The warships of the Royal Navy found safe harbor in American cities and also found them to be fruitful targets for customs interdiction. Still, after midcentury, Halifax, Nova Scotia, was more important than any of the American cities for the outfitting and repair of warships.[14]

Given these realities, how did the imperial leaders in London regard the American cities? On the whole, British imperial leaders were able to take the cities for granted. After all, the colonies were thousands of miles distant from London. Compared to the influence of provincial cities like Bristol and Liverpool on British politics, and compared to the economic importance of Caribbean sugar, Newfoundland fisheries, and Chesapeake tobacco, the colonial cities barely registered.[15] Contemporary British officials generally did not think about these cities as distinct from the colonies, or from "America" as a whole. Still, during the imperial crisis, British leaders offered hints of their deep investment in the idea that American cities were inferior to the London metropolis. The British economist and clergyman Dr. Josiah Tucker imagined "Vice-Roys sent over from . . . Philadelphia, or New York, or at some other *American* imperial city" to rule over the British, and concluded, "The *English* would rather submit to a *French* yoke, than to an *American*; as being the lesser Indignity of the two."[16] The British found the cities useful as outposts of empire; at the same time, they expected their colonial inhabitants to demonstrate due obedience to Crown and Parliament.

From the eastern side of the Atlantic, the cities may have seemed insignificant, but in America the cities had a disproportionately large influence on the surrounding countryside. War, economic shifts, new legislation, and news from around the globe flowed into the urban seaports before they reached upriver to rural places. As a result, American cities became the first places to feel the effects of imperial policies. As another historian of the colonial cities argued half a century ago, these five cities played a crucial "preparatory" role in the coming of the Revolution, as population centers where leaders, crowds, and events conjoined. These cities were often the generators of revolutionary thought and action—they nurtured the Enlightenment in the New World, they helped unleash the dynamic forces of republicanism, they developed a burgeoning sense of American nationality, and they succeeded in spreading their views to the rural hinterlands.[17] Later historians added the idea that the cities also sparked internal upheaval, including religious revivals, economic disorder, and class conflict.[18] Whether we argue that the American Revolution was radical in its overthrow of British government or radical in its inflammation of internal struggle, the American cities were undeniably important as sites of radical change.[19]

This study takes as its starting point the 1740s, a decade of change and unrest across North America and the Atlantic world. Great Britain declared war on Spain in October 1739, the War of Jenkins' Ear. The ensuing War of the Austrian Succession in Europe, known in North America as King George's War, also brought the French and British into conflict from 1744 to 1748. The war devastated Boston, which sent many of its young men into combat. New York, however, grew fat off the profits of privateers, private vessels commissioned to prey upon enemy vessels. Philadelphia did not participate as much in musters or privateering, but during this period it swelled with new immigrants and prospered from its trade with the West

Indies. The cities matured and (except in the case of Boston) grew. As Americans grew wealthier, they began to demand a wider selection of consumer goods. Urban shops and warehouses filled with new merchandise.[20]

Meanwhile, the leadership of Sir Robert Walpole in Parliament had ended in 1742. Walpole had permitted a colonial policy of what Edmund Burke would later call "salutary neglect," largely allowing the American colonies to govern themselves. Under Lord Halifax, the Board of Trade in 1748 began working to establish regular transatlantic mail service to New York City. The board demanded that colonial laws conform to royal instructions, and it began cooking up ways to extract more revenue from the colonies. Such developments were ominous portents for the cities.[21]

Other events helped to make the 1740s a particularly turbulent decade for the cities. The influential itinerant preacher George Whitefield first toured the American seaports from 1739 to 1741, heralding the beginning of a wave of religious revivals. In 1740 a major fire swept through Charleston, destroying hundreds of buildings. In 1741 black New Yorkers burned Fort George and several other buildings in an alleged conspiracy that resulted in more than thirty executions. Philadelphia witnessed a contentious election riot in 1742. Major conflicts over the Royal Navy's impressment of local seamen took place in Boston throughout the 1740s, culminating in three days of rioting in 1747. This event inspired Samuel Adams to begin writing for the radical *Independent Advertiser*, one of many newspapers that challenged the authority of government in the years following the celebrated 1735 trial of John Peter Zenger in New York.[22]

During the Seven Years' War (or French and Indian War), which began in North America in 1754, military contracts and wartime privateering brought prosperity to the cities, but the end of the conflict sank the seaports into a deep economic depression. British decisions surrounding the 1763 Treaty of Paris indicated that the security of the seacoast colonies was the empire's first priority. British statesmen believed Benjamin Franklin's assurances that the colonies would not develop their own manufacturing, and his confidence that the fractious colonies could never unite against the mother country. Ironically, although Great Britain had articulated its war aims with the continental American colonies in mind, its subsequent decisions appeared to take the colonists' dependence on the empire for granted. Imperial policy following the Seven Years' War made life harder for the seacoast cities, as well as for Americans who hoped to move west following the removal of the French threat.[23]

The Seven Years' War, while bathing Great Britain in military glory, had saddled the British Empire with crippling debts and massive troop commitments in the trans-Appalachian West. Parliament therefore began to enforce existing customs duties and to levy new duties on colonial traders to pay for the conflict and the postwar settlement. In trying to earn a return on its investment in the American colonies, Parliament made itself deeply unpopular in America. These new laws concerning trade and navigation, when coupled with the depression that followed the war, struck the cities' inhabitants as a particular hardship, as did naval impressment and the quartering of peacetime garrisons in American cities. The colonists, with their fiercely independent legislatures and proud dissenting traditions, were dismayed to find that Parliament was no longer willing to treat them with the "salutary neglect" that they had enjoyed for most of the eighteenth century. Americans began to fear for their pocketbooks, their liberties, and their lives.

The imperial crisis unfolded in a series of actions and reactions, which are best understood as three periods of controversy: the Stamp Act crisis, the Townshend Acts crisis, and the crisis surrounding the Tea Act and Intolerable Acts. Each crisis forced city dwellers to confront difficult choices that would determine their own fate and that of the world beyond.[24]

Three acts in 1764 and 1765, coupled with more rigid customs enforcement, spawned the first crisis. The Sugar Act altered the restrictions and duties on foreign rum and molasses and mandated more rigorous procedures for the customs service. The Currency Act prohibited colonial issues of paper money. The Stamp Act levied taxes on court documents (including attorneys' licenses), ship clearances, college degrees, land deeds and land grants, mortgages and leases, contracts, bonds, articles of apprenticeship and appointment to public office, liquor licenses, playing cards and dice, pamphlets, newspapers, advertisements, and almanacs. All such items required stamped paper, which the Treasury Office would distribute through its appointees in the colonies. These new laws particularly affected urban Americans, including merchants, brokers, mariners, distillers, lawyers, taverngoers, newspaper printers, and local officials. In 1766, Parliament repealed the Stamp Act, while also passing a Declaratory Act that affirmed Parliament's right to legislate for the colonies "in all Cases whatsoever." Finally, the Revenue Act of 1766 included further restrictions on the trade of sugar and other commodities, designed to help British merchants and manufacturers, as well as West Indian planters, at the expense of American merchants and consumers.

Charles Townshend, as chancellor of the exchequer, initiated the second crisis with a series of new laws in 1767. A new Revenue Act levied duties on paper, lead, painters' colors, glass, and tea. In addition, Parliament expanded the power of the vice-admiralty courts in America and created an American Board of Customs Commissioners, which took up its headquarters in Boston in November 1767. Colonial assemblies began urging a united stand against Townshend's program, and in the meantime legislatures in New York and South Carolina clashed with Parliament over the quartering of troops and the use of provincial funds. The presence of troops in Boston and New York ultimately led to violence in 1770, the same year that Parliament repealed all the Townshend duties except one.

This remaining duty ultimately precipitated the final crisis that led to the American Revolution. The Tea Act of 1773 reaffirmed the tax on tea while giving significant commercial advantages to the monopolistic (and nearly bankrupt) East India Company. By effectively lowering the price of tea, the new law threatened to seduce Americans into paying the duty. Tea ships sailed for Boston, New York, Philadelphia, and Charleston, and in each city, the inhabitants destroyed the tea, turned back the ships, or stored the tea unsold.

An outraged British ministry passed a series of acts in Parliament "for reestablishment of lawful authority" in Massachusetts, which the colonists called the "Intolerable Acts" of 1774. The Boston Port Act closed the city's harbor beginning June 1. The Massachusetts Government Act amended the colony's charter, giving the king greater powers to appoint several types of officials. The Administration of Justice Act allowed royal officials to stand trial outside of Massachusetts if accused of certain crimes. The Quartering Act, which applied to all the colonies, allowed governors to demand quarters for soldiers in uninhabited buildings. Though Parliament had aimed most of these acts at Massachusetts, colonists throughout North America saw them as dangerous precedents for the subversion of constitutional rights and liberties. Bostonians became martyrs suffering for the cause of all America. Americans sent aid to the blockaded city, and twelve colonies sent delegates to the first Continental Congress at Philadelphia in September 1774. These delegates proclaimed the Intolerable Acts unconstitutional and called for a boycott of British goods.

The objections, meetings, and disturbances that followed these imperial actions became impossible to ignore. During the years leading up to the Revolution, the mobilization of people from all social ranks was particularly intense in the urban centers. Because these populous polities were the loci of economic activity and government, they sharply felt the effects of imperial policies. As enforcement of the Navigation Acts and Quartering Acts became vital to the British Empire, American cities increasingly became the headquarters of the customs officials, vice-admiralty judges, naval and military officers, and governors who tried to ensure that city dwellers complied with imperial policies.

The cities also became the flashpoints for legislative protests, committee meetings, massive outdoor gatherings, intercolonial collaboration, newspaper harangues, boycotts, customs evasion, military-civilian violence, and riots. As centers for communication and social life, the cities were the hubs for the transmission of information and recruitment during times of crisis. Eighteenth-century urban political culture flowed through multiple avenues of communication, association, and social interaction—everything from the press to the streets, taverns, and churches.[25] The cities provided places for people to interact, and the imperial crisis accelerated such interactions and stimulated a variety of revolutionary transformations.[26] Americans faced choices about their identity, loyalty, and course of action, and they made their decisions about the revolutionary conflict in an environment of circulating ideas, arguments, and beliefs.

This environment was what scholars of architectural history call the "cultural landscape." City dwellers acted and moved within and among this cultural landscape: the cities' buildings, the spaces between them, and the material objects within them. City dwellers had helped to create, define, and explain their physical surroundings, based on their cultural backgrounds, values, and metaphors. The urban landscape hosted formal, ordinary activities such as court proceedings, ceremonies, and economic exchange, as well as informal or unexpected activities such as riots, smuggling, or clandestine meetings. In addition, city dwellers' use of certain spatial metaphors also revealed their political mindset, such as calling the empire a household. As British policies threatened to transform the cities, Americans' expressions and actions reflected their choices and anxieties. The Revolution changed Americans' understanding of their urban landscapes and the cities' relationship to the Atlantic system.[27]

The urban landscape helped to set the parameters of political mobilization and social change. While John Adams famously said, "the revolution was in the minds and hearts of the people," it is also correct to say that the Revolution took root in Americans' homes, streets, and public buildings.[28] As American city dwellers began to participate in politics on a broad scale, they developed a new brand of political culture. Although they had incongruent, even conflicting goals and motivations, they needed to achieve some degree of common ground in order to launch a large-scale rebellion. The dynamic commercial centers gave people the opportunity to discuss their common purposes and negotiate their disparate interests.

The cities offered several challenges to would-be revolutionaries. First, they needed to wade through the pluralistic urban environment and overcome any tendencies toward a civic impasse. Second, social unrest forced city dwellers to define the limits of mobilization. Third, rebels clashed directly with government countermobilization. Fourth, the cities would have to communicate with one another and with the rural hinterlands. The revolutionaries' attempts to overcome these challenges highlight the cities' significance for the study of political mobilization.

As their first challenge, revolutionaries needed to enlist the cooperation of the diverse range of groups that made up the pluralistic cities. City dwellers in the eighteenth century were not physically separated from one another. Residential clustering by religion or ethnicity was insignificant. Clustering by wealth became more common by the end of the eighteenth century, while clustering by occupation seems to have been the strongest trend. Cities offered increased economic opportunity and economic mobility to their inhabitants, even as the yawning disparity between the wealthy and the poor also stimulated envy and resentment. A mixture of races and ethnicities fostered assimilation and cultural exchange, as well as conflict and repression. The presence of different religions encouraged pluralism and tolerance, as well as more strident delineations of doctrinal differences. Diversity provided city dwellers with a degree of flexibility and freedom, while forcing them to articulate their differences or negotiate a common ground.[29]

A civic impasse might also result, however, from suspicion, disagreement, or apathy among Americans. Radicals emerge in societies all the time, after all, and in many cases (when authorities do not stamp out such radicalism immediately), the complacent majority will laugh or brush them off, and go about their business. Even when the threat to a person's livelihood or liberty is real, he or she may not feel willing or able to risk joining, or identifying with, a political coalition. City dwellers had to learn new forms of behavior to overcome their inactivity and their differences, and mobilize in support of a new and radical political movement.

City dwellers had to invent their own mechanisms of political mobilization, since Great Britain had established no institutions in the colonies for making decisions or resolving conflicts, and colonists had no legal means other than petitions (indirectly through London interest groups, or directly through their agents) to influence the British government—and the influence of these appeals was declining.[30] Such petitions illustrated the bonds of dependence within the larger empire, but the cities had their own internal networks of dependence as well, and they turned these networks into tools of mobilization. The notion of dependence often connoted inferiority, as when city dwellers were employees or debtors, apprentices or slaves, women or children, political clients, devotees of God, or deferential to their social betters.[31] Yet city dwellers depended on one another in so many ways that "interdependence" is a better word for characterizing urban life. As they grew, the largest North American cities developed a sense of interdependence: civic consciousness, civic responsibility, and civic power. When threats arose, revolutionaries could harness this civic awareness in the service of resistance and revolt.[32]

Colonial urban Americans came to have a distinct sense of the public good and began to recognize the value of communal action. People from all ranks could embody this communal spirit: "city fathers" in positions of social, economic, and political power; "middling" organizations such as fire companies, militia companies, or benevolent associations; and the "lower sort" in the form of crowd action. In this book I will show how a civic consciousness developed among Boston's waterfront community, New York taverngoers, Newport congregations, Charleston's elite patriarchy, and the gatherings in Philadelphia's State House Yard. Certainly, urban coalitions were often fragile or fleeting. Nevertheless, the development of such alliances for the public good, in accordance with republican principles, contributed to Americans' sustained resistance to Great Britain. These interactions helped to overcome the turgid inactivity of civic impasse.[33]

The formation of consensus was not always easy, and the civic community rarely acted as an organic whole. As city dwellers mobilized against the British, they faced a second challenge when they found their coalitions unstable and subject to various forms of dissent. Women, antislavery advocates, white mechanics, blacks, seamen, and other groups separately (and sometimes jointly) spoke and acted with regard to the social inequalities they faced or specific social grievances. These grievances occasionally threatened to undermine and distract the Patriot coalition from its central goal, which was the overturning of offensive imperial policies and (ultimately) rebellion. When crowds mobilized against local offenders, committing property damage and violence, elite leaders tended to reject these mobilization tactics. As these Whig leaders tried to maintain control, urbanites on the margins of established society were attempting to expand the boundaries of the polity and test the limits of Patriot mobilization. By definition, revolution involved the contestation and the destabilization of the civic world.[34]

Since society regarded these marginal groups as being outside the political sphere, laws and customs often prohibited them (legally or socially) from moving on an equal footing through the buildings that established citizens constructed. Slaves could not bear arms or testify in court, nor could they gather in public without their masters' permission. Women, non-whites, and the poorest of white men could not vote or hold office. Members of minority religious sects were sometimes forced to pay taxes to an established church they did not recognize. Nevertheless, many of these socially and politically disenfranchised people agitated in their own ways—it would be misleading to say that these marginal groups had no access to the political sphere, or that they slavishly relied upon their social betters for such access. Many city dwellers moved through an alternative "shadow landscape," one that included not just formal buildings, but "the spaces and interstices within and between buildings."[35] Such groups challenged the political establishment from the margins, using the means at their disposal—participation in open town meetings, writing petitions or publishing polemics, and crowd action. If they were not refined enough to argue with gentlemen in the cities' finest taverns, they voiced grievances and made plans in dramshops or illegal watering holes. Sailors and vagabonds may not have been welcome in the countinghouses that ruled the waterfront, but they thrived in the transitional zone amidst the docks and wharves. Many marginal city dwellers searched for salvation at the fringes of spiritual life, when they found that existing congregations did not meet their needs. These groups held out hope that equality before God might translate into political equality. When members of the shadow landscape found themselves excluded from the politics of the courthouse and statehouse, they took to the streets outside them.[36]

In the shadow landscape, city dwellers could escape from traditional mores and hierarchies. They could form alternative communities. They could express their grievances and even undertake social revolution. They challenged prevailing notions of patriarchy and hierarchy, and voiced controversial views about the social, economic, and political order. To be sure, women and non-whites had restricted access to urban networks of sociability and communication, and white men had a definite interest in keeping those restrictions in place. At the same time, the propertied white men who led the legislatures, tavern companies, meetinghouses and countinghouses often showed an intense interest in recruiting the assistance of women, slaves, poor men, and other peripheral groups. The Patriot leaders who were the most skillful at mobilizing ordinary city dwellers mingled in the shadow landscape and participated in ritualized associational life, revelry and leisure, riots and parades. They walked among their fellow city dwellers on the waterfront, in the taverns, and in the streets. Rich men and politicians often supported crowd actions when it served their purposes, even the tarring and feathering of Loyalists, or did little to prevent such actions. Continent-wide boycotts of British goods, and the spinning of homespun clothing, required the assistance of women and lower-class consumers. Rich and poor, black and white might share in religious revivals or the banishment of British troops and customs officials. Thus, elite and ordinary city dwellers shared in the burdens of political mobilization, with a key difference: society did not permit women and non-whites to take advantage of the prestige, the notions of brotherhood, the sense of voluntary civic duty that so distinguished institutions such as the legislature or the Sons of Liberty.[37]

The revolutionary movement was therefore both inclusive and exclusive. Mobilizing groups pushed at and expanded the boundaries of social and political inclusion, but Patriots did not (and could not) entirely discard the concept of limits and boundaries. In the process of revolution and social transformation, Americans constructed a new social order with new structures and limits.[38] Poorer and middling white men ultimately gained inclusion in the civic community and enjoyed greater participation in society and politics. At the same time, the propertied white men who led the Revolution were largely content to leave certain segments of society in the shadows. In some cases, preconceived notions of wealth and status determined the limits of the Revolution; in more fundamental ways, race and gender imposed severe constraints, and some marginal groups remained excluded from social and political life after the Revolution ended. Still, their actions sounded revolutionary refrains amid the wider urban din of the Revolutionary era.

Rebellious Whigs faced another type of significant opposition. Supporters of the Crown did their best to counteract Patriot mobilization, which presented a third challenge to revolutionaries. The largest cities all had high concentrations of Loyalists or Tories, dedicated to maintaining the empire's existence rather than joining the resistance. Friends of government, like rebellious Americans, used many of the available mechanisms of mobilization. These groups engaged in countermobilization, disseminating their own opinions on and interpretations of events, positing their own arguments in taverns, listening to very different sermons in church, and maintaining their own definitions of authority on the waterfront and in the assemblies. Still, supporters of imperial government faced significant difficulties in their attempts at countermobilization. The source of their authority was three thousand miles away, which weakened their ability to exercise their power effectively. Government officials in the colonies and their allies in the legislature (when they had any) could wield some influence over city dwellers, but imperial power often stretched no further than this. Parliament could send British officers and troops to protect state interests, but use of the army and navy as tools of peacetime control tended to backfire. Anglican ministers and laypeople sometimes acted as staunch allies—but here, too, the British found that a person weighed his or her religious identity against other factors.[39]

Some historians argue that most Americans' interests and identity had become too far divorced from the interests and identity of the mother country, so Loyalist mobilization was doomed from the start.[40] Other scholars argue that friends of government were less successful at mobilization than the rebels because Patriot ideology was more coherent and appealing than Loyalist ideology.[41] Indeed, many Loyalists were archconservatives with a firm belief in social hierarchy, who generally disdained politics in waterfront taverns or out of doors, and engaged in it half-heartedly, if at all. In practice, this limited the Loyalists' ability to mobilize city dwellers effectively. Focusing primarily on how Patriot persuasion worked, I suggest that the contours of urban life also helped to shape the reasons that Whig mobilization was ultimately more effective than government countermobilization. On the waterfront, in taverns, in churches, in households, in the streets, and in meeting places, the British and their supporters constantly found themselves outmatched. In the end, the friends of government were unable to enjoy the same success that urban Whigs had at disseminating their opinions, persuading their neighbors, and establishing unity.

The final challenge arose as revolutionaries attempted to spread civic awareness inland and unify Americans throughout the continent. Urban centers played a vital role as nodes of communication, and catalysts of political mobilization did their best to take advantage of the existing networks that linked these cities to one another, to London, and to the rural hinterlands. Personal correspondence and travelers facilitated the transmission of ideas and identity from urban centers, while printed material helped to spread the cause to local communities. Newspapers and pamphlets, "The general source throughout the nation, / Of every modern conversation," transmitted the facts and inflammatory fictions of the Stamp Act controversy or the Boston Massacre and disseminated the opinions of influential writers to the population. One printer, singing the praises of newspapers, wrote that his readers belonged to "that Aggregate called the Town, or the World, or the People." In this way, newspapers helped bring individuals, or as the printer put it, "Atoms," together. Such "aggregates" helped create a shared identity among North Americans living at a great distance from one another. At times, rural people—tenants, backcountry farmers, or debtors—saw urban merchants and politicians working against their interests. Yet if urban Patriot leaders could convince rural residents that they shared a common danger—and therefore a common interest—with each other and with more cosmopolitan communities, the Revolution would become a national cause.[42]

While each of the Anglo-American cities had its peculiar characteristics, unique characters, and distinctive challenges, they had in common an interconnected landscape of layered geographies that was ripe for political mobilization. These urban spaces included the waterfront, taverns, houses of worship, households, and statehouses, as well as the streets that snaked among the buildings. As city dwellers moved among these urban spaces, they could draw upon a wide array of networks for cooperation and mobilization. In this book, each chapter focuses on one of these spaces and explores one city as a case study.

The waterfront was the beating heart of urban commerce. More than any other part of the city, the docks and wharves exemplified the dynamism of the cities, as visitors and migrants came and went, as seamen rolled in and out of port, and as merchants extended their capital throughout the Atlantic world. Because of their close connections with Atlantic commerce, the denizens of the waterfront community were usually the first to feel the effects of imperial policies. From Charleston, South Carolina, to Falmouth down east (in what is now Maine), merchants, shipbuilders, and seamen stood at the forefront of resistance to Great Britain.

The first chapter focuses on the imperial conflict as it unfolded in the maritime and commercial spaces of Boston. No city could be more appropriate for opening a discussion of the imperial conflict. Boston was the name that plagued imperial officials throughout the late colonial period, with its raucous rap sheet of crowd actions—the Knowles Riot of 1747, the Stamp Act riots of 1765, the *Liberty* riot of 1768, the Boston Massacre of 1770, and the Boston Tea Party of 1773. British authorities repeatedly tried to assert control over Boston's waterfront community, and each time, the community mobilized in response to impressment, customs duties, and other impositions of imperial authority. Five times the Bostonians banished imperial officials, soldiers, and other pariahs to Castle Island in the harbor. The central significance of the Boston waterfront had crystallized by 1774, when Parliament singled the city out for punishment. In response, donations poured in from around North America to ameliorate the harsh effects of the Boston Port Act. Rural communities throughout Massachusetts and beyond were inspired to resist the Coercive Acts. Boston's conspicuous (and early) leadership among the waterfront communities of North America warrants special attention because its actions demonstrated how mobilization could unify city dwellers from throughout the social spectrum and across the continent.

When city dwellers wanted a break from the bustle of commercial and maritime life, they often collected together in taverns to eat and drink, converse, exchange news and information, and debate politics. During the imperial crisis, taverns or public houses brought together a cross-class political network that would be necessary for the coherence of a revolutionary alliance.[43] Voluntary societies, which flourished in eighteenth-century cities, functioned as mechanisms of urban mobilization, often gathering in taverns. Local groups could translate their sense of shared interests and civic responsibility into the first stirrings of nationalism.[44] City dwellers (particularly men) gained a sense of community belonging and became actively involved in the local civic life of fire companies, tavern clubs, fraternal orders, and militia companies. Americans demonstrated during these years that they were a "nation of joiners." Commerce and sociability became new reasons for city dwellers to transcend distinctions of age, ethnicity, religion, and occupation. These groups tapped into networks of intercolonial communication and gathered in popular sites of sociability. As a result, they provided templates for the merchants' committees, Sons of Liberty, and committees of correspondence—and thereby helped to bolster intercolonial resistance to Great Britain.[45]

New York City, the case study of the book's second chapter, stood at the pinnacle of alcohol consumption, communication, and sociability in the American colonies. The city functioned as the terminus for official packet boats sending mail from England, and so its taverns benefited from the fastest news.[46] Furthermore, New York's taverns and grogshops frequently played host to British officers, troops, and sailors, bringing Whigs and friends of government face to face. Even as clubs and associations, laws and polite hierarchies were in place to maintain an orderly tavern setting, rebels and other dissenters often capitalized on the entropic, drunken atmosphere of taverns to create societal disorder and political upheaval. In the complex world of New York politics, whichever faction could organize and rally tavern companies would have the greatest success at mobilizing the populace.

The churches, meetinghouses, and synagogues where colonial Americans participated in religious life could be a source of political mobilization or a source of civic impasse. In some parts of America, revolutionaries were able to harness houses of worship for political mobilization. Bostonians were relatively homogenous in their religious belief, and their clergymen historically equated the Church of England with tyrannical authority. The Bay Town's Congregationalist ministers effectively politicized the pulpit during the imperial crisis and formed a network of Patriot preachers that Loyalist Peter Oliver called the "Black Regiment."[47] In other cities, the diversity of religious belief posed particular difficulties for Patriots attempting to build a political coalition. In Philadelphia, Quakers and Presbyterians hurled invective at one another during the controversies of the 1760s. In New York, conflict between Anglican and Presbyterian factions frustrated attempts to build unity among Whigs.[48] In this way the religious landscape sometimes fractured city dwellers rather than uniting them.

The third chapter discusses political mobilization in this religious landscape. Newport is an interesting case study because the political allegiances

of many city dwellers drew upon the prevailing New England denominational conflicts that were so evident in Boston *and* because the religious diversity of Newport's residents fostered a pluralistic political climate resembling
that of the middle colonies. The city was a particularly important gathering
place for Baptists, Quakers, and Jews, and it had influential populations of
Anglicans and Congregationalists.[49] Amidst the acceptance and flexibility
that characterized a cosmopolitan city with Enlightenment ideals, this religious diversity also caused suspicion and contention in Newport, which
created a civic impasse that frustrated political mobilization. In addition, the
urban setting provided fertile ground for religious revivals among women
and blacks. While the attendant social agitation (especially against slavery)
failed to create lasting revolutionary transformation, such revivals nevertheless had a significant impact on public life. The pluralistic mixture of
American cities shaped the characteristics of urban political mobilization,
both in the established cultural landscape and in the shadow landscape.

Households were the individual units that made up the urban body
politic. Each household was a microcosm of the city, playing out political
mobilization and its attendant conflicts in an endless variety. Because
these houses were crowded together in the city, residents depended on their
neighbors. Eighteenth-century Americans had not yet developed the
notions of privacy that became more common in the nineteenth century.
The realms of family, market, coffeehouse, clubs, and court did not neatly
separate into public and private spheres. In the era of the imperial crisis,
business and family concerns had repercussions that were as public as discussions in taverns, churches, courthouses, and assemblies.[50] Colonial laws
governed relationships between masters and servants, as well as men and
women, and neighbors had countless opportunities to observe these relationships. When city dwellers purchased consumer goods, their decisions
had wider effects on the economy and (during the intercolonial boycotts)
carried political meaning as well. Urban households, and the politicized
relations among these households, are the subjects of the fourth chapter.[51]

Urban townhouses framed many important aspects of urban life,
including consumption, gender and race relations, and paternal authority.
In Boston or Philadelphia or Charleston, the wealthiest merchants and
landowners sat atop the pyramid of colonial patriarchal society, and they
built grand houses that bespoke their mastery and refinement. These plush
Georgian mansions sat alongside the more austere townhouses of their
neighbors, where increasing numbers of middling city dwellers nonetheless had the means to participate in the consumer economy and fill their
homes with imported British goods. During the imperial crisis, American
spending habits came under fire from Patriots seeking to boycott imported
goods. Women had important voices in matters of spending, and Patriot
men needed the support and assent of their wives and female relatives.
Wealthy elite masters also had to worry about maintaining social control
over their neighbors, their servants, and slaves, and they clung to tradi-

tional notions of patriarchal regulation to keep their houses and cities in order. Elite city dwellers also found it difficult to maintain rigid, patriarchal domination when rioters might bring pressure to bear on upper-class neighbors who supported obnoxious British policies, when slaves might revolt or run away, and when women asserted their decision-making power. The imperial crisis caused social unrest that gave the urban gentry several reasons to feel less than secure about their households.

In all these matters of domestic life, Charleston was the quintessential example. There the level of wealth, luxury, Anglicization, and high fashion astounded visitors.[52] In Charleston, patriarchy was particularly central to the culture of Lowcountry planters.[53] As the largest port of entry for persons of African descent, the city had the largest colonial populations of slaves and free blacks.[54] Like members of the elite in other cities, Charleston's elite patriarchs had reasons to be suspicious of urban crowds, fearful of their slaves interacting with free blacks in the cities, and anxious that luxury goods from Great Britain would corrupt them. As the revolutionary movement spread, Charlestonians negotiated with one another about the proper arrangement of their households and the appropriate limits of mobilization.

In most of the thirteen colonies, the assembly house became a rallying point for official or semiofficial resistance to British policies. Legislative houses like the Virginia House of Burgesses were notorious in their defiance. At the same time, the legislatures and courthouses were responsible for governing the colonies—some in an aristocratic, authoritarian fashion and others with more democratic responsiveness. In Charleston, for instance, the political elite were so united and so dominant in South Carolina politics that they were able to maintain power while ignoring the will of the electorate. Rhode Island and Massachusetts had more responsive provincial and local governments, and so the people of Boston and Newport were generally able to make their opinions heard in the assemblies and town meetings. New Yorkers and Philadelphians, however, experienced a sharp disjuncture between popular demands and legislative response.[55]

Philadelphia is the case study for the fifth chapter because of the famous political meetings that occurred inside the State House (now known as Independence Hall), as well as the dramatic mobilization of Philadelphians "out of doors." This chapter examines the various types of political activity that took place outside the Court House and the town meetings in the State House Yard. During the decade that preceded the Revolution, groups outside the political elite increasingly began mobilizing just outside the halls of power. By 1774, these outdoor gatherings had cleared the way for the meetings of the Continental Congress at Carpenter's Hall and the State House that ordained Philadelphia the capital of the American Revolution.

These five cityscapes exemplify the processes of mobilization that took place throughout urban America and beyond in the years preceding the Revolutionary War. This book's epilogue shows how things changed, however, during the war years. British military occupation immobilized urban politics, posing a challenge to the rebels that was much more difficult to surmount. While government countermobilization may have been ineffective, George III ultimately attempted to resolve the imperial crisis by sending thousands of troops to the colonies. In doing so, the British were able to smother Patriot political activity in the cities they occupied. In 1774, General Thomas Gage, commander of the king's forces in America, succeeded Thomas Hutchinson as governor of Massachusetts, supported by an occupying British force. Gage attempted to enforce the Intolerable Acts, the most extreme measures of countermobilization Parliament had yet devised, by appointing sympathetic judges and suspending town meetings. Gage moved to seize local stores of arms, powder, and ammunition, and New England rebels gathered to meet him each time. On April 19, 1775, British redcoats exchanged fire with Americans at Lexington and Concord, and within days, militia from all over New England converged on Boston to besiege Gage and his men.

During the subsequent eight-year War of American Independence, all five of the largest American cities played host to major military engagements. As the British armed forces descended on American shores, they found they needed the cities to prosecute the war against the rebellious colonists. The cities had deep harbors, they were commercial centers that could supply the ships, they could provide winter quarters for troops, and they still served as excellent nodes of communication. Furthermore, the British hoped to rely on the cities' Loyalist populations and use the cities as footholds for reestablishing civil government. Thus, from the American standpoint, the very physical characteristics that rendered the cities ideal for political mobilization also made them vulnerable to British occupation or even naval bombardment and destruction. As each of the five cities in this study became untenable as sites of political mobilization, Patriot sympathizers abandoned them for the countryside. The Revolutionary War disrupted the cities' economic functions and displaced the rebellious politicians who had been such a vital force over the previous decade. As a result, the war period witnessed the immobilization of all five of Anglo-America's largest cities, and the movement of administrative, military, and economic management inland, out of the reach of the British navy. The cities had no choice but to capitulate to occupying forces—residents took oaths of loyalty to the Crown and survived by supplying the British army.

This ignominious wartime history has motivated many Americans to gloss over the cities' significance during the prerevolutionary and revolutionary years. No wonder George Washington and Thomas Jefferson privileged farmers over the fractious inhabitants of the sinful urban centers. No wonder they ultimately chose a remote riverbank rather than an established metropolis as the site of the new nation's capital. Although the cities of the United States retained their importance as centers of commerce and manufacturing, it was uncertain whether they would ever again play so crucial a role in political mobilization and the advancement of democratic ideas and practices.

Chapter 1

PORT IN A STORM

The Boston Waterfront as Contested Space, 1747–74

On Friday, Septr 30th, 1768, the Ships of War, armed Schooners, Transports, &c. Came up the Harbour and Anchored round the Town; their Cannon loaded, a Spring on their Cables, as for a regular Siege. At noon on Saturday, October the 1st the fourteenth & twenty-ninth Regiments, a detachment from the 59th Reg^t and Train of Artillery, with two pieces of Cannon, landed on the Long Wharf; then Formed and Marched with insolent Parade, Drums beating, Fifes playing, and Colours flying, up King Street.

Paul Revere tells us about the British troops landing at Boston, but his engraving (fig. 1.1) speaks even more loudly. Boston at first appears to be a placid place, nestled in the heart of the Massachusetts Bay. Church spires climb upward like beacons atop John Winthrop's "city upon a hill." Wharves spike out in all directions, ready to receive trade goods from all over the Atlantic world and to send commodities to distant ports. The abundance of houses, ships, and warehouses indicates a flourishing town, an exciting place of business, and a haven for peaceful travelers. Yet the eye is immediately drawn to the British warships ringed in an ominous, offensive stance around the town's skirts, with their guns lowered. Transports bearing troops converge upon Long Wharf. The two regiments begin their march toward King Street, the heart of business and government in colonial Boston.[1] The scene we are witnessing is an attempt to reassert British control over the city and its waterfront—because Boston in 1768, indeed for much of the eighteenth century, was anything but placid. The previous June, Boston's waterfront dwellers had rioted to protest naval impressment and the seizure of John Hancock's sloop *Liberty*. These Bostonians had staked their own claims on the waterfront. The customs officers in Boston, fearing for their lives, had fled the city—banished, in effect, from this waterfront community. The waterfront was central to this

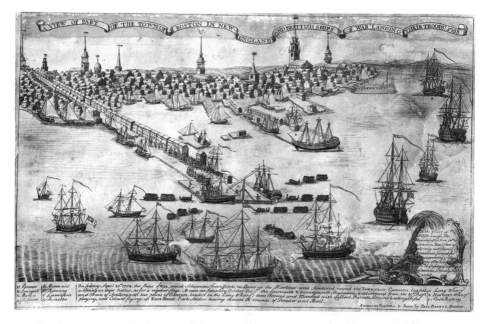

Figure I.I. Paul Revere's print portrays the landing of British troops on Boston's Long Wharf on September 30, 1768, as an invasion by a hostile army. *A View of the Part of the Town of Boston in New-England and British Ships of War Landing Their Troops*, by Paul Revere. Boston, 1770. Boston Athenæum.

conflict, and indeed central to the city's political mobilization in the years prior to the Revolutionary War.

These incidents were highlights in a series of dramatic events that took place along the Boston waterfront in the eighteenth century: impressment riots, violence against customs officials, conflict between townspeople and troops, and of course the Boston Tea Party of 1773. The docks and wharves of Boston had seen the comings and goings of immigrants, travelers, troops, commodities, culture, and ideas for well over a hundred years.[2] From the vantage point at the end of Long Wharf, 2,100 feet long, Bostonians had become accustomed to looking toward the sea for new opportunities, new goods, new neighbors, and new information. Now they looked out from Long Wharf and saw an occupying army. During the imperial crisis, Bostonians mobilized as a cohesive, politicized waterfront community to protect themselves from such encroachments. They came to regard imperial officials as trespassers and outsiders who needed to be expunged, and in five incidents from 1747 to 1774 they actually did force their enemies—governors, importers, and customs officials—to flee the Boston peninsula. In the process of asserting their control over the city and the waterfront, this community eventually articulated a unified identity separate from that of the British Empire. By the eve of Revolution, the

Boston waterfront served as an example to other colonists who sought to wrest control of the larger contested space, North America, from king and Parliament.

During the imperial crisis, the waterfront was a specific site of self-conscious revolutionary activity with its own forms of cooperation and conflict. Merchants, seamen, and shipwrights depended upon a vibrant Boston economy, and they were keenly aware of imperial attempts to encroach upon the smooth operation of trade. This community achieved independence from the British Empire by wresting control of waterfront space. This chapter examines the political mobilization of the Boston waterfront, which made the city a leader of resistance to Great Britain.[3]

From the tip of North End to the Boston Neck was about two miles, and no point in Boston was more than half a mile from the water (fig. 1.2). Although it would be difficult to divide such a small space into neighborhoods, Boston's waterfront had its own social hierarchy, system of communication, and political culture: in this way it was a microcosm of the larger city. Here ship carpenters worked on skeletal keels, worrying as customers increasingly took their business to Salem, Marblehead, and towns to the south. Here oystermen called out to innkeepers, hoping to earn enough to pay rent. Here customs officials, drawing their salary from the Lords of the Treasury, inspected the cargo of the local shipping and made sure the king was paid his due. The wholesale merchant might try to squeeze the shopkeepers, the ship's captain might order about his hands, and prostitutes might beckon a British sailor from the alleyways. The shipyards, docks, and wharves had particular economic functions and a distinct culture, in a town where commercial and maritime activities were at the center of daily life.[4] On a map, these docks and wharves appeared to be mere appendages of the town, but the reverse was true. No rigid or formal boundary existed between the waterfront and the rest of Boston—the waterfront was an integral (if not dominant) part of the larger urban setting *and* a space with a complex community of its own. This community included some of the key participants in revolutionary political mobilization.[5]

Travelers to colonial Boston immediately noted that the waterfront was a distinct place. Aside from the ferries and the difficult road along Boston Neck, the wharves were the primary point of arrival for visitors, transients, newcomers, and other travelers. Population growth in Boston was sluggish compared to the crush of new immigrants that boosted New York and Philadelphia. Nevertheless, Boston's population was experiencing high turnover due to the wars and economic shocks that plagued Massachusetts during the mid-eighteenth century. The wharves of these cities also filled with unfree and dark-skinned workers who arrived as part of the slave trade. The Boston waterfront was a gateway between land and sea, between New England and distant parts, between foreign lands and a homeland.[6]

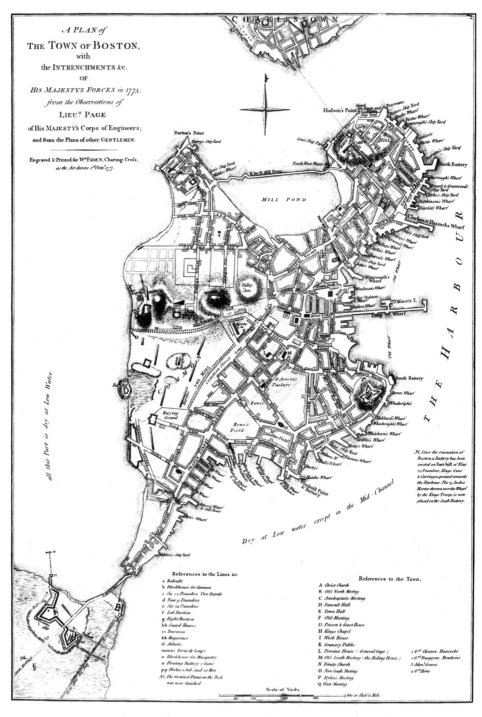

Figure 1.2. The eighteenth-century coastline of colonial Boston was almost entirely ringed with wharves and docks that were integral to its economic life. *A Plan of the Town of Boston, with the Intrenchments &c. of His Majestys Forces in 1775*, by Sir Thomas Hyde Page. [London]; Engraved and printed for Wm. Faden, 1777. *Library of Congress, Geography and Map Division.*

No less important than the people who passed through Boston were the commercial goods that workers shuttled along the waterfront. The "Harbour" and "Shipping" of Boston were principal attractions for new-comers, and the merchant John Scollay called Boston "the grand engine that gives motion to all the wheels of commerce." The town's customs officers emphasized that Boston was of much greater importance than the "lesser Harbours, Rivers, Creeks, and Bays" of New England. Fish and ships had sustained New England's mercantile economy during the century preceding the Revolution, and Boston's distilleries were busy turning molasses into rum. Although much of this activity was shifting away from Boston to other towns along the coast by 1763, Boston was still a competitive ship-builder, and the town flourished in its role as an "entrepreneurial head-quarters," the principal commercial entrepôt in the region. Fish, whale and cod oil, lumber products, naval stores, and foodstuffs went out, while wine, brandy, clothing, ironware and glassware, tea, and sugar came in.[7]

Bostonians from all walks of life depended on this engine for suste-nance, and merchants like Scollay were not the only ones who made this engine run. The seamen who composed between one-tenth and one-quarter of the city's population were workers "without whose lives the wheels of maritime commerce could not have turned," as one historian writes.[8] Artisans such as blockmakers, caulkers, riggers, shipjoiners, and ropemakers built ships and kept them in good repair. Laborers loaded, unloaded, and moved the goods. Coopers made barrels for storage, and many other workers, directly or indirectly, helped turn the machinery of the waterfront. The Tax Taking and Rate Books of 1790, which underrepresent the number of mariners and laborers involved in this waterfront community, demonstrate that merchants and retailers accounted for 16.6% of the Boston workforce, coopers and marine craftsmen for 11.2%, mariners for 8.9%, and laborers for 8.6%. Distillers and tavernkeepers, who often plied their trade near the waterfront, accounted for another 2.8%. Combined, these groups probably comprised more than half the city's population.[9] The waterfront fostered a community of interdependent contributors to the economic livelihood of the city. A political cartoon about the expected Stamp Act boycott in November 1765 made this point clear: Mercury (personifying commerce) reluctantly leaves America, ships lie useless and unsold, and a crowd of unemployed sailors mills about.[10]

News passed through this gateway along with goods and travelers. Seaborne newspapers and letters transmitted information from one port to another, although not all news appeared in print. The waterfront sustained other vital networks of communications: the taverns where people read newspapers and exchanged ideas, the transient population of mariners who carried news and gossip by ship, and the interpersonal trading con-nections that linked the Atlantic seaports. Even elite merchants, who had access to more privileged hubs of communication such as the British Coffee House, depended on what they learned from mingling in the taverns or on the docks. In a major port and information "hothouse" like Boston, people interacted face-to-face. The waterfront community's networks were particularly important for the sharing of general and specialized information, even across social barriers.[11]

Members of Boston's maritime and commercial communities often lived by the wharves and shipyards. This proximity fostered the interactions that made waterfront life unique, giving the people of the waterfront a sense of community identification and allegiance. Members of the community believed that collective progress meant individual enrichment ("a rising tide lifts all boats," as the old saying goes), and vice versa. This attitude facilitated political mobilization, since political coalitions needed to harness individuals' interests for a common goal.[12]

Marine artisans provide the best example of the waterfront community's closeness. Craftsmen with enough money could afford to purchase property, and surviving deeds show that these members of the maritime trades often lived near one another, sometimes near the wharves and shipyards in the South End, West End, or Faneuil Hall area. The waterfront community concentrated primarily in the North End. Although just over a third of Boston's population lived here, this area had the majority of mariners, coopers, and marine craftsmen, along with almost half of Boston's sea captains and laborers.[13] Caulkers, for instance, preferred to live and work on Hull, Charter, and Ellis streets: Alexander Baker, Christopher Clark, Benjamin Gallop, Josiah Holland, Ames Howard and his son Ebenezer, John Perrigo, Nathaniel Woodward and his sons Nathaniel Jr. and John Newell all lived on these three North End streets in the second half of the eighteenth century. Jonathan Tarbox, a caulker whose impressment would help touch off the Knowles Riot in 1747, lived on the corner of Salem and Hull streets until he deeded the property to Eleazer Ingals, a shipwright, in 1761. This area was also popular among mastmakers like Samuel Harris, Ralph Hart, Timothy Thornton, and Joseph Walker.[14] The proximity of the marine artisans' homes to one another engendered a feeling of maritime community among the winding streets of the North End.

This community was not completely insular, of course. A cosmopolitan mix of craftsmen and retailers lived and worked along the numerous wharves, owning or renting shops and houses. Bostonians valued these locations because they were "convenient for Trade." Newspapers regularly published advertisements for goods on sale aboard ships, in warehouses, and in shops along the water. A diverse array of artisans plied their trades on Boston's wharves, such as tallow chandler John Langdon of Clark's Wharf (later Hancock's Wharf); anvilmaker Edward Lack, and jobbing-smith and toolmaker James McElroy, both of whom moved from Scarlett's Wharf to Doble's Wharf; the farrier "Widow Hendry," who moved to Scarlett's Wharf after a fire destroyed her business in Paddy's Alley; and shoemaker George R. T. Hewes, at the head of Griffin's Wharf.[15] A North Ender such as silversmith Paul Revere, who also kept a shop on Clark's

Wharf, grew up among oystermen, lobstermen, and maritime artisans. When Revere protested British actions as a member of the North End Caucus or a courier for the Boston Sons of Liberty, he drew upon his experiences growing up in this waterfront community.[16]

Members of the elite also made their homes near the waterfront. While a wealthy merchant such as John Hancock might reside on Beacon Hill, above the smells and bustle of dockside life, other prominent Bostonians lived near the wharves or in the North End, interacting on a daily basis with fishermen, shipwrights, and dockworkers. Lieutenant Governor Thomas Hutchinson lived a block from Clark's Wharf at the corner of Fleet Street and Garden Court when rioters attacked his house in 1765. Benjamin Hallowell, comptroller of customs, lived around the corner from the Town Dock on Hanover Street between Wings Lane and Union Street. Samuel Adams had a house, brewery, and wharf in the South End. His father and their neighbors on Barton's Ropewalk had purchased the street in 1736 and named it, appropriately, Purchase Street. Hancock, with a direct interest in maritime life, lived away from the waterfront, while Adams, who was less involved with commerce, lived just off the water. While the boundaries between the waterfront and the rest of Boston were certainly porous, the waterfront particularly encouraged physical closeness and social interaction among members of different social groups in the "face-to-face society" of eighteenth-century Boston.[17]

Boston's laborers and seamen crowded into tiny wooden two-family houses or "bachelor's halls," many of which were located near the wharves.[18] Their presence contributed to a distinctive waterfront culture. Seamen and fishermen developed "peculiar toughness" from the hardships of seafaring, they were notorious participants in tavern culture, and they had close associations with the seamy underside of Boston life.[19] Benjamin Franklin, at age sixteen, delighted in the waterfront subculture as he devoted his satirical pen to the "Night-Walkers" of Boston in 1722, in the guise of the widow Silence Dogood. Silence "met a Crowd of *Tarpolins* and their Doxies, link'd to each other by the Arms," who proceeded to regale her with a few choice maritime metaphors. The coffeehouse satirists, prostitutes, and seamen that young Franklin encountered in the streets portrayed Boston's late-night waterfront culture as an impertinent diversion.[20] We might guess that seamen, who were frequently depicted as lower-class transients in this way, merely skulked along the margins of Boston society. Yet it would be a mistake to underestimate these Jack Tars: the unique culture and the close, cooperative working relationship of seamen aboard ship fostered a particularly strong collectivism and antiauthoritarian militancy, qualities that revealed themselves in their history of negotiations and resistance. Nonwhite seamen in particular thrived in the shifting world of seafaring life, proud, skilled workers who acted as go-betweens among people of different races.[21] The recurring eighteenth-century fights against impressment demonstrated that seamen were at the center of their community, not merely at its margins.[22] Since Boston seamen were well integrated in the waterfront society and economy, they could contribute their collective strength and tradition of resistance to the wider community and help inspire revolutionary action.[23]

Amidst these community ties and information networks, the waterfront also had a hierarchy based on wealth and ownership. As John Adams noted, "All the rich men will have many of the poor, in various trades, manufactures and other occupations in life, dependent upon them for their daily bread; many of smaller fortunes will be in their debt, and in many ways under obligations to them." On the waterfront, a subset of the colonial culture Adams described, these obligations would have been even more tightly intertwined. Merchants employed captains (who in turn paid the rest of the crew), pilots for guiding ships into port, dockworkers and cartmen for transporting cargo, coopers to build barrels, marine artisans to build and repair ships, and carpenters to repair wharves and warehouses. Artisans often employed journeymen, apprentices, and laborers, and a variety of wealthy men owned slaves or indentured servants, many of whom were sold on the waterfront. John Greenough offered "a likely Negro Boy, 13 Years old, us'd to Household Business" for sale on a wharf near Winnesimit Ferry, along with a parcel of seasoned timber. Blacks, who clustered in cities, were often heavily represented in maritime life and waterfront crafts.[24]

The merchant John Hancock bought the town's second largest wharf in 1767 and was soon earning £150 a year from wharfage fees and rents. He was so wealthy that countless Bostonians either worked for him or were in debt to him (though he was shrewdly lenient about collecting), which granted Hancock power that few others could match.[25] The customs house tidewaiter Owen Richards testified to Hancock's influence in 1768. Hancock had come on board the brig *Lydia* (docked at Hancock's Wharf) "attended by a large number of People" including the ship's captain, mate, boatswain, and "a Negro with a Lanthern who we supposed belonged to M[r]. Hancock." Hancock ordered them not to let any customs house officers below deck: "if they did he would immediately turn them out of his Employ." Later that night, Hancock discovered Richards in the steerage, and ordered the mate and boatswain to seize hold of the tidewaiter and force him back on deck.[26] Ship's officers, slaves, artisans and laborers acknowledged Hancock's lofty position in waterfront society as a wealthy creditor and employer. Obligation and deference, patronage and livelihood flowed like currency through this network of exchange, employment, and authority.[27]

The ownership of wharves, warehouses, and ships made patrons out of many wealthy Bostonians. Probably fewer than seventy-five people owned the lion's share of wharfage in Boston. Many of these wealthy wharf owners were influential in the militia or town offices.[28] Like Nathaniel Appleton, Joshua Henshaw, George Minott, James Pitts, and Oliver Wendell, most of these men were merchants at one time or another. Others were artisans, tavernkeepers, shopkeepers, mariners, and distillers.[29] These owners were in a position to lade and unlade commercial goods at their wharves, store them in warehouses, and rent out valuable space to artisans, shopkeepers, or residential tenants. Some, like Hancock, John Rowe, Thomas Amory, and James Noble, enjoyed the privilege of hearing Bostonians refer to their waterfront property by their families' names.

Long Wharf was the harbor's most prominent pier. An association of merchants financed the construction of this elaborate public works project early in the second decade of the eighteenth century. Each shareholder divided wharfage revenues and contributed to improvement and repair costs, and in 1772 became incorporated as the Proprietors of Long Wharf.[30] The merchant John Rowe attended several meetings of the Proprietors, generally at the British Coffee House in King Street, where they discussed repairs and the election of wharfingers or supervisors.[31] These Proprietors oversaw a variety of business on Long Wharf: Samuel Hewes offered a 115-ton brigantine for sale, while Arthur Savage and Company called upon creditors to settle their accounts at their store.[32] In addition, the shareholders exercised a great deal of the patron's influence over the shopkeepers, drinksellers, and artisans who maintained smaller businesses along Boston's most important wharf.[33]

Even as the waterfront defined its own hierarchy, the community also fostered interaction among Bostonians of different social strata by providing some room for social advancement and career changes. The ability to rise was often limited, of course, especially in tough economic times. Nevertheless, an orphan without prospects might become an apprentice— almost half of all orphans bound out by the Overseers of the Poor wound up in maritime trades. A young apprentice in the shipyards might establish himself as a journeyman or even a master craftsman. A master shipwright might earn the title of "merchant" or "gentleman" during the course of his career. A mariner might also advance in rank within the hierarchy of "boys," ordinary seamen, able seamen, quartermasters, cooks, coxswains, gunners, boatswains, carpenters, mates, and captains. Seafaring was a youthful profession. Few grew old at sea. Some died at an early age from disease or accident, while others might move on to other trades (a seven-year career at sea was average in the eighteenth century). Since seafaring involved a great deal of experience with rigging and fitting ships, a seaman might "retire" to work on land in Boston as a dockworker, marine crafts-man, or in another trade. George R. T. Hewes, for instance, spent three years of his youth fishing the Grand Banks, but became an apprentice shoemaker, while Ashley Bowen began life at sea as a thirteen-year-old cabin boy, became a sea captain, and ultimately returned to Marblehead to work as a rigger and sailmaker.[34] Whatever later career he chose, a coastal New Englander's ties to seamanship and the maritime community did not simply dissolve.

Ship captains also enjoyed the potential for social advancement. Many rose to become full-fledged members of the merchant community, entering the Indian, West Indian, coastal, and retail trades or becoming general merchants with diversified investments. Even when ship captains remained at sea, they maintained close ties to merchants and other men on shore. Newspaper advertisements for runaways or goods for sale often listed ship-masters with their merchant partners or affiliates. The Boston Marine Society, an incorporated group of ship captains, met to share information about navigation and provide relief in times of trouble. These meetings were undoubtedly social as well, and upwardly mobile captains such as John Bradford and John Homer found themselves mingling with wharfin-gers such as Jabez Hatch and merchants such as William Mackay, William D. Cheever, and Jonathan Snelling. The potential for advancement gave the waterfront community a fluid quality that contributed to its overall stability. Merchants, shoemakers, and coxswains did not forget their friends, neighbors, and shipmates in the trades they had left behind.[35]

Boston's thriving club life encouraged advancement and socialization within the waterfront community. A merchants' club had been meeting in the front room of the British Coffee House since 1751 (the group also met at the nearby Bunch of Grapes tavern), and sometime during the next decade the group incorporated itself into the influential Boston Society for Encouraging Trade and Commerce. By the early 1760s this group had taken responsibility for representing the interests of merchants in petitions to England.[36] Another group of merchants, wealthy maritime artisans, and politicians formed a political organization called the North End Caucus. This group met at the Salutation (also called The Two Palaverers) on Salutation Alley in the North End and the Green Dragon Tavern in Union Street (where St. Andrew's Masonic Lodge met as well), which led to the Town Dock.[37] At these public houses and dramshops, Bostonians from across the social spectrum, as well as travelers, could interact, transmit news and information, conduct business, and engage in politics.[38]

During the imperial crisis, these sources of common ground would shape the articulation of grievances and political interests. At the same time, lopsided distribution of wealth, power, and status often exposed the harsher side of inequality along the waterfront, engendering stratification and friction. Sometimes people on the waterfront expressed their dissatis-faction with such inequality by rioting, burning, or stealing. Others took the initiative to run away from their masters and patrons. The fifteen-year-old "Apprentice Lad" John Regan ran from his master, Captain David Shand of the *Tristram*. Two seamen, Thomas Burton and Thomas Butler, deserted the ship *Anthony* while it was docked at Clarke's Wharf. Daniel Shehane, "an indented Irish Servant," age twenty, fled from Alexander Inglish, master of the brigantine *Sally*. Newspaper advertisements warned masters of other vessels not to harbor, conceal, or carry off such runaways, "on Penalty of the Law." The waterfront's dynamic, anonymous quality gave these disgruntled seamen, servants, and slaves an opportunity to terminate their employment and assert their own notions of freedom. In New York, the plotting of theft and arson in waterfront taverns such as Hughson's and Comfort's led to several fires and executions in 1741.[39]

The smooth operation of patronage relied upon a widespread belief that these cultural, social, and economic exchanges served everyone's interests. On board the *Lydia* or at his wharf, John Hancock wielded real economic power, which gave him the ability to command deference and obedience from tenants and employees. At the same time, Hancock purchased uniforms for celebrants of Pope's Day every fifth of November and commissioned shipbuilding to keep local artisans employed—in this way, he deferred to less wealthy Bostonians in return. For many elite Bostonians, it was worthwhile to maintain such good relations. Otherwise, apprentices and seamen might exercise their power in more disruptive ways, by stealing, running away, participating in a mutiny, or taking their grievances into the streets. Under ordinary circumstances, this is how the waterfront community worked. At the same time, poorer waterfront dwellers sometimes singled out their masters or some other powerful individual as obnoxious, and in those cases they could compel a wealthy merchant to subordinate his interests to what *they* argued were the interests of the wider waterfront community. This type of social conflict bubbled below the surface in eighteenth-century Boston, and sometimes resulted in riots and disorder.[40]

Imperial officials could also command respect and obedience under ordinary circumstances. Before the 1760s, patronage, personal influence, political appointments, Crown contracts, and social authority drew together Bostonians and representatives of the British Empire. The waterfront hosted public shaming rituals in response to military defeats, as well as public celebrations in honor of military victories, holidays, and the arrivals and departures of important personages. For instance, in honor of the birthday of George III in 1763, "all Ranks and Orders of persons" expressed "the greatest Tokens of Loyalty and joy" in a celebration that took place by the water's edge. Cannons were fired from Castle William in the harbor, the shorefront batteries, and the vessels docked by the wharves. The town regiment, an artillery company, and the Company of Cadets marched into King Street and performed exercises for the benefit of the governor and council.[41] A portrait of Captain-Lieutenant John Larrabee, circa 1750 (fig. 1.3), vividly demonstrates one Bostonian's enjoyment of his place in the British Empire. Larrabee stands proudly and authoritatively, hefting a spyglass and resting it on the barrel of a cannon. The painting may be portraying Larrabee on Castle Island, where he lived and served—in the background are British warships in Boston harbor. In 1750, between King George's War and the Seven Years' War, this military officer believed himself well integrated with the harbor, the empire, and his province. When he mobilized, he mobilized on behalf of his countrymen. For Bostonians

Figure 1.3. Captain-Lieutenant John Larrabee displays his pride as a loyal soldier and subject of the British Empire before the imperial crisis. Larrabee lived and served on Castle Island, which would later become the refuge of imperial officers fleeing from Boston crowds. *Captain-Lieutenant John Larrabee, ca. 1750*, by Joseph Badger. *Worcester Art Museum, Worcester, Massachusetts.*

who defended the royal prerogative, whether they were royal officials, wealthy merchants, or ordinary artisans, these attitudes remained unchanged during the imperial crisis—indeed, the violence of the Boston crowds convinced them that the empire was more worthy of their loyalty than the masses.[42]

Conflict between Massachusetts and the empire was relatively subdued before 1760. Wealthy merchants personally knew many of the imperial officeholders, customs collectors, and naval officers. Imperial appointees and local elites mingled together in clubs or at fancy social events.[43] The three branches of imperial government with a presence on the waterfront—the Vice-Admiralty Court, the Customs House, and the Royal Navy—made up a relatively tranquil imperial system in Boston prior to 1763. When new imperial policies caused a shift in this climate, the Boston waterfront became an important site of conflict and political mobilization.

The Vice-Admiralty Court of Massachusetts oversaw legal interactions on the waterfront in a way that provoked few objections before 1763. Appointees of the governor, the vice-admiralty judges had jurisdiction over the high seas and seaborne commerce. Merchants and seamen alike took advantage of the vice-admiralty courts to settle their disputes over wages or customs interdiction. The sessions of the vice-admiralty court allowed Bostonians to stay abreast of seafaring activity throughout New England. Although waterfront inhabitants had little objection to the relatively weak vice-admiralty courts, such attitudes would change after 1763.[44]

The second branch of British government that made its presence felt on the Boston waterfront operated out of the Customs House Office in King Street. The collector made sure that Bostonians entered goods properly and paid duties. He also gave bonds, seized illicit goods, and forwarded customs receipts to England. Other officials included a comptroller who acted as a check on the collector and sometimes as his proxy; a surveyor and searcher responsible for outdoor inspections; weighers and gaugers; landwaiters or portwaiters who stood guard on the wharves; tidewaiters, employed as needed, who stood guard on vessels; and boatmen, also employed as needed.[45] For over a century, colonial merchants had grudgingly tolerated Parliament's restrictions on trade, mostly because the inefficiency, corruption, and disorganization of the "Old Colonial System" precluded effective enforcement. Even if the small group of customs officers had wanted to enforce the Acts of Trade effectively, traders resisted or avoided customs duties by means ranging from legal wrangling, forgery, and bribery to smuggling and open violence.[46]

Prior to the Seven Years' War, city dwellers, including Bostonians, regularly and brazenly evaded the Molasses Act of 1733. Although most traders did not take the risk, smuggling molasses from foreign Caribbean islands was cheaper than legally importing British West Indian sugar. Many merchants, sea captains, and their employees cooperated in siphoning these illicit gains—which deprived British Caribbean planters of their profits and the British Treasury of revenue—into Boston, Newport, New York, and other American ports. Overt smuggling encouraged a burgeoning disrespect for the authority of customs officials. Advocate General William Bollan reported that smugglers would hide or spirit away their seamen so that admiralty judges could not compel the seamen to testify as witnesses. In 1743, he warned that "the Illicit Traders will by their Numbers, Wealth and Wiles have got such power in these parts that Laws and Orders may come too late from Great Britain to have their proper Effect against it."[47] Like crowd action or other forms of protest, smuggling allowed for some dynamism and flexibility within the more rigid system of political patronage and socioeconomic power—yet a revenue-hungry ministry could not tolerate such flexibility.

The Royal Navy, the third branch of imperial power, provoked the beginnings of more explosive resistance. For decades, Bostonians had clashed violently with naval officers—riots over impressment occurred in the early 1690s, 1702, 1741, 1745, 1747, and 1758. Throughout the British Atlantic world, the navy attempted to replace deserters by harassing local vessels, and sometimes even initiated presses on land. Impressment denied seamen their basic freedom, forcing them to serve the navy when they could earn much more aboard merchant vessels. According to custom and Bostonians' interpretation of unclear British laws, the navy could only impress seamen (not land-based workers) during a wartime emergency and needed a warrant from the colonial governor to do so. In Boston, impressment could cause the commercial "engine" to grind to a halt. Laborers and tradesmen hid from the press gang, ships refused to enter the harbor, and the prices of provisions rose. Still, impressment was necessary for the prosecution of Britain's imperial wars. In 1742, Massachusetts governor William Shirley helped the townspeople and the navy to reach an understanding. He insisted that the navy press only non-Massachusetts seamen on arriving vessels (ostensibly the most extrinsic people on the waterfront), so that captains could ship goods along the coast freely and recruit seamen in peace. This policy created "a community of interest," according to historians, among the denizens of the waterfront, merchants as well as seamen.[48]

Naval press gangs continued to antagonize this community of interest, and by the late 1740s, the navy and its press gangs had made themselves intensely unpopular in the Boston. While naval officers complained that the captains of higher paying merchant ships were "enticing away their Seamen," the Massachusetts legislature accused the navy of violating the "Law, and His Majesty's Royal Charter, and the Rights of English Men."[49] A press gang killed two resisting mariners in 1745, and the town complained in 1746 that impressment was driving seamen out of the province. The Common Council, the upper branch of Massachusetts government, responded to these grievances by refusing to approve further impressment warrants. Meanwhile, Parliament passed a bill in 1746 that prohibited impressment in the West Indies but said nothing of North America, filling New Englanders with "a Hatred for the King's Service . . . [and] a Spirit of Rebellion," as Commodore Charles Knowles later wrote. The navy, with the backing of Parliament, had encroached upon what they believed to be the most marginal component of Boston's commercial society. Yet they found that Boston's interdependent waterfront dwellers were ready to rally to local seamen's defense.[50]

The dispute over impressment was still festering when Knowles provoked Boston's waterfront community. On November 16, 1747, his sailors pressed forty-six men from the harbor, including almost the entire crew of the *Mercury*, as well as locals such as Jonathan Tarbox and two shipwrights' apprentices. Bostonians responded by taking some of Knowles's men hostage and demanding the release of the impressed men. The crowd broke windows, harassed authority figures, burnt a boat on the Common, and "distributed themselves at the different Wharves and Ferry places" to prevent any naval officers from escaping the town overnight. Knowles threatened to bombard the town, while Governor Shirley fled to safety on Castle Island. After three days of disorder, the crowd released Knowles's officers, Bostonians welcomed Shirley back to Boston with a parade, and Knowles returned most of the impressed inhabitants and left port.[51] A British naval officer had infringed upon the rights and liberties of the waterfront's "community of interest," and the waterfront had mobilized in response.

Most of Boston's elite disavowed responsibility for the incident. They blamed the riots on foreign seamen, servants, artisans, blacks, "lewd and profligate Persons," and "low sort of people," and they arrested eleven alleged ringleaders, including five mariners and four laborers. While legislators and the governor tried to deflect blame from the town of Boston in this way to save face with the imperial government, most merchants approved of resistance to impressment, which hurt their interests, too. Furthermore, the Knowles Riot inspired Patriot ideologue Samuel Adams, the Harvard-educated brewer's son who was on his way to becoming one of Boston's principal leaders. In the months following the incident, Adams castigated the "great and intolerable Injury of impressments" and the government's inability to provide effective redress. He defended the "Assembly of People drawn together upon no other Design than to defend themselves, and repel the Assaults of a Press-Gang," and believed that the waterfront community had a "natural right . . . to repel those Mischiefs against which they can derive no Security from the Government." Bostonians had used extralegal means to counteract threats from British naval officials and regain control of the waterfront space, providing a model for future resistance and an inspiration for future Patriots. The actions of the navy had disrupted and polarized the waterfront community. Its denizens adopted a new, revolutionary consciousness and acted in concert to defend their liberty, integrity, and economic activity from governmental oppression.[52]

The Knowles Riot also foreshadowed a sequence that was to repeat itself throughout the prerevolutionary decade on the Boston waterfront. In four major instances—the Stamp Act crisis, the *Liberty* riot, the Boston Massacre, and the Boston Tea Party—the sequence would unfold as follows: British officials would attempt to encroach upon waterfront prerogatives through customs laws, armed threats to personal liberty, or a combination of the two. Members of the waterfront community would respond in minor ways at first, until the scuffle for control culminated in a major crowd action. This blatant display of mobilized animosity would compel British officials to flee to Castle Island and step up their plaintive requests for assistance from England. The British imperial command and the burgeoning Whig elite of Boston would respond in the ways they thought most appropriate, leading to repercussions along with a tentative settlement of the contest for control over the port and waterfront. In 1747, the repercussions were small—a grudging compromise and the stirrings of waterfront consciousness. By the decade before independence, the repercussions became more far-reaching, and Bostonians and imperial officials raised the stakes for control of the waterfront.

Changes taking place on the waterfront in the late 1750s and early 1760s exacerbated the oncoming imperial crisis. Boston was already missing out on the grain trade that was contributing to economic growth in New York and Philadelphia. The Seven Years' War brought lucrative supply contracts for merchants, yet also increased the British military presence, impressment, and war casualties. Economic hard times plagued shopkeepers, artisans, and laborers in the northern cities. In the midst of these troubles, the Great Fire of March 20, 1760, broke out in a tanning yard in the center of Boston and swept southeastward to Fort Hill, damaging hundreds of buildings. Then a smallpox epidemic stalked the town in the early 1760s, causing deaths and more poverty. In January 1765, the merchant Nathaniel Wheelwright declared bankruptcy, sending shockwaves through the credit networks of Boston. John Rowe reported that local merchants were "much alarmed." He predicted that "a great number of people will suffer" as a result of Wheelwright's bankruptcy. A severe storm in March 1765 damaged a number of wharves and ships, straining the local economy even further. Unemployment, destitution, crime, and street violence were rampant, and the North End and dockside areas, those most closely associated with the waterfront, seemed to have been hit the hardest. Adding insult to injury, many supporters of the imperial government had moved to the suburbs and appeared determined to ignore the city's plight.[53]

In this climate, British authorities tried, too late, to reform the colonial system and its maritime empire in earnest. Already the British customs service had antagonized Boston merchants by removing Benjamin Barons, Boston's lenient customs collector, from office. Now local customs officers attempted to exercise their right to issue writs of assistance, or general search warrants, for catching smugglers in Massachusetts. The fiery lawyer James Otis became famous for his oratory when he argued against the legality of the writs in Superior Court. When George Grenville assumed the office of chief minister to the king in 1763, he ordered customs officials to their posts in America and had them make regular reports. He also empowered naval officers to counteract smuggling and seize ships. Grenville enacted new duties on wine, coffee, and other commodities, amended previous duties on textiles, and mandated that colonists would have to ship iron or lumber to England before heading on to Europe. The Sugar Act, called the "Black Act" in Boston, prohibited the colonies from importing foreign rum, and halved the duty on foreign molasses to 3d. a gallon, with the idea that a lower duty would discourage American smugglers and encourage legal payment of the tax. The customs service mandated that all American merchants fill out elaborate paperwork to ensure their compliance with the law and the payment of all duties. Judges in vice-admiralty courts had the authority to rule on customs violations and authorize the seizure of ships without the help of juries, and customs officers could bring suit in these courts if they thought that judges and juries in colonial courts would be too friendly to American merchants. Customs officers, informers, and naval officers involved in seizures received part of the profits from the sale of seized ships and their goods. In the event of wrongful prosecution, American merchants had no power to sue British customs officials for damages. The laws were intended to increase revenue from customs duties and facilitate effective enforcement. On the Boston waterfront, their principal effect was to heighten the animosity between the town's inhabitants and the agents of British government. Customs officials, previously known as harmless incompetents, now joined naval officials as obnoxious outsiders who were encroaching upon the waterfront.[54]

The Royal Navy managed to compound its unpopularity in Bostonians' minds by taking on some of the responsibility for customs seizures. The navy had begun enforcing restrictions against trade with other European nations during the Seven Years' War. After the war's end, with persistent strictness, they continued seizing and harassing vessels in and around Boston. Rear Admiral Alexander Colville boasted, "By the Vigilance of the Sea Officers Smuggling is now reduced to very low Ebb." Boston merchants were not so sanguine about this development. One complained, "No vessel hardly comes in or goes out, but they find some pretence to seize and detain her."[55] Meanwhile, impressment continued unabated. In July 1764, Admiral Colville issued orders to his captains to begin procuring men ("without distressing trade") and was deliberately vague about the methods. The navy, armed with these dual offensive tasks, was bound to provoke conflict. A crowd of Newport seamen and dockworkers beat back a press gang trying to recapture a deserter from H.M.S. *St. John* in June 1764. In July a group of New Yorkers attacked a press gang from the *Chaleur* and burnt its boat in front of City Hall. On November 28, 1764, fishermen and mariners responded violently to a British naval officer who boarded the

Betsy & Ruth for the ostensible purpose of examining her for smuggled goods. One of the ship's owners, Robert Gold, was already an active defender of the waterfront community as a member of the Boston Society for Encouraging Trade and Commerce.[56] Animosity toward the navy's press gangs and its interference with commerce was beginning to turn American ports into battlegrounds over imperial encroachment.

Merchants, meanwhile, exercised their own methods of resistance to naval officers—Bollan's prediction that the "Illicit Traders" would gain strength was coming true. In August 1765, an embarrassed Admiral Colville begged his superiors to discount the anonymous letter they had received from Boston, which accused the captains of the men-of-war around New England of harboring "immodest Women" on board their ships. Colville explained the false accusation by arguing "that the Captains on the New England Station are become very unpopular from the nature of their Duty as Custom house Officers; and the Odium against them is greatly heightened [sic] from the necessity they are frequently under of Impressing, before they can proceed to sea." Colville also repeated the navy's frequent complaint that the higher wages offered on merchant ships, combined with "the various Artifices used to inveigle our Seamen from us," had been responsible for desertion among his men. The year before, in October 1764, Boston merchants had instituted a boycott of any pilot who served the king's ships. The pilots, though they appeared to Captain Charles Antrobus to be in a "starving condition," refused to carry him from Boston to Newport, for fear of never working in Boston again. Colville blamed the "smuggling merchants" and their "prejudices" against the navy. Using their economic power for political ends, these merchants enforced a certain discipline on the waterfront. They asked the pilots to sacrifice their livelihoods for the greater good of standing up to the navy's harassment.[57]

Thus, the "Spirit of Rebellion" continued to unite the waterfront as a community of interest even before the Stamp Act riots confirmed Boston's place as the vanguard of resistance to Great Britain. Seamen, crowds, and merchants were demonstrating their ability to draw upon their collective strength and act together in the interests of commerce and the smooth operation of maritime life. To be sure, the merchants and town leaders were senior partners in this alliance: in 1764 they were willing to sacrifice the interests of individual pilots, just as in 1747 they gave up a handful of rioting seamen and laborers to the authorities. Merchants and magistrates justified these acts in the name of the greater good: "the Rights of English Men" and stable commercial activity. At the same time, seamen and artisans were every bit as willing as their patrons to protect the waterfront from infringements of liberty by British officials, as crowd actions and resistance to impressment had illustrated.

The Stamp Act rioting of August 1765 dramatically revealed the Bostonians' uneasiness with British rule. Two institutions were particularly important for mobilizing Boston's crowds against the Stamp Act, and both drew from the waterfront community. First, a group called the "Loyal Nine" helped to coordinate the action from behind the scenes. The club met at William Speakman's South End distillery and included two distillers, John Avery Jr. and Thomas Chase; the merchant Henry Bass; shipowner Henry Welles; and possibly Joseph Field, ship's captain. Second, the Loyal Nine seems to have recruited crowd participants from the North End and South End gangs that annually brawled with one another in anti-Catholic Pope's Day celebrations each November 5. These gangs drew heavily from the maritime population, including seamen and blacks. Henry Swift, a shipwright, was captain of the North Enders, and was among the many waterfront dwellers who also participated in the riots protesting the Stamp Act. Bostonians recognized the importance of mobilizing to protect their waterfront turf.[58]

On August 14, the crowd hung effigies of local stamp officer Andrew Oliver and the king's former tutor, Lord Bute, from the Liberty Tree, a block from the shorefront in the South End. The crowd then destroyed Oliver's "stamp office" in Kilby Street, also located on the water, at Oliver's Dock. Finally, the crowds "stamped" and burned the effigy on Fort Hill, overlooking the water, where British officials could clearly see the bonfire from Castle William. Governor Francis Bernard had heard the unwelcoming message of these waterfront protests and fled to the castle. In the coming weeks and months the stamps themselves would be stored in exile at Castle William. On August 15, Bernard wrote, "I saw a Bonfire Burning on Fort Hill: by which I understand that the Mob is up and probably doing Mischief." As in 1747 (and later in 1768 and 1773), the crowd mobilized on the waterfront as a conspicuous site for public protest against British policies. The bonfires on Fort Hill signified Bostonians' continued control over the waterfront. Such fires, the crowd hoped, would keep obnoxious stamps and obnoxious British officials like Bernard away from the Boston peninsula.[59]

The Boston crowd soon expressed its own grievances, apparently without the sanction of the Loyal Nine. On August 26, the crowd targeted British officials who had extensive authority over the waterfront. They threatened Charles Paxton, the unpopular surveyor of the port and marshal of the vice-admiralty court. They burned the files of William Story, deputy registrar of the vice-admiralty court, destroying records of customs seizures and wage disputes. The rioters wreaked the greatest havoc on the property of Comptroller Benjamin Hallowell and Lieutenant Governor Thomas Hutchinson, who supported the new trade regulations and (according to rumor) had sent depositions about smuggling to Great Britain.[60] Resentment against supporters of royal government had sparked a wildfire of crowd violence that spread to other cities. In Newport, crowds destroyed the homes of Dr. Thomas Moffat and Martin Howard Jr. on August 28. After posting a notice on Newport's Long Wharf, the crowd banished them and their allies to H.M.S. Cygnet in the harbor. In New York City, "Sons of Neptune," ship's captains, and shipwrights took the lead in Stamp Act rioting. While the inhabitants of depressed port towns channeled their economic grievances into political actions, they also demonstrated a desire to retain control over the waterfront and the cities. They had shown their displeasure with officials whose antagonistic actions were beginning to mark them as outsiders. In Boston, the waterfront community had decided that illiberal British officials did not belong. Bernard had fled, and many Bostonians hoped that other imperial officials would take the hint and follow suit.[61]

The debate over policies such as the Stamp Act turned upon broad-based economic grievances along the waterfront. In September 1765, Bostonians threatened to impose a boycott that would compel British merchants to lobby for the repeal of the Stamp Act. Governor Bernard appealed to the waterfront community not to adopt such a plan.

> If trade and navigation shall cease by the shutting up the ports of this province for want of legal clearances, are you sure that all the other ports which can rival these, will be shut up also? Can you depend upon recovering your trade again entire and undiminished, when you shall be pleased to resume it? Can the people of this province subsist without navigation for any long time? What will become of the seamen who will be put out of employment? What will become of the tradesmen who immediately depend upon navigation for their daily bread? Will these people endure want quietly without troubling their neighbors? What will become of the numberless families which depend upon fishery? Will they be able to turn the produce of their year's work into the necessaries of life, without navigation? Are there not numberless other families who do not appear immediately concerned in trade, and yet ultimately depend upon it?[62]

Governor Bernard illuminated the interdependent character of the waterfront, appealing to the interests of Boston's merchants, tradesmen, fishermen, and seamen. Yet he also revealed a certain class bias, intending for his audience of "Gentlemen" in the Council and House of Representatives to recall the August riots and recoil in horror at the prospect of unemployed seamen and tradesmen "troubling their neighbors." Governor Bernard was shrewd to suggest that the proximity of rich and poor near the waterfront might become a source of conflict. The House, for its part, answered confidently that there would be "no danger" of "outlawry," and asserted, "When our sacred rights are infringed, we feel the grievance." They refused to comply with the Stamp Act. Meanwhile, the newspapers hastened to assure the public that all efforts would be made to keep seamen, "this valuable Set of People," employed, and that mussels, clams, and cod were sufficiently available to feed Boston's poor. Two hundred New York merchants agreed on October 31 to refrain from importing British goods, and the merchants in Philadelphia, Boston, and other port towns followed suit. Still, Bernard had exposed a tension that persisted throughout the revolutionary conflict in Boston: though ties of commerce and proximity united waterfront denizens, scarcity, economic discontent, and violence might shatter this unity. For instance, the Sons of Liberty in Charleston acted "instantly" to suppress unemployed seamen who had taken to the streets. In Philadelphia a group of ship carpenters called the "White Oaks" acted to stymie challenges to imperial authority. When Pennsylvania's Quaker party defended the Stamp Act in hopes of convincing Parliament to overturn Pennsylvania's proprietary government, the Philadelphia White Oaks supported them. In Boston, however, town leaders gambled that shared beliefs about the unconstitutional nature of the new Revenue Acts would provide sufficient grounds to preserve the unified political coalition that had arisen out of the waterfront community.[63]

Their gamble paid off, as the waterfront crowds made clear. George Meserve, the appointed stamp distributor for New Hampshire, learned of the Stamp Act's unpopularity while traveling to Boston. As a result, he sent advance notice that he would resign the office. When he arrived at Long Wharf in September 1765, his friends and other gentlemen paid their respects, and when he publicly announced his resignation, "three Cheers were given by a vast Concourse of People, which were repeated at the Head of the Wharff, and again on the Exchange." In South Carolina, the stamp distributors George Saxby and Caleb Lloyd similarly took refuge in Fort Johnson before publicly announcing that they would not exercise their duties. Cheering Charleston crowds greeted them at the wharves. Displays such as this, or the mock execution of stamped papers that arrived aboard a vessel in 1765, allowed waterfront denizens from all walks of life to interact in the public arena and express their political beliefs. Whereas such celebrations had previously demonstrated imperial support, the Stamp Act repeal gave city dwellers the opportunity to celebrate their resistance. In Boston and Charleston, the waterfront spectators' cheers signified approval of the stamp officers' resignation. If they had chosen instead to execute their offices, city dwellers might have treated them as they had treated Hutchinson, Hallowell, Moffat, or Howard—officials whom Bostonians and Newporters were beginning to regard as outsiders. In May 1766, news arrived in Boston that Parliament had repealed the Stamp Act. Bells rang, cannons fired, and "colours were displayed from the Merchants Vessels in the Harbour." Bostonians celebrated their unified defense of the waterfront community, and continued to do so on anniversaries of the repeal.[64] Although the waterfront reached a state of relative calm after the repeal of the Stamp Act, the storms of rebellion were rumbling.

Like the Stamp Act, subsequent imperial policies touched off waves of resistance on the waterfront. The Townshend Act levied new duties on imports of glass, lead, paint, paper, and tea into the colonies. Upon hearing of the new law, the printer and bookseller John Boyle predicted, "An Opposition to this Act no doubt will take place." The ministry also reorganized the vice-admiralty court system into four superior admiralty courts (still devoid of jury trials), one of which would sit at Boston. The Treasury established a Board of Commissioners of Customs for North America, also to reside in Boston, due to its blatant violation of customs laws. Only one of these new commissioners, John Temple, had a good reputation among the Boston merchants. The others were familiar enemies, Charles Paxton of Boston and John Robinson of Newport, or suspicious British newcomers, William Burch and Henry Hulton. This new board quickly began enforcing customs regulations more strictly, much to merchants' dismay. The resulting payment of additional fees, plus the costs of court battles with the customs commissioners, placed a heavy burden on overseas merchants, and an even heavier burden on small-time coastal traders. The board commissioned its own ships to make seizures at sea, increasing the maritime community's animosity toward His Majesty's vessels, and hired more tidesmen, which expanded the official presence on the wharves and ships. Seamen's private trunks, traditionally exempt from official consideration, were now subject to confiscation. Parliament had injected British authority even further into the heart of the city's waterfront, and the waterfront began to crystallize as a frontier zone of mobilization, where the conflict between the representatives of Great Britain and the hostile townspeople of Boston would play out.[65] Bostonians' resistance took a variety of forms. At the urging of Boston's leaders, the Massachusetts House of Representatives sent a circular letter in February 1768 urging the other colonies to take a united stand against Townshend's program. Meanwhile, city dwellers and rural townspeople pressured seaport merchants in Boston, New York, Philadelphia, and elsewhere to sign agreements not to import any goods from Great Britain, in a second attempt to compel a repeal. On the waterfront, resistance also involved the evasion of customs duties (smuggling) and threats against customs officers.[66]

Waterfront dwellers banded together to abet local smugglers and used brazen tactics for defying customs officials, especially the new board. The streets rang with cries such as "Liberty, Property, & no Commissioners" and "Pay no Duties,! save your Money and you save your Country!" Joseph Harrison wrote that the "running of Goods and Smuggling is become public Virtue and Patriotism."[67] When customs officers seized a ship and pulled it alongside the wharves, Bostonians would board it in the middle of the night, unload it, and sometimes even refit it so the vessel could put off to sea. Crowds harassed the commissioners, their families, and anyone who paid the Townshend duties. Insults flew, and effigies dangled from the Liberty Tree in February and on the anniversary of the Stamp Act repeal on March 18, followed that evening by the "loud Huzzaing" of local seamen and apprentices in the streets.[68] In May 1768, Bostonians threatened to banish the customs officials outright: Paxton reported that the townspeople would "put the Governor and the Commissioners of the Customs on board a Ship and send them to England" if Parliament did not repeal the Townshend Acts.[69]

Daniel Malcom, a sea captain turned merchant and member of the Boston Marine Society, was a thorn in the side of customs officials throughout the late 1760s. On September 24, 1766, customs officials had accused Malcom of concealing smuggled wine and liquor in his basement and issued a writ of assistance, or search warrant, to inspect his house. To protest the illegality of their authority, Malcom fortified his house against the officials. His North End neighbors—including Captain John Matchet, wharfinger John Ballard, silversmith Paul Revere, distiller Benjamin Goodwin, merchant William Mackay of the Marine Society, Captain Caleb Hopkins of the Marine Society, and a group of boys from the nearby grammar school—gathered en masse in support. Malcom showed his gratitude by having sailmaker and shipmaster Edward Jarvis distribute wine among them. The North Enders proved to be reliable defenders against British infringement upon liberty and property.[70] In 1768, Malcom was again smuggling wine, and he applied to John Williams, the new inspector general at the customs house, "for the usual indulgences"—that is, he asked whether he could avoid paying any duties. Williams refused to look the other way as previous customs officers had done. If Malcom were caught smuggling, his goods would be seized. That night, thirty or forty "stout fellows, armed with bludgeons" rowed across the harbor in drays and transported Malcom's smuggled wine into several cellars in town. Although this noisy affair was public knowledge, customs officers were unable to turn up any informers or effect a seizure. This type of action required the cooperation of merchants, local magistrates (who were often merchants themselves), captains, seamen, laborers, watchmen, sympathetic neighbors, and possibly low-level customs officials as well. Bostonians from throughout the social spectrum participated in smuggling, sharing a common dislike for British officials and a common loyalty to local waterfront commerce that was reinforced by patronage.[71]

John Hancock, perhaps Boston's greatest patron, also became the most storied adversary of imperial officials. In 1767, Hancock had already declared himself an enemy of the customs commissioners by refusing to allow his Company of Cadets to participate in an official welcome for the commissioners. Hancock's refusal reflected the wider community's lack of respect for these officials, and he was rapidly becoming a waterfront folk hero.[72] On April 8, 1768, two tidesmen boarded Hancock's brig *Lydia* at his wharf to prevent any clandestine unlading of the customable goods on board. With a crowd at their backs, Hancock, his employees, and a coterie including radical merchant-captains Matchet, Malcom, and Mackay confronted the tidesmen and encouraged them to stand down. The bystanders were so delighted with Hancock's actions that they escorted him from the wharf, and he had to beg them not to parade through the town in support.[73] Like Malcom, Hancock demonstrated visibly that he was willing to take a stand against Britain on the basis of waterfront grievances. Because Hancock was a major creditor, landlord, shipowner, wharf owner, employer, and rising politician, his actions were destined to have a greater impact on the waterfront.

Two months later, the Royal Navy provoked Bostonians even further. With threats against customs officials mounting, the H.M.S. *Romney* arrived in the harbor and within a few weeks had sent out a press gang. Bostonians enjoying "the Cool of the Day" on the waterfront helped a few escaping seamen reach the shore, and when the press gang's boats attempted to land, the bystanders answered them with stones and brickbats. In the following days the *Romney* impressed two more men, and the crowd rescued an impressed man. The waterfront had become a hotly contested space, and tensions with British officials were at a high point.[74]

The customs commissioners thus showed a poor sense of timing when they seized Hancock's sloop *Liberty* at his wharf on June 10. A tidesman claimed that Hancock had been smuggling wine and that Hancock's men had attempted to bribe him. Hancock's men then temporarily imprisoned the tidesman below decks and warned him to keep silent. In light of this testimony, or perhaps to punish Hancock for his defiance aboard the *Lydia*, the customs officials announced their intention to seize the *Liberty* by painting the king's arrow on the main mast at sunset on June 10. The commissioners understood that seizure would be dangerous, given that the town's inhabitants "had long before this shewn a great Disaffection to the Revenue Laws," so they endeavored to have the *Liberty* removed from Hancock's wharf and put under the protection of the *Romney*. The workday having just ended, "People began to muster together on the Wharf, from all Quarters" as boats from the *Romney* approached. Captain Malcom, Goodwin, Matchet, and Hopkins, brothers in arms from the 1766 fight over writs of assistance, mobilized yet again to defy this customs seizure, along with "a Number of Sailors, and vagrant Persons who were suspicious of an Intention to put them on board the Ship." In all, some 300 to 400 members of the North End waterfront community attempted to prevent the seizure. They threw stones at the warship's crew, wounding some of them. After the naval officers steered the *Liberty* away from shore, the crowd turned on the customs officials, carrying them "in triumph as trespassers up the wharffe" and pelting them with stones and brickbats. In addition to the usual threats and window-breaking, the crowds took a "particular and elegant" pleasure boat of Harrison's from Oliver's Dock (where the stamp office had been torn down in 1765), and dragged it through King Street and the main road to the Liberty Tree. Here the crowd staged a mock vice-admiralty court and condemned the "seizure." Then they brought the boat to the Common and burnt it "before Mr. Hancock's Door."[75]

The reactions of Bostonians and British officials to this incident illustrate the increasingly polarized relationship that was developing between Great Britain and the seaport city. The customs officers, for their part, felt unsafe on the Boston waterfront. As Joshua Henshaw Jr. wrote: "The Commissioners (excepting Mr. Temple) with their Under-Officers upon this little Difficulty, repaired on Board the Romney, and I believe will be obliged to remain there, as it seems to be the mind of the People that they have lived long enough in this Town."[76] The officers and their families stayed on board the *Romney* for nine days, and on June 21, in the not-so-proud tradition of unpopular British officials, they settled in at Castle William—exiles from the Boston waterfront. Customs Commissioner Henry Hulton's sister Ann wrote, "Every Officer of the Crown that does his duty is become obnoxious, & they must either fly or be sacrificed." According to her understanding of the prevailing waterfront mentality, Bostonians would have been otherwise inclined to treat her brother and his fellow "Gentlemen" with civility, but as commissioners "they are prohibitd [from] setting foot on Shore again at their peril." If the commissioners defied this "prohibition," church sextons with an eye on the docks would alert the town by tolling the bells as if for a fire alarm. Keeping the commissioners out of Boston was as much a public good as keeping the city free of fire.[77]

The officials' families tried to make the best of their exile ("every body seems much happier in their exiled state than on the Land of Liberty") as they remained on Castle Island through November. Governor Bernard, distressed at his collapsing authority, pleaded for troops "to rescue the Government out of the hands of a trained mob, & to restore the Activity of the Civil Power, which is now entirely obstructed." The ultimate consequence of the *Liberty* riot, therefore, was the British troops' occupation of Boston.[78] Bostonians had banished offensive British officials, and would do so again, because they had begun to perceive the "Land of Liberty" as a space independent of an unconstitutional authority. In this way, the harbor became a political border zone of sorts, separating Castle William from the Boston peninsula and keeping unlawful British authority at a safe distance (fig. 1.4).

Although New Englanders were fiercely protective of their charter rights, and waged this fight on several fronts, Bostonians singled out the waterfront as a part of the city that suffered particularly from British policies. Boston's maritime commerce was always vulnerable to market swings throughout the Atlantic world, competition from other ports, and other circumstances beyond the inhabitants' control. The navy and the commissioners of customs had an invidious ability to aggravate (if not cause) trade difficulties, and as a result, waterfront dwellers feared and despised them. Merchants, artisans, shopkeepers, laborers, and their neighbors recognized their economic interdependence and did not relish the prospect of a depression caused by unconstitutional British policies.

The issue of impressment also presented waterfront denizens with the stark realization that liberty might be a precarious thing when British officers wielded power arbitrarily. Violence in American ports had, by this time, already discouraged the navy from using the press gang obnoxiously. Naval officers knew that the waterfront community would rally behind seamen (and land-based local workers) and assert their common culture of resistance to tyranny. The events of 1768 had threatened the interests of all Bostonians, from the wealthy and powerful John Hancock to the impressed seaman. After 1769, the issue of impressment largely faded from view.

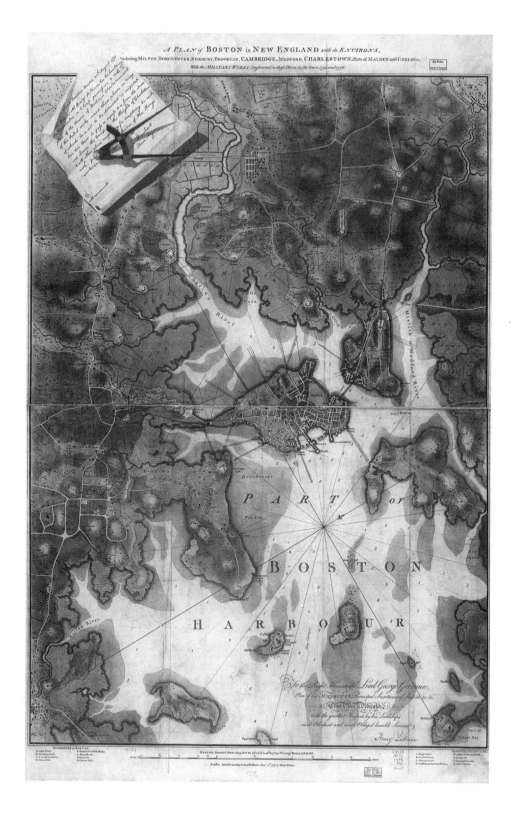

A PLAN of BOSTON in NEW ENGLAND with its ENVIRONS,
including MILTON, DORCHESTER, ROXBURY, BROOKLIN, CAMBRIDGE, MEDFORD, CHARLESTOWN, Parts of MALDEN and CHELSEA.
With the MILITARY WORKS Constructed in those Places in the Years 1775 and 1776.

PART OF

BOSTON

HARBOUR

To the Right Honourable Lord George Germain,
One of his MAJESTY'S Principal Secretaries of State &c. &c. &c.
This Plan is Dedicated
with the greatest Respect by his Lordship's
most Obedient and much Obliged humble Servant
Henry Pelham

In that year, a special court of admiralty heard the case of *Rex v. Corbet*, in which the young attorney John Adams defended a seaman accused of murdering a naval lieutenant with a harpoon during an impressment attempt. Adams prepared to challenge the constitutionality of impressment, when the trial was suddenly and mysteriously adjourned, and the seaman acquitted. Adams later remarked, "No trial had ever interested the community so much before, excited so much curiosity and compassion, or so many apprehensions of the fateful consequences of the supremacy of parliamentary jurisdiction, or the intrigues of parliamentary courts. No trial had drawn together such crowds of auditors from day to day." Adams suspected that the judges had quickly silenced the trial to avoid a public discussion of the navy's right to impress: "Such a judgement would . . . have accelerated the revolution."[79] When faced with impressment or customs seizures, the community of interest on the waterfront reflexively defended itself. The ritual acts of banishing customs officers and burning a "seized" boat belonging to Harrison displayed this community's power to police its waterfront domain.

In the aftermath of the *Liberty* riot, town officials articulated many of these ideas. They reported their "mortification" that Parliament continued to tax the colonists without their consent, depriving them of the "little circulating cash that remained among us for the support of our trade." They were alarmed at rumors of new revenue acts and customs officials, who would "suck the life-blood of the body politick while it is streaming from the veins." They resented the presence of warships such as the *Romney*, "anchored within a cable's length of the wharves," which they knew the Board of Commissioners had summoned for protection. While the purpose of the ships' presence, they wrote, was "to over-awe and terrify the inhabitants of this town into base compliances and unlimited submission," their ultimate effect was a "restraint upon our trade." They pointed to the seizure of the *Liberty* "without probable cause," calling it "violent" and "illegal." And they concluded by calling for an end to "impresses of all kinds."[80]

As they voiced their grievances to the authorities, Boston's merchant-politicians also called for political solidarity among the waterfront community. This became particularly important as agreements not to import British goods created divisions among the cities and conflict within them. Merchants and politicians often failed to address the needs of waterfront workers and seamen, and such conflict might have derailed political mobilization

---

Figure 1.4. This map of Boston harbor shows the distance between the Boston peninsula and Castle Island (now Fort Independence) in the eighteenth century. Castle Island is just beneath the word "Harbour" on this map, toward the left. *A Plan of Boston in New England with its Environs* . . . Engrav'd in aqua tinta by Francis Jukes, by Henry Pelham. London, 1777. *Library of Congress, Geography and Map Division.*

against the acts of Great Britain.[81] Yet even during the nonimportation agreements, the merchants were able to muster widespread support in the maritime community. The same leaders who inspired the waterfront crowds in these years—Hancock, Adams, Malcom, and lumber merchant William Molineux—were also active in the nonimportation movement. It was not the Boston Society for Encouraging Trade and Commerce, a more exclusive club of merchants, but a new, broad-based group of "the Merchants and Traders of Boston" that began calling for boycotts of English goods in 1768 and 1769. The vast majority of Boston merchants and shopkeepers signed the agreements, yet the agreements would have been worthless if any outliers had persisted in importing British goods. The Merchants and Traders endeavored to enforce nonimportation by pressuring those who had imported from Britain to surrender the offending goods. In October 1769, those who refused to sign had to endure the insults and violence of the waterfront crowds, as Whig merchants and shopkeepers sent Bostonians to smear the signs, doors, and windows of importers' shops with "every kind of Filth," sometimes called "Hillsborough paint" after the Earl of Hillsborough, secretary of state for the colonies.[82] Merchants and rioters alike had articulated the common interest of Americans, and marked those who acted against this interest as outsiders. The Boston Town Meeting called nonimportation a "publick Good" that induced merchants to subsume "their own private Emolument" to "the common Interest." By contrast, the town portrayed violators of the agreements as "thoroughly & infamously selfish" and "lost to the feelings of Patriotism." Some of these importers, like smugglers, were able to muster dockhands to clandestinely remove goods from warehouses. The town clerk recorded the importers' names in the town records for posterity, as enemies of Boston—most were Scottish immigrants or young men new to the commercial community, and local merchants argued that these importers, with their British-based commercial networks, threatened Boston's "common Interest." Similar efforts at shaming stubborn importers went on in other cities.[83] Impressment, customs duties, and unfair competition made the waterfront particularly vulnerable to encroachments upon liberty. This was the rationale behind city dwellers' banishment of the customs officers and importers from their midst.

Merchants could only sacrifice their own interests for so long, however, and they began to look for ways to resume their business. While radicals like Molineux used threats to enforce continued nonimportation in Boston (and even in other New England towns, where he met hostility), others feared the crowd's violent acts. The waterfront community split into different factions. Some of the lesser merchants and shopkeepers, suffering from the strained market conditions during nonimportation, began to resent and distrust the merchant princes and smugglers who had prospered by controlling the flow of trade.[84] In the midst of this climate, two Glaswegian shipmasters arrived in January 1770 to arrange for the construction of four 230-ton ships, on the condition that the Boston merchants would agree to permit the importation of the necessary building materials. Seventy artisans immediately signed a petition to carry out the Scots' request, and as they considered submitting it, the corpulent justice of the peace and selectman John Ruddock interrupted the meeting, tore up the petition, and told its sponsor "that he was ruining himself & his Country." Selectman Ruddock's physical heft was probably enough to intimidate such a gathering—but his political and economic heft along the waterfront also ensured that none of the marine artisans objected to his actions, at least according to one source. The Scots, meanwhile, took their business to Newburyport.[85] Still, the selectmen were not completely insensitive to the needs of artisans and laborers: Ruddock and other merchants on a special town committee tried to ensure that nonimportation would not affect the poorer waterfront denizens too adversely. They concluded, "The best method of employing the Tradesmen and poor People in this Town is in the natural branch of Ship building which has been the staple and principal means for employing of the People," and they commissioned three vessels to help alleviate the unemployment problem. The town unanimously approved their report.[86]

Despite this palliative measure, nonimportation had exposed potential cracks in the waterfront's community of interest. Artisans, shopkeepers, and petty merchants went along with nonimportation as long as the influence of patrons like Ruddock and charismatic leaders like Molineux held sway, and as long as they continued to believe the prevailing rhetoric of political mobilization: that they were sacrificing their personal interests for the "publick Good." When the economy suffered, however, these motives could only sustain the nonimportation movement for so long. In the midst of such disagreements, supporters of royal power were able to engage in effective gambits of countermobilization. The Scottish printer John Mein used the same weapon that Boston's radicals used—the newspaper—to expose and embarrass the substantial number of Boston merchants who had continued to import goods. Merchants throughout American cities, who were buckling under their sacrifices while these violators got rich, became disheartened and began to abandon nonimportation. Then in April 1770, word arrived that Parliament had repealed all the Townshend duties except the one on tea. Radical Bostonians hoped to continue the boycott, but the fight had gone out of most American merchants by the summer of 1770. After bitter fights among and within the cities, New York and Philadelphia merchants declined to renew nonimportation agreements. Waterfront mobilization had collapsed along several fault lines— differing political beliefs, as well as economic interests. In the end, however, the disputes of 1767–70 demonstrated that while conflicting economic interests and commercial rivalries among cities had the power to derail radical mobilization, imperial policy also had an impressive capacity to unite Boston's waterfront community. Those merchants who were most responsive to the demands of shipwrights and seamen, and best able to bring other Bostonians to their side, were the ones who mobilized the waterfront community most effectively.[87]

In the midst of these conflicts, the presence of British redcoats united angry Bostonians still further. After the *Liberty* riot, imperial officials decided to station troops in Boston to protect the customs officers in the performance of their duties. While Revere's engraving captures the solemn reaction to the troops' landing on Long Wharf in September 1768, relations between waterfront dwellers and troops would not remain so sedate for the next year and a half. The "lobster backs" attracted fierce resentment, like the customs officers, as outsiders encroaching upon the waterfront. Initially, resistance was largely limited to grumbling against the governor and customs officers and demands that the troops be quartered at the town barracks in Castle William across the harbor. By winter the regiments were encamped close to the waterfront, in sugar refineries, sail lofts, warehouses, and distilleries near Dock Square, on Water Street and Atkinson Street, Pitts's Wharf, Griffin's Wharf, and Wheelwright's Wharf. One journalist marveled, "What an appearance does Boston now make! One of the first commercial towns in America, has now several regiments of soldiers quartered in the midst of it, and even the Merchants Exchange is picquetted." Many of the soldiers, allowed to do odd jobs while off duty, competed with waterfront workers in the tight labor market. In New York, such competition helped provoke angry seamen and dockworkers to chase British troops off the wharves and ships, leading to the Golden Hill and Nassau Street riots of January 1770.[88]

Violence had already broken out in New York, and incidents continued to escalate in Boston. Accusations of the troops assaulting men and women were common. One officer cursed and threatened the Town Dock sentries when walking abroad past midnight. Small groups of Bostonians, at the encouragement of agitators like Molineux, harassed the British sentries in return, initiated brawls, and encouraged desertion among the soldiers. On February 22, Bostonians rioted to intimidate the Scottish importer Theophilus Lilly. Once again, Captain Matchet was present, as well as the merchant Edward Proctor and seaman Robert Paterson. Ebenezer Richardson, a customs informer, attempted to disperse the rioters, then entered his house and, from a window, fired into the crowd. Paterson's pants were torn, and eleven-year-old Christopher Seider was fatally wounded. A brawl between ropemakers and soldiers at John Gray's ropewalk (between Hutchinson and Atkinson streets in the South End) on March 2 angered Bostonians even further.[89]

In this prevailing climate of tension, the fight for control over Boston's waterfront soon elicited further casualties. Skirmishes broke out between the townspeople and the soldiers in Boylston's Alley on March 5, 1770, near the barracks, in front of the customs house in King Street, and in Dock Square. Hearing the noise of shouts and ringing fire bells, seamen and other maritime workers poured into King Street. Familiar faces appeared: the seaman Paterson, a seventeen-year-old shipwright's apprentice called Kit Monk, and a brawling ropemaker named Nathaniel Fosdick. John Adams called them "a motley rabble of saucy boys, negroes and molattoes, Irish teagues, and out landish jack tarrs." Inevitably the troops fired, and when the smoke cleared five men were dead or mortally wounded, including the mixed-race seaman Crispus Attucks, second mate James Caldwell, and ropemaker Samuel Gray. These deaths helped widen the rift between Great Britain and the townspeople, who subsequently commemorated the "Boston Massacre" to rally the colonists in opposition to the mother country. Those troops who were not subsequently thrown in prison marched to Wheelwright's Wharf under the escort of William Molineux and departed for Castle William on March 10 and 11—banished, as two governors and the customs officers had been, from the city they had unsuccessfully tried to control. In the months following, crowds directed their anger at importers and customs officials. Commissioner Henry Hulton and his family fled to Castle Island again that summer after an attack on their country home.[90] British officials, apparently chastened by the waterfront show of force on March 5, did nothing for a time—though in concert with Governor Thomas Hutchinson they did, as Dr. Thomas Young wrote, commit "fresh insult upon us by wresting our Castle out of the hands of the Province Garrison" and putting it under direct royal authority as a place of refuge from the Boston mobs.[91]

Meanwhile, waterfront crowds had been using some vicious new tactics. Bostonians tarred and feathered seaman George Gailer in 1769 because they believed he had informed on his own ship. The tidesman Owen Richards turned down a bribe and seized the schooner *Martin* in 1770. In response, one Boston crowd tarred and feathered him, while another rescued the seized goods. When customs official John Malcolm struck George R. T. Hewes in the head in 1774, a crowd tarred Malcolm to such a brutal extent that a portion of his skin peeled off, which he preserved for a voyage to England as a demonstration of his sacrifice. The usual procedure was for the crowd to assault the victim, strip off his clothes, cover him with feathers from a pillow and tar from a nearby wharf, and parade him around town for hours, often in front of the customs house (fig. 1.5). The practice of tarring and feathering had distinct maritime antecedents—Richard I had prescribed it as a shipboard punishment in 1189—marking it as a product of Anglophone waterfront culture. Seamen had apparently brought the practice to North American port cities, where in the late eighteenth century it surfaced as a working-class ritual punishment. Although Whig merchant-leaders attempted to discourage the practice (Dr. Thomas Young and wharfinger John Ballard convinced the crowd to settle for banishing the Scottish importer Patrick McMasters at the Roxbury town line), Boston's waterfront workers favored it on these three occasions against men who had positioned themselves as enemies on the waterfront battleground by seizing vessels and informing on smugglers. Like the burning of boats in 1747 and 1768 or the banishment of customs officers to Castle Island, tarring

The BOSTONIAN'S Paying the EXCISE-MAN, or TARRING & FEATHERING

Plate I.   London Printed for Robt. Sayer & J. Bennett, Map & Printseller Nº 53, Fleet Street as the Act directs 31 Octr. 1774.

Figure 1.5. Americans, including Bostonians, sometimes viciously punished offenders by tarring and feathering them. In a fictional scene beneath the Liberty Tree, a sailor and four other men force tea down a tax collector's throat, while in the background another group of Bostonians dumps the rest of the tea in the harbor. *The Bostonian's Paying the Excise-man, or Tarring & Feathering,* artist unknown. London: Printed for Robt. Sayer and J. Bennett, 1774. *Library of Congress, Prints and Photographs Division, LC-USZ62-9487.*

and feathering was a ritual articulation of waterfront justice—Bostonians used it to assert control over waterfront space and against offending British officials and informers.[92]

Crowd actions such as tarring and feathering offenders and burning boats were not limited to Boston. In fact, there is some evidence that crowds in different cities coordinated their activities, most likely using informal networks of communication. South Carolina lieutenant-governor William Bull complained in November 1765, during the Stamp Act crisis, that Charlestonians had "imbibed & propagated" their principles from vessels arriving from Boston and Rhode Island; in 1770, elite Charlestonians ordered the town watchmen to "prevent disturbances among disorderly negroes and more disorderly sailors."[93] From 1764 to 1775, crowds burned (or threatened to burn) the king's boats in Casco Bay, Newport, New York City, Providence, and Wilmington, North Carolina. In 1768, a crowd marched from Boston to Roxbury to find Commissioner John Robinson, who fled to Newport only to find another crowd looking for him there. Gloucester, Massachusetts, customs official Jesse Saville met with torment in Providence, Rhode Island, as well as in his hometown. George Gailer was tarred and feathered in 1769 at least in part for his service aboard the customs sloop *Liberty* (formerly John Hancock's), whose crew had irritated inhabitants of New London, Connecticut, before Newport seamen destroyed the ship. The Bostonian Nathaniel Rogers, a violator of the nonimportation agreements, went to New York on a business trip in 1770. There the Sons of Liberty carried his effigy through the streets and warned him to leave the city; in another incident of banishment, he fled to Shelter Island. Ebenezer Richardson, the customs informer who had shot Christopher Seider in Boston in 1770, later met with hostility in Philadelphia. John Malcolm, tarred and feathered in Boston in 1774, had received the same treatment at the hands of seamen in Pownalborough, New Hampshire, two months before. Crowds in different cities were evidently communicating with one another about persons' offenses and ritual methods of punishment, and more than likely the seamen were the ones carrying the messages from port to port. Through waterfront networks and shared ritual practices, urban waterfront dwellers throughout North America were achieving a unity of grievances, values, and identity. By the critical years of 1774 to 1776, they had transmitted the ritual practice of tarring and feathering, as well as this notion of a shared identity, to the countryside.[94]

The Boston Tea Party, an action that involved city dwellers and rural townspeople alike, was the climax of prerevolutionary resistance on the waterfront.[95] Parliament passed the Tea Act in 1773, offering drawbacks to the monopolistic East India Company for shipping dutied tea to America. Smugglers of Dutch tea in Boston, New York, and Philadelphia had much to lose from such legislation. New York partners Pigou & Booth, contracted to import tea under the terms of the new law, believed that they would encounter difficulties from local smugglers, who "will of themselves be able to raise a considerable mob, including a great number of retainers, such as boatmen, alongshoremen, etc."[96] Indeed, local broadsides there and in Philadelphia threatened any merchants who would store or sell the tea, and any ship captains or pilots who would bring the tea ships into the harbor. In New York, Philadelphia, and Charleston, Patriots successfully convinced the merchants commissioned to receive the tea, called "the consignees," to resign their offices or convinced authorities to keep the tea from landing on their wharves. Waterfront showdowns resulted in victories for the protesters in each instance. Meanwhile, committees of merchants and distillers attempted to dissuade the consignees in Boston. When negotiations failed, the waterfront crowds tried to intimidate the consignees into resigning their commissions. On November 3, William Molineux and the crowd forced Richard Clarke and the other consignees to barricade themselves in his warehouse at the foot of King Street for an hour and a half. Two weeks later, when news arrived that the tea ships were not far behind, the mob attacked Clarke's residence in School Street. Then the residents watched and waited for the tea, while unleashing a storm of protest in the press and in mass meetings that deliberately allowed non-voters—seamen, waterfront laborers, and residents of neighboring towns—to participate in the gatherings.[97]

The *Dartmouth* anchored off Long Wharf with 114 chests of East India Company tea on Sunday, November 28. In the days that followed, the Patriots roped the *Dartmouth* and two other tea ships to Griffin's Wharf, and they maintained control of political events by controlling the wharf. Once again the waterfront became a zone of separation between the maritime community and its enemies. On Monday, November 29, a handbill notified Bostonians of the arrival of the tea: "the hour of destruction or manly opposition to the machinations of tyranny stares you in the face." The bill summoned an extralegal town meeting known as "the Body," with merchant Jonathan Williams presiding. The Body posted twenty-five men, including a substantial coterie of waterfront denizens and marine artisans, under the command of merchant Edward Proctor and distiller Ezekiel Cheever, to stand watch, both to discourage violence and to ensure that the tea stayed on board. The customs commissioners and those consignees still in town (who were *also* dubbed "commissioners," marking them as outsiders) fled to Castle William for safety, fearing tarring and feathering by the crowds. At Griffin's Wharf, the town's sentinels (and not the navy) could maintain control over the ships and the tea. A stalemate ensued: the consignees would not return the tea to England, Governor Hutchinson would not allow the ships to get past the Castle, the townspeople would not allow the tea to land, and the customs officers could forcibly seize the tea by December 17.[98]

At Old South Meeting House on December 16, "the Body" of Bostonians made one final attempt to force merchant Francis Rotch to order his family's ship, the *Dartmouth*, back to England. When this effort failed, Samuel Adams proclaimed, "This meeting can do nothing more to save the country." Possibly on cue, a war-whoop rose from the gallery, along with shouts of "Boston harbor a tea-pot tonight!" and "Hurrah for Griffin's Wharf!" The meeting dissolved, and the crowd poured down Milk and Hutchinson streets to Griffin's Wharf. As thousands gathered along the shore to watch quietly, three groups of men, each with a commander and "boatswain," went to work. The tea party included a number of waterfront denizens and workers: Edward Dolbear and Henry Purkitt were apprenticed to cooper Samuel Peck, one of the "chiefs." Henry Bass and William Molineux were among the several merchants present. Lendall Pitts, son of the wharf owner James Pitts, was a "captain" at the tea party. Shoemaker George R. T. Hewes and Paul Revere, both of whom owned waterfront shops, also played active roles. Blockmaker James Brewer, the young oarmaker John Hooton Jr., shipwright Samuel Howard, ropemaker Edward C. Howe, wharfinger Thomas Moore, and shipjoiner Thomas Urann also represented the waterfront community aboard the tea ships. With their skill and waterfront experience, they were able to unload the ships in an orderly manner. Using block and tackle, the squads of "Mohawks" hoisted 340 chests of dutied tea, broke them open with hatchets, and spilled the tea over the side. The next day a trail of tea still remained floating in the water, and a party of volunteers went out in boats to break it up, thus completing this waterfront task.[99]

The Knowles, *Liberty*, and King Street riots as well as the Tea Party had involved community responses to grievances that affected the local waterfront: impressment, unconstitutional seizure, and military intimidation. The Tea Party also incorporated participants from inland towns, indicating wider regional support. This support, and the resistance to the Tea Act in other cities, ensured that Boston harbor ("a tea-pot tonight!") and the Boston waterfront would become powerful emblems outside Boston.

By 1774, the network of exchange that operated from the Boston waterfront had taken on revolutionary significance. The usual networks of communication—newspapers and shipping—had forged the political and economic links that made possible the Sons of Liberty, nonimportation associations, and Committees of Correspondence. Tarring and feathering and boat-burning, as we have seen, were also elements of waterfront exchange. Other towns often looked to Boston as the vanguard of radical action, and so the communication of news, grievances, political mobilization, and Revolutionary ideology among colonists would frequently bear the stamp of the Boston waterfront. One only needed to follow the trail of Liberty Poles, masts rising up in town squares throughout the Bay Colony, to see this phenomenon in action.[100]

Communication networks were crucial for mobilizing the hinterland of Massachusetts as well. Samuel Adams first began enlisting the support of the inland towns in the final months of 1772, and by 1773, men from other towns were regularly attending public meetings in Boston.[101] While John Adams was drying off in a Shrewsbury tavern in 1774, he overheard a group of farmers discussing the latest news from the provincial capital. When one farmer criticized the actions of the Boston crowds, his companions convinced him that the unconstitutional nature of parliamentary taxation held an implicit threat to his own liberty and property as well. One of them said, "If parliament can take away Mr. Hancock's wharf and Mr. Rowe's wharf, they can take away your barn and my house." When taxation threatened the proprietary interests and eminent leaders of the waterfront, the repercussions of British encroachment could easily spread to the Shrewsbury farmer. The prominent place of the waterfront in Massachusetts life made this physical space an important rallying point for the province: farmer, wharf owner, householder, and waterfront resident alike faced a common danger, and the skeptical Shrewsbury farmer would do well to heed the example of the resistance on the Boston waterfront. This transmission of ideas helped transform the Revolution from a waterfront cause to a countryside cause, and ultimately an intercolonial cause.[102]

The closing acts of the drama on the Boston waterfront would resonate throughout the thirteen colonies. The Boston Tea Party was the latest in a string of conspicuous acts of waterfront mobilization against imperial policy. In response, Parliament voted to punish Boston severely by isolating its waterfront from the commerce that sustained it. The Boston Port Act moved the hated customs office to Plymouth and the Board of Customs Commissioners (its officers fully banished at last) and provincial government to Salem. It further stipulated that no ship could enter Boston after June 1, 1774, and no ship could leave after June 15. Coasting vessels with provisions for Boston had to be cleared at Marblehead. The accompanying "Intolerable Acts" attempted to resolve a few formerly contested points on the waterfront by allowing the quartering of troops inside Boston proper and granting customs officers the right to a friendlier trial outside Boston. Finally, the ministry sent General Gage to replace Hutchinson as governor, supported by eleven regiments of royal troops. Bostonians' image of Hutchinson at this time, where Death wields a fisherman's harpoon pointed at "the wicked Statesman" (fig. 1.6) stands in marked contrast to the portrait of Captain-Lieutenant Larrabee. In 1774, Massachusetts was mobilizing against Governor Hutchinson, seeking to exile him from the waterfront and province that (as they perceived it) he was threatening. As with Revere's engraving, Bostonians used visual representations to express their views on authority, and the contested space of the waterfront became a proxy for the Atlantic conflict.[103]

The importance of Boston's waterfront as contested space became most visible to the rest of America when Parliament shut it down. Members of the "Late" Virginia House of Burgesses were horrified at Britain's disregard for the colonists' constitutional rights, and pointed to the Boston Port Act as "violently and arbitrarily" depriving Bostonians "of their property, in wharfs erected by private persons, at their own great and proper expence." Thomas Jefferson, Patrick Henry, and their colleagues recognized Boston's waterfront as a place of property ownership, and latched onto this principle to support their arguments against the infringement of constitutional rights.[104]

Waterfront denizens had grumbled at the exercise of royal power before, yet nothing could have prepared them for the might unleashed upon them now. John Boyle wrote in his diary, "By this cruel edict of the British Parliament, Thousands of our Inhabitants will be involved in one common

Figure 1.6. This almanac cover shows Death brandishing a fisherman's harpoon at the unpopular Thomas Hutchinson, governor of Massachusetts. "The wicked Statesman, or the Traitor to his Country, at the Hour of DEATH," possibly by Paul Revere, cover of Ezra Gleason, *The Massachusetts Calendar; or An Almanack for the Year of our Lord Christ 1774.* Boston, Isaiah Thomas, 1773. *Courtesy of Houghton Library, Harvard College Library.*

undistinguished Ruin!"[105] He and diarist Thomas Newell noted the blockade in the harbor, the landing of the regiments at Long Wharf (so reminiscent of 1768), and the troops' encampment in town at Boston's most cherished public spaces: the Welsh Fusileers on Fort Hill, and the rest on the Common. In winter these troops quartered themselves in distilleries, at Griffin's Wharf, and in several dockside stores and houses.[106] Bostonians began fleeing the town in droves, leaving Boston an empty and "gloomy place." On June 15, a rainy afternoon, Newell wrote, "Most of the stores on the Long Wharf are now shut up [;] thus are we [surrounded] with Fleet and Army the harbor shut, all Navigation cease & not one Topsail Vessel to be seen but those of our Enemies. Let not posterity forget our Sufferings."[107] The remainder of North America, at least, did not forget. Six weeks later, Boyle reported that the maritime community was making the best of the situation: "Every part of this extensive Continent, appears to be deeply interested in the Fate of this *unhappy Town.* Many and great are the Donations we have already received, and many more we have reason to expect. Even our poorest people have not yet suffered for the want of Bread." The waterfront had been the site of heroism. Now it would be the site of martyrdom, a fearful example for the other colonies to heed. As George Washington wrote, "The Cause of Boston" was now "the cause of America."[108]

After the imposition of the Coercive Acts, events were largely out of the waterfront community's hands. The first shots of the Revolutionary War echoed in the Massachusetts countryside. The response of the militia during and after the Lexington and Concord engagements demonstrated the extent to which the Revolutionary movement had spread inland. The waterfront, cut off from its commercial activity, suffered grievously until the evacuation of British forces in March 1776. When the Continental Congress broke from King George III in the Declaration of Independence, they based their grounds for separation in part on the grievances that Boston's waterfront denizens had expressed during the previous twelve years.

The center of revolutionary mobilization had moved westward from Long Wharf to Concord's North Bridge. While inland towns like Concord and Shrewsbury were slower to rebel than Boston, a scholar of Concord writes that "where you lived" in rural towns "was often as important as what you owned in determining how you participate . . . in town affairs." In a town like Concord, "where you lived" was a question of physical location. In a small city like Boston, it was more a question of where you were located in the town's economy, culture, and society—the waterfront as space determined its denizens' participation in revolutionary politics. By 1765, Boston had been polarized into two factions: the government faction, with its sources of political power and policy in London, Halifax, and Castle William; and the radical faction, with its sources of political power and mobilization in the public spaces of the city—the churches, the town meeting, the Liberty Tree, the taverns, and the waterfront. While an inland town such as Concord could largely concentrate on its own internal squabbles and remain oblivious to the imperial dispute with Britain (at least before the end of 1772), the Boston waterfront was a zone of greater conflict because its residents were continually aware of their connections to the Atlantic world and the political and economic ramifications of those connections.[109]

Revolutionary ideology also reflected the spatial differences that separated town from city. Massachusetts farmers responded to their fears that feudalism was reviving, and so their rebellion against Britain was based on relatively abstract and remote notions of retaining land ownership amidst the threat of lordly authority. Members of the radical waterfront community, by contrast, had a greater stake in colonial policy and the Atlantic world. As a result, their rapid, conspicuous, and sometimes violent acts of mobilization were responses to grievances they felt more acutely than their neighbors, grounded in an ideological framework that resonated with particular strength. These grievances—unjust taxation, corrupt placemen, prerogative vice-admiralty courts, impressment, and military occupation—were vivid and tangible examples of the dangers of British policy, personified by Boston's community of government supporters. Furthermore, waterfront dwellers throughout the social spectrum could apply their global outlook to the revolutionary struggle and thereby invest it with even greater importance. From seaman to merchant, the waterfront rebel was more likely than other colonists to channel his or her cosmopolitanism into a belief that "the cause of America" was a libertarian "cause for all mankind."[110]

Thus, the waterfront revolution was a crucial and catalytic component of the urban revolution, which was in turn a crucial and catalytic component of the American Revolution as a whole. Waterfront mobilization contributed to the wider Patriot mobilization, with seamen and merchants resisting British authority and achieving independence alongside Boston's Patriot clergymen like Samuel Cooper, lawyers like John Adams, and printers like Benjamin Edes. Although Boston was distinctive for its earlier and more radical resistance to Great Britain, the mobilization of the waterfront community also occurred in the other major seaport towns of North America. The communication networks of the Atlantic maritime world linked these wharves and warehouses to one another, and waterfront spaces in Newport and Charleston became visible and useful places from which to launch challenges to imperial authority.

The revolutionary movement required broad support within the microcosmic community of the Boston waterfront. The city's radical coalition mustered this support time and again over the course of the imperial crisis. Although social tensions and political disagreements sometimes surfaced in this contested space, the cultural and economic interdependence of the waterfront gave its residents grounds for unity in response to a common threat. Bostonians came to define Loyalists and British officials as outside this unified community, as the distance from Castle Island to Long Wharf became the cultural equivalent of the distance from London to Boston.

Chapter 2

ORDERLY AND DISORDERLY MOBILIZATION IN THE TAVERNS OF NEW YORK CITY

On January 3, 1775, one of John Case's acquaintances invited him to Jasper Drake's tavern. Case was a sixty-year-old Loyalist from Suffolk County, and Drake's was an odd place for a Loyalist. The tavern was a popular gathering place for seamen and Patriots, and Drake was the father-in-law of the Patriot leader Isaac Sears. The tavern's patrons that evening included Sears and another Patriot leader, Alexander McDougall, who invited Case into a discussion of politics and "attempted to convince him" that his political views were wrongheaded. When Case would not back down, Sears and several of his companions nearly bowled him over "with the force of their eloquence and noise." Seeking to restore order to the conversation, Case suggested that the taverngoers discuss the imperial crisis from its origins, the Stamp Act. At that point Moses Dudley Jr. of Connecticut became exasperated and said that in his home province, Case would be "put to death" for his Loyalist views. Members of the company then declared that they would "not suffer a Tory to sit in company with Gentlemen," and they caught Case by the arm and forced him into a chair in the chimney corner.

Sears then called over a young slave of Drake's and tried to order him to sit in the corner as well, announcing that Case belonged in the company of slaves, since he was as dependent on the British Empire as a slave was on his master. The company agreed to ostracize Case, or put him "in Coventry," meaning that none should speak with him "under the forfeiture of a nip of Toddy" (though Case claimed the penalty was a whole bowl). As he nursed his wine alone, Case tried to provoke members of the company into answering him, and he succeeded twice. One taverngoer may have threatened to brand Case's backside with a red-hot gridiron (though the Patriots later claimed the threat was much milder) and had stayed his hand only because of Case's age. Ultimately, Case got the hint and retreated from the tavern. Such actions, Case concluded, ought to "convince every friend to order and the constitution, how dangerous a situation we should be in," if the Sons of Liberty "are suffered to assume the lead in our public trans- actions." He urged his fellow citizens to unite against such "men whose actions prove, that instead of freedom, their aim is to establish disorder, oppression, and anarchy."[1]

During the third quarter of the eighteenth century, taverns were the perfect venues for revolutionaries seeking to surmount the challenges of political mobilization. As key nodes in Atlantic networks of communica- tion, taverns encouraged a broad spectrum of white men to engage in voluntary action, and as a result they helped revolutionaries to overcome a civic impasse by bringing together the pluralistic urban community. Case's encounter illustrates how Sears and McDougall met the challenge of Loyalist countermobilization. As Case attempted to engage the Patriots in an orderly discussion about imperial policy, he was adhering to the prevail- ing standards of polite discourse in the tavern setting. Yet the assembled Patriots had their own notions of how to organize a tavern's patrons. They set up a drinking game in which anyone who talked to the Tory would have to buy the group some toddy. According to Case, this encounter degener- ated into threats of violence and disorder, and this was the risk that politi- cal actors took when they mixed alcohol with politics.

Public houses, which allowed for the mixing of inhabitants and visitors from different social groups, were important sites of interaction in New York and other cities.[2] Men found unity and disunity as they discussed politics in taverns, and their disagreements with one another often spilled into the newspapers or even pell-mell into the streets. Some New Yorkers attempted to restore order to this drunken, anarchic climate by insisting upon civilized discourse, organizing social clubs and associations, prose- cuting "disorderly houses," and establishing hierarchies based on gender, race, class, and political viewpoint. Yet despite these attempts to establish an orderly resistance to British policy, noise, drunkenness, and violence were bound to accompany tavern life. Since the resistance to Great Britain arose from taverns, such resistance encompassed drunken disorder as well as orderly mobilization. As New Yorkers found mutual affirmation among their tavern companions, political leaders attempted to harness and mobi- lize taverngoers—rich and poor, orderly and disorderly—to resist British policies.

Drinking alcohol was almost certainly more prevalent in colonial New York City than in Boston or Philadelphia. By 1768, the province of New York had seventeen distilleries, each pumping out an average of 45,000 gallons of rum a year. The province consumed about 1,119,000 gallons of rum in 1770. This was 6.7 gallons of rum per New Yorker annually—a slightly skewed figure since some of the rum went to New Jersey. Still, New Yorkers probably drank rum at a higher rate than other Americans, who each drank 4.2 gallons of rum on average that year, or more than seven one- ounce shots every day. New Yorkers drank rum because the shortage of drinking water in the city necessitated that alcoholic beverages be affordable and available. Rum also allowed New Yorkers to imbibe large amounts of inexpensive calories to help them cope with the climate and the workday.[3]

Visitors found New Yorkers' consumption of alcohol to be remarkable. Unfettered by the cultural predominance of the strict Quakers or Puritans, New York City's ethnically diverse population had long found common ground over bowls of punch and tankards of ale. The Dutch who had originally settled New York had used two different taverns for municipal business before they built City Hall, and Common Council meetings and jurors' inquisitions also helped to establish the tradition of using public houses for public business.[4] The English traveler Alexander Mackraby wrote in 1768 that New York was "a better place for company and amusements than Philadelphia; more gay and lively."[5] Dr. Alexander Hamilton of Maryland would have agreed; in 1744 he had written, "in this place you may have the best of company and conversation." Nevertheless, by the time he left New York he confessed, "I was glad to remove from a place where the temptation of drinking . . . threw it self so often in my way."[6] The Philadelphian William Gordon marveled in 1754 that in a few years the next generation of New Yorkers might consume the whole vintage of Madeira wine. "Never did I see the like, Never do I believe there [existed a] city more thoroughly devoted to Bacchus. He orders [where] ever they meet."[7] With 365 liquor licenses issued in the twelve months following March 1771, a ratio of one tavern or retailer for approximately every sixty city residents (or one for every thirteen adult white men), New York had around double the number of drinking establishments per capita than other large colonial American cities (see appendix 2). The lawyer William Smith Jr., who disdained heavy drinking and wanted to attract immigrants to New York City, tried to claim that the city's "common drinks are beer, cyder, weak punch, and Madeira wine." Yet taste spoke louder than rhetoric, and John Watts, a prominent liquor merchant, regularly told his suppliers that New Yorkers insisted on their liquor being distilled at high proof. Such demand for strong alcohol was apparently distinct from demand in other colonial seaports.[8]

New Yorkers did much of this drinking in taverns, also called public houses, located throughout the city (fig. 2.1) and operating in a close and symbiotic relationship with the city's commercial life. Taverns were common at the head of the waterfront, they catered to City Hall and the Exchange, and they lined principal roads such as Broadway, Wall Street, and Pearl Street. Public houses were particularly prevalent at the tip of lower Manhattan, the oldest part of the city, and sprang up in all parts of the city as it grew—usually ahead of churches or other public buildings.[9]

Taverns and grogshops were vital parts of colonial urban life, as flexible and dynamic as the city itself. There were more taverns in a colonial city than any other type of building besides houses, but in a sense this distinction is meaningless.[10] The same building, after all, might become a tavern, dwelling,

Figure 2.1. New York City, densely concentrated at the tip of Manhattan island, issued enough liquor licenses that there was one drink seller for every thirteen adult white men during the early 1770s. *To His Excellency Sr. Henry Moore, Bart., . . . This Plan of the City of New York, Is Most Humbly Inscribed, by . . . Bern[ar]d. Ratzen. T. Kitchin, sculpt.* London, Jefferys and Faden, 1776. *Library of Congress, Geography and Map Division.*

retail shop, or workshop. In all probability, neither the city's taverns nor its houses were "built with any uniformity."[11] The city's best taverns tended to resemble the finest houses; for instance, Samuel Fraunces's Queen's Head and Edward Willett's Province Arms were both originally DeLancey family mansions (fig. 2.2).[12] More middling or humble establishments might be converted from dwelling houses with only one or two rooms for public use. The lawyer Alexander Graydon described one of these in Philadelphia, when at dusk he and a friend dropped into "an obscure inn in Race street" where "we were led by a steep and narrow stair-case to a chamber in the third story, so lumbered with beds as scarcely to leave room for a table and one chair, the beds superseding the necessity of more."[13] An illegal grogshop might operate out of a kitchen building or the main room of a poor person's dwelling. Newspaper advertisements from the period demonstrate that tavernkeepers frequently switched locations, hung out different signs, started businesses and failed, converted public houses into dwellings, and vice versa. Finally, many urban places could serve as ad hoc sites of intoxication and entertainment, including City Hall, the Fort, the Fields, the streets, the harbor (for the firing of cannon during celebrations), and private households.[14]

Figure 2.2. Fraunces Tavern still stands at the corner of Broad and Pearl streets, though the original building, a DeLancey mansion, is no longer extant. In this image a twentieth-century artist imagines how the eighteenth-century building looked. "Fraunces' Tavern, N.Y.C., 1777," in *Old New York*, by Samuel Hollyer. New York, 1905–19. *Picture Collection, The Branch Libraries, The New York Public Library, Astor, Lenox, and Tilden Foundations.*

New York's network of tavern sociability and communication was closely related to the city's far-flung mercantile networks and was therefore intimately connected with the Atlantic world. "New-York is one of the most social places on the continent," wrote William Smith Jr. in his 1757 *History of the Province of New-York*, a work that he hoped would serve as a booster for New York City and its places of sociability. While New Yorkers invited the world to their taverns for commerce and socializing, New York taverngoers also used public houses as their conduits to the rest of the Atlantic world. New York was a principal stop for the packet boats that traversed the Atlantic Ocean, and these ships deposited mail, gossip, and newspapers—all of which found their way to the coffeehouses (such as the Merchant Coffee House) and taverns, both of which served alcohol to the merchants, officials, and other literate New Yorkers who gathered there. These patrons could absorb, digest, and discuss matters of economic and political importance, both local and worldwide. Hamilton wrote of one occasion when he and a tavern companion "smoked a pipe after dinner and chopt politicks."[15] As Great Britain extended its reach across the Atlantic Ocean during the eighteenth century, it relied not only on the apparatus of the state but also on less formal institutions like newspapers and the mail to connect New York with the metropolis at London, seaports from Kingston, Jamaica, to Norwich, Connecticut, and the hinterlands. Though not everyone had equal access to these literate networks, taverns granted most white men the opportunity to participate in the Atlantic web of communication and commerce. Such networks would become vitally important as mechanisms for political mobilization.[16]

The Merchant Coffee House and other fine taverns were at the pinnacle of New York's loose, shifting hierarchy of taverns—they offered the best food and drink, hoping to attract the wealthiest clientele. Further down in this loose hierarchy, other taverns provided places of rest and communication for working New Yorkers. Abraham De La Montagne's tavern on Broadway across from the Fields was an unofficial headquarters for the city's cartmen, who could hitch their horses and wagons in the courtyard or the street, receive their mail, and find out who was hiring that day. Taverns were natural places for labor recruitment (just as they would be for military enlistment at the start of the Revolutionary War).[17] During the privateering bonanza of the midcentury imperial wars, junior officers from merchant marine vessels would post notices in taverns, offer the ship's articles for examination, and sign up seamen (often plied with alcohol) in search of fortune. Tavernkeepers put clothes on a mariner's back, extended credit, and provided other services. Seamen, in turn, sometimes gave tavernkeepers a share of their prize money or bequeathed their money and possessions to them in their wills. For that matter, seamen provided ready support for taverners, soaking themselves at Benjamin Pain's Jamaica Arms in William Street, the Sign of the Globe, and the Sign of the Prince of Orange. Singing, carousing, whoring, brawling, gambling, toasting, laughing, telling sea stories, and celebrating, patrons made the taverns raucous places during the prosperous war years. In 1740, the printer John Peter Zenger claimed he was unable to learn the particulars of a recent voyage by the aptly named Captain John Lush because the ship's crew was "too busy in making merry with the Money."[18] Once a successful privateering voyage was over, taverns such as Mark Valentine's or the Widow Lawrence's on the New Dock hosted auctions of the prize ships and their cargo.[19]

As taverngoers drank, they sometimes disrupted law and order in New York, yet the restrictions on taverns and drinking were far from strict. New Yorkers at the provincial and municipal level enacted two types of laws and ordinances regarding alcohol: those designed to encourage and derive revenue from its sale, and those that sought to prohibit its sale to certain groups.[20] At the imperial level, customs duties ensured the flow of specie to the Treasury: as John Watts wrote in 1765, "The Dutys on Rum Wine & Negroes have heretofore supported our Civil List."[21] As for molasses that might be distilled into rum, the collection of duties on its importation (for reexport or local consumption) was a major source of revenue for London in the years after the Sugar Act of 1764.[22]

At the provincial level, import duties and excise taxes brought revenue to New York's coffers, and the colony took steps to ensure that the hogsheads and casks were measured fairly. While these activities ensured the growth of the provincial bureaucracy, the practice of farming out the collection of the excise tax to the highest bidder had led to extortion and corruption by the 1750s. Using arguments against taxation without representation, New York's *Independent Reflector* managed to motivate the Assembly to amend the law in 1753.[23] Under the new provincial system, appointed commissioners collected the excise fee, while the mayors of the city, as they had done for decades, granted licenses to and collected fees from those they judged capable of keeping "an orderly house according to the Law" for the sale of strong liquors.[24] Such licenses also provided currency for the colonial system of patronage; influential New Yorkers might wheedle a license to help a client, or convince the Common Council to waive the fee.[25] Thus, at the imperial, provincial, and municipal level, the government sanctioned and benefited from the sale of alcohol. Though the city's mayors had the power to exercise their regulatory power by limiting the number of drinking establishments, the steady growth of taverns throughout the eighteenth century demonstrated that such limitation was not their goal.

The authorities did, however, try to inhibit certain types of drinking in the service of upholding the social order. Taverns and disorderly houses often fostered crime, vice, and disorder, and it behooved New York's leaders to limit such excesses. Court records do not survive for prosecutions for drunkenness, which historians assume must have been legion.[26] New York's coroner witnessed a number of deaths arising from alcohol poisoning or fatal accidents that arose from drinking. After one such accident in 1773, the *New-York Journal* suggested, "The Suppression of these Houses, which subsist only by furnishing the Means of Drunkenness and Debauchery to Servants and mean disorderly People, would be highly agreeable to the Inhabitants in general."[27] Serious acts of violence and mayhem also occurred in legal and illegal drinking establishments: attempted rape, assault, trespass, rioting, pickpocketing, manslaughter, and murder.[28]

Numerous records survive for an increasing number of prosecutions for the keeping of disorderly houses that corrupted the morals and manners of New Yorkers.[29] The definition of disorderly houses was imprecise: in some cases, innkeepers or tavernkeepers kept their taverns open late, encouraged misbehavior, or served the wrong clientele.[30] In other cases, the authorities charged soldiers, storekeepers, laborers, mariners, and artisans, along with their wives and widows, and "spinsters" with selling liquor without a license.[31] During the eighteenth century, Crown attorneys in New York City prosecuted several men (in 59.6 % of the cases) and women (in 40.4% of the cases) for keeping disorderly houses. The number of female defendants was disproportionate to the number of women accused of all crimes (9.9% of the total accused), and it is worth noting that the percentage of New York City women who held tavern licenses (15% in the 1760s) was much lower than the ratio in other cities (24.4% in Philadelphia, 41.6% in Boston, and 48.3% in Charleston).[32] New Yorkers apparently believed that the presence of women in taverns particularly threatened the social order.

The authorities prosecuted keepers of disorderly houses for variations on "Quarrelling, fighting, gaming" along with "drinking Tipling Whoring and misbehaving themselves to the great Damage and common Nusance" of the polity. Many disorderly houses also encouraged theft, the receipt of stolen goods, and the entertainment of slaves. What was most striking about the prosecutions was how few of them were resolved. Relative to other crimes, indictments for keeping disorderly houses had a low percentage of convictions and a high percentage of acquittals. Evidently it was extremely rare for the authorities to convict keepers of disorderly houses, either because such accusations were difficult to prove, or because New York's magistrates had neither the means nor the desire to try to stop the flood of alcohol.[33]

Another set of laws and ordinances helped to define the culture of taverns by regulating who could consume alcohol in New York. New York laws prohibited the sale of strong liquors to servants and apprentices; prevented tavernkeepers from taking clothing or goods as payment; forbade tavernkeepers from extending too much credit (especially to seamen); and tried to ensure that no one bet on billiards and shuffleboard and that no sailors, servants, youths under twenty-one, or apprentices bet on dice or cards where alcohol of any kind was sold.[34] The Common Council ordered that tavernkeepers refrain from selling drink to town residents on the Sabbath, and tavernkeepers had to report the name and profession of their out-of-town guests so that "men Or Women of E[v]ill Name" might be discouraged.[35] These laws particularly targeted non-whites in the cities.[36] Legislation of 1730 prevented anyone from selling "rum or other strong Liquor to any Negro Indian or Mulato Slave or Slaves" or from entertaining another person's slave without that person's permission. It was unlawful for "above three Slaves to meet together" without their masters' consent, and manumitted blacks and Indians were particularly proscribed from entertaining slaves.[37] The leaders of New York wanted to prevent certain types of violent mobilization by limiting certain types of people from gathering in taverns.

City dwellers particularly feared the disorders that might arise from drinking among blacks. After Fort George burned down on March 18, 1741, followed by thirteen other fires, Lieutenant Governor George Clarke reported that blacks in New York City had hatched an insidious arson plot in taverns run by traitorous whites. The subsequent trial proceedings, resulting in thirty-four executions and dozens of slave banishments, revealed a black culture of drinking, fiddling, dancing, cockfighting, gambling, and resistance. John Hughson, tavernkeeper and receiver of stolen goods, hosted "great feasts" on Sundays. After the music and eating subsided, the group initiated fellow conspirators during a ring ceremony involving the Bible, knives, and a circle of chalk. Blacks (many of them runaway slaves), Indians, and whites gathered at Hughson's and elsewhere on market days, holidays, or even "every other night." Some formed gangs or secret societies like the Geneva Club (after the bottles of liquor they had stolen from a tavern cellar). After the fires, the Assembly tightened the penalties for serving liquor to slaves because "the great Number of Publick Houses in which Negroes have been entertained" had been the "principal Instrument to their Diabolical Vilanies."[38]

Such regulations were often quite difficult to enforce, however, and so blacks found ways to gather, drink, and celebrate—often in mixed company with whites.[39] Mariner's wife Catherine O'Neal, according to prosecutors, "did cause and procure certain Evil and illdisposed Persons, Negro Slaves and others of . . . dishonest Conversation to frequent and come together" in her house in the West Ward at all hours, day or night, in 1766.[40] Two coopers, a laborer, and a mixed-race slave named Eneas all faced prosecution in 1771 for stealing forty-two bottles of beer and two pounds of sugar from Theophylact Bache.[41] After the slave conspiracy of 1741, blacks could not have been optimistic that their social gatherings would ever translate into political upheaval. While blacks participated in multiracial crowds and engaged in acts of resistance, the fierce reaction of New York's authorities ensured that blacks would face an uphill battle in their struggle for freedom during the era of Revolution.[42]

Though New Yorkers were often lax in their application of direct forms of control over drinking, many still wished to impose forms of order upon taverns and drinking, preferably by less overt means than the law. Where the law was silent, social convention further regulated the racial and gender hierarchy of the taverns. Lower-class women often found ways to drink, but the links between drinking, prostitution, and disorder discouraged elite and middle-class women from damaging their reputations by entering a tavern. Women did not normally participate in New York's many clubs and associations; instead, they attended balls and concerts and promenaded through pleasure gardens or Bowling Green.[43] When women worked alongside men in taverns, their role was subordinate. Hamilton gives us a glimpse of how a male tavernkeeper might treat a member of his household establishment. He heard the Scotsman Robert Todd yell from upstairs, "Dam ye bitch, wharefor winna ye bring a canle?" It is unclear whether the woman he addressed was his wife or another female member of his household. Blacks also received harsh treatment in taverns. Hamilton remarked upon "the stupid negroe wench" who "forgetting her orders to the contrary," brought a bowl of peas to the table after one of the customers had specifically requested that peas not be brought. During the confrontation between Sears and Case at Drake's tavern, Sears similarly attempted to make "a Negro boy, who belonged to the house" sit in the chimney corner next to him, so as to prove a political point that a person with such views "was only fit to sit in company with Slaves." The boy, however, "had too much understanding to comply" with Sears's baiting.[44] Blacks and women might achieve a certain freedom in unlicensed houses, but in licensed taverns, despite the presence of a few female retailers and tavernkeepers, white men did their utmost to maintain their control.

Although white male New Yorkers had circumscribed the ability of women and blacks to congregate and drink, they had much more trouble managing the disorders that arose among themselves in taverns. Alcohol led to the loss of self-control, and so it might lead to the weakening of controls over the community. Bachelors, the young men who would become particularly active in the Revolutionary movement, particularly threatened an orderly society. Since the end of the seventeenth century, writers had stigmatized the bachelor as licentious, impulsive, greedy, ungovernable, wicked, foolish, and unrestrained in his sexuality. A predator, he was the ruin of women and the father of bastards.[45] Alexander Graydon recalled his younger days when alcohol made him feel "valiant in the novel feeling of intoxication" as he and a companion "sallied forth in quest of adventures. . . . In a word, we aspired to be rakes, and we were gratified."[46] He continued, "The pleasures of the table, the independence of tavern revelry, and its high-minded contempt of the plodding and industrious, were irresistibly fascinating to me."[47] A writer to the *New-York Weekly Journal* feared these imprudent bachelors, "loose and profitless Creatures" who "brought about their own Wretchedness by Whoring and Gaming," and plagued families and towns.[48] James Murray found that his impudent and deceitful apprentice, a "perverse and disorderly Youth," behaved along these lines: Murray's neighbors complained "of his endeavouring to ruin their Apprentices, enticing them to go to tavern."[49] New York was a town that respected industry and profit, and so they looked askance when young men frittered away their time and money carousing in taverns.

The cacophony of bad language in New York's taverns also struck many observers. A minister left one tavern in a huff when the landlord sang a bawdy song. He told the company that this "was a language he did not understand." A correspondent to the *New-York Weekly Journal* similarly criticized the "drunken Jests" he heard at taverns, as well as "a bawdy Song, or two, a few drunken Healths, and about a dozen or two Puns and Quibbles." The pseudonymous "Alcanor" wrote that the "Obscene toasts" he heard in taverns served only to "disgust the sensible, to disconcert the modest, and to expose the depravity of taste as well as manners" of the brutes who relished them. Hamilton further observed that the most esteemed "dons" in town derived "a certain odd pleasure . . . in talking nonsense without being contradicted."[50] Drunkenness did nothing to improve one's eloquence: a doctor burst into Todd's tavern one night "so intoxicated with liquor that he could scarce speak one connected sentence."[51] The prevalence of disorderly bachelors and the jumble of tavern speech were having a broad impact on society: William Smith Jr. wrote, "Our common speech is extremely corrupt, and the evidences of a bad taste, both as to thought and language, are visible in all our proceedings, publick and private."[52] The Massachusetts lawyer John Adams, who recognized Smith as a kindred spirit, agreed: "At their Entertainments there is no Conversation that is agreeable," he said of New Yorkers. "There is no

Modesty—No Attention to one another. They talk very loud, very fast, and alltogether." A New Yorker would ask a question, and then interrupt the respondent before he had a chance to utter three words.[53] The provincial degeneracy of New York City was most visible in the tippling house.

Visitors judged their fellow taverngoers by Atlantic standards of gentility and refinement, and New Yorkers often failed to withstand the scrutiny of outsiders. In 1774, John Adams wrote, "With all the Opulence and Splendor of this City, there is very little good Breeding to be found. . . . I have not seen one real Gentleman, one well bred Man, since I came to town."[54] Hamilton wrote of New Yorkers in 1744, "These dons commonly held their heads higher than the rest of mankind and imagined few or none were their equals. But this I found always proceeded from their narrow notions, ignorance of the world, and low extraction." Colonists, Hamilton said, had never understood "the different ranks of men in polite nations."[55] As the eighteenth century progressed, such criticisms made New Yorkers more and more insecure about their provinciality. In response, genteel New Yorkers (like other Americans) elevated the more refined pursuits of cards, dancing, eating, music, and conversation above the rowdy tavern culture of more common folk.[56] Hamilton and others knew the cure for disorder in New York: a civil discourse that they attempted to pursue through the formation of clubs that encouraged the expression of a more refined wit.[57] Such a discourse might raise New York above its provincial status and set it on a more equal footing with the metropolitan standards of Great Britain (though any visitor to London's taverns knew that one would find the same rowdy behavior there).

New Yorkers met in a variety of clubs and associations, hoping to introduce structure and polite formality to tavern life. Drinking clubs and drinking rituals were the most basic way for taverngoers to create a more orderly tavern setting. Tavernkeepers encouraged such clubs, whose drinking and feasting paid the bills. As Graydon of Philadelphia reminisced, "Nothing was more delightful to me than to find myself a member of a large bottle association sat in for serious drinking; the table officers appointed, the demi-johns filled, the bottles arranged, with the other necessary dispositions for such engagements." As William Smith Jr. described in his booster history, New York "men collect themselves into weekly evening clubs." For instance, Hamilton drank with the "bumper men" of the Hungarian Club, while John Watts had a number of friends in the Oyster Club.[58] These drinking clubs often had elaborate rituals for screening, initiating, and integrating members, such as a sequence of toasts. In 1769, "Alcanor" criticized toasting, as "Many a sober inclined man is forced into excesses he dreads and detests, by fear of offending the company, or appearing wanting to the sentiment the toast conveys."[59]

Organized drinking helped encourage feelings of harmony, fellowship, and collective identity in the tavern. Drinking rituals encouraged an open social atmosphere where taverngoers judged a man based on his ability to hold his liquor rather than his wealth or seniority. Graydon remembered placing a high value on his "potency in potting," while a satirist writing to the *New-York Weekly Journal* thought it whimsical and lamentable for people "to Value themselves upon this strange property" of "strong Constitutions" for drinking.[60] One evening in 1744 at Robert Todd's tavern, Hamilton observed, "Two or three toapers in the company seemed to be of opinion that a man could not have a more sociable quality or enduement than to be able to pour down seas of liquor and remain unconquered while others sunk under the table."[61] Drinking with the Hungarian Club, he added, was "the readiest way for a stranger to recommend himself, and a sett among them are very fond of making a stranger drink."[62] Newcomers, visitors, and inhabitants could meet and ingratiate themselves with one another in taverns. Since the ability to get drunk was open to all men, it was a leveling experience filled with possibilities for social flexibility.

This invocation of drinking rituals, and their attendant leveling effects, created a tension between those who were comfortable with the integration of drinking with New York's political and social life, and those who were not. To the former group, the organization of drinking rules put all taverngoers on an equal footing with one another, encouraging sociability and perhaps the mobilization of tavern companions for political ends.[63] Not all such clubs revolved solely around consumption and intoxication, after all. New York had ethnic societies and Masonic lodges, as well, by the 1740s, which strengthened connections to transatlantic networks of membership.[64] These clubs allowed elite New Yorkers to structure their visits to taverns.

On the other hand, this orderly sociability might only succeed in placing tenuous restraints on drunkenness and its leveling effects. To critics of these drinking rituals, alcohol inspired a disorderly disregard for hierarchy, an atmosphere of boorishness that threatened civilized society. These critics believed that the leveling effects of alcohol would lead to drunken anarchy. J. Hector St. John de Crèvecoeur wrote that "the frequent use of spirituous liquors from the repeated Inebriation it causes swells [us] with an Idea of Equality" when New Yorkers conversed with their betters.[65] Men of any rank, fortified with drink, might breach the bounds of propriety and authority. A couple of pieces in New York newspapers in 1748 and 1749 highlighted the irony of using drinking rituals to impose order on alcohol consumption. The author of "An Essay on Bumpers" called intemperance a foolish and destructive vice: "To love Drink for Drink's sake . . . is a shameful, an unnatural and a detestable Practice." The writer criticized the organized, intentional drinking of bumper toasts (a bumper was a glass filled to the brim), and scrupled to call "*sober Men*" those "who get drunk once or twice *every* Week or two." While the author professed to love company, he decried the practice of forcing someone "to drink more *Bumpers* and *Toasts* than the Person's Inclinations, Habit of Body, or Circumstances admit." The pseudonymous "Sam. Swallo" printed a response to "An Essay on Bumpers" (perhaps a follow-up by the same author), which satirically described a company of "clever, jovial Fellows" reading the first article aloud in a tavern. Tom Fuddle assumed that "every Body, from the highest to the lowest" drank bumpers, while Will Tipple declared, "I wou'd not give a Farthing for a Man's Company that won't be social!" The company laughed at the essayist's favorable example of Philadelphia, saying that its inhabitants drank bumpers less frequently because of the Quaker City's "*Stinginess*." As essayists evaluated the benefits of sociable drinking, they walked the line between politeness and bawdy wit, just as the tavern clubs themselves did.[66]

In a satire on the "Customs of the Province of Drinkallia," a contributor to the *New-York Weekly Journal* described a town resembling an English tankard, fortified with barrels and roofed with the boards of broken casks. The city arms depicted leeches (alcoholics and hangers-on were often called sponges or leeches), with the motto "When full we are at Rest." Inhabitants drank morning and night. "All claim a Liberty of speech on any Subject," the author wrote, "and from this claim, two or three generally speak at once," on philosophy, love, commerce, and debauchery. "They generally discuss Points of Religion when they have drank most, and settle the State best when they can stand least." According to the laws of Drinkallia, all bargains were sealed with half a bottle, all oaths were void after 3 P.M., no one could drink alone more than two days in a row, and no one could preach temperance. Upon entering any house, the host or tavernkeeper offered strong wine or liquor to the stranger—to refuse labeled the visitor not just ill-bred but traitorous. Such was this satirist's view of New York City—a place that, for all the Hungarian Club's pretensions to regularity, was fundamentally soaked in disorder.[67] The tavern's regulations and rituals either represented an empty contradiction or a useful polite fiction, depending on one's perspective. Meanwhile, these satires perpetuated the notion that taverns were open to all men and all viewpoints.

Many critics called for good manners, which would organize men according to their politeness and erudition. Hamilton mocked an "incoherent" tavernkeeper who proclaimed the equality of souls before God, and he scorned a musician whose conversation was fit only for "ignorant blockheads."[68] In response to such offenses, many New York taverngoers aspired to even greater heights of orderly sociability. They adopted refined manners, dress, speech, and conversation in a tavern, which would allow them greater access to polite respectability, and perhaps social and economic advancement. Men of wealth and status might face social exclusion if they did not learn and follow the standards of polite sociability.[69] Even governors were not immune to lapses in politeness. The lawyer William Smith Jr. heard that Lord Dunmore, "fuddled" with drink, had acted like "a silly extravagant Buck" and "a damned Fool" at a feast of the Sons of St. Andrew in 1770. "He grounds all upon his being noisy and clamorous in giving the Toasts . . . at the Table" and had "sunk himself to the vilest baudy Healths." The company was astonished and ashamed, according to the witness, and Dunmore had "done for his Reputation forever." With Dunmore sure to be "lampooned and despised," Smith resolved to be more circumspect "involving my own [reputation] with a Character that will be disreputable among all sorts of People, & perhaps expose what I gave him in Confidence."[70] Raucous behavior offended men like Hamilton and Smith, who attempted to elevate themselves above their neighbors at the next table. Yet such hierarchical categories could be fragile, as the rising insistence on gentility clashed with the leveling nature of the tavern. This would be an important lesson to those who sought to mobilize their neighbors during the imperial crisis.

In the midst of this discussion of sociability and manners, three young Presbyterian lawyers introduced new forms of club life and civilized sociability to New York. Smith, William Livingston, and John Morin Scott were Yale graduates who went on to hold political office in colonial New York. These three sought to mobilize city dwellers to contribute to the public good by launching a number of projects for civic improvement and the pursuit of knowledge as counterweights to state and church.[71] In the process, they criticized the drinking that comprised so much of New York's public life. As a young man, Livingston had written, "Minerva has a few votaries among this ignorant generation." Instead, "Bacchus and the Queen of Love own the greater number." For his own part, Livingston asserted, "Drunkenness I really think is the last Vice that ever I shall fall into." His subsequent reputation as "the Philosopher" seems to have borne this out: the Loyalist Thomas Jones wrote that Livingston was sullen and uncouth. Smith was similarly resistant to the tavern culture. Jones noted that Smith had "a steady, demure, puritanical countenance," and even the apparently dour Livingston criticized his friend Smith's "Ministerial Severity" and "Compunction of Conscience" when it came to drinking. Though Smith seems to have taken a drink now and then, he felt uncomfortable with the evenings he spent "soaking at Tavern with a set of noisy Fops," as well as the general "Damned Hurly burly of the town." Scott was more at ease in a tavern company than the other two; as Jones wrote, he "possessed a jovial, hearty, free and engaging disposition, loved company and was a boon companion." When he later ran for office, Scott's enemies told voters to look for him at "Sot's Hall," criticized a mind "much impaired by Debauchery and Excess," and said he "damns all but Favourites when drunk."[72]

Livingston and his companions wrote essays in the *Independent Reflector* attacking New Yorkers' luxurious drinking practices and the leveling effects of gambling, comparable to the well-known fulminating of moralists such as John Adams of Massachusetts or Anthony Benezet of Philadelphia.[73] The three also founded the Society for the Promotion of Useful Knowledge, which offered its members edifying, polite conversation as an alternative to the bawdy songs, smoking, gossip, effeminacy, ignorance, licentiousness, and drunkenness of the "various Companies of Men, that collect themselves into Weekly Clubs, and Societies." Their goal was "to improve the *Taste*, and *Knowledge*, to *Reform*, and *Correct*, the manners of the Inhabitants of this *Town*" through enlightened conversation. The society kept merchants at arms' length, since they "live without Study, and converse only at the *Coffee House*." While a far cry from the bumper toasts of the Hungarian Club, the society still allowed "a Glass of Wine, to exhilarate the animal Spirits, enliven and sharpen their Apprehensions, and wet their Eloquence." Over the coming months, satirists trained their barbed pens on the new club. "A Brother Philosopher" praised the society for its goals of "universal Love, and Regard for Mankind" without respect to religion. Still, he noted that the society's indulgence in wine might sink them into "*Ribaldry*, and malicious *Billingsgate* [obscene abuse]."[74] Another essayist attacked Smith directly, writing that "the Arguments, you have so frequently belch'd out at the *Coffee-House*, militate against your Conduct" in spreading false rumors.[75] Once again, the balance between politeness and wit was important. According to the critics of the new society, the difference between meeting to discuss manners over drinks and meeting for drinks in a mannerly way was a difference only of degree. Nevertheless, Livingston and his allies helped introduce orderly and intellectual outlets for socialization and civil discourse, the means to spend their tavern time more purposefully.

All in all, one quarter of New York's adult white men belonged to voluntary associations by the end of the colonial period, according to one scholar, not including the various social clubs. Livingston, Smith, and Scott organized the New York Society Library in 1754 and a forum for legal discussion called the Moot in 1770. After the Seven Years' War, groups of New Yorkers formed another library society and more ethnic societies, a hospital society, a Macaroni Club for horse racing, an elite Social Club, and a society for the promotion of manufacturing in response to new customs duties. Religious Dissenters established a short-lived society in response to local electoral defeats at the hands of Anglicans. In an endeavor that was doomed to failure, the Society for Reformation of Manners and the Suppression of Vice in the City of New York imitated similar clubs in England, calling for better enforcement of laws against drunkenness, lewdness, cursing, Sabbath-breaking, "and many other dissolute and irregular practices," and called upon its members "not to tarry unnecessarily in companies where such evils are practiced." In the late 1760s, merchants, mariners, and artisans organized as the Chamber of Commerce, the Marine Society, and the Friendly Society of House Carpenters. Such associations generally met in taverns and coffeehouses. The New York Society Library subscribers first elected trustees at the Exchange Coffee House in Broad Street on April 30, 1754. These trustees held their first meeting a week later at Edward Willett's Province Arms tavern on Broadway, and continued to meet at a variety of taverns over the coming years, including Samuel Francis's Queen's Head and Sarah Brock's tavern near City Hall on Wall Street.

The Moot Club's rules expressed the subscribers' determination "to meet in the Evening . . . every Month, at Barden's or such other Place" as the members might appoint, which over the following year included Francis's tavern as well as Bolton's. The club's bylaws laid down explicit rules for settling the tavern bill. The New York Marine Society favored Captain Thomas Doran's tavern, while the Social Club met at the Queen's Head.[76]

The Scottish philosopher David Hume had predicted that men would "flock into cities" in order to "receive and communicate knowledge; to show their wit or their breeding, their taste in conversation or living, in cloaths or furniture." Such men would form "clubs and societies" and thereby "feel an increase of humanity." As club members, New Yorkers harnessed private interests and the pursuit of happiness to promote public benefits, civic spirit, and solidarity. In New York and throughout the British Empire, such societies went hand in hand with urban growth and refinement, commercial expansion, and promotion from tavernkeepers and newspapers. Tavern clubs, channeling the spirit of public good, represented an integral part of the eighteenth century's developing transatlantic network of migrants, consumer goods, and ideas. Particularly after 1760, these networks were becoming essential parts of life in North America's largest cities.[77]

Subjects of the eighteenth-century British Empire increasingly saw their society as a loose collection of voluntary societies.[78] This voluntaristic impulse became an important component of political mobilization in the decade before the Revolution. Initially, New Yorkers joined clubs based on ethnic ties, Masonic rites, and the civilized pursuit of knowledge. After 1763, many of the newer clubs were rooted in economic self-interest, though such associations did not necessarily translate their organization into explicit political action. Many clubs disallowed political discussion, in fact—the Moot threatened to expel any member who introduced "any Discourse about the Party Politics of this Province." No particular club could contain New York's fluid political alignments. The Moot Club, therefore, made clear that each night's president "shall take Care to keep due Order and Regularity." To inject politics into club life was to invite conflict and disorder.[79]

Tavern clubs provided structure and support for otherwise rowdy bachelors, encouraging their drive for self-improvement and upward mobility as well as the wider public interest. Voluntary associations were supposed to uphold cultural standards of sociability and order, but William Smith Jr. did not believe that incorporating the Marine Society would "be of public Utility[,] but rather [would] increase the Wantoness of the Populace."[80] Smith revealed his class bias by voicing suspicions of a club in which mariners predominated, though the mariners received their charter anyway. New Yorkers tended to separate themselves into a hierarchy of taverns, yet they never forgot that companionable drinking might make different kinds of men into peers of one another. From the Marine Society to the Moot Club, the civic and sociable world of New York was an aggregate of voluntary impulses, cross-class cooperation, and tavern interactions that the elite authorities could never quite contain. Smith, Hamilton, and other proponents of organized sociability believed in mobilizing tavern companies for polite, refined conversation that contributed to the public good. At the same time, they scorned acts of rudeness or drinking to excess in taverns. As a result, their view of mobilization in taverns was specific, not to say narrow, especially in New York's alcohol-soaked culture. One newspaper contributor wrote, "It is indeed possible to be *merry* and *wise*."[81] Among polite companies, merriment did not have to be the antithesis of reason; sociability and civic improvement could go hand in hand.

This debate over merriment and civic improvement was difficult to resolve, and it was destined to become embroiled with politics and political mobilization. Critics expressed particular concern about the mixing of liquor with politics in New York. They worried that voters were judging candidates for office based on tavern gossip. When members of political factions tried to influence voters, Crèvecoeur wrote, "People at those Times neither Know nor forsee of what Eminent service this Man will be to their country more than [any] other," except what "they hear . . . said of him at Tavern & other publicke Places." As Crèvecoeur decried this process, he also noted the democratic pride that such tavern talk might encourage. As an American freeman interacts with political factions, he "Knows & Feels all his Influence which perhaps he had never before Experienced — this gives him a high opinion of himself." While the freeman could argue his views "with all the Knowledge he can muster," he could expect to grasp no more than "the coarse Rudiments of Provincial Politicks."[82] Taverns inspired feelings of individuality and equality by encouraging civic awareness and participation.

Contemporary critics expressed further concern over the presence of alcohol at elections. A song printed in the *New York Weekly Journal* urged voters to "Stand up to save your country dear, / In spite of usquebaugh [whiskey] and beer." Livingston expressed "Grief and Indignation" at "our Practice of making Interest for Elections, and intoxicating the People to influence their Voices." These "Election-Jobbers" were destroying British liberty and virtue by selling their voices for "Beer and Brandy," "a brutal Carouse," "a Pound of Beef," "a Song," "a Treat, or a Frolick!" By acting this way, a politician invited suspicion that his candidacy threatened the public good: "Why else such hawking of Liquor, and purchasing of Interest?" Livingston urged his fellow citizens to vote freely, "and scorn to be either brib'd, or dram'd, or frolick'd, or bought, or coax'd, or threaten'd out of your Birthright." While the author did not mean to suggest that every previous candidate who had treated voters had intended to bribe them, he pointed out that "the Practice had obtained the Sanction of Custom," and so candidates were idly "following the Mode." Plying the voters with alcohol was crucial to getting elected, and this worried not only Livingston and his partisans but critics in other large cities as well.[83]

In 1769, Livingston and his friends suggested one way to remedy the effects of treating: conducting votes via secret ballot rather than having voters call out their choice (which subjected them to dangerous influence). Livingston's enemies countered that alcohol might just as easily corrupt voters with secret ballots. "J. W." described Connecticut's secret ballot system, where "all the Taverns and Ale-Houses" were still open to everyone on election days, with candidates footing the bills.[84] "Popular Whigs," as historian Alan Tully calls them, were particularly engaged in this "Mode" of treating. The powerful DeLancey and Jones families, leaders of one of colonial New York's principal factions, practiced a style of politicking that lent itself to the raising of the punch bowl in taverns. Governor George Clinton, before he broke with the DeLanceys, was particularly esteemed as "a jolly toaper." James DeLancey was known for his fondness for alcohol and companionship, his brother Oliver for killing a man in a tavern brawl, and House Speaker Adolphe Philipse for his sexual exploits.[85] Their political allies had reputations as sociable, swaggering glad-handers and men of action who were generous with their liquor. Smith bristled at DeLancey's broad-based cronyism: "His revels with low company, his daily coffeehouse haunts. . . . [He] was all his days addicted to company and knew mankind well from the highest to the lowest orders."[86] When the DeLancey faction unleashed its antilawyer screeds in the 1760s, Livingston countered (with a dart aimed at Captain James DeLancey) that if only merchants were fit to represent the city in the Assembly, then apparently "every Cockfighter, Horseracer and Whoremonger, is in the Politics of the present Day a Merchant."[87]

Livingston, Smith, and Scott, the critics of convivial politicking, were the political rivals of the DeLanceys. The Livingstonite faction corresponded to an idiom of "provincial Whiggism" that they had inherited from Lewis Morris Sr., Lewis Morris Jr., and James Alexander. Their temperament was generally more stingy, prudish, literary, and aloof. As Tully writes, "For all of them a good evening was not backgammon and bumpers but conversation with other educated men."[88] Whig essayists had long written that drunkenness and idleness sapped the people's ability to be vigilant against tyranny.[89] Instead, these men used taverns to found a number of civic-minded clubs. These provincial Whigs were idealistic and forward-looking about the ways of mobilizing sociability for civic ends: in December 1765, the Society for Promoting Arts held a meeting where Richard Deane produced a local liquor distilled from malt as a means to reduce importation of foreign spirits. At the same time, as we have seen, they were not averse to a glass of wine to stimulate active minds. By trying to keep tavern politicking at arm's length, these provincial Whigs demonstrated a certain willful naiveté about the best way to mobilize most New Yorkers.[90]

One striking practice, characteristic of both the provincial and popular Whigs, was emerging: both groups sought to use tavern sociability for political ends, sidestepping both church and formal state structures as a basis for public action. The weakness of such structures in colonial

New York helped to enable the growth of urban pluralism (including political factions) and the need for voluntaristic action. These developments would be particularly significant during the Revolutionary era.[91] Indeed, by the 1760s, the intellectual divisions between provincial and popular Whigs had become less relevant in the vertiginous world of New York politics. Ultimately, the Livingston faction had its charismatic taverngoers, too, among privateers like Philip Livingston. Indeed, John Morin Scott's enemies accused his supporters of selling their votes to him for a dram.[92] Successful politicians recognized that it was better to operate among the beer-houses than to try to rise above them.

As they schemed to dominate New York politics, the DeLancey and Livingston factions formed alliances with the new leaders of the street and tavern. Beginning in 1765, the Sons of Liberty authored patriotic pamphlets and petitions, made popular speeches against imperial encroachment, and formed committees and military companies. The merchant Alexander McDougall, after years as a successful privateer captain, "quitted the sea and settled in New York, where he kept what is known among sailors by the name of 'a Slop-Shop.'"[93] Isaac Sears, another merchant and privateer captain, married Sarah Drake, whose father's tavern on Water Street was known as a hangout for seamen and revolutionaries.[94] John Lamb, as a wine and liquor merchant, must have had dealings with retailers all over the city; his wife's sister's husband, Joseph Allicocke, a Son of Liberty in 1765 who became a Loyalist, also sold wine and liquor.[95] Marinus Willett, a later addition to the Sons of Liberty, was also related to a tavern-keeper; the Edward Willett who kept the Province Arms was likely Marinus's father.[96] After the Seven Years' War, New York's leading Sons of Liberty faced the challenge of mobilizing the convivial drinkers who made up the city's sociable world, while also maintaining order among them. When riots erupted in New York (actions that elite Livingstonites deplored), these leaders tried their best to maintain order so that the imperial government might respond favorably to the colonists' grievances.[97]

The imperial crisis created disruptions and disorder in all the cities on the eastern seaboard of North America. Riots and other acts of resistance commingled with the already turbulent state of politics in New York. Parliament's harsh imposition of a new imperial order turned taverns up and down the American seaboard into central sites of cross-class political mobilization. In Boston, New York, and Charleston, and in numerous towns in between, Sons of Liberty met around the punch bowl to discuss resistance to imperial policy.

Taverns had already hosted both orderly and disorderly resistance to the enforcement of customs duties. When George Spencer alerted the provincial authorities to the prevalence of smuggling in 1759, sundry New Yorkers abused him at the Coffee House; the following day, a group convinced one of Spencer's creditors to have him arrested. The deputy sheriff Philip Branson stopped with Spencer at a tavern on the way to jail, "where he

Called for Wine & other Liquor." During this deliberate delay, a "Mob of Sailors & Others" formed, hauled Spencer into a cart outside the tavern, and pelted him "with Mud & Filth of the Streets" as they dragged him about the city.[98] Not all tavern protests were so chaotic, however. In January 1764, when New York's economy was faltering, "a very considerable Body" of the city's merchants met in the long room of George Burns's Province Arms tavern to discuss issues of debt and commerce, and to form a committee that drew up petitions to the provincial Assembly and to Parliament. The merchants stamped the meeting with the legitimacy of the public good: "Every Gentleman who is a Friend to the Trade of our Mother Country or has Property in this Province, must conceive himself interested in the Success of this Undertaking."[99] Two months later the merchants called a meeting at Samuel Francis's Queen's Head "on Business of great Importance to Trade."[100] In June, Robert R. Livingston reported that some New Yorkers would not drink dutied wine, knowing such duties would devastate the local wine import trade.[101]

These meetings for the airing of imperial grievances became even more heated once New Yorkers learned of the provisions of the Stamp Act of 1765. Various contributors to New York newspapers had railed against the new tax, and a New York City crowd had threatened to attack Maryland stamp officer Zacharias Hood at his lodgings at the King's Arms Tavern in September, prompting the landlady to pack him off to Fort George. Furthermore, the delegates to the intercolonial Stamp Act Congress met at New York's City Hall in October to voice their protest. These delegates often sought out Burns's City Arms Tavern for lodging and entertainment, which provided opportunities for intercolonial sociability and political mobilization. John Dickinson, one of the delegates, wrote to his mother that he was afraid the "long sittings" at dinner "will consume the greatest part of our afternoons." In this way, New Yorkers initially relied on the printing press, the Assembly, and the Stamp Act Congress to counter British attempts to extend imperial taxation. New Yorkers did not mobilize outside of these legal channels as quickly as Bostonians did. Bostonians were more economically desperate, historically more touchy about their civil and religious liberties, and more homogenously united around the institutions of Commonwealth and Congregationalism. In New York, on the other hand, the "Sons of Liberty" did not meet openly until late November 1765 (though shadowy meetings probably took place earlier), while major mob action roiled New York much later than the riots in Boston and Newport.[102]

Stamp Act rioting in New York began in late October, five days after Lieutenant Governor Cadwallader Colden ordered that the colony's stamped papers be stored in Fort George.[103] On October 31, the day before the Stamp Act was to go into effect, several protest displays emerged. Crowds roamed the streets dressed in mourning for liberty. At the Merchant Coffee House, the dice were wrapped in crepe and the backgammon boxes were swathed in black. More than two hundred merchants met at Burns's tavern and resolved not to import goods from England until Parliament repealed the act. As they met, a crowd of seamen and boys gathered at the door of the tavern, having heard that there would be a ritual procession to "bury Liberty" (this was probably based on an allegory they had read in John Holt's *New-York Gazette*). Though the merchants were leading no such procession, the crowd paraded anyway, "whistling and hurraing" through New York streets and breaking lamps along with thousands of windows. The dual strains of orderly resistance and disorderly disruption were both apparent.

The following night, a relatively organized procession took a nasty turn. Colden ordered troops to ready Fort George for defense on November 1, as crowds hoisted effigies of the hated lieutenant governor and the devil about the streets "with the greatest order, carrying candles and torches in their hands." Rioters hanged the effigies, paraded them before the Coffee House, dared the fort's garrison to fire on the crowd, and carried the gallows along with Colden's chariot to Bowling Green to be burnt. From there the rioters went to Major Thomas James's Vauxhall, since James had said "he would cram down the Stamp Act upon them with a hundred men."

Major James of the Royal Artillery occupied a stately mansion in Bowling Green that he named Vauxhall, after London's pleasure gardens. By choosing this name, he adopted a posture of refinement and separation from lower-class New Yorkers, and a haughty expression of military grandeur. London's Vauxhall offered wealthy gentlemen a way to legitimate their exclusive sociability, yet even here, people transgressed social boundaries. Effete, narcissistic "Macaronis," or stylish fops, paraded their consumer goods through London's Vauxhall and threatened the stability of traditional social roles. London dealt with these contradictions in its own way. The rough-and-tumble drinking city of New York, meanwhile, was no place for Major James's display of military arrogance. New Yorkers refused to allow Parliament to impose its imperial will upon them, and they refused to allow Major James to parade his wealth, refinement, and tyrannical views. Instead, the crowd took everything moveable out of James's house, drank his alcohol (three or four pipes of wine, each ninety-two gallons), burned his possessions, and gutted the house of all its doors, window frames, and partitions. Afterward, they attacked some "bawdy houses" (perhaps because they catered to soldiers) and retired for the evening.[104]

The mobilization of resistance to the Stamp Act had become too frenzied, and so New Yorkers hoped to restore order. While Isaac Sears boasted inside the Coffee House on November 2 that the inhabitants would have the stamps in their possession within the next twenty-four hours, Robert Livingston and others patrolled the streets and tried to pacify the crowd. The next day, November 3, the "Sons of Neptune" posted a notice at the Coffee House telling New Yorkers to ignore these patrician attempts to restore order. Other letters threatened violence to Colden and customs officials. Still, New Yorkers were beginning to agree that things had gone too far—their real grievance was with the imperial government, not with local leaders. On November 4, various tavern companies declared their intention to restore order to the city. An open group of "all the Citizens" met at the Coffee House in the morning and agreed to keep the peace that night. "Several Captains of Vessels and others" met at a tavern and offered their support to Colden, while asking that he remove the stamps from Fort George. Radical New Yorkers threatened drunken violence, while others coaxed Colden and his allies with more orderly demands. A number of taverngoers had been drunk and belligerent, a "perfect anarchy," as the fearful Governor's Council described it. At the same time, other taverngo-ers retained the capacity to impose order, organize protest, and mobilize resistance with restraint. Yet the use of taverns as sites of mobilization was risky. The restoration of order was never assured.

Years later, tavernkeeper Samuel Francis revived Major James's Vauxhall as a provincial version of the English pleasure gardens that the house's name was intended to invoke. (New Yorkers had prevented Major James from restoring his house and delivered threatening notes warning the Assembly not to indemnify James for his losses.)[105] At Vauxhall, the city's gentry could socialize and enrich themselves, but they probably could not relax. The violence of the Stamp Act riots made elite New Yorkers anxious about the conduct of their urban neighbors.

New York's culture of politics and sociability could never be solely the province of the polite. Disorder, dissatisfaction, and disaffection fermented alongside the beverages. While the Stamp Act riots and other outbreaks of street violence did not primarily express class resentment, these events nevertheless challenged the local gentry's ability to maintain order in New York City. Historian Pauline Maier has argued that the Stamp Act crisis taught New York's resistance leaders that disorderly violence was counterproductive. Therefore, organized resistance sought to "contain disorder" in the future. This was certainly true of some New Yorkers, many of them affiliated with the "provincial Whigs" who had supported the creation of voluntary associations, standards of polite sociability, and the imposition of laws. For these Whigs, the 1765 riots were yet another example of the results of unbridled drunkenness.[106]

It must have been clear to other New York leaders, however, that they could not merely reapply naive provincial Whig ideals as a way of directing resistance. The writer "Cethegus" struggled with this very issue in 1769. In response to the Townshend duties, he called for boycotts, declaiming luxury, prodigality, lavish imitation, "Idleness and Extravagance," and "the danger of tumults" in the same language the provincial Whigs had used to criticize taverns. "Cethegus" applauded the Hollanders who had rebelled against Spain "with no other drink than water." Although he admitted that "mobs are sometimes necessary evils," he worried "that there is no appointing bounds to a mob beforehand." As they sought to maintain order and control, New Yorkers faced a dilemma. They could not rely on legislation, since laws might be either ineffective or *too* effective. Most colonists agreed that inflexible laws were the worst means of curbing disorder, since they lent themselves to further abuses of power. A significant current of Whig thought, after all, still believed that rioting and disorder were natural responses to oppression, integral parts of society, and perhaps conducive to the public good.[107]

New Yorkers seized upon the tavern, therefore, as a particularly important place to coordinate resistance to imperial policy. The network of drinking houses, from refined taverns and coffeehouses to unlicensed grogshops, already incorporated the organized sociability of ritual drinking and club life, geared toward civic improvement. Taverns also sponsored drinking and disorderly behavior, helping to distill rum-induced courage and patriotic rage into a potent punch. The ever-present power of drinking in taverns, as a social lubricant and as a source of purposeful disorder, was even more useful for cross-class political mobilization than petitions or newspaper articles, the more idealized, orderly means of resistance to imperial authority.[108]

Public displays and assemblages of people increasingly took place in front of the Merchant Coffee House, a refined establishment in a central location. Shadowy crowd leaders often posted broadsides there that called for meetings, announced approval of crowd action, or threatened persons who were obnoxious to the community. Just as in Boston, New York radicals used certain sites as prominent platforms for defending their turf. In all cities, taverns worked particularly well. Visitors and inhabitants often found themselves stopping by a tavern or coffeehouse for a drink and a political discussion. As "Belinda" lamented to a female friend in a 1766 newspaper satire, self-absorbed young men had formerly never entertained a thought in their head "but such as we or their glass inspired." Now these young men breathed politics along with tobacco smoke and coffee fumes in public houses all over the continent.[109]

New Yorkers promoted (and later celebrated) the repeal of the Stamp Act in tavern meetings designed to recruit taverngoers for resistance to imperial policy. Secret meetings among radical opponents to the Stamp Act may have begun as early as September 1765. On November 25, 1765, leaders of the resistance to the Stamp Act called a "General Meeting of the Freeholders, Freemen and Inhabitants of the City and County of New-York" at George Burns's tavern the next day, to which "Persons of all Ages, Ranks and Conditions" were welcome. They assured the newspaper-reading public that they would act according to "the strictest Rules of Society," and "that their Proceedings shall be conducted with the utmost Solemnity and good Order." The meeting was preparing an address to the General Assembly to press for repeal of the Stamp Act when elite DeLanceyites and Livingstonites wrested control of the meeting and adopted more moderate resolutions than those the radicals had advocated. Undeterred, the Liberty Boys organized an outdoor meeting on December 6 to urge lawyers to conduct business without stamps. Although the threat of violence loomed over New York during the rest of the month, one historian attributes the relative calm to James DeLancey Jr.'s savvy alliance with the Sons of Liberty. On January 7, 1766, the Sons of Liberty met publicly at William Howard's tavern and resolved to defend New York against the Stamp Act with their lives and fortunes and to preserve "the Peace and good Order of this City." The group would meet thereafter once a fortnight.[110]

City dwellers did not just exchange ideas among themselves in taverns and coffeehouses. They initiated a correspondence among tavern companies throughout the Atlantic seaboard, forming an intercolonial organization of the Sons of Liberty. On September 23, 1765, Colden suspected that the colonies were engaged in a "secret Correspondence," plotting to destroy stamped papers and force stamp officers to resign. An organized gathering of the Sons of Liberty in late October or early November, possibly at Burns's tavern, initiated an intercolonial effort centered in New York City. On December 31, Gershom Mott and Hugh Hughes, two of New York's Sons of Liberty, traveled to a tavern in New London, Connecticut, to urge joint resistance to the Stamp Act. The New York Sons of Liberty formally established a committee of correspondence at their February 4 meeting, and soon resolved, "We conceive the general safety of the colonies, and the British constitution, to depend on a firm union of the whole." Mott and Hughes personally delivered their message again at Norwich and Windham and Boston, where the Sons of Liberty in turn established connections with smaller Massachusetts towns and Portsmouth, New Hampshire; the network ultimately included Albany, Providence, Newport, Schenectady, Oyster Bay, Huntington, Philadelphia, and towns in New Jersey, Maryland, and Virginia, while another network drew together Georgia and the Carolinas.[111]

Thus, meetings that began in a New York tavern provided a model for— and corresponded with—organizations that met in cities and towns (probably quite often in taverns) in all thirteen of the colonies that ultimately rebelled against Great Britain. The very name "sons of liberty" was reminiscent of the fraternal bonds of tavern clubs. In a published December 1765 letter, New York's Sons of Liberty called upon their "brethren" to attend to "the public good" and "let all divisions cease." As the British Captain John Montresor reported, the Sons of Liberty "Keep an office and enter minutes and record them & all their correspondence to their licentious fraternity throughout the different Provinces." The Sons' processes and nomenclature drew on tavern idioms of unity, order, masculinity, and civic improvement, articulating the voluntary ethos that would come to characterize the Revolutionary movement and its institutions.[112]

New Yorkers made it clear, through feasting and drinking, whose political opinions were welcome in the tavern. On February 6, 1766, Montresor reported that the Sons of Liberty "declare that they will fight up to their knees in blood rather than suffer the Stamp Act to be put in force in this

Province and if they can assist even in any other." By the end of the month, he wrote that the Sons "make no scruple of publickly declaring that they are for shaking off the Yoke of Dependency, of their Mother Country."[113] We can imagine New Yorkers making such statements in taverns: places where authority was largely absent, yet men could fortify and encourage one another with strong words and strong drink. Though "the Company of every Well-wisher to their Country" was acceptable to the Sons of Liberty, such language was meant to exclude as well as include.[114] When school-master John Stranger announced his determination "not to have a Word to say, either against my King or Country" during the Stamp Act crisis, New Yorkers "told me plainly I should eat no more of their Bread & that I might go about my Business," and so he returned to England in 1766.[115] As North America became polarized over questions of imperial policy, an observer could see the antagonists close ranks most clearly in the cities, particularly in the city taverns.

New Yorkers learned of the repeal of the Stamp Act on May 20, 1766, and the next day the "True Sons of Liberty" held an "elegant Entertainment" at William Howard's tavern, "their usual House of publick Resort." In addition to music and dining, the company made twenty-eight toasts. The evening concluded with bonfires and illuminations, though townspeople noted sourly that the houses of military and naval officers remained dark. "The vast Concourse of People" were exuberant with joy, firing pistols and breaking windows and doorknockers. Montresor was disgusted at the crowd of Liberty Boys that marched to the fort to congratulate Governor Henry Moore, "three of which, drunk as they were, had admittance." Nevertheless, the Sons of Liberty made sure to note that "the whole Transactions of the Day was conducted and finished with the greatest Loyalty, Harmony, and good Order." Such celebrations echoed in distant taverns; as far away as Antigua, a "very elegant entertainment" marked the happy event. For the king's birthday on June 4, New Yorkers attempted to restore the town's harmony by hosting a joint celebration of the birth-day and the authenticated arrival of the Stamp Act's repeal. The town dispensed "Beer and Grog for the Populace, and an Entertainment or Dinner provided at the City Arms for the General, Governor, officers military, Naval and civil, at the Expence of the Inhabitants and cannon fired at each Toast, accompanied with Huzzas." This time the entire town was illuminated.[116]

Celebrations of the Stamp Act repeal echoed not just across space but through time as well. For years, New Yorkers celebrated the March 18 anniversary of the repeal. In 1768, the "Friends to Constitutional Liberty and Trade" met at the nearby taverns of John Jones and Edward Bardin in the Fields. The company enjoyed an elegant entertainment with flags, music, and fireworks, as well as "a pleasing Flow of social Affections." The newspaper account emphasized the company's "proper Decorum," reported that they sent their leftover food and "a suitable Quantity of Liquor" to the city's imprisoned debtors, and recounted toasts to the monarchy, the

Virginia and Massachusetts assemblies, "Friends of America," John Dickinson of Philadelphia, and "Unanimity to the Sons of Liberty in America."[117] Such ritual toasts, and their reprinting in newspapers, helped to forge links and communicate political ideas among the literate and illiterate in New York City and beyond.[118]

While the Sons of Liberty did their best to emphasize decorum and social unity at this event, New Yorkers knew all too well that the entropic forces of drunkenness and political strife could threaten such orderly sociability. Montresor wrote that the Sons of Liberty sat down for supper on January 19, 1766, "but upon some disagreement (which is generally the case) they broke up and dispersed as soon as it came on the table leaving only half a dozen."[119] In February, New Yorkers read of a tavern meeting in Savannah, Georgia, that was interrupted by "a son of liberty who had been engaged most part of the day in the wars of Bacchus"; supporters of the governor ejected him from the tavern and beat him.[120] Not all resistance meetings ran smoothly, particularly when drinking was involved. Nevertheless, the Sons of Liberty accepted a certain level of disorder as a way of doing business—or politics—in taverns.

Politics was a complicated business in New York, and people's allegiances sometimes shifted. As a result of this dynamic urban political culture, political mobilization was not always a simple matter of government supporter against Liberty Boy. In 1769, as nonimportation meetings were taking place at Bolton and Sigel's, two groups of Liberty Boys planned separate repeal anniversary celebrations at the taverns of Edward Smith and Henry Van De Water.[121] On the day of the celebration, a committee from the Van De Water company (which included Alexander McDougall) tried to extend an orderly courtesy to the company at Smith's tavern: "Their Constituents drank their Healths, &c." Captain Isaac Sears and John Lamb, at Smith's, believed that McDougall and his companions "only *assumed* the Appellation" of Sons of Liberty, and returned no answer. The Van De Water company tried to extend courtesies again, sending a single emissary, upon which Lamb's companions debated whether the emissary "should not be *shewn* they Way out of a *Window*." The emissary wisely opted for front door instead.[122] Political factions were mobilizing their followers in rival taverns, and such disorder threatened to create a civic impasse in New York City.

For radicals who worried that a civic impasse would hamper resistance against Great Britain, the clashes between city dwellers and British troops must have given them renewed hope. Taverns and disorderly houses often provided the fuel for such disagreements. Before 1763, members of the armed forces had been smoothly integrated into New York City's tavern life. Many officers participated in New York's clubs: in the early years of the Seven Years' War, for instance, the majority of new members of the Saint Andrew's Society were military men.[123] Colonel James Montresor described his life in 1758 and 1759 as filled with balls, dinner invitations to the Glass House, supper at Scotch Johnny's, and club meetings.[124] During the Seven Years' War, the merchant John Watts had delighted that the "Tipling Soldiery" were "exceedingly publick Spirited in the Consumption of strong Liquors."[125] When business was booming and New Yorkers were happy with their role in the British Empire, soldiers and civilians enjoyed one another's company in a cheery display of imperial unity and goodwill.

Yet the Seven Years' War also exposed the fault lines where cooperation might break down between New Yorkers and the military presence among them. The admiralty blamed American grog shops for enticing sailors away from their service in the Royal Navy.[126] The townspeople in turn complained that sailors hiring themselves out at the dockyards for low wages made it tougher for locals to find work.[127] The military commander Lord Loudon had cursed the mayor, John Cruger, and forced the city to quarter troops during the war. In January 1764, a group of soldiers broke Major Robert Rogers, an imprisoned debtor, out of jail and wounded the jailer. Late in 1764, New Yorkers refused to supply firewood to the barracks and the mayor would not let General Thomas Gage quarter his troops in the city's public houses.[128] This issue of hospitality prompted serious conflicts between soldiers and New Yorkers.

By June 1765, John Watts was no longer celebrating a "public spirit" shared by civilians and the military. He reported that people would "rather part with their Money . . . than to have a parcel of Military Masters put by Act of Parliament a bed to their Wifes & Daughters."[129] It turned out New Yorkers wanted neither: members of the New York Assembly defied Parliament by refusing to obey the Quartering Act of 1765, with its appropriation of taverns as quarters and its requisition of rations of alcohol. In March 1766, the crowd threatened to burn Sir Jeffrey Amherst in effigy for his proposal to send more troops to America to enforce the Stamp Act. The Assembly refused Governor Henry Moore's request for quartering appropriations again in June 1766, and most colonies denied the army the liquor that the Quartering Act mandated. William Pitt, the Earl of Chatham, commented acidly that "New York has drunk the deepest of the baneful cup of infatuation, but none [of the colonists] seem to be quite sober and in full possession of reason." Parliament responded with the Restraining Act of 1767, which harshly curtailed New Yorkers' rights by forbidding the Assembly to meet until it complied with the Quartering Act. The Assembly evaded the punishment by passing a blanket appropriation of funds to the governor. A controversy also erupted during the late 1760s and early 1770s between military and civil officials in New York over who would take precedence at public entertainments, once again demonstrating the importance of sociable rituals in settling questions of political power.[130] These debates over lodging and drink contributed to the tension between troops and townspeople, prompted suspicions of standing armies, and gave new ammunition to those who sought to counteract imperial encroachment in New York.

Soldiers had long been associated with the despised bachelor in the Anglo-American tradition: drunk, debauched mercenaries who were estranged from the bonds of family and nation, frequenting prostitutes and living a life divorced from liberty.[131] Bostonians expressed their resentment toward British soldiers on numerous occasions, culminating in the banishment of soldiers to Castle Island after the Boston Massacre in 1770.[132] In Philadelphia, Alexander Graydon recalled the terrifying, mirthful, debauched rampages of two soldiers and concluded, "The common observation, that when men become soldiers they lose the character and feeling of citizens, was amply illustrated by the general conduct of the British officers in America." Soldiers' contempt for "mohairs," or civilians, Graydon wrote, contributed to the resentments that led to the separation from Great Britain.[133]

Examples of soldiers' atrocities were legion. In December 1755, the Common Council noted the desertion, "Breaches of the peace," "Tumults and Outrages," and "Disorders and Irregularities" that had resulted from the sale of strong liquors to garrison troops. As a result, the council passed a law prohibiting the sale of liquor to His Majesty's private soldiers after sundown, or the entertaining of soldiers in licensed houses. The magistrates reminded New Yorkers of this law in November 1766, after a number of soldiers from the 46th Regiment broke into the home of cartman Casper Hart, wounded him with a bayonet, and hamstrung his horse. Competition for employment had likely been the cause.[134] Other incidents that year had also caused turmoil: a group of inebriated soldiers stabbed a tavernkeeper in June; and a group of armed soldiers menaced several houses in the Field one night in October, in retribution for the treatment they had received at a disorderly house.[135] In 1769, Lieutenant William Jones of H.M.S. *Hussar* pleaded guilty to rioting, breaking into the disorderly house kept by laborer John Campbell, and entering it with more than thirty companions.[136]

Aside from these incidents of drunken violence and harassment, many of the brawls between soldiers and civilians had explicitly political overtones. New Yorkers had not forgotten the arming of Fort George against the inhabitants during the Stamp Act riots, or the fact that military officers had refused to illuminate their houses during the celebration of the Stamp Act repeal.[137] The repeal inspired New Yorkers to erect the Liberty Pole, which soon became a revered monument in commemoration of their resistance against the Stamp Act (fig. 2.3).[138] The townspeople were enraged in August 1766 when officers cut down the Liberty Pole, and brickbats flew through the air. Over the next week the townspeople insulted the troops and their officers, and even tried to unhorse an officer, while passing around proposals "for the Innholders & Inhabitants not to have any Intercourse with the military or even to admit them in their houses." To refuse to drink with military men was to exclude them from the city. Eventually the authorities restored order, despite the soldiers cutting down a second Liberty Pole on September 23. After the first anniversary celebration of the

Figure 2.3. This sketch shows New York City as a site of contest between British soldiers on the left and Sons of Liberty, huddled together in a tavern, on the right. New Yorkers had raised the Liberty Pole to commemorate the repeal of the Stamp Act, and the troops regarded it as a symbol of sedition. "Raising of the Liberty Pole in New York City," in the collection of Pierre Eugene Du Simitière. New York, ca. 1770. *The Library Company of Philadelphia*.

Stamp Act's repeal in 1767, the troops destroyed the third Liberty Pole. The inhabitants erected a fourth, bound with iron, and troops attempted without success to destroy this pole. After that the inhabitants kept watch, and in frustration the soldiers fired their muskets at Bardin's tavern. Drunken violence and disagreements over imperial policy had created an uneasy rift between New Yorkers and the imperial troops who were supposed to act as their protectors.[139]

As debates over troops and the Townshend Acts raged, the taverns became places where civilians and soldiers expressed their opinions about the imperial crisis and clashed violently. On November 14, 1768, demonstrators heard speeches in front of the Coffee House, where effigies of Boston's Sheriff Stephen Greenleaf and Governor Francis Bernard were hanging, as New Yorkers protested the stationing of troops in Boston, as well as the Townshend Acts. This in turn impelled the Assembly to answer the Massachusetts circular letter protesting against imperial policy.[140] On Saturday night, January 13, 1770, a party of the 16th Regiment made an attempt to saw down the fourth Liberty Pole. Running into trouble, they attempted to bore a hole in it and blow it up with gunpowder. A group of inhabitants observed these proceedings and rushed into De La Montagne's tavern (formerly Bardin's) across the street, which a group called the "United Sons of Liberty" had chosen as its monthly meeting place the previous summer. The taverngoers gave the cry of "fire!" to alarm the inhabitants and taunted the soldiers with hisses. In response, the redcoats drew weapons and attacked the gathered inhabitants, who withdrew inside the tavern. The soldiers broke the tavern's front windows, forced their way into the building, assaulted the waiter, and destroyed some of De La Montagne's lamps and bowls. When the soldiers succeeded three nights later in destroying the pole, they cut it into pieces and piled them in front of De La Montagne's door. The incident touched off a mass meeting in the Fields and a series of violent encounters between civilians and soldiers, culminating in two days of armed fighting at Golden Hill and Nassau Street on January 19 and 20.[141]

In the midst of these scuffles, the realignment of political factions and the imprisonment of a prominent Patriot became the occasion for further drinking rituals and conflicts over taverns. The merchant Alexander McDougall, under the pseudonym "A Son of Liberty," wrote a broadside in December 1769 entitled *To the Betrayed Inhabitants of the City and Colony of New York*. The piece castigated the New York Assembly for its appropriation of funds for the armed forces. McDougall urged New Yorkers to follow the example of Boston and Charleston by refusing to obey the Quartering Act. The broadside called the people to gather at the Liberty Pole (in front of De La Montagne's tavern), to which 1,400 people responded. John Lamb moderated the meeting—he, Sears, and McDougall had apparently resolved their differences since the uncomfortable rivalry between the two taverns during the repeal celebrations of 1769. On January 30, 1770, eleven days after the fight at Golden Hill, Sears and McDougall, along with tavern-keeper Joseph Drake and two other radicals, asked New York's Common Council for permission to erect a new Liberty Pole opposite Vandenbergh's tavern in the Fields. The Council rejected their request, and so Sears bought a lot just north of the Fields (and closer to the barracks than the pole's original site) for the raising of an almost indestructible Liberty Pole, twenty-two feet high. Thousands attended the ceremony on February 6. Over the next two days, the council met and ordered McDougall imprisoned for his authorship of *To the Betrayed Inhabitants*.[142]

The unified radical tavern leaders now had a martyr for their cause, a subject of a newspaper war that carried on for months, until McDougall was released in late April and the charges dismissed. As Thomas Jones remembered it, McDougall "was dubbed 'a second [John] Wilkes,' 'a patriot,' 'a defender of the rights of mankind and the liberties of the people.'" In tribute to the Wilkes analogy (Wilkes had gone to prison for his authorship of another pamphlet, *North Briton No. 45*), groups of forty-five men or women would dine with McDougall, while "Peter R. Livingston . . . sent him 45 bottles of Madeira, some Scotch traders 45 bottles of ale." Jones wrote, "Sometimes we were told of 45 bottles of wine being drank at a sitting, of

45 lbs. of beef being eaten, and 45 patriotic toasts given."[143] Such gustatory, lubricated pageantry demonstrated that alcohol and meals had the power to unite groups of political actors.

Yet at the same time, the celebration of the Stamp Act repeal on March 18, 1770, would wear a very different cast than the meetings in previous years. McDougall was in prison; the battle of Golden Hill was still a recent memory; New Yorkers had cooperated for months on the nonimportation agreement that joined them with the other port cities; and Sears, Lamb, and McDougall—all important political actors—were reunited as radicals. De La Montagne, who had formerly hosted the "United Sons of Liberty," found himself compelled to advertise that "I shall not be able to entertain any other company than those gentlemen and their connections who engaged my house for that day." The DeLanceyite "Friends to Liberty and Trade," who claimed the mantle of having met in past years at the taverns of Bardin, Jones, and Smith, had summoned their own anniversary meeting at De La Montagne's. The radicals therefore bought their own tavern, Hampden Hall, near the Liberty Pole.[144]

Soon after, fifteen soldiers who were about to ship off from New York attempted to destroy the new Liberty Pole on Saturday night, March 24, 1770. When the citizens rebuffed them, they returned with reinforcements as an armed group of forty. Four or five of the citizens retreated to Hampden Hall. The soldiers surrounded the tavern and attempted to force the door. As the proprietor Henry Bicker defended the entrance with fixed bayonet, the soldiers vowed to burn down the tavern. Once again the fire bells sounded the alarm, and Colonel James Robertson ordered the soldiers to be confined until they departed the city.[145] Bardin's tavern in 1767, De La Montagne's tavern in January 1770, and now Hampden Hall became sites of contestation during these instances, focal points for the assertion of authority and control.

The De La Montagnes found that casting their lot with a particular faction brought benefits as well as perils. The DeLanceys rewarded De La Montagne in 1770 by granting him the post of inspector of pot and pearl ash, replacing Isaac Sears. Thereafter, those opposed to the radicals found De La Montagne's a safe place to meet. General Charles Lee allegedly avenged the radicals in February 1776. He stayed at De La Montagne's (now managed by his widow), entertained guests with provisions and liquor, and then refused to pay her bill when he left for South Carolina. According to the Loyalist historian Thomas Jones, "He damned her for a tory, cursed her for a bitch, and left the house without paying her a six-pence."[146] Tavernkeepers might make enemies by allying themselves too closely with one party or the other. These were businessmen, after all, and most probably decided that the safest course was to keep the doors open to people of all political opinions, since political coalitions, like tavern businesses, often shifted in prerevolutionary New York.

Some observers echoed William Livingston's warning that mixing politics with liquor was dangerous. Wine intoxicated even the wisest, leading to jovial conversation and less moderation of one's words. "The expanded breast is but too ready to kindle a political sentiment, not universally relished," wrote "Alcanor," which "may change the festive harmony to riotous anger productive of the worst consequences." Drinking toasts put dreadful pressure on tavern patrons: "For who can decline drinking to this Gentleman's best beloved, or that friend's fire-side? Who shall refuse the King, in a bumper? Or who more bold, will hazard being kicked out of company, if a band of Patriots, take it in their heads to drink 45 rounds to Wilkes and Liberty?"[147] "Alcanor," like "Cethegus," Livingston, Smith, New England elites, and the founders of the Society for Reformation of Manners, held true to their Whig ideals of political mobilization and sociability free of tumults and disorder. Yet they failed to recognize the realities of prerevolutionary New York: disorder, drunkenness, and rioting were just as useful tools of political mobilization as the Whigs' ordered ideology of self-improvement.

The political climate of the taverns worried cautious Livingstonites like William Smith. In March 1773, he happily watched as "the De Lancey Dominion crumbled away fast in the House in the Council & in the Coffee House."[148] Yet as New Yorkers expressed their outrage over the Tea Act that autumn, Smith became fearful of renewed crowd action and held fast to his idealistic notions about the way that New Yorkers should conduct their resistance to British policy. Smith, observing the unity of "Vertue and Vice," hit upon an apt description of New York's resistance movement, which was essentially a tavern-style union of self-improvement and riotous unrest.[149] As New Yorkers contemplated the approach of the tea in December 1773, Smith reported that the local artisans "convene at Beer-Houses, where Sears Mc.Dougal & al meet them to concert Measures for the Day of the Shipp's Arrival."[150] When the *London* finally did arrive in New York in April 1774, a local committee of observation and the ship's owners immediately escorted the captain to the Queen's Head Tavern to hammer out a solution.[151]

McDougall and Sears called New Yorkers to gather at the Queen's Head on May 16, soon after city dwellers read the Boston Port Act that had just arrived from London. The radicals posted signs at the Coffee House and urged merchants to meet at Francis's tavern to nominate a committee of correspondence. Three hundred people gathered, exceeding the tavern's capacity, and the company adjourned to the Exchange. James DeLancey Jr. and his allies tried to discourage nonimportation, to wait for Boston's reaction to the act, and to quash the formation of a committee of correspondence. When the latter effort failed, DeLancey's allies inflated the size of the committee in order to sow confusion. This group successfully hijacked this overgrown tavern meeting, claiming to have nominated men "whose zeal for the public good cannot be doubted" rather than, as Colden wrote, "hot Headed Men." From the perspective of those interested in countermobilization, order had seemingly triumphed over disorder. They might have stopped to consider, however, that New Yorkers were now congregating in taverns to debate public affairs, rather than delegating this responsibility to legislators.[152]

The radicals soon struck back, calling a meeting of "Mechanicks" at Bardin's tavern (formerly Hampden Hall) and nominating a rival slate of committee members. After receiving Paul Revere from Boston and seeing him off to Philadelphia, supporters of both slates—merchants, artisans, and Sons of Liberty—met at the Coffee House, agreed to more moderate steps, and formed the moderate Committee of Fifty-one. Soon radical New Yorkers became dissatisfied with this committee. In July, when New York's moderate delegates to the Continental Congress attempted to ignore the sentiments of a popular meeting that had gathered at the Coffee House, the populace managed to wring a compromise from the more conservative delegates.[153] New Yorkers bristled when conservative, cautious leaders attempted to assert too much control or contradicted the will of the majority. By taking advantage of beerhouses, Hampden Hall, or the Queen's Head, radical tavern leaders were much more successful than these moderates at including a wide swath of New Yorkers in the political process.

Over the coming months, New Yorkers discussed and acted upon the rapid changes taking place throughout the British Empire. The first Continental Congress met, and Americans throughout the continent divided into Whigs and Tories. Members of the latter group convened in taverns as well—indeed, in the summer of 1776, revolutionary authorities in New York City listed six tavernkeepers who provided safe houses and meeting places for Loyalists, or otherwise supported the king.[154] William Smith described a meeting on January 9, 1775, of the DeLancey party— John Watts, Oliver DeLancey, Hugh Wallace, William Axtell, James DeLancey Jr., and John Harris Cruger—at Hull's Tavern "to consult whether it would be advisable to prevent the Assembly from approving the Acts of the [first Continental] Congress or not."[155] Supporters of imperial policies had long taken advantage of drinking halls for political ends. As early as 1744, Hamilton spotted in a tavern "one of these despicable fellows whom we may call c[our]t spys," an intimate of then-governor George Clinton. "This fellow, I found[,] made it his business to foist himself into all mixed companies to hear what was said and to enquire into the business and character of strangers."[156] New York's Loyalist mayor Whitehead Hicks must have toasted with like-minded city dwellers in taverns; Thomas Jones described him as "a *bon vivant*," who "loved company, and was a jovial fellow."[157] No doubt, given a different political climate, supporters of Crown policies might have operated more effectively within taverns as sites of Loyalist countermobilization.[158] Instead, the city's taverns proved to be most useful to radical Whigs at the forefront of resistance to the Crown. Radicals like Isaac Sears and John Lamb were more effective than prudish Livingstonites and skittish DeLanceyites at fusing the forces of drunken disorder and orderly sociability into a weapon of political mobilization.

Such complaints about drunken anarchy reveal the Loyalists' implicit recognition that Whigs had become more effective at mobilizing companies in taverns. The very word "liberty" apparently had "the power of intoxication" in the colonies, while anyone who urged moderation would style himself "A Friend to Order" or "Sober Citizen."[159] When arguing for moderate measures about storing the dutied tea, William Smith wrote, "I wished the People would be sober."[160] In May 1774, John Watts noted approvingly that "by the interference of most people of Wright, a soberer Counsel takes place," since "the lower Class of people were taking it up exceeding high here & wo[ul]ᵈ have carryᵈ things to extremitys."[161] Thomas Jones, writing years later, described how a crowd in August 1775, "after swallowing a proper dose of Madeira" one evening in a public house, planned to rouse Dr. Myles Cooper out of bed at midnight, shave his head, slash at his ears and nose, strip him naked, and banish him from the town.[162] A student warned Cooper before this plan could be carried out. On another occasion in March 1776, a party of radicals, "after swallowing . . . a sufficient quantity of Rumbo" at Drake's tavern, attacked the house of printer Samuel Loudon, broke his windows, pulled him from his bed, and destroyed the copies of a pamphlet that would have attacked Thomas Paine's *Common Sense*.[163]

In both of these instances, Jones observed that alcohol fueled these Whig crowd actions—either he was reporting these incidents with accuracy or he was slandering the Liberty Boys in a fit of resentful, elitist pique. Nevertheless, Loyalists throughout North America agreed with Jones. As "Bellisarius" wrote to New York from Boston, New Englanders were blindly worshipping the Liberty Tree, newspapers and congresses, and instead of diligently pursuing their occupations they "attend at taverns, where they talk politicks, get drunk, [and] damn King, Ministers and Taxes." The Sons of Liberty, the writer added, "by their debaucheries and ill conduct in life, are reduced almost to poverty" as they (and the ministers who hypocritically preached sobriety) contributed to "the turbulency of the times" and stoked "the heated imaginations of the populace."[164] Loyalists and many moderate Whigs insisted on claiming the mantle of order and sobriety, and they associated radicals with leveling tendencies, alcohol, and heated disorder—John Adams noticed their fears of leveling during his visit to New York in 1774.[165] By disavowing disorder and alcohol, the Loyalists and moderates conceded the most important political territory New York had to offer: the taverns. Radical Whigs, by contrast, achieved their goals by embracing orderly sociability in addition to these drunken lurches at the Crown's supporters.

The organized tavern network of the intercolonial Sons of Liberty was particularly active during the crucial years of 1774 to 1776. In March 1774, William Goddard reported that he and a tavern full of "the first Characters" in Boston had had "the Pleasure of drinking the Health of the Committee of N.Y.[,] Mr. Lamb, & other Fr.ᵈˢ of Liberty in your City."[166] Bostonian Paul Revere similarly asked John Lamb to convey his compliments "to the sons of Liberty in New York, particularly to those, with whom we dined at Black Sams," or Samuel Francis's Tavern (the Queen's Head).[167] Meetings of the "Body of Freeholders and Freemen" or just the "the heads of the [Liberty] party" might take place at the taverns of William Marriner, Edward Bardin, or the Widow Van De Water.[168]

In the Coffee House in March 1775, Dr. Robert Honyman found the people "much divided, & Party spirit is very high, contrary to what I found at Philadelphia where people only minded their business, but here nothing is heard of but Politics." Honyman heard New Yorkers "Talking Politics almost incessantly, & I am well situated for that, this house [the Connecticut Arms tavern] being much frequented by the Liberty party; & one lodges in it now, one of the Comittee [sic] for Suffolk county, & a very sensible, honest man."[169] The following month Honyman found this tavern "continually crowded with high Whigs & comittee men," as the noisy company kept him awake that night.[170] Honyman had the opportunity to observe tavern mobilization in action, even among the "Company at breakfast; staunch liberty men." Honyman cried, "Politics, Politics, Politics! There are numbers of Hand bills, Advertisements, Extracts of Letters on both sides daily & hourly printed, published, pasted up & handed about. Men, women, children, all ranks & professions mad with Politics."[171] Political discussion flowed among all ranks in the taverns, from breakfast until late at night.

Drake's tavern played host to various forms of political mobilization throughout this period. Marinus Willett later recounted that "the warm friends of the opposition to the British measures used to meet dayly" at Drake's and that "the most zealous partizans in the cause of Liberty used to have dayly and nightly meetings" there.[172] Here, on Beekman's Slip, the Sons of Liberty had protested New York's withdrawal from nonimportation agreements in 1770.[173] Earlier that year, committees organizing petitions for electing New York representatives by ballots met at Drake's nightly; New Yorkers might sign petitions at Drake's as well as at the taverns of Bicker and David Phillips.[174] Alexander McDougall recorded a meeting at Drake's with William Goddard from 8 P.M. until midnight on May 28, 1774, discussing a plan for a North American postal service.[175] In June 1775, Willett and half a dozen of his companions at Drake's moved to intercept British troops, who were attempting to transport arms to Boston. Willett boldly announced his intentions with a notice posted at the Coffee House, and afterward the weapons were stowed on property owned by tavern-keeper Abraham Van Dyck.[176] After the outbreak of fighting at Lexington and Concord, Drake's tavern served as a recruitment center for a militia that kept order in town and intercepted supplies intended for the regular troops.[177] Thus, taverns served multiple functions: as places to assemble a crowd, as sites of encounter and persuasion or meeting and recruitment, and as local and intercolonial centers of communication.

When New Yorkers heard the news from Lexington and Concord, militia companies drilled and legislative meetings slowed. "The Taverns filled with Publicans at Night" and "Little Business [was] done in the Day." New Yorkers ran to the Coffee House to sign the articles of Association, and rich men nervously formed committees to rein in the growing power of Isaac Sears and his military companies.[178] Two months later, George Washington and Governor William Tryon arrived in New York City on the same day in June 1775. Whig leaders, militiamen, and a crowd of inhabitants escorted Washington from a dinner at Lispenard's inn to Hull's tavern. Loyalist leaders, in the meantime, conducted Tryon to a private home.[179] Politically charged entertainments still helped to define the city's political culture. Nevertheless, Americans were beginning to put down their mugs and pick up their muskets as the emphasis shifted from political mobilization to military mobilization.[180]

Taverns had done a great deal to foster resistance to British authority, as mixed companies enacted the rituals of sociable interaction. Furthermore, an American network of taverns was helping to politicize the countryside as well. When rural folk came to town, they might be swept up in the frenzy of mobilization. At the Connecticut Arms in March 1775, Dr. Robert Honyman "sat about an hour talking Politics with people from the Country."[181] Social gatherings such as dances, balls, horse races, cockfights, court day fairs, and especially taverns throughout rural towns provided sites for the transmission of important news from the cities, the signing of protest resolves, the administration of loyalty oaths, and militia musters.[182]

The development of a revolutionary political culture in taverns always incorporated a variety of challenges and conflicts. Taverns brought together a broad array of white men and made them feel equal to any army officer, merchant, or member of Parliament or the Assembly. Elite New Yorkers could not always control tavern activities, nor was it easy for political leaders to forge a consensus among New York's diverse inhabitants. Livingstonites, DeLanceyites, Whigs, Tories, and Liberty Boys needed to persuade and recruit allies tavern by tavern, person by person. In these places of shared conviviality, like-minded people could encourage one another as part of the process of political mobilization. No doubt it was a slow and difficult process, and much of it was unrecorded by contemporaries. Yet ultimately New Yorkers succeeded in mobilizing their neighbors and their countryside counterparts to revolt.[183]

The taverns' legacy of democratic social mixing failed to endure. New York's clubmen were beginning to meet in private rather than public houses. The city's artisans converted a playhouse to "Mechanicks Hall" in 1776, while the elite Social Club had been holding their summer meetings at "Kip's Bay, where they built a neat large room, for the club-house." The majority of elite and middle-class New Yorkers in the late eighteenth and early nineteenth centuries retreated to hotels that discouraged social mixing. These groups no longer embraced or legitimated tavern disorders, and increasingly relied on troops and police to quell disturbances.[184]

The legacy of prerevolutionary tavern mobilization in New York and in cities and towns throughout North America was nonetheless significant. Not all cities had the same religious or ethnic mix as New York, the same factional climate of family rivalry, or the same clash of ideologies among popular Whigs, provincial Whigs, and radical crowd leaders. In every town, to be sure, Loyalists and cautious Whigs wrung their hands over disruption and disorder; and in every town they dealt with these problems of mobilization in different ways. Yet most cities (and smaller towns) succeeded in finding leaders who knew how to mobilize tipplers and taverngoers: men like Boston's Samuel Adams and Paul Revere or Philadelphia's Timothy Matlack. City dwellers met and mobilized in taverns throughout the continent—Boston's Green Dragon or Cromwell's Head or Philadelphia's Old London Coffeehouse—to plan resistance against Great Britain.[185]

Furthermore, taverns such as these often played host to committees that corresponded with their counterparts in other towns. New York City was a leader in this movement, which was perhaps natural given its access to transatlantic networks, entrepreneurial climate, freewheeling drinking culture, and pluralistic population. To the extent that Americans in other cities reflected these elements, they, too, participated in an intercolonial network of taverns that encompassed orderly and disorderly resistance. Taverns fostered fraternal bonds among white men in a diverse society and encouraged an open debate of political issues. They helped to organize groups of men as voluntary participants even as they occasionally allowed for disorderly resistance to British authority. Through a variety of methods, taverns allowed city dwellers to draw the line between Great Britain and America. Taverns opened up the public world to ordinary New Yorkers and helped shape the coming of the Revolution.

Chapter 3

"AND YET THERE IS ROOM"

The Religious Landscape of Newport

While taverns and the waterfront workplace were natural sites for political mobilization, houses of worship did not become politicized as easily. To be sure, religion inspired passionate commitment that could be harnessed for revolutionary purposes. William Smith Jr. of New York accused Americans of being "civil and religious Enthusiasts," criticizing the rabid way in which the Whigs cried for "civil and religious liberty" in the same breath.[1] The religious revivals that swept through the American colonies during the eighteenth century gave many Americans new ideas and a new language for questioning established traditions and authorities.[2] Yet when most Americans walked into a synagogue, a meetinghouse, or a church, they did not necessarily see these places as appropriate venues for taking a political stand. Religion played a complex role in the Revolutionary movement—people's beliefs inspired political action, but a diversity of such beliefs often frustrated attempts to muster unified resistance to the British Empire. The American Revolution was an ecumenical movement in many ways, but the urban experience demonstrates just how difficult it was for Patriots and Loyalists to reach across religious lines to build political coalitions.

Like the other large American cities, especially New York and Philadelphia, Newport had a pluralistic environment, or a multiplicity of religious groups. Newport had developed an attitude of latitudinarianism, or the toleration of other beliefs, yet the variety of religious groups also led to disagreements about various issues, doctrinal and otherwise. The crowded urban landscape forced these groups to articulate their differences in close quarters, often with acrimonious results. As they waged these battles, Newport's churches could muster the power, ideas, and resources of their sister institutions in other parts of the Atlantic world. As prominent urban congregations, Newport's churches commanded particular access to (and influence within) these networks. Their words and friendships had the potential to influence coreligionists throughout America. Yet this local acrimony—and the transatlantic connections that helped fuel it—also hampered the formulation of a Whig coalition.

Newporters proved to be reluctant revolutionaries, but their mixed response to the imperial crisis does not tell the whole story. Religious beliefs destabilized other social relationships during the 1760s and 1770s. Poor white men in Newport did not forge their evangelical zeal into political mobilization, as poor white men would do in other parts of America, but women and blacks did respond to the "spirit of liberty" that eighteenth-century revivals encouraged. As a result, while neither of these groups would make extensive inroads into political participation, their religious activities represented an achievement of significant revolutionary transformation during a period of political upheaval.

In the eighteenth century, houses of worship were no ordinary buildings. The sight of a church was unmistakable, while a tavern was little more than a house with a license to sell drinks, and a waterfront's wharves were piles of wood extended into the harbor. Throughout human history, societies have designated certain buildings and spaces as sacred—and even American Protestants, for all their heritage of iconoclasm, recognized that the places where they gathered for worship were special. In most small colonial villages, the church was the largest building and the only one that belonged to the entire community, rather than a private individual. Even in cities, churches were among the largest structures. Eighteenth-century maps and views of towns highlighted the locations of churches and the steeples that rose above the shops and residences (fig. 3.1).[3] Houses of worship represented the transmission of culture, knowledge, and salvation. They represented authority, sanctuary, and a place of gathering for a higher purpose.

Colonial North America played host to a variety of competing denominations—almost all Protestant—and most individual congregations belonged to larger institutional networks: ecclesiastical hierarchies like the Church of England or more loosely connected organizations like "Independent" Congregationalists.[4] Such networks of associates, organizations, or letter-writing correspondents, which connected cities to one another and to smaller towns, brought disruptive outside ideas to a city, and they lent strength to urban congregants for the purposes of political mobilization. Urban churches, large and small, depended on their contacts in North America and overseas for information about Atlantic world events and the cause of God (and the sect) in other places. As the imperial conflict unfolded within the urban landscape, the city and its houses of worship felt the reverberations of conflicts occurring elsewhere.

A stroll around Newport, New York, or Philadelphia would have revealed a lively conversation or interaction among these houses of worship, a conversation weighty with long-standing disagreements among these denominational networks about infant baptism, taking communion, ecclesiastical

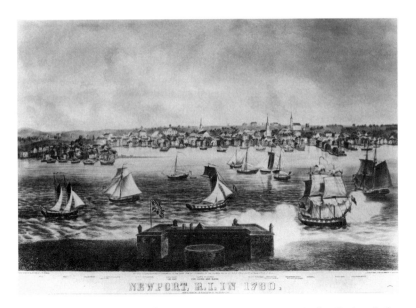

NEWPORT, R.I. IN 1730,

Figure 3.1. Most eighteenth-century city views prominently displayed the church steeples that rose above the other buildings. This view of Newport shows the variety of denominations that competed for the attention of the inhabitants. *Newport, R.I. in 1730*, by John P. Newell. 1865. *Collection of Newport Historical Society, 01.953.*

hierarchy, and other issues (fig. 3.2). Newport had its own unique religious landscape. The Baptists and Quakers who founded Rhode Island continued to dominate the colony, while Anglicans and Congregationalists, who were much more common in the rest of North America, were relative latecomers to Newport.

Walking up Church Street from the wharves, one could not fail to notice the Anglicans' Trinity Church, crowned with a steeple. Completed in 1726, Trinity was 70 feet long and 46 feet wide, plus "6 foot more for the break of the altar and 16 for the belfry," according to its rector at the time (appendix 3). In 1762, Trinity became the largest building in Newport, with thirty-six new pews and an extension of twenty-six feet.[5] Its layout differed significantly from the meetinghouses of Dissenters (fig. 3.3). It was longitudinally oriented with a recessed chancel for the Lord's Supper, traditionally regarded as a more "churchly" form. There were aisles running from belfry to altar, which presented a weekly opportunity for a hierarchical processional of the minister and the most prestigious parishioners to display their rank. Trinity had baptismal fonts at the belfry end; and the gorgeously worked three-decker pulpit at the other end had a preaching desk (for the sermon), reading desk (for the rest of the liturgy), and clerk's desk. Trinity Church thrust upward from the landscape in a physical assertion of the power and prominence of the empire's established church in Rhode Island.

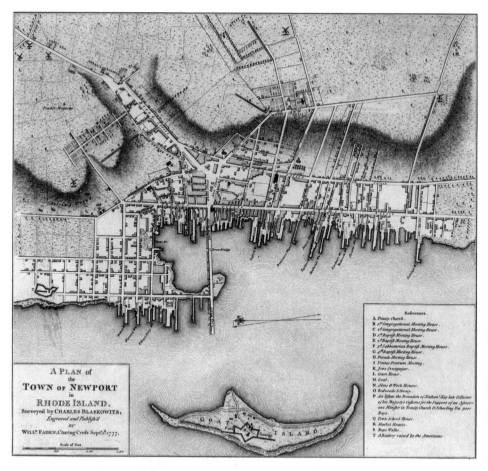

References.
A. Trinity Church.
B. 1st Congregational Meeting House.
C. 2d Congregational Meeting House.
D. 1st Baptist Meeting House.
E. 1st Baptist Meeting House.
F. 3d Sabbatarian Baptist Meeting House.
G. 4th Baptist Meeting House.
H. Friends Meeting House.
I. Trinta Fratrum Meeting.
K. Jews Synagogue.
L. Court House.
M. Goal.
N. Alms & Work House.
O. Redwoods Library.
P. An Estate the Donation of Nathan Kay late Collector
of his Majesty's Customs for the Support of an Assist-
ant Minister in Trinity Church & Schooling Ten poor
Boys.
Q. Town School House.
R. Market House.
S. Rope Walks.
T. A Battery raised by the Americans.

A PLAN of
the
TOWN of NEWPORT
in
RHODE ISLAND.
Surveyed by CHARLES BLASKOWITZ,
Engraved and Publish'd
by
WILL.m FADEN, Charing Cross Sept.r 1 1777.

Scale of Feet.

Figure 3.2. City maps generally listed places of worship among the city's public buildings in the legend. A stroll around Newport revealed several meetinghouses. *A Plan of the Town of Newport in Rhode Island. Surveyed by Charles
Blaskowitz, Engraved and Publish'd by Will.m. Faden.* [London], 1777. *Library of
Congress, Geography and Map Division.*

Its congregants were less suspicious of church ornamentation than
Dissenters—Trinity placed a higher emphasis on the visual aspects of the
liturgy with its processional aisles, raised pulpit in front of the altar, elaborate vaulted ceiling, and gleaming silver sacramental pieces. Even the
soundscape was more assertive, with bells and an organ that had been a
gift from the Irish philosopher George Berkeley in 1732.

Figure 3.3. Trinity Church, Newport's Anglican church, had a long, processional aisle leading to the pulpit and altar. Contemporaries considered this a
more "churchly" form. Arrangement of pews at Trinity Church of Newport,
Rhode Island, 1762, in Mason, *Annals of Trinity Church*, 172. *Collection of
Newport Historical Society.*

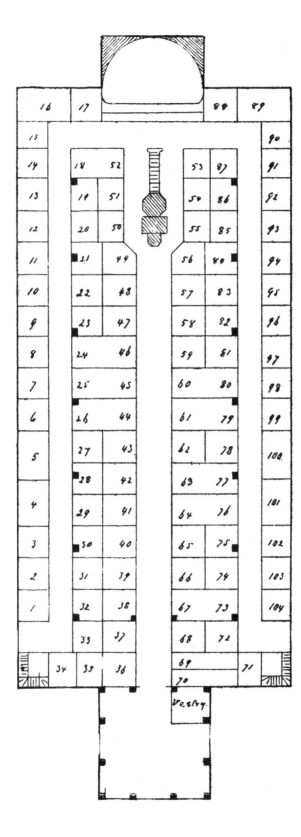

Trinity Church had a disproportionate share of the town's wealthiest merchants, in addition to mariners, British officials, and recent immigrants from Great Britain.[6] Such people had networks all over the Atlantic world, and so Newport Anglicans were particularly linked to Great Britain's political and commercial empire. Furthermore, the society had a source of wealth most other Rhode Island congregations could not match, since the Society for the Propagation of the Gospel (SPG), a missionary organization for the British colonies, helped fund Trinity Church until 1771. Even after the church became financially independent of the SPG, its clergymen and congregants likely maintained contact with ministers and coreligionists in Great Britain and North America.[7] All Anglican clergymen took oaths of loyalty to the king and Parliament at their ordination, and all services included prayers for the king and his family. Enemies of the Church of England, particularly in New England, identified the Anglicans with the government. Not surprisingly, the minister and congregation of Trinity Church would overwhelmingly support the government during the imperial crisis. The church was an important site of Loyalist countermobilization in Newport.[8]

Just around the corner from Trinity were two meetinghouses that sheltered the Anglicans' principal rivals: First Congregational Church met just up Banister Street, while the Second Congregational Church building, larger and more prosperous, was a mere two blocks north of Trinity. The two Congregational societies met in simple-looking meetinghouses that announced their distrust of outward ornament (fig. 3.4). Looking through nineteenth-century eyes, George Channing remembered the Second Congregational meetinghouse as "lacking in every thing deserving the name of architectural order, proportion, or convenience, without form or comeliness." He wrote that the meetinghouse "was cold as the north pole in winter, and at fever-heat in summer. The windows . . . clattered violently when there was any wind. . . . Fire was deemed an element utterly irreconcilable with devotion in our meetinghouse."[9] Calvinist theology taught that physical meetinghouses were not sacred "churches," and associated ornamentation with Roman Catholicism. In this way the Congregationalists used their buildings to proclaim their doctrines to the streetscape—a simple meetinghouse was a challenge to the more ornamental Anglican Church building. Still, the laity apparently regarded the buildings as sacred spaces. The devout Sarah Osborn, for instance, repeatedly referred to her meetinghouse as the "House of the Lord."[10] Societies located their pews so that all parishioners could hear the Word from the pulpit, while the secular forms of social hierarchy determined seating arrangements.[11]

Congregationalism was the dominant sect in New England—though not in Rhode Island or Newport—and its Newport practitioners actively communicated with their coreligionists in New England and beyond. The religious revivals that began heating up in 1739 had sparked transatlantic correspondence among evangelicals and their opponents, and the surrounding region of southeastern New England fostered a particularly eclectic

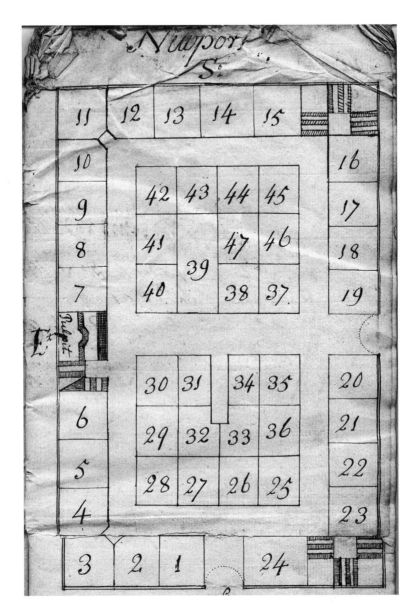

Figure 3.4. Dissenters organized their meetinghouses differently from Anglicans, and situated pews so that every congregant could hear the minister speak from the pulpit. This seating plan for the First Congregational Church assigned pews to specific families. Arrangement of pews at First Congregational Church of Newport, Rhode Island, circa 1745. [First] Congregational Church Records, Book 836. *Collection of Newport Historical Society.*

mix of sects. Ezra Stiles, the pastor of Second Congregational Church after 1755 and a future president of Yale College, and Samuel Hopkins, pastor of First Congregational Church after 1770 (appendix 4), both had extensive networks of correspondents, especially in Massachusetts and Connecticut, where Congregationalism was the established religion. One cause that occupied Stiles in particular was the threat of an Anglican conspiracy to establish state-supported bishops and ecclesiastical courts in America. In Boston, Jonathan Mayhew and Charles Chauncy were leading the fight against this conspiracy, trumpeting the cause of civil and religious liberty. Stiles was an active participant in this network, while Hopkins maintained connections with fellow followers of the theologian Jonathan Edwards. While these fighting Congregationalists did not agree on many things, they were ready to provoke fiery exchanges on religious and political issues.[12]

Spread around the northern and eastern edges of Newport were three long-standing Baptist meetinghouses. Together these churches formed the largest denomination in town. The congregants of the popular Second Baptist Church were "six-principle" Baptists who believed in laying on hands. When George Whitefield preached at their meetinghouse, it housed a thousand persons in the downstairs seating, three hundred in the galleries, and four or five hundred more.[13] First Baptist Church, with its stricter principles of predestination, also had wealthier congregants than the other Baptist societies, from prosperous artisans like William Claggett to prominent political figures like merchant Josias Lyndon, Rhode Island's governor in 1768. In 1773, the society elongated its church by 25 feet, reflecting increased attendance during this period. The Sabbatarian, or Seventh-Day, Baptist Church, which held services on Saturdays, was the smallest meetinghouse in town.[14] These meetinghouses were similar to the Congregationalist houses in structure (fig. 3.5); the primary difference was that none had steeples or bells. Stiles reported that the Baptists "would as soon erect a Crucifix as a Bell" atop their meetinghouses.[15]

The Baptists, as a growing presence in the northern colonies, had certain disadvantages in establishing and mobilizing widespread American networks. They were underrepresented among merchants and mariners, and they had limited contact with Baptists south of Pennsylvania. Nevertheless, Baptists raised money throughout North America for Rhode Island College. The Sabbatarians corresponded with a sister church in London. The Second Baptist Church belonged to the General Association of Baptist Churches formed in 1692. Its pastor, Gardner Thurston, attended a meeting of the Warren Association, a regional Baptist group, in 1768, though he did not join. He and the other elders welcomed a variety of visiting Baptists: Isaac Backus, James Manning, Hezekiah Smith, Samuel Stillman, Morgan Edwards, and John Gano. Thus, even Baptists, with their weaker intercolonial contacts, had links with other towns. The 1770s would be years of strident advocacy for American Baptists, and Newport, with its large Baptist population, could not fail to notice these changes.[16]

The Quaker meetinghouse of Newport was on the northern side of town, roughly between the First and Second Baptist Churches. Before 1762 (when Trinity Church was enlarged), the Quaker meetinghouse was the largest building in Newport, packing in crowds of 2,000 in 1722 and 1766 and

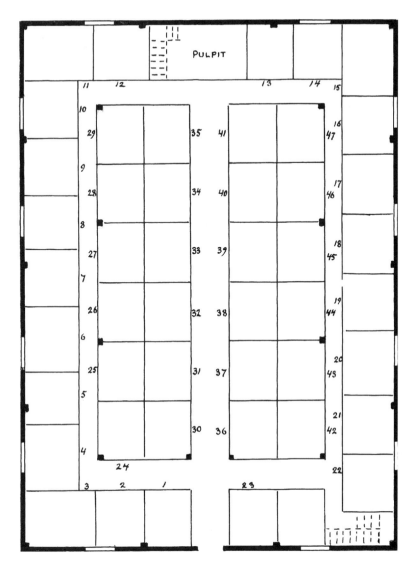

PULPIT

Figure 3.5. The meetinghouse of the First Baptist Church was somewhat similar in shape to the First Congregational Church meetinghouse, though it had even less outward ornamentation. "The Meeting House of the First Baptist Church, Built 1738—Enlarged 1773. Arrangement of pews as per plat of 1833." First Baptist Church Records, Book 1167. *Collection of Newport Historical Society.*

5,000 in 1743 during Yearly Meetings, when Friends from throughout the region gathered. A "generous segment of the rich and powerful" considered themselves Friends well into the eighteenth century.[17] The Friends meetinghouse displayed many of the architectural features common to its denomination (fig. 3.6). Since Quakers did not hire ministers or believe in a church

GROWTH OF THE MEETING HOUSE

GRAPHIC SCALE—FEET

NORTH ⊙ SOUTH

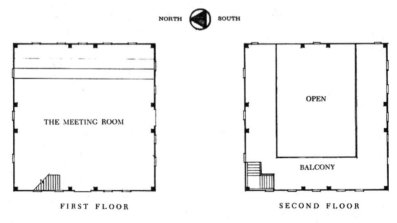

THE MEETING ROOM

OPEN

BALCONY

FIRST FLOOR   SECOND FLOOR

THE ORIGINAL BUILDING
1699 TO 1705

NO EVIDENCE FOUND OF THE SIZE OR LOCATION OF ADDITION 1705 TO 1729

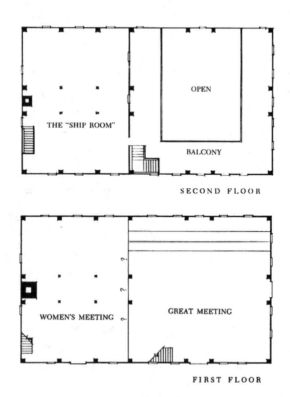

THE "SHIP ROOM"

OPEN

BALCONY

SECOND FLOOR

WOMEN'S MEETING

GREAT MEETING

FIRST FLOOR

THE THIRD STAGE
1729 TO 1807

hierarchy, they had no pulpit. The house had little adornment on the exterior or interior. A partition permitted simultaneous men's and women's meetings, and worshippers could remove the partition when large Yearly Meetings took place. A large building, the meetinghouse had two rows of galleries for those in attendance. At the same time, the Newport meeting-house had a unique characteristic: a ten-foot cubic tower atop its roof. Apparently a controversial adornment in 1700, this "cupola" would have trumpeted the Quaker meetinghouse as a dominant religious institution; for a short time, it was the only "steepled" building in Newport until the first Anglican Church added a steeple in 1703.

Newport Quakers welcomed Friends from all over New England during the Yearly Meeting, and so Newport rested at the top of the New England network of Quakers. When the Philadelphia Quaker speaker John Pemberton visited Newport in 1774, he specifically mentioned that "Friends were well respected at Court & had great Influence there."[18] Throughout the year, the Friends hosted visiting preachers from England or the middle colonies, including women such as Mary Weston of Southwark and Rachel Wilson of Westmorland. Quakers also had correspondents, mercantile and spiri-tual, in Great Britain, the Delaware Valley, and elsewhere. These outside influences came to have profound effects on Newport's Society of Friends. In the years after Samuel Fothergill's 1755 visit and John Woolman's 1760 visit, many Friends began to drift away. The New England Yearly Meeting faced increasing pressure from Great Britain and the Delaware Valley to enforce a more strict compliance with the Discipline, and many of the rural meetings in New England were eager to comply. Some Newport Quakers took these strictures seriously, dealing harshly with Friends who intermar-ried, took up arms, drank alcohol, participated in political affairs, took oaths, or owned and traded slaves. Others either flouted the Discipline or withdrew from the Society.[19]

The Moravian meetinghouse, built in 1768, doubled as a residence for the minister and his wife, who apparently lived on the ground floor, while the congregation met in an upper chamber. The couple supported them-selves by conducting a school for sixty children, because, as the visiting John Ettwein recorded, "the little congregation is poor and small and could hardly support a couple in any other way." Even this tiny congregation had a network of correspondents, since the congregation owed their initial gathering to Newport's trade routes. The Moravian pastor Albert Rudolph

---

Figure 3.6. By 1729, the Quaker Meeting House was large enough to seat thou-sands of worshippers for annual regional meetings. The meetinghouse had a partition to allow for separate men's and women's meetings. The Society of Friends, which did not hire ministers, included no pulpit in its meetinghouse. Growth of the Quaker Meeting House of Newport, original building (1699–1705) and third stage (1729–1807). *Newport History* 42, 2 (spring 1969): 51. *Collection of Newport Historical Society.*

Russmeyer had "sundry Letters from different Parts of the World, collected & circulated among the Unitas Fratrum."[20]

The Jewish synagogue, built from 1759 to 1763, stood mere steps from First Baptist Church and the Sabbatarian Baptists (fig. 3.7) and was the second-smallest house of worship in town. The Anglican customs official Peter Harrison, inspired by Christopher Wren's English churches, designed the synagogue somewhat like a basilica, though with an ark for the

Figure 3.7. When Newport's Jews completed their synagogue in 1763, it contained an ark for the Scriptures and a *bimah* for prayer-reading. The synagogue, which still stands, was the only brick house of worship in Newport at the time. Touro Synagogue, Newport, Rhode Island. *Collection of Newport Historical Society, P2788.*

Scriptures rather than a chancel, and a *bimah* for prayer-reading rather than a pulpit. The building had galleries (where the women sat) supported by Tuscan-Doric columns. The synagogue owned candlesticks, a *ner tamid* (cternal light), silver *rimonim* (Torah caps) and breastplates, and candelabræ of the finest quality. With two levels of large, round-headed windows and an integrated central space, the synagogue created an atmosphere of light, spaciousness, and unity. The building itself (now called Touro Synagogue) stood at a rakish angle to the street, oriented toward Jerusalem. The Jews welcomed visiting rabbis from a variety of distant lands, sent away to New York for a *mohel* to perform ritual circumcisions, and had mercantile contacts in other cities.[21]

For all their apparent outer differences in size and structure, many of these meetinghouses were often strikingly similar in their ornate interior display of urban elegance. The Seventh-Day Baptist Church, for instance, had a beautifully carved pulpit, gilt-lettered tablets with the Ten Commandments (added in 1773), and a vaulted ceiling; in many respects, its interior closely resembled that of Trinity Church (figs. 3.8, 3.9). Like the other Baptist churches, it presented a plain, humble face, not to mention the smallest square footage in town. While the exterior characteristics of Trinity Church and the Sabbatarian meetinghouse expressed their very different beliefs to the outside world, on the inside both congregations bespoke their urbane cosmopolitanism and the commonalities that Newporters cultivated among one another. The cityscape had room for its doctrinal differences, as well as the concord that urbanity demanded.[22]

The similarities among Newport's denominations even crept into the liturgy. Ezra Stiles of Second Congregational attempted to be broadly inclusive when offering baptism or communion; yet only two-thirds of his congregants were baptized and less than 10% were full members.[23] At First Congregational, only one-third of the congregants were baptized. The discrepancy between the two societies sometimes caused tension, as when Stiles agreed to baptize persons who had been refused the sacrament at First Church.[24] The disinclination to baptism among both congregations was due, Stiles wrote, to "a Discouragment by Baptist & Quaker Influence."[25] Descended from Baptist or Quaker families or merely convinced by their beliefs, Newport's Congregational laity took seriously the New England debates over the privileges of the unregenerate and their children, and furthermore internalized the other sects' opinions on baptism. Marmaduke Browne of Trinity Church also observed the influence of dissenting beliefs on his congregants' attitudes toward the sacraments. The reluctance of his parishioners to take communion "does not proceed so much from their leading unblemished lives, as from the wrong notions they have imbibed and persist in adhering to of that sacrament."[26] At Trinity Church, the minister found it just as difficult to convince his parishioners to accept the host as any other New England minister. City churches expressed theological differences even as the laity often held similar views across congregations.

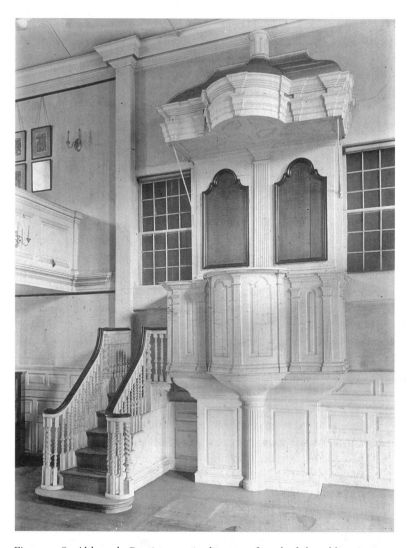

Figure 3.8. Although Baptist meetinghouses often had humble exteriors, Newport's Seventh-Day Baptist Meeting House, which still stands, had an elegant, finely worked pulpit inside. Stairs and pulpit, Sabbatarian Meeting House. *Collection of Newport Historical Society, P579.*

Newport was a New England city, yet, as the visiting Dr. Alexander Hamilton noted, "They are not so strait laced in religion here as in the other parts of New England."[27] In many ways, Newport's diverse population resembled that of New York City or Philadelphia rather than that of the more homogeneous Boston.[28] Rhode Island, like Pennsylvania or New Jersey, had no established church, and Newport was too large and diverse even to have a church that was preeminent by default.[29] Newport's most prominent citizens included Baptists, Quakers, Anglicans, and Congregationalists. By law,

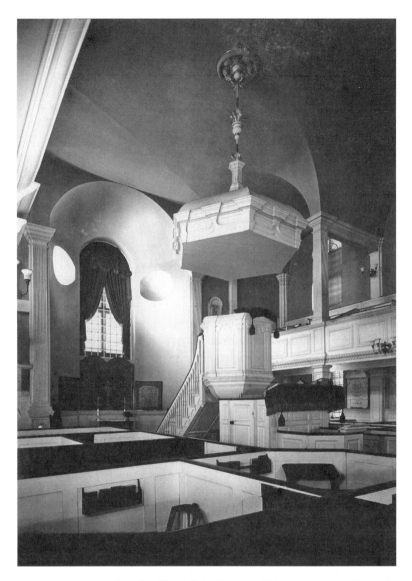

Figure 3.9. Trinity Church still stands in Newport. This interior view shows the church's elegant pulpit and recessed chancel. The church bears striking similarities to the Sabbatarian Meeting House. Trinity Church showing the Pulpit, Newport, RI. *Collection of Newport Historical Society, P1576.*

Jews' failure to follow the New Testament excluded them from voting and holding office; nevertheless, even a few of the wealthiest Newport Jews enjoyed high social status. Travelers to cities like Newport were almost certain to find a place to worship with like-minded congregants, and they often toured a city's meetinghouses and churches to sample different preaching styles (or exhibit different preaching styles, if they were ministers) or to gawk at the architecture.[30] The pluralistic religious landscape of the cities, with its multiple communities of faith, fascinated visitors.

Newport's own residents also took advantage of the flexibility of this landscape. Some of them remained with the denominations of their childhoods throughout their adult lives. Religious variety infused many city dwellers with a greater commitment to their own sect, and they fought to prove the worth of their own doctrines and to keep heresies at bay. They found comfort and community in church, in an otherwise worldly and unwieldy city of thousands. Some welcomed the eighteenth century's spirit of religious experimentation and enjoyed hearing seafaring preachers like George Whitefield, John Murray, and Rachel Wilson. Still others changed their affiliation for reasons of status, disgruntlement, or revelation, and sought out new places to contemplate the afterlife.[31] Finally, others welcomed the opportunity to escape the organized religions altogether—although few people were truly anonymous in colonial cities, a person could remain safely undisturbed if he or she overslept on a given Sunday.[32] Based on Stiles's list of Newport congregants, it appears that around half of all Newporters were unaffiliated (appendix 3). The pluralistic landscape liberated the religious and irreligious.

In a heterogeneous city, a person's choices were more extensive than in the countryside. Sarah Rogers requested (and received) a dismissal from First Baptist Church so she could join the Second Baptist Church. She was confident that her request would be granted, "as each of you highly esteem this Privilege of uniting in Church Fellowship where you can be best suited."[33] Baptist Elder John Callender's daughter Mary became a prominent Quaker preacher.[34] Mary Mellen, reared a Congregationalist at the First Church, became a Moravian in 1756 and donated the land for the Moravian meetinghouse; about two hundred people attended her funeral in 1772.[35] Other Newporters converted from Baptist Churches or the Quaker Meetings to Congregationalism or Anglicanism; people changed religious affiliation as a result of marriage or ill health. Husbands and wives, like the Almys, sometimes chose different churches.[36] Two of the leading Patriots in Newport had a flexible relationship with a variety of religious affiliations during their lifetimes. John Collins, a wealthy merchant who would eventually represent Rhode Island in the Continental Congress, was born into a Quaker family. Boston's Jonathan Mayhew presided over Collins's marriage into the Congregational Avery family in 1757, Collins held a pew at Trinity Church in 1762, and Stiles called him a Quaker in 1775. Solomon Southwick, the Whig printer of the *Newport Mercury*, descended from the persecuted Quakers of Salem, Massachusetts; his brother and his patron belonged to the Sabbatarian Baptist church. Southwick studied at the Presbyterian College of Philadelphia, married in the Second Baptist Church, and published a wide variety of religious tracts. Stiles described him as having "forsaken all religious Worship" in 1775, and he apparently received a certificate of Quaker membership in 1777, perhaps to avoid military service.[37] For many, the scattered sacred buildings around Newport represented the opportunity to change one's mind, one's affiliation, one's network of coreligionists. Hundreds of Newporters, meanwhile, belonged to no society at all, and local clergymen lamented these "nothingarians."[38]

As a result of this flexibility, the revivals and schisms of the eighteenth century did not shake Newport's religious landscape with as much rancor as they did in the countryside. Although the town's three Baptist Churches had experienced a number of rifts and disagreements during their early history, by 1765, Isaac Backus wrote, "The bars between them are so broken down as to interchange in preaching."[39] The Congregationalists' schism of 1728 also predated New England's more divisive rifts.[40] As a result, the institutional composition of Newport's religious landscape was largely settled by the middle of the eighteenth century. George Whitefield drew large crowds in Newport because of his charisma and his inclusive, evangelical message, but he did not cause too much upheaval. During his visit in 1770, he preached at both Second Baptist and First Congregational, and he dined at the home of Quaker merchant John Wanton along with Stiles, Hopkins, Thurston, Russmeyer, and a variety of gentlemen. The next night his host was Congregationalist church member Jonathan Otis.[41] Although many of Newport's pastors, such as Stiles and Nicholas Eyres, could be characterized as Old Lights who opposed this new wave of evangelicalism, Stiles called William Vinal "a great Whitefieldian."[42] Nevertheless, unlike other towns in New England, including Providence, Newport remained relatively free of painful religious divisions.

Two small New Light (or evangelical) Baptist congregations sprang up between 1740 and 1776, exceptions to this placid pluralism. The first split from the Second Baptist Church: the former itinerant Timothy Peckom led a schism in 1742, though his group dissolved by 1748. A linen draper and transatlantic troublemaker named Henry Dawson set off another wave of disruption in 1770. Stiles wrote that he was "forming a Baptist Church here in opposition to Baptists & all sects in Town." By the summer of 1772, Stiles recorded that Dawson had about twenty communicants and "forbid any but the regenerate to sing or joyn in any parts of public Worship." At his baptisms and communions, Stiles observed "Great Indecency & Confusion in the p'ple present." In 1773, Dawson renounced Sunday Sabbath in favor of becoming a Sabbatarian, throwing his tiny congregation into an uproar. Although he preached well, most Baptist elders considered him a "false bretherein" and Dawson was "rejected by all the Baptists in America." Dawson had moved on to New Jersey by 1774.[43] Two waves of separatist revivals rocked the complacency of Newport's settled Baptist congregations, though neither took hold for an extended period of time.

Many religious leaders, believers, and traditions in Newport and the surrounding countryside fell even further outside the rubric of the six established denominations. Newport gave shelter to Irish Methodist John Martin;

a Scottish Seceder or antiburgher; a Catholic priest traveling from Hispaniola to Quebec; the *converso* James Lucena; Lutheran minister John Christopher Hartwick; and German Calvinist Elder Kaulbach.[44] The itinerant John Murray attracted a number of Newport laypersons to his sermons on universal salvation, to the horror of the town's ministers. Murray was asked to refrain from speaking at Quaker meetings; he panicked Stiles by preaching from the Second Congregational pulpit during Stiles's absence in 1772; and Trinity's George Bisset published a sermon denouncing him.[45] Still, Newporters tolerated a number of unconventional neighbors. Stiles preached from Deuteronomy 14:10–11 against enchanters and necromancers, calling "the Powaws of the American Indians . . . a Relict of this antient System of seeking to an evil invisible Power." He added, "Something of it subsists among some Almanack Makers and Fortune Tellers" such as Joseph Stafford in Tiverton, as well as midwives like Newport's seventy-year-old Granny Morgan, who divined using urine cakes stuck with pins.[46] Despite the coercive nature of many of the established churches in Anglo-America, the folk beliefs of these urban residents and travelers demonstrated that unorthodox practices usually associated with rural life (especially that of southeastern New England) also found room to thrive in a cosmopolitan urban setting. These beliefs coexisted with iconoclastic "free thinking" and universalism, as well as a mosaic of established doctrines.[47]

Newporters' worldly concerns help to explain their permissive attitudes about religion. They imported, distilled, and shipped thousands of hogsheads of molasses, and participated in the slave trade more than any other port in British North America.[48] Wealth in Newport flowed from the mercantile network of rum, molasses, and slaves; successful participants included Congregationalists, Jews, Anglicans, Quakers, and Baptists.[49] The economic interdependence of Newport's waterfront community fostered a climate where residents generally tolerated one another's religious practices. Residents tolerated slave trading because they depended on it. (Few eighteenth-century religious leaders spoke out against slavery in any case.) They tolerated smuggling and bribery because customs restrictions and duties often cut into profits. During the imperial crisis, Newporters arrived at their political allegiances based in part on their estimation of which regime would best allow them to continue turning a profit, and not just based on their religious backgrounds. For many, especially Newport's "nothingarians" and nominal congregants, material concerns (and attendant political concerns) no doubt outweighed godly concerns. The churches and meetinghouses stood only blocks away from the shops, warehouses, and wharves. Even the deeply devout understood that pews would not be rented, steeples and roofs could not be repaired, fancy furnishings—like the Sabbatarians' tablets with the Ten Commandments or Touro Synagogue's silver *rimonim*—could not be purchased, were it not for Newport's brisk commercial activity. Commerce encouraged religious pluralism in Newport, and pluralism in turn was good for business. New Yorkers and Philadelphians similarly attempted to overlook religious rifts for the sake of trade.

Newport in its golden age before the Revolution was not just a town of prosperity and wealth, of course. Hundreds lived in crushing poverty. Every day in Newport, hundreds of non-white people lived under the brutal regime of racism and slavery.[50] If socioeconomic conditions in Newport were a source of turbulence, then Rhode Island politics certainly provided no relief, whether the issue was paper currency or smallpox inoculation. Rhode Island bore witness to the Ward-Hopkins controversy, a struggle for local office between two factions that both hoped to prevent Great Britain from encroaching upon the colony's charter. The struggle was an ugly fight, tainted by dirty tricks, bribery, and corruption that infected all branches of government.[51] Politics in the colony fostered an intense game of self-interested political office-seeking—a game that yielded great profits and benefits—motivated by "other motives than Love of God and Country."[52]

With people switching their religious affiliations, with money to be made and votes to be wooed, most Newporters found it in their best interests to uphold the idea of "liberty of conscience" that Roger Williams had introduced to Rhode Island. Berkeley famously reported in 1729, "Notwithstanding so many differences, here are fewer quarrels about religion than elsewhere, the people living peaceably with their neighbors of whatsoever persuasion."[53] As long as Newporters could find common ground with one another in theology, ecclesiology, organization, and building practices, they could develop a tradition of common action in the service of the public good. At the ordination of William Vinal, therefore, the ordaining minister Joseph Fish urged the new pastor to show "the several Denominations of Christians" that their religion was "courteous, affable and kind."[54] The Baptist elders of Newport were also publicly conciliatory. John Callender published a number of overtures to Bostonians and Congregationalists, and an obituary for him in the *Boston Gazette* noted his "catholic & christian Temper." Edward Upham reflected on his career at "Newport, where I had lived for more than 22 years in peace and agreeable Harmony with all Men, Jews, gentiles &c."[55] In the mid-eighteenth century, Newporters of all religious beliefs regarded pluralism as essential to a healthy urban environment.

The urban atmosphere motivated many people to think in broad, communal terms. Samuel Hopkins's New Divinity movement developed from Jonathan Edwards's theology, and the urban landscape heightened rather than diminished his uncompromising ardor. In *An Inquiry into the Nature of True Holiness*, Hopkins illustrated his doctrine of disinterested benevolence and the common good. By urging individuals to adopt a social Christianity rather than an individualistic search for salvation, he advanced a more aggressive catholicism—not a mere acceptance of others' religious beliefs, but a mandate to uncover sin everywhere in the city and aim toward its repair. A city dweller should be willing, he said, to give up his house, "how-ever magnificent and costly," if its demolition would save the city from fire: to do so was to "promote the greatest good of the whole community" rather than acting the "sordid part" of selfishness and vice. In a city with diverse property interests, people typically did not seek the common good except in moments of extreme crisis. Hopkins, who saw great moral crisis in his adopted city of Newport, urged his audience not only to live a life of disinterested benevolence but even to subsume the quest for personal salvation beneath this social Christianity.[56] Most Newporters agreed that the religious landscape was part of the wider public space, and therefore a potential source of political mobilization. The problem was that most Newporters recoiled from Hopkins's strict ideals. City dwellers could never rally around a single settled preacher. Religion was bad for politics.

Newporters instead strived to enact a pluralist, "catholic spirit" that would allow for the formation of broad political coalitions and civic partnerships. Members of a variety of sects founded the Redwood Library in 1747 to be "catholic & without respect of Sects," and the established clergy in town held honorary memberships; the Freemasons' Lodge and the upscale Hand-in-Hand Fire-Club similarly drew from most of the town's denominations.[57] Russmeyer and Stiles swapped their impressions of Anglican clergymen and Moravian treatises over dinner.[58] Hopkins and Stiles were pallbearers at the 1771 funeral of Marmaduke Browne, who Stiles called "a tolerable Figure for a Chh Clergyman, for in N. E. they are generally of very ordinary Talents."[59] A measure of toleration even extended to Jews of Congregation Yeshuat Israel; Newport's gentiles accepted them as members of the commercial community and as neighbors. On a tombstone inscription for Aaron Lopez, Stiles praised his manners, hospitality, benevolence, business acumen, and integrity, calling him "esteemed and loved by all."[60] Gentile Newport businessmen understood that Jews would not conduct business on the high holidays.[61] Jews in turn contributed to the genial spirit of cosmopolitanism by financially supporting the buildings of other denominations. Jacob Rodrigues Rivera was happy to purchase lottery tickets toward the construction of a Baptist meetinghouse in Providence, since it answered two goals: "That of pleasing the very Worthy M.'r [Nicholas] Brown, which I wish ever to do; & Secondly my great Inclination to promote & forward, every Publick Building to the Utmost of my Extent."[62] When it came to the public good, public ceremonies, public business, and the public peace, the several denominations often evinced a sincere willingness to get along.

Despite this cooperative climate, Newporters failed to harness their town's pluralism in the service of rebellion. Suspicion and prejudice among the sects still lurked within their breasts, and the imperial crisis brought these tensions to the surface. New England's legacy of antipathy between Anglicans and Congregationalists caused scorching disagreements in Newport. When Berkeley visited in 1729, he wrote that Newporters were "a strange medley of different persuasions, which nevertheless all agree on one point, viz. That the Church of England is second best."[63] By the 1770s, Stiles reported that Anglicans returned the sentiment: "The [Anglican] Congregation is large maybe 200 Families, consists of the principal Families in T°[wn] for Riches & Politeness, all possessing in common a sovereign Contempt of all religious Denomin^a but themselves."[64] Although the Redwood Library had been founded on ecumenical principles, by 1773 Stiles (its librarian) bitterly observed, "The Episcopalians slyly got into it & obtained a Majority w^c they are careful to keep." The Freemasons, too, were hatching Anglican plots.[65] While Stiles had served as a pallbearer at Browne's funeral, he also called the Anglicans "Superstitious" for not holding services on the Sunday after the minister's death, and he had unkind words for Browne's successors as well as his predecessors, a collection of despots and apostates. The Rev. John Lockier had scandalously dallied with a young woman posing as his live-in maid; the Rev. James Honyman was "a Non-Juror Jacobite Highflying Chhman, who inspired his Flock with the most rigid principles of Religion & Government & an inveterate Hatred of Presbyterians."[66] Even the polite dinner of Stiles and Russmeyer included catty remarks on the ways in which urbanity among divines sometimes went *too* far. The two criticized the Moravian Bishop August Gottlieb Spangenburg for having "no Steadiness and Fixedness, only to accomodate himself to every Company," and George Whitefield for having "too much of this conformability to the World in his Conversation." Stiles wrote that his colleague, Hopkins, was even more intolerant: "He believes the Moravians have no Christianity—most Christians embrace Delusion—and I never find him approving the Doctrines usually preached in any Churches now in Christendom whether Congregational, Presbyterian or &c."[67] Pluralism and mutual forbearance kept Newport in business, but few expected any sort of "union" among the town's worshippers. This would present difficulties for those who sought to mobilize Newporters during the imperial crisis.

Stiles was overtly suspicious of the Anglicans two blocks away, though historians have not fully appreciated the degree of resentment he harbored toward Newport's other denominations as well. Stiles held many ideas that Rhode Island Baptists and Quakers would have found abhorrent. In *A Discourse on Christian Union*, a famous statement on Christian pluralism, Stiles declared, "The right of conscience and private judgment is unalienable" and called for forgiveness among Calvinists and Arminians.[68] To read the *Discourse* simply as a statement of religious unity, however, would be a mistake. Stiles originally addressed the *Discourse* to a convention of Rhode Island Congregational ministers, "my brethren," in April 1760.[69] He called for a union of Congregationalists and Presbyterians against the Anglicans, made little mention of Quakers and only scant overtures toward the Baptists.[70] Moreover, his demographic projections must have irked non-Congregationalists. Stiles estimated that the number of people across Europe who believed in Presbyterian ordination (which, he did not say, excluded Quakers and many Baptists) was double the number of the Church of England: "If therefore the matter was to be decided by numbers, it must resolve in our favor by a very ample majority—tho' truly not numbers, but the *scriptures alone* ought to decide the truth." Stiles expressed smug satisfaction "to find the largest body of protestants on our side." He calculated, furthermore, that in one hundred years Congregationalists in New England would number seven million, while the Anglicans, Quakers, and Baptists would rack up meager numbers in the hundreds of thousands.[71]

While Stiles called for peace within the Congregational churches, his *Discourse* must have struck other Rhode Islanders as a provocation. Stiles claimed that Connecticut, Massachusetts, and New Hampshire successfully enacted a "happy policy of establishing one sect without infringing the essential rights of others," such that "other sects scarcely know that they are tolerated dissenters, so happy and mild is our dominion."[72] While Stiles intended to contrast this "public liberty" with the shabby treatment of Dissenters in England and the southern colonies, the pamphlet must have prompted incredulous scoffing from New England's Quakers and Baptists. If Rhode Island was destined to become overwhelmingly Congregationalist in the future, Newport's other denominations must have wondered what Stiles planned to do with them for the present. Baptists and Quakers, knowing well their bitter legacy of flayings, mutilation, and executions in Puritan Massachusetts, probably had an inkling.[73]

Rhode Islanders discerned some of the feelings between Congregationalists and the other denominations during the debate over the founding of Rhode Island College. The Newport Baptists got along well enough with Stiles that they asked him to draft a charter in 1763. Upon seeing the results, however, the Providence Baptists accused Stiles of trying to hoodwink them into founding a college where Congregationalists—still a minority in Rhode Island—would have too great a share in governance. (For his part, Stiles claimed that he and his parishioner William Ellery had drafted a "catholic plan.") The charter signed into law on October 24, 1765, gave Baptists the lion's share of control and stipulated that the college's president be a Baptist. The Providence Baptists also succeeded in wresting the college's location away from Newport.[74]

This controversy engendered harsh feelings; Baptist Elder Morgan Edwards of Pennsylvania later wrote that "the baptists narrowly escaped being jockied out of their college," while Stiles insisted that "the Baptists deserted the Congregationalists."[75] In the *Newport Mercury*, Ellery anonymously accused the Providence partisans in the Corporation of Rhode Island College of "bribery and corruption," and particularly castigated the four "hypocrites" (all Newport Baptists) who had basely sold out Newport's future.[76] In March 1771, a writer (probably Baptist) in the *Providence Gazette* ridiculed Stiles as "*Doctor Propheticus*" and the leader "of the *puritanic* Part" of Newport. In Stiles's demographic projections the satirist saw the minister's desire "of having all Power and Authority, both in *Church and State*, soon in [Congregational] Hands."[77] Later that year, the representatives for Providence at the General Assembly opposed an application on the part of Newport's Second Congregational Church for a charter of incorporation. The Newport deputies ("tho' both Chhmen," Stiles wrote) spoke in favor of the charter, which won by a scant majority of three.[78] In Providence, too, poor relations between Baptists and Congregationalists motivated the latter group to consort with Anglicans, perhaps as a way to express the depth of their displeasure. Stiles recorded a rumor in October 1771 that the Providence Baptists "were determined to root . . . the Presbyterians out of Providence & convert the whole Town to the Baptists," upon which the Providence Congregationalists declared their enmity to the college and even knelt in worship with the Anglicans onc Sunday.[79] Newport's catholic Baptists and Congregationalists, who had been making overtures toward one another for decades, must have lamented the decline in relations between the denominations.

Jews endured even sharper antipathy. Although they were able to operate their businesses freely in Newport, the town's gentiles denied their Jewish neighbors the full benefits of citizenship. In 1761 and 1762, when Aaron Lopez and Isaac Elizer applied to the superior court and the General Assembly for naturalization, they were denied on the basis of their Judaism. Stiles wrote, "Providence seems to make every Thing to work for the Mortification to the Jews, & to prevent their incorporating into any Nation; that thus they may continue a distinct people. . . . The Opposition [that the naturalization of Jews] has met with in Rh. Island, forbodes that the Jews will never become incorporated with the people of America."[80] Rhode Islanders knew how the influential thinkers in Massachusetts and Connecticut regarded them: as lawless in politics as they were in religion. Perhaps, in their zeal to prove that pluralism would not bring the Antichrist to Newport, Rhode Islanders went out of their way to show that theirs was a *Christian* colony by preventing Jews from being full colonists.

This landscape of mutual suspicion created barriers to political mobilization during the imperial crisis, in spite of urban pluralism—not just in Newport, but in New York and Philadelphia as well.[81] A French traveler wrote that Great Britain took advantage of America's multiplicity of denominations to keep the colonists divided and thereby thwart mobilization. He accused the British ministry of keeping the denominations "at vareance amongst themselves and Consequently wholly Dependent on them and subject to their will." The traveler also noted that the British strategy was misguided, "for the Inhabitants of north america Can lay asside their religion, when their Interest requires it, as well as the English Can, and allways have done."[82] Newport's houses of worship may have looked different on the outside, after all, but they still expressed shared cosmopolitan values in their interiors. While religious controversy was a salient feature of Anglo-American political history, Anglo-Americans had also developed a tradition of putting aside their differences for the sake of a larger cause. In the past, American Protestants had rallied to the larger cause of fighting external enemies such as Catholic France or heathen Native Americans. Similarly, Newport's different sects united in resistance to the Stamp Act of 1765: the city's Sons of Liberty included Baptists (Henry Ward, Josias Lyndon, and Charles Spooner "from among middling and lower life"), Anglicans (Robert Crooke, Metcalf Bowler, and Thomas Freebody), Congregationalists (John Channing, Jonathan Otis, Henry Marchant, William Ellery, Christopher Ellery, and possibly Samuel Hall, whose wife at least was a Congregationalist), and the motley John Collins.[83] Nevertheless, the imperial crisis also exposed rifts among the many religious denominations in North America, and the colonists would find it challenging to overcome their religious differences to mobilize against British policies.

For instance, many Anglicans supported the British government during the Stamp Act crisis, and a group called the Newport Junto even proposed that Parliament revoke Rhode Island's charter. These new developments exposed disunity among the city dwellers of Newport. Most of the Junto members were Anglicans, and Stiles singled out "the Custom House Officers, officers of three men of war, and about one hundred gentlemen Episcopalians" as supporters of the Stamp Act. The principal targets of the Newport Stamp Act riots on August 27–30, 1765, were also Anglicans. Junto members Martin Howard Jr. and Thomas Moffat were burned in effigy and saw their houses gutted before they fled to the warship *Cygnet* in the harbor.[84] An Anglican minister (presumably Browne) expressed the congregation's sentiments about these disturbances in a Christmas sermon on Proverbs 4:25–27 in 1766. Browne professed to advocate a moderate position "between an undue compliance with arbitrary & illegal power, & a factious or seditious behaviour." Throughout most of the sermon, Browne enjoined his hearers never to act "rashly & precipitately," to "see that thou act by rules, & upon certain principles," to "Take no indirect courses, but use such methods as are manifestly just & honest," and to live lives of "active & passive obedience" to civil government and its penalties. These words must have resonated among a congregation whose pew-holders had been hanged in effigy and whose houses had been attacked, particularly when Browne asked, "How many injuries have been done to innocent & righteous men, under a <u>pretence</u> of Zeal for God & true religion[?] . . . And hence have proceeded innumerable disorders in states & kingdoms, when the publick peace has been disturbed, & all good order violated out of a pretence of promoting the honor of God, & the good of men."[85] An effort at countermobilization, this sermon demonstrates the Anglican attitude toward the Stamp Act disturbances. The sermon echoed other British and Anglican critics who associated American resistance with religious enthusiasm and a "pretence of Zeal." Since the king was the head of both church and state, Anglican theology encouraged obedience to both. Many Trinity parishioners did join the resistance against Parliamentary measures; Stiles's paranoia notwithstanding, Anglicans did not universally support the Stamp Act, nor did Congregationalists have a monopoly on support for charter rights in New England.

Nevertheless, Congregationalists would prove to be the backbone of resistance to Great Britain in Newport. This would be a mixed blessing. Granted, the Congregationalists' dominance in New England made them fitting leaders. At the same time, the other sects retained their suspicions of Congregationalists, which would hamper the colonies' ability to present a unified front toward the mother country. Whig Congregationalists would have to establish an ecumenical, cosmopolitan network of correspondents if they hoped to mobilize an intercolonial network of protest, a covenant chain of Whig resistance. The revolutionary movement, under the banner of "civil and religious liberty," needed to create the broadest possible coalition of Anglicans, Congregationalists, Presbyterians, Lutherans, Quakers, Baptists, Pietists, Catholics, and Jews. As a result of the colonists' widely divergent opinions about religion, unified continental statements of resistance such as the Declaration of Independence lacked strong religious content.[86]

Stiles became a key player in the resistance network. A well-known Enlightenment thinker who kept in touch with a diverse community of intellectuals, Stiles was participating in one of the greatest transatlantic experiments of the age. His network of correspondents translated their disparate ideals and values into a common vision of Whig resistance, a vision that could be interpreted in different ways by different religious traditions. Stiles's own views sprang from a distinct interpretation of church structure and salvation. Like most clergymen of his day, he believed in keeping out of politics directly.[87] Yet on a daily basis, Stiles encountered neighbors from a variety of other theological traditions, and he attempted to communicate his most cherished ideals so that they would be acceptable to the widest possible audience. Stiles became indispensable as a "connector" whose cosmopolitan contacts helped to nourish political mobilization.[88]

When the Whig attorney Henry Marchant traveled to London in 1771, he made use of such transatlantic networks. Marchant's mission was to settle a lawsuit and to gain recompense for Rhode Island's expenses in the Seven Years' War. He carried recommendations from Stiles that affirmed him as "a Man of Sobriety & Virtue & at present firmly Congregational; & a friend to Civil & religious Liberty."[89] To the English Dissenter Richard Price, Stiles spoke of Marchant's interest in forming "a Connection with the Heads of the Dissenting Interest" in London. He assured Price that Marchant would not follow other New Englanders by forgetting his religion once reaching England.[90] Marchant's other letters revealed his network of Whigs, Congregationalists, merchants, colonial leaders, and Enlightenment figures: he had letters from Harvard mathematics professor John Winthrop and Massachusetts House Speaker Thomas Cushing to Benjamin Franklin; from Boston's James Otis to the English historian Catherine Macaulay; and from Samuel Adams to Arthur Lee, the Virginian lawyer who served as an agent for Massachusetts. He also carried letters from Jewish and Quaker merchants of Newport to their connections in London.[91] In every British town he visited, Marchant recorded the number of Dissenters. Marchant enjoyed Great Britain's cultural offerings, but he also kept an eye out for coreligionists who could support his allies at home. Marchant's mission failed, but upon his return to Newport he helped to fortify the network of Dissenters and Whigs. In a letter to Price he recommended Stiles as a regular correspondent: "In this Sir, I had the Publick Good at Heart & particularly Religious Liberty . . . and the Cause I conceived might be served by frequent Communications of Facts and Sentiments from each Side the Water from Honest and ingenious Men. If there is any Thing worth living or dying for, I think it is civil and religious Liberty."[92] If a Revolution for these liberties were to take place, it would happen because Marchant, Stiles, and others had mobilized these transatlantic networks.

Yet Newport's diverse sectarian landscape militated against the pattern of religious mobilization that formed in Boston, where a "Black Regiment" of Patriotic Congregationalist preachers encouraged their congregants. Many Newporters regarded Congregationalists as dangerous, which frustrated Whig Congregationalists' attempts to mobilize their neighbors who belonged to other churches. The other denominations outnumbered the Congregationalists, and they were too suspicious of them to blithely hand over the reins of power. For those who hoped to resist Britain's imperial policies, success would be contingent upon their ability to overcome these suspicions. For instance, Newporters were notorious laggards among the seaport cities during the Townshend duties crisis. While the nonimportation controversy created political rifts in every city, radical colonists believed that Newport's agreement was particularly weak. These colonists were outraged when Newport was the first major city to break its agreement and begin importing goods in early 1770. Merchants in other cities began cutting off trade with Newport. Newport's political, social, and economic structure helps to explain why the town was slower to mobilize than these other cities. Rhode Islanders never had an imperial governor to serve as a foil for rebellion, Newport merchants were enjoying good profits, and perhaps the town's large slave population gave potential white agitators pause. Beyond these factors, the town's religious diversity contributed significantly to its civic impasse, just as it often frustrated mobilization in diverse cities like New York City and Philadelphia.[93]

Stiles had no doubt that Anglicans were obstructing the mobilization of Congregationalist Whigs. "The Ministry dread the Population of New England and want to break up their religious and political principles, alter Times, Customs, Names, and all usages having Liberty and Charter powers connected with them," Stiles wrote in February 1773. "But two Things will survive the general Shipwreck. 1. American Liberty. 2. Congregationalism." Although both of these were under attack, and Stiles expected that many Congregationalists would desert the American cause "and bow the Knee to Baal," he remained confident that Americans would multiply, increase their territory, become independent, and (in the north) become predominantly Congregationalist. "It will be easy 100 years hence to give the Name New England to all the original Territory from 40 deg. and Northward [i.e., the Mason-Dixon line], and to declare a Primacy to the Congregational or Presbyterian Religion," he wrote, while "Episcopalian and deistical Crown Officers" would some day be reviled in the same breath as Pharoah, Nebuchadnezzar, and other biblical villains.[94] Such impolitic predictions would have shocked members of Newport's other denominations. Members of these sects could take some comfort that the Ellerys, Vernons, Marchant, and Stiles's other Whig congregants behaved in a more conciliatory fashion; yet many non-Congregationalists understandably lumped the laymen in with their pastors as emissaries of the Congregational juggernaut. If Congregationalist Whigs were unwilling to compromise in a diverse city like Newport, their meetinghouses would prove inadequate as sites of mobilization.

In Philadelphia, the fear had long persisted that "whenever this righteous People [Presbyterians] have power in their Hands, they will tolerate no other profession or Opinion but their own, and never cease till they establish themselves in such a Manner, so as to exclude all other Sects."[95] Foreign visitors to North America took note of the resentment in Rhode Island against Massachusetts Congregationalists, as one diarist wrote in 1765: "Rhode Island was setled first by people Banished from Boston, and was for some years the general asilum for such as sufered from the spirit of persecution that reigned then at Boston. . . . In Boston they are [still] ranck Bigoted presbiterians."[96] Suspicion against Congregationalism found many voices during the prerevolutionary years, which threatened to create rifts in the burgeoning movement of resistance against Great Britain.

Baptist Elder Morgan Edwards of Pennsylvania joined the criticism of New England Congregationalists. He wrote that the Congregationalists were "supercilious in Power, and mean in Conquest." Stiles sputtered defensively that Massachusetts and Connecticut treated Baptists and others much better than Anglicans treated Dissenters. Stiles noted Edwards's efforts in 1770 to compile all the New England Baptists' complaints of persecution to send them to London: "This was a Scheme of the Ministry to set the Baptists against the Congregationalists, & prevent the former from joyning the Latter in opposing an American Episcopate, under the notion that they should meet with more Liberty & less oppression under episcopal than presb. Government." According to Stiles, the strategy was working. If the Baptists would not join the Congregational crusade against Anglican bishops, he wrote, they might as well roll out the red carpet for Episcopal bishops in America—the Dissenters' worst nightmare.[97]

These tensions affected congregants' decisions about where to place their loyalties in the years between the Boston Tea Party of 1773 and the Declaration of Independence in 1776. With Bostonians baldly defying Parliament and Parliament dealing harsh punishments in return, it became more difficult to remain neutral. When Rhode Island Patriots burned the British customs cutter *Gaspée* in Narragansett Bay on June 9, 1772, the colony's fate became more closely tied to that of the rest of New England, but Newport's leaders of the resistance still had difficulty mobilizing their neighbors. In January 1774, John Collins attended a Newport town meeting where the debate over answering a letter from the Boston Committee of Correspondence "rais'd some ill natured Reflections about han[g]ing the Quakers and Whiping the Baptist."[98] Moderates and Loyalists postponed a public reading of the letter for three weeks, which dismayed Collins's correspondent, the Baptist Patriot leader Samuel Ward. Ward lamented "that such vile Reflections should at this Juncture be revived and pointed against a People [Congregationalists] Who are making all possible Compensation for the cruel Errors of their Ancestors, by giving the greatest Indulgence to both Quakers and Baptists and by exerting their utmost Influence under every possible Discouragement to secure the civil and religious Liberties of Christians of every Denomination." He added, "I hope the Baptists and Friends have too much good Sense and public Spirit to be catched by the Bate so stale and ridiculous and will heartily join in the intended Union of all the Colonies."[99] Ward, who as governor had spent a good part of his life trying to reconcile the political factions in Rhode Island, understood the importance of pluralism, compromise, and a flourishing "public spirit" to maintaining Patriot unity against Great Britain.

Many younger Rhode Islanders, however, may not have been as familiar with the history of the town's pluralism; alternatively, they may have believed that freedom from New England Congregationalists, preserving imperial trade networks, or loyalty to Great Britain were more important than joining the cause of the tea-destroyers in Massachusetts. Rhode Island College President James Manning raised this objection when he said "he did *not know why we should fast for Boston.*"[100] By the fall of 1774, Boston was suffering from the closing of its port and military occupation, and Whig leaders were doing their best to unite the colonies. To Congregationalists, the reasons for mobilization on Boston's behalf would have been self-evident; to Baptists a Congregational cause was more dubious.

In Philadelphia, New England Congregationalists faced the same historical accusations they had in Newport. At a meeting in Carpenter's Hall on October 14, 1774, Massachusetts Baptists protested the persecution they had faced and implicitly threatened to withhold their support for the First Continental Congress unless their demands for religious freedom were met. Philadelphia Quaker John Pemberton reportedly "bellowed loud on N. England persecution and Hanging the Quakers &c." Stiles reacted caustically: "In truth the Baptists intend to avail themselves of this opportunity to complain to England of Persecution—because they hate Congregationalists who they know are hated by the King Ministry & Parliament. They will leave the general Defence of American Liberty to the Congregationalists to the Northward and Episcopalians to the Southward;—& make Merit themselves with the Ministry, who are glad to play them off against us, & for this

End promise them Relief. Their Partiality & Malice are great." Stiles expressed shock that the Baptists would complain about the comparatively lenient policies of Massachusetts, when the unjust taxation of Dissenters was much worse in the southern colonies. He was outraged that Baptists were trying to force Whigs into a civic impasse. "We shall not forget this Work of our Brother Esau," Stiles promised darkly.[101] Of course, to Baptists in Massachusetts, leaving Congregationalists and Anglicans to the "Defence of American Liberty" was like leaving a dog to the defense of the family bacon.

The Quakers, including Newport's Friends, disappointed Whig Congregationalists as well. In December 1774, Quaker speaker John Pemberton of Philadelphia passed through Newport with an English Quaker woman. Stiles believed that Pemberton intended to dissuade Friends from taking part in American opposition to Parliament, in accordance with the Philadelphia Yearly Meeting's epistle to that effect. In other words, he saw it as an act of countermobilization on the part of Quakers who supported the Crown. Stiles, suspecting that Quakers were playing into the Ministry's design of dividing the colonists, confronted Pemberton, who replied that he "had only advised their Friends to keep in their own Line, be in a humble & low standing." Stiles, who interpreted this answer as "sly Cunning & Evasion," responded that the Quakers carefully avoided saying "any Thing on the Cause of public American Liberty at this critical Time when it became them to be explicit," and their silence "implied an oblique Reflection upon the Congress & the present public Measures which had been concerted by the united Wisdom of the Colonies."[102]

Stiles recognized that face-to-face persuasion was an important part of mobilization, and so he used all the tools at his disposal in his discussion with Pemberton. At one point, Stiles cited the Catholic specter of the Quebec Act as a threat to all Americans. Though few Catholics lived in Newport, many Protestants feared the free exercise of the Catholic religion in Canada. There were limits, after all, to Americans' cosmopolitan sensibilities, and old prejudices against Catholics could be an effective tool of mobilization.[103] Then, touching indirectly upon his favorite theme of Congregational demographic projections, Stiles warned that "the Time might come when Empire, or the sovereign Power should be transferred or erected on this side [of] the Atlantic, & wished him & the *Friends* to consider that a Time might come when they must seek Protection & political Favors from American higher Powers." According to Stiles, history would condemn the Quakers for failing to join a united American stand against Parliamentary taxation and the revocation of charter rights. Stiles was confident that the Congregationalists and Presbyterians in the North and the Anglicans in the South could maintain a "Defense of American Liberty" by themselves, without having to depend upon any other "Sects" in the Northern Colonies. Nevertheless, it was "ungenerous" of these sects "to take part against us in this important & interesting Crisis." Stiles apologized for his "Warmth," yet insisted that Pemberton and the Friends know "*in what Light that Letter & their Conduct are viewed by other Sects.*" This confrontation between a Quaker speaker and a Congregational minister illustrates how Newport's diverse religious landscape was a persistent challenge for proponents of revolutionary mobilization.

On the eve of the battles at Lexington and Concord in April 1775, Stiles assessed the Northern Anglicans, Quakers, and Baptists, and he did not like their lack of dedication to the Patriot cause: "A Languor prevails thro' these Bodies. Tho some few Baptists & Quakers are hearty with us, yet too many are so much otherwise, that was all America of their Temper or Coolness in the Cause the Parlt. would easily carry their Points & triumph over American Liberty. Perhaps the Junction of the *Baptists, Quakers,* northern *Episcopalians, Canadians,* and the *Crown Officers* may form here among us a Body of near Two Hundred Thousand or less than a *Quarter of a Million* in an anti-American Interest." Again, Stiles put his faith in demography: "Of the Whites I judge we have near *Two Million* Souls hearty and uncorrupted Friends of Liberty. These I trust in God will finally prevail—when the Baptists & Quakers may hereafter have Occasion to make their Court to us. . . . Perhaps the Baptists may open their Eyes—but there is no hope of the Quakers so long as they are dictated by the London General Meeting, & until the Seat of Empire is transferred or erected in America."[104] Stiles was confident in his own cosmopolitan network, yet he feared that the anti-Puritan sentiments floating around the Baptist, Quaker, and Anglicans' networks would lead them to obstruct the cause of America against Great Britain. Stiles expressed the fears of many Congregationalists about their neighbors in Newport and their uncertain allies in the middle colonies, fears that were grounded in the sectarian suspicions that colonial Americans had been harboring for generations.

Many of these neighbors and allies were just as fearful of the Congregationalists. Three weeks before the outbreak of fighting at Lexington, James Rivington's Loyalist *New-York Gazetteer* launched a vicious satirical attack (another tool of persuasion) on the transactions of the Newport Whigs' Committee of Inspection meeting on March 5, 1775. Rivington or his contributor mentioned Solomon "Sapscull" Southwick, Stiles ("Doctor Magpie"), and some of his most prominent Whig parishioners (Dr. John Bartlett, Henry "Mushroom" Sherburne, Henry "Bluster" Marchant, William "Wormwood" Ellery, and William "Smuggle" Vernon). The piece cunningly endeavored to link Congregationalists and their quest for supremacy in New England governments with Puritanical religious suppression, Oliver Cromwell and the regicides, smuggling, tarring and feathering, the *Newport Mercury*, and Whig committees, and the Patriot cause. The satire also attempted, as Stiles observed, to alienate Quakers, Anglicans, and Baptists "from the common cause." The piece had the Congregationalists calling Quakers "a very pernicious and antichristian sect" and "a great eye sore to the people of God," all of whom they would have hanged had it not been for the intervention of the king. In the satire's fictitious recounting of events, the committee criticized the Quakers for reading epistles of "peace, meekness, and obedience to government" at meetings and threatened to punish such epistles "by whipping, imprisonment, banishment, or hanging, in conformity to the salutary example of our pious forefathers." The committee of the satire went on to call the Baptists "troublers of an Israel to the commonwealth," and attacked their "loud clamours and injurious remonstrances," particularly their complaints against persecution in Massachusetts at the First Continental Congress in 1774. Rivington's committee threatened to "extirpate them whenever our republic is properly confirmed" and to seize Rhode Island College from their control. To pique Anglicans, Rivington also had the committee threaten to ban the Book of Common Prayer as a "prophane canonization of the wicked Charles."[105]

Rivington singled out Stiles for a few wicked jibes. Poking fun at Stiles's pedantry, the satirical piece portrayed the suppression of the King James Bible in favor of "a very antient Syriac edition of the Old Testament" and a Geneva edition of the New Testament prepared by Oliver Cromwell's chaplain. Furthermore, the piece lampooned Stiles's population projections for New England (a beloved target since the *Providence Gazette* piece of 1771) and "his great abilities displayed in calculating so accurately, the prodigious swarm of Independants [i.e., Congregationalists] that will cover the face of the western world toward the close of the [year] 9999." The satire may also have targeted the jingoism of Stiles's *Discourse on Christian Union*. It accused the committee of resolving "that unanimity is the tone of all the public deliberations, and that nothing more fatally tends to destroy that unanimity . . . than a difference in religion." The satirical committee resolved that only Congregationalists could vote in the committee, since their religion "deserves the preference to all others" for having sponsored the execution of Charles I. The piece concluded with a charge that Stiles hotly denied even in his diary, that he had set a "laudable example . . . in ceasing to pray for George the third." Still, Stiles did not pretend to deny that he had cast aspersions upon the ill-timed complaints of the Baptists.

If these attacks read like the bitter harangues of a Loyalist printer, some of this suspicion, fear, and bitterness toward Congregationalists was later evident in Whig writings as well. John Collins, as Rhode Island delegate to the Continental Congress, believed that he had been the victim of political attacks for having "stood much in the way of what they Called the New England Prisbeyterian interest." Collins had previously written to General Nathanael Greene, his relative by marriage, "that a certain Sect was seeking the downfall of all the rest," and in the summer of 1779 Greene eventually agreed that these "suspicions were not altogether groundless." Collins angrily predicted that Samuel Adams and William Ellery would "use all their influence to damn me with the People, but they may be Damd them Selves for what I Care for them or their party. I will Act my part as I think best for the public good, and Suffer no junto or party to influance me or lead me from what I think best for the good of the whole. It is well known I am not a begot to any party, Religious, or Sivel, but have Endeavered to Support the Carracter of an honest independant man." Despite his anger at the Congregationalists, he was hopeful that "that party are loosing ground in Congress fast." Greene agreed, calling the New England faction "very prejudical to the true interest of America." Collins and Greene shared their suspicions of Ellery and Henry Marchant. In their reflections on the two Newport Congregationalists who represented Rhode Island in Philadelphia, Greene and Collins had some of the same fears of a New England conspiracy as Loyalists and Anglicans had expressed for many years.[106] Rhode Island Baptists probably expressed some of the same sentiments, particularly as they observed the continued struggle of their brethren in Massachusetts. In 1780, Boston Baptist minister Samuel Stillman spoke of "the designs of a <u>Certain Body of People</u> to Crush the B[a]p[ti]st. Interest," and George Benson, recounting these remarks, lamented, "in Vain then do we Oppose the British Lyon While we Tamely Submit to the all Devouring Jaws of the P[urita]n Bear." Stillman predicted that if Congregationalists' "devouring" continued unabated, the Massachusetts Patriots "<u>will make us all Tories</u>."[107]

Despite these threats, Baptists supported the Revolutionary War, though their participation had something of a neutral cast. Samuel Ward, delegate to the Continental Congress, was often a guest at the Sabbatarian Meeting House in Newport. The Sabbatarians ordained Ebenezer David, who later died serving as a Continental Army chaplain, and their deacon John Tanner was a Patriot. Their own minister, John Maxson, was excused from taking a loyalty oath to the Whigs because of his age (he was 63). Stiles called him "a pious & inoffensive Man, whom I never heard to be a Tory, but it seems his honest Mind was not strong eno' to digest this Revolution."[108] Second Church's Thurston appears to have been a relatively passive player. He was "not suspected" of being a Tory in 1776, though he subsequently stayed in Newport after the British captured and occupied the city in December of that year. At the same time Thurston's friend Hezekiah Smith of Haverhill, Massachusetts, became a Continental Army chaplain, and his coreligionists the Browns of Providence were ardent Rhode Island Patriots.[109] The Rev. Erasmus Kelly of the First Church was waiting to see which way the wind blew, thinking the king's troops would prevail; at the same time, Stiles grumbled that he was "not a little affected with Baptist Politics." Kelly strangely disavowed the taking up of arms in all cases (not a typical Baptist stance) "tho' he said if any was lawful, the present American War was so; and that he could pray for success to the Americans."

Stiles ultimately sympathized with Newport's Baptist ministers, wishing that Newport's Patriot committees had left them alone and believing that none of them was inimical to the American cause.[110] Newport's Baptists may have felt that Congregationalists were untrustworthy, aggrandizing salesmen. At the same time, the product—resistance to Great

Britain—appeared to be more attractive than the alternative. Still, the Baptist meetinghouses would prove unlikely sites of Patriot mobilization. The Baptists recognized that they would have to keep an eye on the Congregationalists. In postrevolutionary America these groups and others would have to delineate a new landscape of pluralism if their republican government and commerce were to prosper.[111]

For all of Stiles's complaints about Quakers, officially they could not take part in politics: the Friends disowned Governor Stephen Hopkins for violating this rule. Still, many Quakers had left or would leave the meeting over issues of oath-taking or military service. Other Quakers expressed strong Tory or Whig sympathies while remaining within the Discipline. Moses Brown of Providence sympathized with his Patriot brothers, and doubtless many Newport Quakers did as well. Stiles named many Quakers in his list of people who remained in Newport after the British occupation. Several dozen Quakers signed an address to the British general Sir Henry Clinton, wishing him success in restoring peace and tranquility to America and asking him to treat "such who have not deviated from their Allegiance to the King in an leniant & tender manner."[112] Unlike the Baptists, Quakers had little theological affinity with Congregationalists. Their pacifism, their belief in supporting secular rulers, and their correspondence with the London Meeting generally kept them in the Loyalist camp, in Newport as in Philadelphia.

If Second Congregational Church was a hotbed of Patriot mobilization, Trinity Church remained the beacon for Loyalist countermobilization in Newport. Stiles noted that the Anglicans made only a half-hearted observance of a Continental fast day on July 20, 1775, "for they abominate this Fast." After the signing of the Declaration of Independence in July 1776, the Rhode Island General Assembly at Newport passed a resolution that mandated a hundred pound fine or imprisonment "if any Person within this State, shall under Pretence of *Preaching* or *praying*, or in any Way or manner whatever *acknowledge or declare the said King* (of G. Brit.) to be our rightful Lord & Sovereign, or shall pray for the Success of his Arms." Stiles reported that "instantly thereon the People of the Chh. of England in Newport cried out of Persecution, went and removed all their Prayer Books &c & shut up the Church; and had no Service in it last Lordsday, tho' M[r] Bisset their Parson was well & walking the Streets." Trinity Church proclaimed its loyalty with closed doors and silent bells.[113] In August, Newport's Anglicans announced their refusal to meet or worship in the "Raccoon Boxes" of the Baptists and Congregationalists as an alternative. Where once the similarity of church and meetinghouse interiors in Newport had been a source of unity, now the Anglicans were openly disparaging the interior architecture of the Calvinist meetinghouses. Another symbol of pluralistic sentiment had collapsed. Houses of worship had failed to unify Newporters.[114]

In December 1776, the British army captured Newport without opposition: the British boasted superior naval support, and the rebels melted away.

George Bisset gave a Christmas sermon appropriate to the occasion, referring to the multitude of angels as a celestial army and bringers of peace.[115] He deplored "a state of enmity & hostility," adding that God "beseeches guilty men to lay down ye weapons of their rebellion, but yet if they will hold fast their enmity to God & madly reject the divine goodness . . . they cannot blame any but y^m selves, if they are distroyed as enemies instead of being received & rewarded as the friends of God." Bisset surely referred to the restoration of Crown rule in Newport, and not just the anniversary of the Nativity, when he welcomed "the return of this most auspicious day, wch brough us a deliverance f^m ye tyranny of the prince of darkness, f^m ye imperious dictates of our passions." He urged his parishioners to celebrate the holiday and its "unutterable salvation" with gratitude, "not in rioting & drunknness," but in taking communion, attending the offices of the church, and relieving the poor. Although a few Newport Anglicans supported the Revolution, and Rhode Island's other Anglican ministers remained neutral, Bisset and his Newport parishioners found it difficult to bury their resentment toward the Patriots. Bisset became a Loyalist, and several Anglicans had their property confiscated for being Loyalists during the war.[116]

Newport's smaller congregations had no identifiable relationship to the Revolution. Stiles observed, "The Unitas Fratrum are a small Body, & tho a pious good people, yet meddle not in this Cause." He also noted that they kept the Continental Fast of July 20, 1775. The Rev. Russmeyer declined to take a loyalty oath and "took the Affirmation that his Conscience was against War," yet Stiles wished that he, too, had been left alone, and declined to list the leader of this pacifistic sect as a Tory during the war.[117] Many of Newport's Jews, though they could not participate directly in politics, took strong positions in the Revolutionary conflict. For a small congregation, they were far from unified in their sentiments—some sided with the British, while others evinced clear sympathy for the rebellion.[118] Newport's Jews faced an added complication because both supporters and opponents of Parliament voiced prejudice against them. In 1770, Thomas Vernon noted that "the Trifle of Goods we have Imported here chiefly by the jews . . . has caus'd the resentment of the Colonies." John Collins worried in early 1774 about "the Circumcised and Uncircumcised Jews, that may import teas," and he and Samuel Ward briefly suspected Aaron Lopez, an avowed Patriot.[119] When the General Assembly tried to administer the Test Act to Moses Hays in the summer of 1776, Hays responded to the prevalent climate of prejudice by refusing to take the test, even as he affirmed his "Sentiments in favor of America" and his belief that the ongoing war was just. Hays noted that as an "Israelite" he was "not allowed the Liberty of a vote or a voice in Common with the Rest of the voters" and noted that the Test was "not Generall" to all residents of Newport."[120] While gentiles had the freedom to make their own decisions about the Revolution, they often pigeonholed Jews, constraining their options and imposing difficulties on them, even those in sympathy with the Patriots.

The Revolution in Connecticut, Massachusetts, and New Hampshire was clearly a Congregational Revolution, but it was based on networks of mobilization, not solely on theological or ideological abstractions.[121] In Rhode Island, too, the Congregationalists were eager to join Boston in its fight against Great Britain, while other denominations were not so sure. The Baptists blinked; even though many of them joined the Patriot cause, they made sure to make their grievances known to Congregational authorities and ultimately achieved greater freedom of worship as a result. Quakers followed the fissures that had already been developing. Some quit the faith and joined the Patriots, while others aggressively tried to maintain their neutrality or openly supported the British cause against the grasping Congregationalists. Anglicans generally supported the king, but in this sect as in all Newport sects, denomination did not necessarily determine one's political proclivities. The Jewish community of Newport provides the best evidence of this. Few in number and surrounded by a mass of gentiles who excluded them from political participation, one would expect them to cling to each other. Yet disagreements plagued many eighteenth-century Jewish communities, and in Newport the Jews cleaved along Patriot and Loyalist lines.

While religion did help contribute to the political decisions of many city dwellers, the urban environment also called for flexibility. Just as some slept through a Sabbath morning or switched faiths, so, too, did they have the ability to break away from their fellow congregants and make decisions based on material calculations, perceived military dangers, or personal rivalries. City dwellers of all political stripes sought houses of worship and their attendant networks for aid, information, salvation, and comfort, but more cosmopolitan places like taverns, the waterfront, or the town square were generally better suited to political mobilization.

If houses of worship were not always appropriate sites of political mobilization, they did inspire other forms of mobilization. The Revolutionary era was not just a time when Americans broke from Great Britain—it was also a period of social change, a chance for ordinary folk to make the world anew and gain greater acceptance in the public sphere. Ordinary white men were able to participate in this revolutionary upheaval, and this was evident in taverns and on the waterfront. At the same time, it was equally evident that women and blacks achieved little in these secular places. These groups of city dwellers had more success achieving social transformation in houses of worship.

Given the prevalence of women among church members and the importance of the church in society (particularly in the covenanted communities of New England), the church was an ideal site for the mobilization of women. During the Townshend duties crisis, Newport men made appeals to women to help them take a stand on imported goods. When Baptist Job Bennet married Patience Burdick in 1768, they appeared at church the next day "dress'd in the Manufactures of this Colony."[122] Newport's Congregational ministers made their homes a public platform for the homespun movement, and they urged their female congregants and other local women to support the nonimportation effort. Six hundred spectators came by to observe a spinning match at Stiles's house on April 26, 1769, with thirty-seven wheels: the spinning women included two Quakers, six Baptists, and twenty-nine women from Second Congregational Church. The following month, another spinning match at the Stiles home (there would be three others) included "Ninety-two daughters of Liberty" behind seventy wheels, "of all Denominations, Chh. [of England], Quakers, Bapt. & Cong. &c." On May 24, 1770, Samuel Hopkins oversaw eighty spinning wheels during a match at his home.[123]

These spinning matches did not take place in the meetinghouses themselves, yet the presiding presence of the ministers lent a religious blessing to these public ceremonies of domestic manufacture. Spinning meetings demonstrated Congregational women's desire and ability to mobilize—an extension of Congregational women's revivals (Boston Loyalist Peter Oliver called it "the Enthusiasm of the Spinning Wheel"). Furthermore, this outlet for Patriot sentiment was more orderly, disciplined, and pious than the rioting and drunkenness that characterized men's political mobilization.[124] Finally, the spinning groups encompassed more than one denomination: Baptist and Quaker women also participated (if in smaller numbers) in this statement of resistance. In this way, networks of religious women joined the male-dominated Patriot networks that were mobilizing during the imperial crisis.

The egalitarian elements of eighteenth-century evangelical religion had been a boon to women in the public sphere, and this would become a source of women's political mobilization. Women often comprised the majority of church members: in Second Congregational Church they outnumbered men by a ratio of almost three to one in 1772; elders at First Baptist Church baptized two women for every man from 1739 to 1776.[125] Women's participation in church decisions varied among the different congregations in Newport, but they appeared to be more active in churches with a more evangelical or pietistic bent. Women were excluded from formal religious participation at Trinity Church, Second Congregational Church, and the synagogue (where they were relegated to inferior seating). At the Quaker meetinghouse, they held their own meetings, elected their own elders and committees, handled money, and administered discipline. At the Moravian meetinghouse, Russmeyer's wife helped perform the sacraments. At the Seventh-Day Baptist Church during the early part of the eighteenth century, women handled money and served on committees to visit errant congregants. Deacon James Barker of Second Baptist sought Stiles's advice in 1771 about "whether Sisters have a right to vote in the Chh." Women made up about two-thirds of church members in Thurston's church, but only nine male members were necessary to transact business at Thursday meetings—and church members had raised an objection to this practice. Precedent seemed to favor women's voting: the sisters had voted to retain Nicholas Eyres in the 1740s, they had helped to elect the deacons, and they participated in the examination of those offering themselves for baptism or communion. Stiles concluded "that it is a Usage & practiced Principle among the Baptists of this Colony (especially the two antient Chhs of Newport & Providence under Hands) to admit Sisters to equal Votes in the Chh meetings, & this by *Lifting up of Hands*." Apparently this practice was more common among older sisters, while "the younger sisters keep their places and say nothing . . . probably their Voting is growing into Disuetude—so that the usage may be intirely dropt in another Generation in these old as well as in the new Churches." Of course, Stiles may have just been wishful that this would provide a basis for Baptists to concur with Congregational theology, since he "never knew or read of the Sisters voting" in Congregational churches.[126] Some women apparently took their cues from their urban neighbors and declined to participate in church votes, while others found each other within the urban setting—at female society meetings, communion services, spinning matches, or Whitefield's sermons—as they reached for a place closer to God.

When Sarah Osborn and her female society helped install Samuel Hopkins at the pulpit of First Congregational, their influence was notable even though the decision-making committee had been composed entirely of men.[127] As the health and sobriety of William Vinal declined in the 1760s, Osborn increasingly compensated for the resultant dearth in leadership. She had led the female religious society of the First Congregational Church since 1741—the women met at Osborn's home at least once a week, fasted, confessed their sins, prayed, and contributed alms. By the mid-1760s, Osborn was facilitating a major revival: during the course of one week, 525 people met in her home, including young men, young women, Baptist men, Baptist women, Congregational men, children, free black men and women, and slaves. Osborn had close contact with Nathaniel Clap, Vinal, Stiles, Maxson, Thurston, and a number of visiting ministers, including Whitefield. Although she detested separatism, she largely overlooked sectarian differences and praised a Baptist laywoman of "catholick spirit."[128] Osborn became one of the most important figures in the religious life of the congregation—and of the entire town—even as she respected Newport's pluralistic values.

The Rev. Samuel Hopkins began meeting with Osborn's female society as soon as he arrived in the summer of 1769. When the parishioners disagreed about appointing him their pastor, he withdrew himself from consideration and gave a farewell sermon that moved many of the full church members to tears. Stiles recorded with some disapproval that in the society as a whole, a majority was against Hopkins's settlement, many of the remaining congregants disliked him, and only about a quarter were genuinely in favor of him. Still, "Mrs. Osborn & the Sorority of her Meeting are violently engaged and had great Influence. They & the 2 Deacons & Two Thirds of Chh [i.e., the full members or communicants] were warmly engaged for Mr. Hopkins." More liberal Calvinists in Boston and New Haven warned that Hopkins's strict views would drive away congregants, but Hopkins's allies prevailed.[129] The society's most devout, especially its women, determined the settlement of the famous pastor at the First Congregational. Women sometimes had the means to mobilize in a religious landscape ostensibly controlled by men.

Women's religious rhetoric often invoked the same language of freedom as the Patriots' political responses to British policies. Sarah Osborn adopted Jonathan Edwards's imagery invoking the grace of God striking off the chains of Satan from an enslaved soul: in 1753, she wrote of a "God of boundless Perfections" who "made way for my escape" from temptation.[130] When considering a second marriage, she said she "could not think of being unequally yoked" to a man who was not a real Christian.[131] Her diaries frequently invoke the phrase "Yoke of Bondage," which she applied to the Stamp Act and also to slavery in a letter she may have written introducing the first antislavery letter ever to appear in the Newport Mercury.[132] This was a language of liberation, of breaking constraints and boundaries when it came to free grace and the freedom to participate in urban revivals. Osborn was concerned "To avoid Moving beyond my Line" by catechizing to black men and women in her home, yet "if no weathers this winter stops them from Enjoying it," she could do no less.[133] Osborn looked forward to forming a new network of like-minded believers: the gatherings in her house "are rather a Sweet Sementing bond of union that Holds us together in this critical day."[134] Her friend Susanna Anthony also hoped to "enjoy unbounded felicity" as she was transported near God, and she prayed that he would "set the prisoner free from every interruption." Once united with God, "Nothing should have tempted me to have wished myself from under these bonds and seals."[135] These women forsook worldly entrapments, seeking unity with other believers and with God in the city.

Osborn apparently led Newport in the quest to extend this unity to blacks as well, and her mobilization of a revival was potentially revolutionary in its own way. Members of all the Newport churches had made overtures to convert blacks to Christianity to some degree, but unlike the humble Sarah Osborn, the wealthy laypersons who helped build and maintain Newport's houses of worship and their luxuriant interiors balked at allowing blacks to share in their weekly sacred rituals.[136] The Anglicans, through the SPG, were probably the first to minister to Newport's blacks. Trinity Church's James Honyman baptized a number of blacks and Indians throughout his ministry; he reported fifty to seventy Indians and black slaves in attendance at services in the 1720s, and one hundred blacks by 1743 (of whom five were communicants).[137] The Rev. Thomas Pollen reported less success in 1755: most blacks were unbaptized, and black Christians reported that slave owners did not baptize their slaves because "the Masters thought that their servants would by baptism come too near themselves." In 1762, the parish appointed Mary Brett as schoolmistress to the slave children, although Marmaduke Browne again referred to an "unaccountable prejudice entertained by many in the Plantations that learning and instruction has only a tendency to render Negroes greater Rogues than they would otherwise be." Almost a decade later Browne made reference to whites' "contempt incident to the colour & slavery of the Blacks . . . they consider them as living purely for the service & if their instruction interferes in the least with this servitude it must be entirely neglected." Trinity Church and its missionary backers made sincere efforts to improve the school; by the spring of 1774 it had thirty-eight pupils, which George Bisset said was "as many as one person can instruct."[138] Trinity Church's spiritual leaders had more interest than their parishioners in the religious education of blacks.

Quaker laypersons also seemed to have little interest in black conversions. An anonymous Quaker document, "An Epistle of tender Love and Advice to the Negroes at Newport and other Parts of New-England," condescendingly asked blacks to refrain from "Indulging your selves in carnal pleasures in rioting and drunkenness" and from "Lying, swearing, bac[k]biting, adultery, and every inchastity," especially fornication. The speaker warned slaves to obey their masters and mistresses not only with "eye service" but in fear of a vigilant God. The writer recognized the great "disadvantages that you lie under" and the slaves' "sighs and groans" and concluded, "therefore of all people you have the greatest need to be inward with God." He or she assured them that "altho' under Bonds . . . you may be the lords freemen and free women." If God inspired some masters to free their slaves, he hoped that these freed people would use their freedom in a worthy manner, with industrious labor "accompanied with a life of piety and virtue demonstrating a due gratitude unto your masters and unto him the all wise disposer of events, that others may be Encouraged to set their Slaves your Countrymen at liberty, for it is the abuse of your freedom that is the great objection made by many against freeing their Slaves." The speaker was "not asham'd to promote his righteous cause amongst the poor Blacks," but the Friends' efforts to convert and incorporate blacks into the Society were ultimately lacking.[139]

Ezra Stiles sincerely ministered to his black parishioners. In July 1772, he hosted six black communicants in his study: "We all fell upon our Knees together, and I poured out fervent Supplications at the Throne of Grace imploring the divine Blessing upon us, and commending ourselves to the holy Keeping of the Most High. We seemed to have the delightful presence of Jesus." In 1773, Stiles mourned the death of his church member Phyllis Lyndon, the slave of former Governor Josias Lyndon. Her husband Zingo Stephens was also a communicant: "Upon becoming religious and joyning my Church, [he] had an earnest Concern for his Wife and Children, and labored greatly to bring her into a saving Acquaintance with her Redeemer; and I doubt not his Endeavors and prayers were blessed to her saving Conversion." Stiles also praised her exemplary conduct, which perhaps inspired the discourse to his black parishioners a few days later on

2 Cor. 5:20–21: "Now then we are ambassadors for Christ, as though God did beseech you by us: . . . For he hath made him to be sin for us, who knew no sin; that we might be made the righteousness of God in him."[140] Although some historians have associated Stiles's catechizing to blacks with Jonathan Ashley's Deerfield sermon on obedience, Stiles chose biblical passages for his black students that primarily emphasized conversion and salvation.[141] Stiles included blacks in the equality of souls before God. When he baptized and admitted three blacks to communion in March 1770, his morning sermon to the entire congregation was on Mat. 12:49–50: "Whosoever shall do the will of my Father which is in heaven, the same is my brother, and sister, and mother."[142] In this urban setting, many blacks and whites prayed, studied the Bible, and took communion together.

The messages of ministers in Newport repeatedly stressed this message of inclusion. The Baptist minister Hezekiah Smith of Massachusetts visited Newport in 1764 and preached a Sunday sermon on a passage from the Gospel of Luke. Later that week, Smith and Thurston preached at one of Osborn's meetings. Smith wrote that Osborn "informed me of a Negro wᵒ was greatly awakened under my Afternoon's Discourse ye Sabb[ath] before, from these Words, & Yet there is Room & since wᶜ Time has met a Change, so yᵗ He can give a satisfactory Account of yᵉ Work of Grace on his Heart." Here was a metaphor from a biblical passage that had profound meaning for this black Newporter. Christ's parable about the rich man having room for more unfortunates at his table taught more than generosity toward the poor. The passage promised salvation for the meek and humble, who would be more welcome in heaven than the wealthy and cosmopolitan.[143] These were words of spiritual mobilization that had the potential to galvanize a spiritual community.

While Hopkins argued that blacks "have imbibed the deepest prejudices against [Christianity], from the treatment they receive from professed Christians," he wrote this with the rhetorical purpose of convincing pious whites to free their slaves.[144] Blacks appeared to have a genuine interest in Christianity. Stiles discoursed to "a very full and serious Meeting of Negroes at my House, perhaps 80 or 90," on the same chapter of Luke in February 1772. He described them as "attentive and affected; and after I had done, many of them came up to me and thanked me . . . for taking so much Care of their souls."[145] Stiles reflected, on this occasion, that there were not above thirty communicants out of 1,200 blacks in Newport—six or seven Baptists, four or five Anglicans (they claimed seven in 1766), six or seven at First Congregational, and seven at his own church.[146] If this number seems small, one should put it in context: in 1770, Stiles recorded six black communicants in his church (he had one more by 1772), 9% of his seventy black congregants. At the same time, Stiles's sixty-six white communicants represented about 11% of the 608 whites in his society. Admittedly, a much smaller percentage of Stiles's black congregants (17%)

than white congregants (66%) were baptized, and the Baptists and Anglicans seem to have had lower proportions of black communicants.[147] Nevertheless, in the years after 1772, a number of church records indicate further catechizing to blacks, black baptisms and marriages, and inductions into church membership. By 1784, 11% of the communicants at the Sabbatarian Baptist Church were black.[148]

Overall, the number of black communicants in town was far from insignificant, and the number of blacks in Newport attending Christian worship was probably substantial as well. Historians of the region's African American culture have argued that black conversions and religious societies were the exception rather than the rule in late eighteenth-century New England. Even if true, such a finding only highlights the way in which an urban center like Newport provided unique opportunities for spiritually curious black people to find uplift, fellow congregants, and fellow communicants. Christianity and religious education inspired spiritual and intellectual transformations for Newport blacks, and their voluntary participation in Protestantism eventually led to the formation of more churches, associations, and institutions—in this way the Revolutionary era wrought social, political, and religious transformation for African Americans.[149]

Despite the egalitarian message of Christianity, most Newport whites were still slow to embrace the idea of social transformation for blacks. African Americans suffered discrimination within the religious landscape. If whites and blacks mingled tears over the graves of slaves, they did not ordinarily mingle during regular church services.[150] In the Sabbatarian Church, the pews in the east gallery were designated for non-whites.[151] Trinity Church removed its black hearers in 1772 to the west end of the church in the pews behind the organ "provided it be agreeable to the proprietors of the pews behind the organ," while the blacks, apparently not consulted, would be "as well accommodated as they are at present."[152]

Some whites, observing the horrors of the slave trade and the contradictions of slavery, criticized the institution. Newporters said that Elder Thurston, who apparently worked as a cooper as well, refused to make barrels for the shipment of rum to Africa because of the association with the slave trade.[153] After Stiles closed the eyes of his deceased communicant Pollipus Hammond, he reflected, "He was many years a Guinea Captain; he had then no doubt of the Slave Trade. But I have reason to think that if he had his Life to live over again, he would not chuse to spend it in buying and selling the human species."[154] Many of Stiles's slave-owning parishioners probably disagreed. In 1780, when the Congregationalists of war-torn Newport considered unification, the members of Second Church demanded Hopkins's dismissal as a condition. "They dislike my doctrines in general," Hopkins wrote, "and especially my opposition to the slavery of the Africans."[155] Nevertheless, during the Revolutionary era a number of Newporters advocated the abolition of the entire institution of slavery.

The participation of Quakers in the antislavery cause is well known, although the urban Quakers of Newport were slower to manumit their slaves than any other Monthly Meeting of Friends in New England.[156]

Samuel Hopkins reacted with horror to Newport's worldly culture of slave trade and self-interest.[157] After the Revolution he would declare "that this town is the most guilty respecting the slave trade, of any on the continent, as it has been, in a great measure, built up by the blood of poor Africans; and the only way to escape the effects of Divine displeasure is to be sensible of the sin, repent and reform."[158] Hopkins noted the Quakers' endeavors to expunge slavery from the Society. Most other denominations attended the Lord's Supper, and Hopkins agreed that the Friends neglected this important ritual. Nevertheless, he pointed out, "while you are condemning them for this neglect, your . . . omission of that righteousness and mercy which they practice [i.e., manumission of slaves], is inexpressibly more dishonorable and offensive to Christ, than their neglect."[159] As Christians gathered together to take the Lord's Supper in Anglican, Baptist, and Congregational churches, Hopkins called upon them to think of their oppressed black slaves and follow the Quakers' example in manumitting them. The meetinghouse was not a place to shut oneself away from the concerns of the world, however much this attracted many serious Christians. Instead, it was also a place to exercise mercy toward slaves, in Newport and beyond. As Hopkins sent his *Dialogue Concerning the Slavery of the Africans* to the Continental Congress, he hoped to transmit the lessons he had learned in Newport to the national leaders in Philadelphia.[160]

Hopkins and Osborn were participating in an ecumenical, cosmopolitan network of mobilization, one with the goals of conversion, uplift, and social change for non-whites in New England and abroad. This network included fellow parishioner Susanna Anthony, who frequently traveled to Boston (where another female religious society met); Boston poet Phillis Wheatley; Phillis's mistress, Susanna Wheatley; Phillis's black friend Obour Tanner of Newport; Bristol Yamma and John Quamine, the two black men of Newport that Stiles and Hopkins were preparing for an African mission; and Newport Gardner, who ultimately became a deacon of First Congregational Church, founder of a school for black children in Newport, and a missionary to Africa. Further abroad, this network drew in Hopkins's allies in the New Divinity movement throughout New England: the Boston Patriot clergy; George Whitefield; the black Anglican pastor Philip Quaque in Ghana; the Indian minister Samson Occom; Selena Hastings, the Countess of Huntingdon; Dr. John Erskine of Edinburgh; a transatlantic network of Quakers; and English antislavery advocate Granville Sharp. Within these groups were black men and women who had to mask their call for emancipation and social change in subtle, poetic language; white women who wielded influence in the church but needed to tread carefully in the public sphere; and white men who could speak more boldly and publicly against slavery, even if it cost them friends and reputations (a path that many New

England clergymen did not take).[161] The urban landscape of Newport inspired these various groups and facilitated their connections to one another. If their mobilization was insufficient to do away with slavery, at least a port city like Newport had the potential to make room for radical ideas.

Some would attain salvation. Some would attain liberty. But not all. Calvinists would say that such fates were predestined, and for liberty as well as salvation, perhaps this was so. For blacks, women, and Jews, their lack of liberty was predetermined by the prejudices and ideals of Anglo-American society. The urban setting exposed these inequalities to Newporters and demonstrated the limits of their celebrated catholicism: they could choose to fight against encroachments upon liberty, as some did in the battles against British taxation and coercive religious establishment; or they could choose to preserve these inequalities. The Revolution inspired some radical outsiders (like Hopkins, the First Congregational female society, and the Quakers) to extend the benefits of God and the polity to all; at the same time, a prevailing civic impasse exposed the limits of revolutionary transformation. In a diverse city like Newport, New York City, or Philadelphia, disagreements over religion and its place in public life made it impossible for political mobilization to encompass everyone—hundreds of Anglicans, Quakers, materialist nothingarians, and neutrals rejected the Whigs' resistance to Great Britain, and most white city dwellers rejected the antislavery movement. Taverns or the streets, devoid of religious baggage, were ultimately more effective sites of mobilization against Great Britain, if not against slavery.

The American Revolution failed to bring significant social change to female or non-white Americans, but it enacted significant changes nonetheless. Radical Baptists joined a Congregational Revolution to attain religious liberty, and their gamble paid off. Hopkins and his antislavery allies, meanwhile, were forced to compromise with a Revolution (and later a Constitution) that protected slavery, and their gamble had only limited success. Compromise was a necessary part of urban life and urban mobilization, and so sinful slave traders and secular urbanites joined with urban evangelicals in the Revolutionary movement. At the same time, the revivals of the prerevolutionary era helped plant the seeds that eventually flowered into more significant gains. The Second Great Awakening would further democratize American life. Religious women found new public roles during the nineteenth century. Black Christianity became an even stronger source of black community and empowerment. The antislavery movement, with its deep religious roots, was ultimately successful in the northern states.[162]

The American Revolution in the cities had at best an indirect link to evangelical religion. The ministers and laypersons who battled over religious revivals formed networks of friendly correspondents, centered in urban seaports like Newport, which communicated ideas about resistance and the Revolution. In addition, evangelicalism *did* work revolutionary transformations for people on the margins—although these "little revolutions" may not have had the same goals as elite white men's resistance to Great Britain, they certainly helped expand the transformative meaning of the American Revolution. Newport was a city that owed much of its growth to Quakers, yet by the 1770s, Quakers had largely retired from politics. The Congregationalists helped push Newport into war, even though the Baptists who dominated Rhode Island distrusted their Puritan neighbors. The residents of Newport celebrated liberty of conscience as a necessary lubricant for business, yet when the war destroyed Newport's commerce, they found that deistic southerners like Thomas Jefferson had taken center stage in the cry for religious liberty. Though a few influential ministers had exhorted their followers for political causes throughout America, most ministers found they had lost stature by the end of the eighteenth century, and disestablishment robbed churches of their public power.[163] Women attained greater spiritual freedom during the colonial era, only to find their femininity subsumed within Protestant culture after the Revolution. Perhaps the most enduring revolution was that of black city dwellers and their allies—this loose group of spiritually questing individuals would ultimately have a lasting impact on black organization and emancipation in the postrevolutionary era. The Revolution was full of contradictions and frustrated ambitions. And yet there was room, as the Gospel of Luke reminded Newporters. The urban religious landscape allowed for communication, conflict, and sometimes political mobilization, while also providing space for experimentation, religious conversions, and new forms of spiritual organization.

Chapter 4

CHANGING OUR HABITATION

The Revolutionary Movement in Charleston's Domestic Spaces

Can we change our habitation remove our effects from one House to another without Some trouble, without some damage to the furniture or without Some Struggle among the branches of the family for the best apartments in the new Mansion? Surely not can we expect then to change Governors to establish a new System & to have no murmuring in so large a family? tis impossible. the exercise of Wisdom & discretion by Leaders is necessary in both cases, especially in the latter, in order as far as 'tis possible, to accomodate, & to pave the way for Satisfaction to every one.

A month after the Declaration of Independence, the South Carolina planter Henry Laurens was wrestling with the challenges of political mobilization. Laurens observed the internal struggles that arose out of the break from British rule: the elite "Leaders" of South Carolina now had to manage the "murmuring" of a variety of groups if they hoped to establish a new, more representative government. This required wise accommodation, the granting of "satisfaction," or concessions to various segments of society. Mobilization was also a rough business, with "some damage" involved in the turbulent process of revolution. The planters and merchants who dominated Charleston and South Carolina, like the gentry in other colonies, did their best to attain social cohesion and political consensus. More than the elite leaders in other colonies, Charleston grandees were particularly successful at retaining control as they mobilized their city and province to resist British imperial policies and eventually separate from Great Britain.[1]

It was no accident that Laurens used a household metaphor to express his experience of the American Revolution. Americans conceived of the Revolution from the vantage point of their households. The prospect of leaving the monarchical household was daunting enough; at the same time, Americans needed to ensure that the entire family would get along in the new, republican household that they were establishing. Under ordinary circumstances, urban households were places where elite city dwellers maintained control over their society. Yet the crowded streets teemed with potential intruders, external threats that might undermine the gentry's authority. Furthermore, the mobilization of disempowered groups within the household—such as women and slaves—also raised the possibility for social and political upheaval. Planters like Laurens worried about the destabilization of their households and, more generally, the patriarchal slave society of South Carolina. Urban crowds, the potential for slave revolts, and questions about the domestic economy and political economy of South Carolina all made resistance to Great Britain a risky endeavor. Householders in the American cities worried about threats from a variety of quarters during these turbulent transformations, and the urban house-hold was critical in helping to shape the Revolutionary movement.

The ferment of the Revolutionary era subjected elite urbanites to new challenges and threats. These challenges sprang from within their own households among women and slaves, from their neighbors in the back-country and among less wealthy white city dwellers, and from countermo-bilizing forces that supported the imperial government. Within the household, Charlestonians in power sought to mediate between man and woman, parent and child, master and slave, black and white, metropolis and province, city and hinterland. In a burgeoning republican society, Charlestonians confronted new notions about the household as the basis of their society and polity. Excessive luxury, enslavement of blacks, conflict with Great Britain, and social challenges from women, urban artisans, and farmers from the Carolina backcountry caused anxieties among the Charleston planters, yet these planters maintained a striking degree of social cohesion by the end of the eighteenth century.[2] With a sufficient exercise of power and a judicious management of political mobilization, the gentry found it conceivable to change their habitation, while still rest-ing on the strong foundation of social and political power that they had enjoyed before.

Like urban churches, urban households engaged in a spirited conversa-tion or interaction with one another amid the grid of streets. City dwellers built their houses within the limits of space and construction costs. These houses announced their owners' status and preferences and drew upon both local and transatlantic cultures. Although the local culture of a town like Charleston encouraged some similarity among the houses, the dynamic colonial cities also displayed a rich variety of building types. Some houses had first-floor workrooms or storefronts facing the street; others tried their best to replicate the pastoral ideals of the colonial countryside; still others emanated the sort of grandeur and wealth that would have been familiar on the finest streets in London.[3]

Homeowners infused their households with many layers of significance and meaning. In its most basic respect, the house was a place of security: shelter from the weather (in its mundane and cataclysmic forms) and security from intruders. The household comprised the most basic social and economic unit—the family—which, among wealthy Carolinians like Henry Laurens, generally included extended kin networks and black slaves. In the traditional, hierarchical world of colonial South Carolina, the household was a place of paternal protection and of deference, a place to manage and contain chattel slaves. Northern households had such hierarchies, too, with the head of household managing a family as well as apprentices, servants, and slaves. The household was also property—an estate for transmission to one's heirs and a place to affirm one's status through the conspicuous display of objects. The household was a place to receive guests: to offer hospitality and extend shelter, repast, and entertainment to visitors.[4]

South Carolina planters making a fortune in rice (and later indigo) often split their time between Charleston townhouses and country plantations. As a result, many planters attempted to replicate the social patterns of the plantation household on their urban house lots in Charleston.[5] The owners of these townhouses discovered that city life presented a very different landscape from that of their rural plantations, which militated against an exact duplication of the plantation ideal. The politics, economy, sociability, and demography of the city presented unique opportunities and challenges for the wealthy leaders of Charleston. With roughly 12,000 residents on the eve of the Revolution, Charleston by far contained the greatest concentration of people in the South, the wealthiest families in all of British North America, more black slaves than Boston, New York, and Philadelphia combined, a unique aggregation of free black Americans, and more non-slaveholding whites than any parish in the Lowcountry.[6] Economically, Charleston's merchant "houses" dominated the foreign trade of South Carolina, North Carolina, and Georgia. Many elite Charleston families had economic concerns within the urban center, as well as the rural plantations.[7] Elite Charlestonians sought connections with their regional neighbors for trade and sociability, which helped strengthen a South Carolinian identity. At the same time, Charleston's urban environment brought it closer to the northern American cities and the metropolis of London.

After the fire of 1740 and the hurricane of 1752, Charleston was teeming with newly built houses. Moses Lopez believed in 1764 that the city had doubled in size since he had last been there in 1742: "One cannot go anywhere where one does not see new buildings and large and small houses started, half finished, and almost finished."[8] Charlestonians were building to accommodate their families and slaves or rent properties (at exorbitant rates) to less wealthy neighbors. They fashioned workspaces in their back lots where they hoped to supervise their bound laborers. They imported the finest furniture, tableware, and clothing or had local craftsmen closely emulate such imports, and conspicuously displayed the Englishness of their fine wares within their households. As they played host to visitors and travelers throughout the Atlantic world and the Carolina hinterland, they

Figure 4.1. During the middle of the eighteenth century, even many of a town's wealthiest residents lived in close proximity to the bustle of commercial life. This view shows the houses along Bay Street on the Charleston waterfront. *View of Charleston, South Carolina*, by Bishop Roberts. Charleston, South Carolina, 1735–39. *The Colonial Williamsburg Foundation.*

positioned themselves as the leading members of their society and as Anglicized consumers in the transatlantic economy.[9]

Bay Street, the hopping commercial thoroughfare along the wharves, provides a taste of Charleston houses in relationship to one another (fig. 4.1). In 1751, Governor James Glen recorded one hundred houses and lots on Bay Street, "the principal part of the town for carrying on most kinds of business." Fifty-two of the lots were inhabited by merchants and their warehouses, seventeen were vacant lots, nine were taverns, dram shops, or "lodgings," five entries had names (Gibbs, John Remmington, "Pinckney Law," Alexander Vanderdussen, Esq., and Scott), and four housed widows. There were two ship carpenters and two more attorneys, a druggist, physician, dancing school, barber, collector's clerk, milliner, bricklayer, blacksmith, and goldsmith. The lowest annual house rent was £40, a widow's, while the highest was £900, a merchant's. In 1774, an English traveler described these houses as "good large sized houses tolerable regularly built, some of brick, but for the most part intirely of wood decently painted." The houses' balconies "command a fine prospect of the ships in the bay and of the open sea without the bar." Families lived in the upper part of the houses, maintaining some privacy and restriction as they observed the scene below. At the same time, even the inner recesses of the house were never far from the noisy world of commerce, the customers shuffling in and out of the shops on the first floor. On Bay Street one observed "a perpetual moving scene of what is doing at the wharfs and in the street below."[10] Streets bustled with customers seeking a drink, a haircut, a dancing lesson, or legal counsel. While the wealthiest Charlestonians stood out on such a streetscape, Bay Street also demonstrated their proximity to other inhabitants of the contentious city streets.

In the middle of the eighteenth century, Henry Laurens conducted his successful commercial enterprise from his counting house on Bay Street, while maintaining a residence on Broad Street.[11] In this part of Charleston he would have observed a city that was noisy, sweltering, dirty, crowded, cramped, noisome, squalid, and prone to fires.[12] Residents complained that their neighbors threw rubbish in the streets, built uncovered necessary houses for their slaves, or sold spirits to blacks at disorderly houses.[13] Travelers noted that Charlestonians "must generally keep their windows open all the time because of the great heat," but open windows meant that sand from the roads would annoy anyone in the front rooms, "together with swarms of mosqueto's and flies," which were "excessive troublesome and disagreeable all the warm weather season."[14] To escape the heat, Charleston residents generally located their bedrooms and dining rooms on the second floor, and the wealthiest tried to build houses at a distance from their neighbors: a German visitor wrote, "In proportion to its circumference, Charleston could really have more houses. However, . . . the houses are mostly built so far apart that the breeze can blow into the streets from all sides."[15] Although the Charleston gentry boasted "large handsome modern built brick houses," there were also merely "decent looking large houses," while "the greatest part are middling looking wooden ones."[16] Charleston offered a diverse array of households, where the estates of the wealthiest were prominent landmarks amidst a complex urban landscape.

In this dense part of the city (fig. 4.2), the household's public nature helped define its public role. Each household had a responsibility to ensure the welfare of the entire community. The city's fire-masters, for instance, could enter "the houses, out-houses, stables and yards, of every owner or tenant" to make sure they had their buckets and ladders or search for combustible materials, and to extinguish fires and even destroy buildings.[17] Thus, interdependence characterized the urban world of Charleston. The city may have been the fourth largest in British North America, but the narrow stretch of blocks between the Ashley and Cooper rivers encouraged face-to-face interactions and even networks of mutual assistance. While the proximity of urban households encouraged interdependence, a man of property and esteem was ideally *in*dependent as well. Charlestonians, especially among the elite, worked to maintain this independence and exert control over the relationships among households.[18]

By the early 1760s, Laurens was ready to retire from the stresses of mercantile life and city living as he devoted more of his assets to plantation lands. To signify his retirement and his new landed lifestyle, he began construction of a house on a sprawling four-acre property in the suburb of Ansonborough (fig. 4.3). Charleston was expanding northward into this area during these years, as residents sought new lots just outside the crowded confines of the old walled city.[19] Laurens had a Scottish carpenter named Robert Deans build the new house, which he initially called "Rattray Green" after a previous owner of the property, and the Laurens

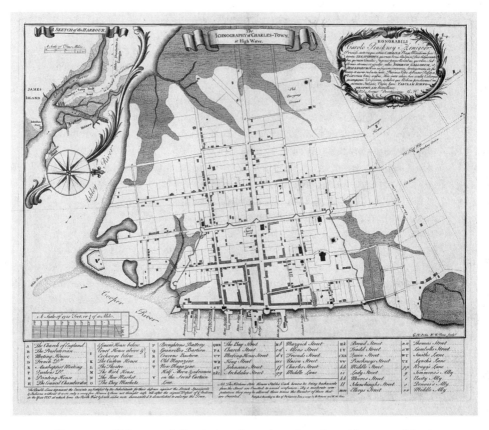

Figure 4.2. This map of Charleston shows how densely residences and business clustered along Bay Street at the bottom of the map and Tradd Street and Broad Street, which run westward from the shoreline. *The Ichnography of Charles-town, at High Water*. A sketch of the harbour, by William Henry Toms, after Bishop Roberts and George Hunter. 1739. *I. N. Phelps Stokes Collection, Miriam and Ira D. Wallach Division of Art, Prints and Photographs, The New York Public Library, Astor, Lenox and Tilden Foundations.*

family was occupying it by the beginning of 1764.[20] Rattray Green was an elevated house with four rooms per floor and a jerkin head roof (i.e., a roof with a clipped gable). Distinguished visitors entering the house probably first encountered the hall (the largest room on the first floor) or the ornate library; for meals, they might be invited upstairs to the dining room or withdrawing room. Servants coming from the work yard probably entered through a rear door, where subsidiary rooms were typically located. As in most wealthy South Carolina households, urban as well as rural, many subsidiary functions at Rattray Green were relegated to outbuildings, such as the stabling of horses, the preparation of food, and Laurens's business transactions in the counting house.[21]

Figure 4.3. Henry Laurens's house, known as Rattray Green, was a large and impressive suburban mansion when the family first occupied it in 1764. Here Laurens cultivated his garden, managed his land and slaves, and displayed his fine consumer goods. The family took a photograph of the house before it was demolished in 1916. Photograph of Henry Laurens House. Date unknown. *Collection of John Laurens III, Charleston, SC.*

Rattray Green represented Laurens's arrival among the colonial planter elite, a class of gentlemen who sat relatively unified atop the pyramid of social, political and economic control in city and country. They extended their power over the wider community as civic leaders and property owners, over their families as patriarchs, and over their slaves as masters. With their economic success and cultural achievements, these Charlestonians also expected to enjoy liberty under the British constitution and their rightful share of social dignity. South Carolina's leaders surrounded themselves with objects of luxury that bespoke the grandeur and refinement of their metropolitan exports, their cosmopolitan membership in a transatlantic empire, and their preeminent status within that empire. Through the glittering array of objects and the grandeur of their houses, elite Charlestonians were able to identify one another and distinguish themselves from the lower orders of society. Their urban neighbors and their visitors could only envy, covet, or resent their conspicuous and aggressive display of objects of refinement and authority. The members of the Charleston gentry also kept their own *political* objects in view, one of which was to protect their status and authority.[22]

Laurens regarded Rattray Green as a country house in the fashion of an English squire, and he emphasized its rural qualities. When Laurens returned from a long trip to England in 1774, all he wanted was to be "left with the Freedom of an English Man, encouraged to plant & Cultivate my

Vine & my Fig Tree, from a well grounded assurance that I may Sit quietly under them & enjoy the fruit of my Labour, as my own property, not to be taken from me but by my own Consent."[23] The pride of the Ansonborough property was not just the house itself but the gardens, reminiscent of those found at villas along the Thames (fig. 4.4). In 1768, Laurens wrote, "Mrs. [Eleanor] Laurens takes great delight in Gardening & we content ourselves upon moderate Fare in a quiet rural Life . . . . And I am so well contented with my Situation that no other Motive but the Good of my Country or Family could tempt me to remove from it."[24] Laurens looked forward to the experimental products of his garden providing "public benefit," as he shared in the scientific endeavors that occupied many gentlemen of his day.[25] He appreciated another significant benefit of his new suburban location during a heat wave in 1765: "I am now as cool as a cucumber & not a moist thread, while the People who come from below say that those in the midst of the Town are suffocating."[26] Rattray Green still stood close to Charleston proper, and Laurens encouraged his friends to stay there on their way downtown.[27] Thus Rattray Green served all of the functions of the Southern and Charlestonian household: it provided security and shelter for the family, and it allowed for supervision of slave labor. The house allowed Henry Laurens to demonstrate his paternal authority, distinguish himself as a member of the elite, and announce his patriarchal status, in part by offering hospitality to guests. The house allowed him to compete with other wealthy homeowners in town (and in other Atlantic cities) through the display of genteel finery, and it helped him to maintain his connections to Charleston and its networks of communication, socialization, governance, science, and trade. Yet Laurens was not living in his new house for very long when the internal and external threats to the Charleston household became vividly apparent.

The Laurens home may have been located at some distance from the bustle of Charleston, but it was still within easy reach. When building his house, therefore, Laurens, like other householders, needed to consider the situation of his house in relation to the rest of the city, and resolve questions of access to his house. The floor plan of Rattray Green probably included a formal means of access for the processional welcoming of distinguished guests. Whenever Laurens mentioned his house in his correspondence, it was to invite visitors to stay with him during their travels to Charleston.[28] Social life in Charleston often revolved around the private household. Horse races, plays, operas, concerts, balls, lectures, a library, and clubs enlivened the city's public social life, and the private home was a crucial element of this network. Visitors such as Josiah Quincy Jr. and Pelatiah Webster recounted their stays in Charleston as a series of dinner invitations.[29] Even John Tobler, who averred that in Charleston, "as everywhere, the wicked outnumber the godly," also noted that Charlestonians "are very obliging and kind to strangers and poor people."[30] The rules of hospitality and household access were known to all South Carolinians.

Figure 4.4. This map of Charleston shows the location of Rattray Green and its large gardens in relationship to the town. Laurens may have moved away from his neighbors in 1764, but local crowds still knocked at his door during the Stamp Act disturbances of 1765. "A Sketch of the Operations before Charlestown, South Carolina, 1780 [and] A Sketch of Sr. Peter Parker's Attack on Fort Moultrie June 28th 1776," by T. Conder, sculpt. Excerpt. In *History of the Rise, Progress, and Establishment of the Independence of the United States of America*, by William Gordon. 4 vols. London, printed for the author, 1788. *The Library Company of Philadelphia.*

When Laurens's neighbors violated these rules during the Stamp Act Crisis, therefore, it must have struck him as a terrible affront.

On October 19, 1765, crowds carried effigies through the streets, culminating in an assault on the house of appointed stamp inspector George Saxby. Supporters and opponents of the Stamp Act interpreted the incident differently. Lieutenant Governor William Bull issued a proclamation describing how "a number of persons unknown, did, on Saturday night last assemble together, and in a riotous and tumultuous manner, enter the house . . . , and did there commit several outrages and acts of violence." Peter Timothy's *South Carolina Gazette*, however, reported that the two thousand protesters did only "small injuries to the windows. . . . No outrages whatever were committed during the whole procession, except the trifling damage done to Mr. Saxby's house, whose furniture, 'twas said, had been mostly removed into the country ten days before." Timothy emphasized that many exercised "great prudence" and "influence" to restrain the large crowd. Had the house's caretaker replied more rapidly to the crowd's inquiries about whether there were stamps within, even the broken windows might have been prevented. After searching the house and finding no stamps, the crowd proceeded onward. The crowd had acted with such restraint that its participants merely bumped up against Saxby's windows. But Timothy and Bull were both well aware that the assault on Saxby's house might have been worse—just as house assaults had resulted in much more damage in Boston, Newport, and New York City.[31]

Four days later, the crowd focused on Henry Laurens. Laurens himself had wondered what would become of "our Estates, particularly ours who depend upon Commerce," if Parliament passed even more ruinous laws for North America. Yet unlike many Americans, he consequently advocated compliance with the Stamp Act.[32] This position was not sufficiently radical for supporters of Christopher Gadsden, a South Carolina representative to the Stamp Act Congress who months later would write that he was "ready to sacrifice at a Moment's Warning on the Altar of Liberty & in the Cause of my Country" his life and "clear Estate."[33] While Gadsden was quick to sacrifice his estate rather than live under British tyranny, Laurens was more cautious about gambling his estate on a rash protest against Parliament. Such caution might be risky in an urban setting, however, when the majority of one's neighbors disagreed. Laurens miscalculated the strength of political mobilization against the Stamp Act.

At midnight on October 23, Laurens "heard a most violent thumping & confus'd Noise at my Western door & Chamber Window, & soon distinguish'd the sounds of *Liberty, Liberty & Stamp'd Paper, Open your doors* & let us Search your House & *Cellars*." Confronting a crowd of sixty to eighty sailors and townsmen (many of whom he recognized), Laurens claimed he had no stamped paper, and "when I found that no fair words would pacify them I accused them with cruelty to a poor Sick Woman far gone with Child & produced Mrs. Laurens shrieking & wringing her hands." The crowd assured him that they merely wanted to *search* his house, not damage it, its contents, or its inhabitants. Laurens, still offended at this affront to his elite status, hesitated until it seemed the crowd was two minutes away from beating down his door. The rioters conducted a superficial search of his house, counting house, cellar and stable, and tried unsuccessfully to compel from him either an oath or a renunciation of certain friendships. As they retired, they gave Laurens three cheers, wished him good night, and said, "We hope the poor Lady will do well." Laurens was amazed that the drunk, armed crowd "did not do one penny damage to my Garden" and not fifteen shillings damage to his fence, gate, or house. At the same time, the event had so distressed his pregnant wife that Laurens spent the next few days giving her constant attention at home. The child, James, died ten years later, and Laurens would recall the 1765 incident and lament that misfortune had followed the boy since before his birth.[34]

Laurens was mortified that these uninvited guests had compelled him to allow a search of his house and grounds. In his own home, the crowd had threatened the standing that he should have enjoyed as a Charleston patriarch. Like Andrew Oliver, Charles Paxton, William Story, Benjamin Hallowell, and Thomas Hutchinson in Boston; like Dr. Thomas Moffat, Augustus Johnson, and Martin Howard Jr. in Newport; like Major Thomas James and Charles Williams in New York; and like John Hughes in Philadelphia, Laurens and Saxby were forced to confront the powerful forces of mobilization that coalesced in the cities as a result of the Stamp Act. Just as firemen mobilized to pull down a burning house to save the entire town, so urban crowds had mobilized to pull down the houses of offenders to save the entire town from the threat of oppressive taxation. No doubt this was why mechanics organized as the "Charleston Fire Company," resolving in 1766 to destroy the persons and property of those who facilitated the use of stamped papers. To attack a house was to ritually attack the owner, to purge a city of a disease in the interest of the public good. The house was a symbol of a person's political and social authority. These urban townhouses were not isolated manor houses—instead, homeowners had to contend with their near neighbors. At moments of crisis, elite city dwellers might be dependent on the goodwill of these neighbors for their authority and even their safety.[35]

In the following days, after Saxby declared he would not execute his office, Charleston celebrated in grand style. "By three o'clock," the *Gazette* reported, "every one had retired to his own home, and all was peace and good order . . . the town has ever since been remarkably composed. The damage done to Mr. Saxby's windows, (not amounting to five pounds sterling) and whatever loss has been sustained, *if any*, we are told, is, or will be, made good. And thus happily has ended an affair from which the most terrible consequences were apprehended."[36] Most Charlestonians could now remain secure in their homes, awaiting Parliament's repeal of the detested act. Unlike other cities in the North, Charleston had sustained very little damage, and the gentry had managed to keep order. Nevertheless, Laurens and other members of the Charleston gentry would carry the lessons of the Stamp Act crisis with them over the next decade. As Laurens emerged as a leader of the resistance to matriarchal Great Britain, he and his wealthy allies would need to maintain their neighbors' "Satisfaction," lest their own houses fall victim to urban unrest. Elites who wished to remain safely in power could not afford to separate themselves too much from their neighbors or from the popular will.[37]

In all cities and towns, the tavern might be a place for social organization, the courthouse and town watch often served as institutions for political authority and policing, the marketplace helped organize economic management, the church and schoolhouse supervised cultural fulfillment and perpetuation, and the streets became avenues for the formation of identity. Yet at the end of the day, city dwellers returned to their houses to enact these functions all over again—and in Charleston, the household was arguably the most important site for such enactment. The leaders of resistance to parliamentary taxation needed the taverns, government buildings, churches, and the streets, to mobilize their neighbors. Above all, they needed to persuade their neighbors within and among the houses of the urban landscape.[38]

During the Stamp Act crisis, the gentry's homes and estates faced threats from both unconstitutional British taxation, on the one hand, and unlawful riotous destruction, on the other. The goal during subsequent conflicts with Britain would be to restrain the populace while combating the more enduring threat from Parliament. In the aftermath of the Townshend duties, the household became a crucial site of political mobilization. Americans had come to embrace the exciting new variety of consumer goods that had come ashore during the eighteenth century. Those who sought to resist British taxation hit upon the idea of boycotting these goods as a way of disrupting the British economy and motivating Parliament to repeal its new laws. Household consumption was reinforcing American dependence upon Great Britain, and self-abnegation might be the key to preserving American liberty. Charlestonians, who were particularly prosperous and especially devoted to British goods, could not avoid contending with this question. Nine of the ten richest men in British North America were South Carolinians, and Charleston District was the wealthiest in North America, with a mean aggregate wealth per inventoried estate that tripled the mean of its closest rival. Charleston houses spilled over with an abundance of these expensive goods; china, clocks, silver plate, mahogany furniture, and looking glasses represented the epitome of expense and elegance.[39]

A lightning strike on November 14, 1771, illuminated the interior of Henry Laurens's house for posterity. The blast shattered a large China bowl, a pair of tureens, several glass toys, three large looking glasses, a thermometer, and two sconce glasses; splintered a closet door, shelves, and the top of a chest of drawers; cracked some of the wainscoting and plaster;

ruined a portrait frame; drove glass shards into a mahogany desk; damaged two clocks, the chimney, and some prints; and melted pewter dishes and the silver handles of knives and other plate, as well as "a Brass warming Pan and a Tin japanned Waiter." Bed quilts flew from the closet. A harpsichord was, incredibly, unharmed. The glass panes of a book case were in shards, but the case itself survived. Of the nine or ten people on the property, only one sustained serious injury: "Satira," a black slave, "had her right Arm & hand much burn'd by the Lightning" as she was working near the chimney in a separate kitchen building.[40] Laurens wept with joy that on this occasion his brother's family and most of "their innocent Dependants" had been "miraculously preserv'd."[41]

By conveying the dominance of the gentry, these objects had enduring political importance. During debates over nonimportation, the political character of material goods took on a more controversial cast. Americans' first attempt at nonimportation, in response to the Stamp Act, had been somewhat haphazard.[42] The Townshend Acts of 1767, however, politicized the consumption of imported goods in dramatic ways. All over the continent, newspapers trumpeting nonimportation agreements drew Americans together in their protest against imperial taxation. In 1769, South Carolinians protested the acts by resolving to promote North American manufactures and refrain from importing most British goods: "We will use the utmost OECONOMY, in our Persons, Families, Houses, and Furniture." Charlestonians thought of nonimportation in terms of family. One writer asked his "Brother" planters, "How can we look at our children" if Carolinians did not protest the Revenue Acts by means of nonimportation? "Let us then, AT LAST, follow the example of our brother sufferers in the Northern Colonies, and encourage the making our own manufactures."[43] Radicals enjoined each other as brothers, for the sake of their children, to defend their right to be taxed only by their own elected representatives. Political mobilization required South Carolinians to look outward, toward the northern cities, to find like-minded urban thinkers. At the same time, Charlestonians also looked inward, thinking of their own households as both a reminder of the stakes and a platform from which each individual family could stage its protest.

During the Townshend duties crisis, Laurens's retirement to a luxurious life at Rattray Green made him the object of criticism. Supporters of the British government challenged his new life of comfort and his position of provincial authority. Aggressive British customs officers seized two of Laurens's ships and Laurens sued for damages. He published pamphlets in his own defense, warning of the tyranny of customs officials. In the process, he purported to decry objects of imported luxury, since these articles "tend to impoverish the Community, by promoting Luxury, Idleness and Debauchery."[44] Egerton Leigh, the vice-admiralty judge who ruled on the case, replied by attacking Laurens's hypocritical sanctimony. Laurens professed to have retired from the slave trade for moral reasons, after having built Rattray Green with his mercantile wealth (including that from slave imports). Now Laurens lived aloof as "the first man in a new street," casting an "idle gaze from his parlour window" at the world. Leigh suggested that his opponent's ungentlemanly actions made him better suited for "lodging in the common [gaol] of Charles-Town" than the "*pure air* which Ansonborough affords."[45] Laurens scorned this empty threat as a "vague swaggering Assumption of Power which was never vested in him," though he seemed defensive about Leigh's remarks on the slave trade.[46] By mocking Laurens's idleness, comfort, and hypocrisy, Leigh challenged Laurens's self-possession and, by extension, the legitimacy of his domestic and political authority. In the mind of Leigh and other supporters of government, such authority rightly belonged with king and Parliament. The judge decried Laurens's life of luxury, implying that anyone who resisted Parliament was unfit to enjoy his seat of power.

Radicals criticized luxury with almost the same thought in mind—any patriot who continued to import British consumer goods and who refused to express solidarity through a boycott was conceding his or her dependence upon Parliament and Great Britain. These radicals needed to make strident appeals, because consumption was at the center of Charleston's household life, and the city would need to set the example for the surrounding hinterland. Ebenezer Hazard wrote that Charlestonians "appear to pay more attention to dress than any thing else."[47] J. Hector St. John de Crèvecoeur remarked on "the elegance of their houses, their sumptuous furniture, as well as the magnificence of their tables," while Carl Bauer in 1780 could attest, "We seldom entered a house in which we did not find almost all furniture of mahogany and also very much silverware." Governor James Glen wrote in 1751 of the "many houses that have cost a thousand and twelve hundred pound sterling. The furniture in those houses must be very considerable and plate begins to shine upon their side boards, and in proportion as they thrive they delight to have good things from England."[48] Wealthy Charlestonians conspicuously displayed the English trappings of their fine wares within the households and out-of-doors; David Ramsay feared they were becoming "fond of British manners even to excess." Consumer goods had corrupted American cities all over the continent, and the countryside was not far behind.[49]

Charleston planters worried that their slaves, too, not just their white families and neighbors, were participating in this consumer economy. Slaveholders worried that if black slaves had access to markets, they would steal from their masters in order to trade for consumer goods. Furthermore, these goods might provide slaves with a sense of self-esteem, allowing them to break out of the masters' paternalistic thrall. It was bad enough (though generally tolerated) when rural plantation slaves claimed a right to the produce they grew in their gardens on Sundays. Slaves sometimes defended this right quite fiercely, even though technically a slave could not own property, because a slave *was* property. Slaveholders intended that liquor, food, and clothing be privileges or rewards that the master granted to slaves, not something that might become a source of independence. Slave porters were holding out for higher wages. Boatmen were running rum on the side. Black men and women in the Charleston marketplace charged hefty prices for country produce. These savvy, defiant participants in the market could spend the money on consumer goods for their families, on gambling, or on wearing "clothes much above the condition of slaves," as the South Carolina legislature and Charleston grand jury complained. While whites intended that their own consumption (or withholding of consumption) would be a statement of economic or political independence, they did not intend for their own slaves to follow the same logic. Conservative elites in northern cities made some of the same complaints about lower-class whites, criticizing those that dressed above their station or otherwise presumptuously participated in the elite world of goods. The confidence man Tom Bell, who operated up and down the American coast during the middle of the eighteenth century, challenged the exclusivity of the colonial gentry by dressing like wealthy people and displaying their polite mannerisms. A poor white thief with the right skills and background could pass as a gentleman by dressing and behaving in the right way. Blacks, separated from whites by their visible racial characteristics, did not have the same opportunities as a trickster like Tom Bell. Nevertheless, for poor blacks and poor whites, consumer goods could create avenues for social mobility and challenges to authority. As a result, many elite city dwellers nursed a desire to limit the expanding scope of consumption.[50]

As a result of their strong attachments to a life of consumption, many Charlestonians retained their fondness for new and imported clothing well after the Townshend Acts went into effect. When supporters of nonimportation asked them to wear homespun, they replied, *"That's not the thing,"* and resisted the critics of fashionable culture.[51] A civic impasse threatened to strangle the boycott in its cradle, and as long as Charlestonians continued to consume, radicals and moralists would continue voicing their concern that luxury was polluting the city. Eventually, through extralegal policing and the drawing up of subscription lists, South Carolinians convinced more and more merchants to forgo importing British goods. While some were reluctant to suspend consumption for the sake of country, Charlestonians mobilized to remind their neighbors of the importance of acting in accordance with the public good.[52]

During the nonimportation debates, Charleston patriarchs who favored resistance to Parliament attempted to enlist the help of women. Women generally had a subordinate role in the household. Men had already appropriated exclusively male spaces such as the tavern and statehouse for political mobilization, and they dominated the dining room, parlor, and hall, when mixed groups mingled in these spaces. Married women were expected to remain dependent upon their husbands, and even wealthy women were limited to a select group of refined (not to say confined) leisurely activities.

Eliza Lucas Pinckney maintained a civil correspondence with her extended kin network and managed the family's resources in the absence of her husband and sons. She could discuss intellectual treatises and exercise her interest in botany, but then she was a relative exception. There is some evidence that elite women might have had the opportunity to carve distinct spaces for themselves in certain household rooms, such as the bedroom or at the tea table, and even discuss politics in such venues. Women had the greatest opportunity to negotiate a social, economic, and political role for themselves in the household, where they shared in the responsibility for entertaining, economic management, communication with friends and relatives, display of social status, their children's education, transmission of inherited property, the purchase of consumer goods, and shaping the household itself. If they were to take a role in political mobilization, the household—particularly the urban household at the center of influence—would be the best place for them to make their stand.[53] Charleston's white women did not take up the spinning wheel like women in Newport and Boston. The mobilization of Charleston's white women more generally invoked their role as consumers rather than producers.[54]

In 1769, Gadsden wrote that it would be "impossible to succeed" without the help of women, and he was optimistic about their participation. "None in the world are better œconomists, make better wives, or more tender mothers, than *ours*," he wrote. "Only let their husbands point out the necessity of such a conduct; convince them, that it is the only thing that can save them and their children, from distress, slavery, and disgrace; their affections will then soon be awakened, and co-operate with their reason." Women, with their interest in preserving the family and the household, would see the logic of the radicals' arguments. Even as Gadsden elevated these virtuous women, the stipulation that husbands would "point out" the advantages of nonimportation may better reflect the reality of how men believed household decisions should be made. Gadsden insisted that women "are not such absolute slaves to dress as hath been too often and too sneeringly represented." Women would obey their husbands, therefore, or they would be likened to slaves.[55]

An opponent of Gadsden's, meanwhile, mocked women's "entire complaisance to their Lords and Masters," and wrote satirically that he did not doubt that their dutifulness, obedience, hospitality, and diligent attendance to "domestic affairs, will lead them to be directors in matters of the highest consequences; and by their frequent attendance upon political debates, and being so often admitted to the gentlemen's council, they certainly will be much the properest persons to manage an affair of so much consequence to the American world." Radicals attempted to enlist women in their cause, even if it entailed subtle coercion, while their opponents made it clear that women, as subordinate, nonpolitical beings, did not matter at all. Many believed that a person's attention to domestic affairs and admittance to "gentlemen's council" were mutually exclusive.[56]

One writer, posing as "MARGERY DISTAFF—CONDITIONALLY," used nonimportation as a vehicle for criticizing the luxurious and sinful life of Carolina men. "*Women* think, it would tend to but very little good Purpose, were they to *card* and *spin*, whilst the *Men* are racking their Brains, in contriving how to *dissipate* their *Time* and *Money*, in what they call PARTIES OF PLEASURE." Distaff lamented that each night of the week, men would frequent clubs or taverns, gamble away their money on cockfights and horse races, stay up late and "*impair their Healths* by the intemperate Use of Spiritous Liquors." Women, by contrast, pursued "innocent Amusements" such as attending balls or assemblies, spending time with acquaintances, and attending to their families. Thus, women's spinning of homespun cloth would be contingent, the author wrote, on men's less profligate behavior and improved domestic economy.[57] The household had become a key site of mobilization in the battle over nonimportation, where firm commitments to virtue and domestic economy were crucial for staving off the pernicious influence of British goods and government. Yet Distaff's gestures toward spinning also strike the reader as rather idealized and detached, perhaps because slavery divorced many white women from actual spinning.

During the tea boycott of 1774, colonists enjoined one another to adopt agreements of nonconsumption, not merely relying on merchants for signing articles of nonimportation. Nonconsumption would involve an even broader segment of the American population to participate in political mobilization. In the aftermath of the Boston Tea Party and the forcible rejection of tea shipments in Charleston, as well as New York and Philadelphia, city dwellers led Americans to develop a new, shared identity that was linked to the abjuration of tea drinking. The physician David Ramsay called tea drinking "a political absurdity" that threatened to "blow up the liberties of America." Married women, in particular, Ramsay wrote, ought to have regard for their "unborn posterity." Radicals could now encourage every household in America to participate in the rejection of a consumer good and a rejection of the mother country from whence it came.[58]

Tea tables were a fixture in Charleston households, including Laurens's, where multiple "tea tables" were mentioned as having been damaged during the lightning strike of 1771.[59] Women's role became particularly important during the boycott of tea (fig. 4.5). In the *South Carolina Gazette and Country Journal*, Presbyterian minister William Tennent addressed "the Ladies of South Carolina" as "an admirer of your sex" and urged them to learn about the dispute surrounding the 1773 Tea Act. Knowing the effects of "long habit," British officials judged that rather than give up the "darling tea-dish ceremony," Charleston women would "suffer this empire to be enslaved and your husbands throats to be cut." Tennent reminded them, "It is tea that has kept all America trembling for years. It is tea that has brought vengeance upon Boston; and you may thank your tea-tables that thousands are now cruelly deprived of their bread." As he appealed to their compassion, fear, and love of family, Tennent insisted that he was not asking women to give up

Figure 4.5. Although this cartoon appears to lampoon American women who boycotted the consumption of imported tea from Great Britain, it also recognizes these women's participation in political acts during the Tea Act crisis. *A Society of Patriotic Ladies, at Edenton in North Carolina*, artist unknown. London: Printed for R. Sayer and J. Bennett, 1775. *Library of Congress, Prints and Photographs Division, LC-USZ62-12711.*

their comfort or daily necessities, only "a mere ceremony—worse, a time consuming poison; a thing which no one can pretend ever did any good." Boycotting tea would chastise Parliament and the East India Company, "convince them that American patriotism extends even to the fair sex, and discourage any future attempts to enslave us." A grateful nation of husbands would add their respect to "the deliverers of their country" to their usual tenderness as husbands and lovers. Tennent's epistle lacks the sarcasm or coercion of earlier appeals to women; instead, he evinces gratitude as he criticizes the tea ceremony rather than its matrons.[60]

South Carolina leaders, while allowing that women might have more political agency than they had suspected in 1769, still expected to draft women into the measures against Britain. Men needed women, and their decision-making power now seemed to count. Women used this opportunity to enter the public sphere, harness their household responsibilities to imperial resistance, and promote the tea boycott. Henry Laurens paid a visit to Gabriel Manigault on June 7, 1775, and found that the aging patrician had reluctantly signed the Association, the nonconsumption agreement that the Continental Congress had adopted in October 1774. Referring to Manigault's wife Anne, Laurens wrote: "the poor old Lady!, from expressions which She dropped, I concluded her persuasions had prevailed."[61] If many Charlestonians had embraced nonimportation and its limits upon consumption with reluctance, some women used the agreements as opportunities to make their voices heard within the patriarchal household. Debates over private domestic economy were now central to the public debate. The household was crucial in shaping the resistance to Great Britain, and women were in turn crucial in shaping the household.

Women in Charleston and other cities recognized the role that they were playing in the resistance to Great Britain. After participating in spinning bees in Newport, after contributing to nonimportation, and after marching with crowds in Boston, white women could feel that they had contributed to the public good.[62] It was in this spirit that Abigail Adams famously wrote to her husband, John, in Philadelphia that he ought to "Remember the Ladies." She continued, "Do not put such unlimited power into the hands of the Husbands. . . . If particular care and attention is not paid to the Ladies we are determined to foment a Rebellion, and will not hold ourselves bound by any Laws in which we have no voice, or Representation." Abigail Adams was of course not representative of all female Americans, and a social rebellion by American women never materialized. Yet the domestic upheaval of the months leading up to the Declaration of Independence impressed itself upon John Adams's mind. "We have been told that our Struggle has loosened the bands of Government every where," he wrote. In addition to the "numerous and powerfull" discontented women, he had heard "That Children and Apprentices were disobedient—that schools and Colledges were grown turbulent—that Indians slighted their Guardians and Negroes grew insolent to their Masters." John Adams laughed off his wife's admonishments, but understood (or at least tried to reassure her) that men would be "obliged to go fair, and softly." To gentlemen with a conservative bent, the American resistance was stirring up a hornet's nest of domestic crises, and concessions would be necessary.[63]

In this lament Adams echoed Henry Laurens, who had found early in 1775 that he and his fellow Lowcountry planters were "miserably Situated between two Fires." One danger was "Kingly tyranny," and "popular" tyranny the other. Charleston's enlightened patriarchs would need "Skilful pilotage" to steer between the two. Laurens feared that "habit & Custom" would reconcile the people to royal tyranny—that British goods coupled with imperial prerogative would corrupt Americans. Having experienced mob disturbances in his own home during the Stamp Act encounter, Laurens believed popular tyranny to be even worse, since it was more violent, although at least mob disturbances were "only temporary."[64] The events of the Revolutionary crisis repeatedly taught Charleston planters that their households were under threat, either from the corrupting influence of British goods within, the violence of popular elements without, or the abuse of imperial power withal.

In this particular discussion of "popular tyranny," Laurens referred to backcountry agitators. As the imperial crisis led to the outbreak of violence in 1775, Charleston planters hoped that they could turn to their white neighbors, the residents of the Carolina backcountry. Unfortunately, since 1765, backcountry residents had fumed at Charleston and the Lowcountry for failing to protect them. These "Regulators" sought to restore order in a land torn by war against the Cherokees and brutal criminal gangs. They burned the houses of those suspected of aiding the criminals. Underrepresented in the legislature, they castigated "the Selfish Views of those, whose Fortune and Estates, are in or near *Charlestown*—which makes them endeavour, That all Matters and Things shall center there, however detrimental to the Body Politic." The selfishness of Laurens and his fellow Charlestonians had left "the Back Country without Law, Gospel, or the least Advantage, of Civil or Religious Life—No Churches, Ministers, Schools, Order, Discipline No Roads Cut—Bridges built—Causeys made for them."[65] Thus, during the Stamp Act crisis Christopher Gadsden had written, "Very little depends on the Example of the Towns in any part of the unpensioned part of the Continent."[66] Where Charleston patriarchs did not perform their obligations, casting only an idle gaze from their parlor windows, they could not expect dutiful neighbors.

As they attempted to drum up support for the Continental Congress and its resolves, Laurens and his fellow aristocrats needed backcountry residents on their side. Elite Charlestonians therefore made political concessions that they hoped would pacify their fellow colonists upriver. To some extent they worried that upcountry settlers (who tended to have fewer slaves) and other nonslaveholding farmers would push for policies that threatened the slave society and domestic arrangements of Lowcountry planters. The Charleston gentry also did not want these farmers from upriver expressing their grievances by breaking windows, trampling gardens, or burning houses in Charleston—after all, armed farmers had marched toward provincial capitals to air their grievances in both New York and Pennsylvania during the 1760s. Even more worrisome was the fact that the royal governor, William Campbell, was encouraging backcountry loyalists who were arming in support of the British government.[67]

During a 1775 debate in the General Assembly over measures against Great Britain, Laurens called upon his backcountry "Brethren" and emphasized the importance of staving off "disunion." The backcountry residents "murmured against delay & procrastination," suspecting that "the Rich Rice-Planter & the Towns-people had Schemed to weary them out in order to thin the House & transact business their own way." To ward off these complaints, Laurens "proceeded to make an offer of my own House for the accomodation of any whose pockets were not Sufficiently Stored for defraying the expence of Town Lodgings." The backcountrymen responded positively: "Several Voices were heard as in a Shout 'they were Satisfied contented & determined to Sit out the necessary time.'" Laurens may have intended this as a sincere expression of goodwill or a gambit for exacting obedience in return for paternal hospitality. In either case, the exchange is significant because Laurens displayed his willingness to share his house, as well as the larger house of a burgeoning republican South Carolina, with these heretofore underrepresented farmers.[68] Months later, the Council of Safety (Henry Laurens presiding) sent William Henry Drayton and the Reverend Tennent with Baptist minister Oliver Hart to recruit backcountry farmers for support of the new Provincial Congress.[69] Laurens had learned that it was not enough to enjoy the fruits of his life's labor from Rattray Green: he needed to extend paternal protection to his neighbors, too, if he wanted to retain his household authority. Eventually, South Carolina leaders would learn that the expansion of slavery was the surest way to create a common interest among the province's white farmers.[70]

Closer to home, the mechanics of Charleston also challenged the hegemony of the gentry. In 1773, the visiting Josiah Quincy of Massachusetts muttered that the South Carolina legislature failed to serve the interests of the entire polity: "Who do they represent? The laborer, the mechanic, the tradesman, the farmer, husbandman or yeoman? No. The representatives are almost if not wholly rich planters. The Planting interest is therefore represented, but I conceive nothing else (*as it ought to be*)."[71] Many of Charleston's mechanics agreed, and they had been mobilizing since their formation of the Fellowship Society in 1762 and the participation of many of that society's members in the protests against the Stamp Act. Although many mechanics owned slaves, some feared competition from enslaved urban laborers, and such dissension (which arose particularly in the 1780s) might also threaten the planters' interests. Mechanics had helped to build the houses and furnishings of Charleston, and they felt they had a stake in the governance of the city and polity. While some elite Charlestonians had scoffed at the political participation of mechanics in 1770, four years later the mechanics began to enjoy greater representation in extralegal committees protesting the actions of Great Britain. This phenomenon was reflected in cities throughout America. The power of the Charleston mechanics was evident in March 1775, when they made "sharp opposition" and raised "a clamour" and "harangues" against the landing of furniture and horses in violation of the Articles of Association. Planters who had homes in Charleston, and who witnessed the crowds who tarred and feathered three supposed Loyalists in 1775, must have worried about keeping themselves safe from their radical neighbors. The earlier Stamp Act riots and subsequent crowd actions in the northern cities had already demonstrated that a dissatisfied urban populace could be a direct threat to the household.[72]

It was crucial for Charleston's resistance leaders to attract widespread, orderly allegiance to the Revolutionary regime, and to cut the cords tying South Carolina to Great Britain. In a letter to Loyalist backcountry planter Thomas Fletchall in July 1775, Henry Laurens illustrated the various components of society that patriot planters wished to incorporate into their orderly republican household. Laurens wrote that the thirteen colonies were associating as armed opponents of unjust British power. "When this Colony in particular is alarmed by threats of Invasions by the British Soldiery, of instigated Insurrections by our Negroes, of inroads by the Neighbouring Tribes of Indians & of what is far more to be dreaded the practices & insidious acts of false Brethren it cannot be wondred at, that we are anxiously desirous of enrolling the number of our freinds upon whom we may firmly rely for aid in the day of trial.[73] Other North Americans were now brothers. Domestic rebellions were among the Carolinians' greatest fear. And the treachery of "false Brethren" left the patriots searching for friends upon whom they could rely in a crisis. If the Charleston gentry could not keep its house in order and mobilize its neighbors successfully, Great Britain would be successful in its mission to enslave them.

Elite city dwellers wanted to avoid the dangerous possibility of a disorderly city where workers and blacks asserted themselves, and so they attempted to use their legal, political, economic, and social power to keep their extended urban families in check. Visitors noted that members of Charleston's gentry were "accustomed to tyrannize from their infancy, they carry with them a disposition to treat all mankind in the same manner they have been used to treat their Negroes."[74] Henry Laurens might have agreed. "We cannot trust any other eyes or judgement but our own in every minute article," he wrote. "Negroes are faithless, & Workmen exceedingly careless."[75] Thousands of runaway slaves mocked elite pretensions to control, and asserted their own self-worth with their skills, language, and clothing. The cosmopolitan cities such as Charleston were often ideal destinations for these runaways, where blacks could attain anonymity and blend in as free city dwellers themselves.[76]

Members of the Charleston gentry shared their households with these black slaves whose labor they exploited. A Hessian officer observed that in Charleston "Everything is done by Negroes, whom one finds in great numbers in all houses, and to excess in many. Those who serve their masters in the city and in the country are kept well." These slaves lived "either in the house with the master, or else an adjacent house serves as their dwelling."[77] The fantastic wealth and aristocratic style of the gentry depended upon the labor of slaves, and Charleston, more than any other city in British North America, was the urban center of slave trading and slave households. As elite slave-owners divided their time between their plantations in the Carolina hinterland and their Charleston townhouses, they often maintained paternalistic control at a distance from their plantations.[78] While in Charleston, these white masters also supervised slave laborers in the yard and kitchens: whites idealized these workspaces as plantations in miniature, shrunk to fit the geographically confined urban landscape. Whites and blacks experienced different landscapes within a Charleston estate. Whites had access to normal avenues of movement through entrance halls, drawing rooms, and dining rooms. Blacks either used the same routes (though invisibly) or used less formal routes of access such as the passageways between rooms and the carriage way outdoors, routes that provided them with intimate access to the household, even as whites intended them to remain subordinate.[79]

Whites could not keep blacks confined to household control. Blacks ventured onto the streets of Charleston, into the marketplaces and their own social gatherings, adding to the dynamic character of the city. An English traveler in 1774 exaggerated the ratio of blacks to whites as being three to one,[80] while a naval officer began his 1769 poem on Charleston with the line, "Black and white all mix'd together."[81] Blacks often enjoyed a certain degree of privacy in the urban spaces and interstices where they congregated. They had time and space to hire themselves out, to participate in public markets, and to compete with whites. In other words, blacks had time and space for a certain degree of freedom, including for activities their masters regarded as subversive. With greater economic and socializing opportunities, Charleston's black residents seemed to "have a peculiar kind of pride and bearing; without degenerating into insolence, it at least gives the impression that they regard a man who is not their master simply as a man, not a tyrant."[82] This was the kind of kindling that might spark revolutionary action in Charleston—just as it had inspired acts of arson in New York City in 1741, or a coordinated legal push for emancipation in Massachusetts. Small wonder, then, that after the Revolutionary War Charlestonians would pass an ordinance limiting the gatherings of blacks.[83]

White Carolinians imagined that they could maintain the same stable supervision over black people in the city as they did on the plantation. Yet disruptive urban conditions continually frustrated their pretensions to control. Henry Laurens famously admonished his brother's slaves "to behave with great circumspection" and warned them against the "treatchery of pretended freinds & false witnesses" if they associated with blacks outside the family.[84] Years before, his slave John (also called Footbea) had "Strolled away from my house, about midnight" in an almost casual way. Since Footbea apparently spoke no English, "he is supposed to have been decoyed away by some other negro."[85] Just as customers and families penetrated the boundaries between street and household, so the free blacks who were often seen gaming in the streets might form contacts with domestic servants inside the master's domain. Laurens hoped that by sending his errant slave Abram "away from some pernicious connexions that he has made with Slaves in Charles Town I do believe he will behave much better and become a Valuable Slave."[86] Laurens idealized the patriarchal relationship he had with his slaves, where he exchanged humane protection for dutiful and grateful obedience. Thus, when a slave was recalcitrant or ran away, he blamed the outside influences of the urban black community.[87] While such an attitude may have been self-serving, this interplay between the city's broader social forces and the household was a key factor in Charleston's domestic life.

Henry Laurens's views on slavery were in some ways more moderate than those of his neighbors, although he, too, expected obedience from his slaves and declined to manumit them and thus deprive his children of an inherited "Estate."[88] Not choosing to free their slaves, therefore, planters needed to use the traditional means of coercion to keep their households in order, using corporal and capital punishments within a set of laws that the visiting Josiah Quincy found depraved and disgraceful.[89] Charlestonians had long suspected that blacks were holding secret councils outside of town or within the city proper, at dram shops, "the houses of *free negroes*, apartments *hired to slaves*, or the *kitchens* of such Gentlemen as frequently retire, with their families, into the country, for a few days." These urban spaces and other interstices could become seedbeds of slave revolt if they were not cautiously monitored and patrolled.[90] Southern planters had reason to be nervous: already antislavery sentiments were flowering in many of the northern cities, blacks were suing for their own freedom in Massachusetts, and manumission was all the rage among Philadelphia Quakers.[91] Perhaps planters could keep their country slaves out of the loop, but not so the cosmopolitan blacks of Charleston. Maintaining control over slaves would protect Charleston's domestic tranquility and, not incidentally, the patriarchal power of Charleston's elite planters.

Quincy reported in 1773, "Many people express great fears of an insurrection." Indeed, slave insurrections had taken place previously in South Carolina's history, and Charleston was very often the focal point. In March 1759, a free black (or mixed-race) man named Philip John (or Jones) was whipped and branded for plotting a black revolt against Charleston whites. When John refused to give up on his plans for an uprising and the establishment of an independent black government, the South Carolina government had him executed. During the imperial crisis, blacks demonstrated that they were paying attention to the language of liberty that rolled off presses and tongues—it was a language with great potential for mobilization. Whites anxiously swapped rumors of possible insurrections, patrolled the streets even more diligently, and responded harshly when they suspected rebellion. In December 1765, the wife of merchant Isaac Huger overheard two slaves plotting a Christmas Eve insurrection, which led to panic and an increase in armed patrols over the coming weeks. In mid-January,

Laurens reported, "some Negroes had mimick'd their betters in crying out '*Liberty*'" in the streets, and the colony banished a "sad Dog" of a man to save appearances. After the outbreak of the Revolution in April 1775, things heated up further. In the spring of 1775, the merchant Josiah Smith Jr. wrote, "Our Province is at present in a ticklish Situation, on account of our numerous Domesticks, who have been deluded by some villainous Persons into the notion of being all set free." Blacks took advantage of wartime chaos with all its potential interruptions of authority, and thousands made their own bids for freedom by deserting their masters. As Christopher Gadsden wrote to Samuel Adams, "We are a weak Colony from the Number of Negroes we have amongst us, and therefore exposed to more formid[able?] ministerial Tricks." In December 1775, the panicked Council of Safety in Charleston sent a force to attack a group of runaways—these blacks had collected on nearby Sullivan's Island to harass the Patriot war effort in conjunction with British warships.[92]

The suppression of black rebellion was a crucial component of white unity—not just for the elites, but for middling and lower class whites too. During the summer of 1775, the South Carolina Council of Safety accused Thomas Jeremiah, a successful free black fisherman, harbor pilot, property owner, and firefighter, of insurrection. Jeremiah, who may well have been a leader among black city dwellers, had allegedly declared his anticipation of a "great war coming" that would "help the poor Negroes." A number of prominent whites believed Jeremiah's protestations of innocence, among them Governor William Campbell. Henry Laurens, president of the Council of Safety, ignored these objections. He upheld Jeremiah's conviction and subsequent execution not only to set an example for urban blacks but also to pacify urban whites. "Although I know none of the out of Door Secrets of the people, & carefully avoid Such knowledge," he wrote, "yet I had heard enough to fill me with horror from a prospect of what might be done by Men enraged as Men would have been if a pardon had been Issued." Laurens did not want to repeat the events of 1765, when the resentment of Charleston crowds had threatened the sanctity of his home in retaliation for his unpopular actions. Instead, Laurens sought to maintain the domestic order as the prevailing opinion of Charleston understood it. Jeremiah's white neighbors feared his prominence. Crowd action and the criminal justice system worked in tandem, encouraging slaves and free blacks to remain in humble submission and thereby denying them the fruits of Revolutionary political mobilization.[93]

Historians have long remarked on the connection between Carolinians' fear of British enslavement and their own possession of blacks as chattel. Christopher Gadsden, like his neighbors, sought to avert "the abject Slavery intended for us and our posterity."[94] Slave owners ferociously defended their liberty because they witnessed the suppression of blacks firsthand. Charlestonians most likely perceived this issue in terms of domestic order. More than anywhere else in the colony, Charleston planters stood at the nexus of connections to Great Britain and to the rural plantations in the city's vast southern hinterland. The threat of slave insurrection and the impending break from Great Britain each loomed large in Charlestonians' minds. Charlestonians sought to maintain order in their own houses partly out of fear and partly because they knew they were about to cause significant disruption in the imperial household.

Charlestonians' ideas about the ordering of their society and polity had significant overtones of domesticity: each household represented another family, another building block that comprised South Carolina society. The ministers of Charleston's two Anglican churches each deployed domestic ideology as a means of keeping elite society afloat during the turbulent Revolutionary period. In February 1775, the Reverend Robert Smith of St. Philip's Church enjoined his parishioners to ask themselves, "Whatever is my part in life, do I act it well,—and contribute my share to public happiness? As a member of *the Community*, a parent, a master, or a servant; is my behaviour such as the eye of Heaven can approve?" He continued, "Let each of us in our sphere & station contribute our share.—let those on whom *a kind Providence* has lavish'd her favours, *Men of large fortunes and extensive influence* lead the way, & thousands will catch the fashion from them. . . . they will find it in the willing obedience of their children, in the duty & faithfulness of their dependents; . . . in the *love &* approbation of their country;— and the admiration & fear of their enemies." Moderation and reverence for God would help men of influence maintain a mighty household in which dependents and neighbors obediently took their cues from their masters and betters.[95] Laurens himself had called upon his "Country Men, the Rich & opulent" to make a "virtuous opposition" to Parliament.[96] Smith had armed the wealthy members of his Charleston congregation with the ideological weaponry that would help them retain control.

John Bullman, the rector of St. Michael's Church, had given an earlier sermon that proved to be much less palatable to his audience. In August 1774, he railed against the sedition of the "illeterate Mechanic," a man "who cannot perhaps govern his own household" or pay his debts, and who "presumes he is qualified to dictate how the State should be governed." Such men had no right to take advantage of urban proximity and pry into his "Neighbour's Secrets." When Bullman offered some of the same distaste for crowds as Laurens had expressed, the parishioners resented Bullman's implication that white mechanics had any less ability to govern their households and voice their opinions in government. The vestry had Bullman summarily dismissed from his pulpit. It was one thing to invoke slaves and Indian tribes to play upon the fears of white Carolinians; it was quite another to impugn the white mechanics, backcountrymen, and (to a lesser extent) women who were fighting to gain acceptance as members of the emerging provincial polity.[97]

When the Continental Congress signed the Declaration of Independence in Philadelphia, the Charleston gentry reacted with fears for their own households foremost in their minds. Laurens captured the dual position of the Charleston gentry: on the one hand, revolutionaries were moving to a republican household to replace the imperial house they had outgrown; on the other hand, provincial patriarchs were trying to maintain control over the dissident, "murmuring" elements of South Carolina society: disenfranchised backcountry residents, despised mechanics, haughty Loyalists, and oppressed blacks. As he worried about these squabbles, Laurens waxed nostalgic about the royal house he left behind. "Even at this Moment," he wrote, "my heart is full of the lively sensations of a dutiful Son, thrust by the hand of violence out of a Father's House into the wide World."[98] Political mobilization thus induced fear in those householders who had the most to lose.

Laurens's use of a paternal metaphor rather than the more common maternal metaphor was significant: in the aftermath of the Declaration of Independence, it was not just the ministers in the vaguely defined "mother country" who had abandoned them. Two years earlier, Christopher Gadsden limited himself to a criticism of "our Mother-in-Law's Intentions" toward Boston, while William Henry Drayton lamented, "Alas! instead of parental tenderness, we experience a step-mother's severity—instead of justice, we receive marks of the most unfeeling ingratitude!"[99] Now, in the year of Thomas Paine's king-killing harangues, it was the king and father who had violently brought America to swordpoint. Although Laurens objected to Britain's methods for chastising America "as a Child," he looked forward to the possibility that Anglo-Americans could "restore mutual Love & a happy intercourse between the Roots & the transplanted branches of the family."[100] Charleston's ruling aristocracy, masters of their domains, tried to resolve a whirlwind of domestic conflicts while retaining power in the American republic. The royal, paternal, imperial household was the only one that they had known, yet they were becoming increasingly unified in their rejection of British control.

The planters knew it was time to abandon the royal household. As early as February 1775, Henry Laurens was having visions of his "pretty Garden" as "the parading Ground of Some Scots Regiment & my House occupied by a half Score Red Coats their Motto 'down with America.'"[101] Laurens now saw British encroachment as a direct threat to his house and grounds. A relative moderate compared to radicals like Drayton and Gadsden, Laurens advocated "compassion & indulgence" to those slow to embrace the Revolutionary cause. "Some people live in a House contentedly till it is disjointed & ready to tumble about their Ears, they Say it will last their time without the trouble or expence of repairs[:] an Instance of great Indolence, but tis generally found in quiet in offensive people."[102] The lifelong cultural, economic, and political attachments to Britain were hard to shake; nevertheless, Laurens and his fellow Patriots became more aggressive about repairs—they knew the time had come to tear down the old house and erect a "new Mansion." By 1776, Great Britain could no longer be called "home."

Perhaps it is fitting that the final chapter of civil government under the Crown in Charleston took place in one of its finest houses in the summer of 1775, the home of slave trader Miles Brewton. According to a family legend, Brewton and Laurens met with Lord William Campbell, South Carolina's last royal governor, warning him that it would be dangerous to remain in the city. Charleston's radicals were itching to place the governor under house arrest. Brewton sympathized with the British, while Laurens himself probably mused over his own encounters with Charleston crowds a decade before. One wonders if Campbell noted the irony of these Charleston grandees heralding the collapse of British government in Brewton's sumptuous home, one of the most opulent examples of Georgian architecture, fashionable craftsmanship, and imported furnishings in the city—"the grandest hall" Josiah Quincy had "ever beheld." Although Charlestonians would continue to import consumer goods into their homes after the Revolution, after the destructive years of war and occupation they would forever decline the hospitality and authority of the Crown. The fearful Campbell took refuge aboard the H.M.S. *Tamar* in Charleston harbor on September 15, and Brewton would perish at sea later that year. Laurens remained with his fellow genteel rebels to manage the "new Mansion," and the slaves Brewton and his competitors had sold them, to their satisfaction. They trusted, as the Reverend Smith had promised, that men of opulence and influence would lead the way.[103]

Elite city dwellers in the northern colonies also shared the same hopes that their leadership would continue unquestioned. In New York City in 1774, Gouverneur Morris stood on a balcony and reflected that the gentry was increasingly fearful of the poor and would never be able to secure its superiority by expecting people to remain ignorant. In Boston, Thomas Hutchinson could never understand why the people did not show their due obedience to government, although he had earlier expressed his concern that "the common people in this town and country live too well." Such feelings very often motivated elite city dwellers and suburbanites to work against revolutionary mobilization and to align themselves with the British crown as Loyalists.[104] As war escalated, and as many Americans reevaluated their economic and political relationship to Great Britain, they also set about building a new republican household, with a new political and social order. Women, especially elite white women, found their roles as consumers, hostesses, wives, and mothers (and sometimes, principally in the north, as traders and producers) achieve political significance. Working and middling-class city dwellers and backcountry farmers saw the Revolution as an opportunity to expand the polity, so that the American political world might no longer be the exclusive dwelling of the coastal gentry. Blacks saw the Revolution as an opportunity to resist, escape, or otherwise assert greater control over their own lives. All of these movements made urban merchants and planters anxious, but the isolated protests of household dependents never translated into widespread collective action. The gentry continued to dominate colonial politics, economy, and society, suc-cessfully perpetuating their lifestyle of luxury and mastery.[105]

After all, the household was the repository of tradition, and although slaves and women found occasions for escaping their bonds, unequal treat-ment of women and slaves persisted after peace returned, particularly in Charleston. The Charleston gentry successfully retained their dominance atop the urban social system and the colony as a whole, continuing to enjoy a preponderance of wealth, status, and political power even as they contin-ued to contend with the fluidity and disruption inherent in urban life. The political leaders of the Continental Congress and the Constitutional Convention helped the South Carolina elite by shying away from instituting any changes in the tricky areas of slavery and household government. Charleston's upper crust, allied with other urban elites, continued to express their authority, and their mansions continued to project power and self-assurance. Where they could, they attempted to tighten their authority. Where they could not, they grudgingly permitted new liberties or allowed new groups to assert their rights within the republican household.[106]

Colonial city dwellers were accustomed to ordering their world along the lines of master and servant or slave; black and white; man and woman; adult and child; and elite, middling, and poor. Although the turbulence of the Revolutionary era invited challenges to this political and social order, Charleston planters (minus some of the outright Loyalists) remained atop their perch after the formation of the United States. Unified politically and socially, they were better placed than the legislators in most of the other thirteen colonies to rule without much dissent. They owed their domi-nance in part to their ownership of the most enviable houses in the city and country; from their management of plantations, they had learned how to exact obedience, through negotiated persuasion or concession where pos-sible and through coercion as an ever-present last resort. Through their management of urban households, they had learned how to defend their sta-tus in a competitive local environment and in a wider transatlantic context. As the leaders of a slave society, Charlestonians used the club of racial subjection and thereby found it easier to maintain white solidarity than their counterparts did in northern cities, where social relations among whites were more fractious.[107]

Chapter 5

PHILADELPHIA POLITICS, IN AND OUT OF DOORS, 1742–76

In the middle of May 1776, only four colonies of the thirteen in rebellion—all of them in the Mid-Atlantic—had not granted their delegates permission to vote for American independence in the Continental Congress. Though Congress was meeting in Philadelphia, Pennsylvania's own Assembly had instructed its delegates not to vote for independence—and in a recent election, the candidates in favor of independence had suffered a narrow defeat. Then on May 8, Philadelphians heard cannons booming on the Delaware River. They learned that the king was sending Hessian mercenaries to crush the American rebellion. Suddenly they began brushing up on the writings of Thomas Paine and Massachusetts delegate John Adams. On May 20, four or five thousand people gathered in the rain in the State House Yard. Looming over them was the State House, where the Continental Congress met and where Pennsylvania's leaders had governed the province for two generations. In the Yard, the crowd denounced the Assembly's instructions to the province's congressional delegation and called for a constitutional convention that would supersede the Assembly. Beaten, the Assembly had little choice but to allow the delegation to vote as they saw fit on the question of independence. Soon afterward the Assembly itself dissolved, and Pennsylvanians set about establishing a new government.[1]

Philadelphians mobilized to question and then reject the formal authority of Parliament, the king, and their provincial Assembly. Much of this activity took place "out of doors," or outside of formal legislative sessions. Philadelphians embraced independence more slowly than the residents of many other cities, partly because of the entrenched power that Pennsylvania's leaders held inside the State House. From this towering edifice, the governing forces of the province had consolidated their power in an oligarchic system and projected this power over a wide distance. The king and Parliament in London also projected their power through their emissaries in Pennsylvania's government. While Pennsylvanians respected the strength of the State House, they also challenged the authority of their government. During the eighteenth century they gradually began to chip away at the power of Penn's successors and the Assembly. The provincial leaders of Pennsylvania could see these challenges unfolding in the open spaces that lay before the city's public buildings. Politics "out of doors," literally and metaphorically, became a significant factor in Philadelphia's political life in the decades before the American Revolution.

The use of the phrase "out of doors" to refer to extraparliamentary activity probably arose during the middle of the seventeenth century. Before 1640, parliamentary proceedings in England were largely secret, and public opinion had little role in government. Critics of government did find some outlets for raising political awareness such as ribald verses, leaks from politicians, and some limited petitioning. Nevertheless, communication between "indoor" and "outdoor" political actors was limited.[2] English people began speaking and writing even more openly about politics out of doors during the English Civil Wars, as censorship lifted and the production of printed material exploded. Petitions to Parliament and public opinion "without-doors" increasingly became sources of politicians' fears and concerns. After 1660, people were regularly discussing politics in taverns. This exchange of public opinion in turn contributed to party politics in England. Members of political parties found themselves compelled to respond to the opinions of people out of doors.[3]

For much of the eighteenth century, the legislatures of Great Britain and Pennsylvania were essentially under one-party rule or "political oligarchy." A vibrant culture of opposition, the "politics of the excluded," developed as the wider populace found room for political expression in the streets, taverns, clubs, churches, and the press.[4] During this period, Henry St. John Bolingbroke wrote that the people had a good effect on Parliament by restraining its excesses. "The cries of the people, and the terror of approaching elections, have defeated the most dangerous projects for beggaring and enslaving the nation; and the majority without doors hath obliged the majority within doors to truckle to the minority."[5] The politics of the people without doors, in other words, could counteract an entrenched cabal within Parliament.

Legislators and their supporters sometimes criticized their opponents for acting in secret, underhanded ways "out of doors," outside the purview of an orderly parliamentary debate.[6] As the lines between parliamentary politics and extraparliamentary politics became blurred, rival politicians might accuse one another of manipulating crowds or the electorate. Legislators sometimes spoke of grumblings "out of doors" as a way of taking the pulse of the people they represented—or as a way of dismissing them as "rabble."[7] Members of the so-called governing classes often expressed disdain for popular politics and its practitioners; they referred to "the poor unthinking and deluded multitude" or "the mob," as distinct from propertied men.

Alternatively, politicians might invoke "the people" as an inclusive term that applied to all adult men.[8] Those who were themselves outside of the legislature could claim the mantle of righteousness if their opinions had currency "out of doors," especially when they perceived the legislature itself as unrepresentative of the people's interests. The different uses of the phrase "out of doors" cut to the very heart of important questions about representation, openness, sovereignty, and public opinion.[9]

Politics out of doors could encompass petitioning; expressions of public opinion in speeches and in print; political interactions in places such as the tavern; machinations and negotiations outside Parliament; and crowd action, from parades to riots. Many of these activities flourished especially in cities, alongside (and sometimes in coordination with) politicking *within* doors.[10] As we have seen, much of urban political mobilization took place out of doors during the imperial crisis in America: crowd action on the waterfront and in the streets and, more broadly, the discussions and actions that unfolded outside courthouses, legislative assemblies, and Parliament. This chapter will examine the Court House and State House of Philadelphia, the city's formal structures of power, as well as the ways in which Philadelphians operating out of doors helped to subvert Pennsylvania's formal political institutions.[11]

The first formal structure of government in Philadelphia was the Town Hall or Court House, which was later demolished in 1837 (fig. 5.1). Ashamed that Philadelphia magistrates were presiding over courts in an alehouse, the Provincial Council began work on a Court House in 1709 and completed construction in 1718. For its location, town leaders chose the center of the densest part of the city: the middle of High Street (Market Street) at its intersection with Second Street, across the street from the Friends' "Great Meetinghouse." In time, mapmakers measured distances from Philadelphia using the Court House as their starting point. The Town House was literally central, the hub from which all spokes extended, and it was central to the political culture of the province and the city (fig. 5.2).[12]

This court complex projected civic power and reinforced a sense of civic consciousness and responsibility. During construction, the city council rearranged the city's market stalls to run behind the Court House, up Market Street to the west, and eventually established the public markets in a permanent brick market house. The courtroom was on the second story, atop an open arcade used for markets and auctions in a "medieval style." These markets (announced by bells and the Court House clock) helped to foster a sense of interdependence and economic exchange among Philadelphians and the inhabitants of the surrounding countryside. Immigrants took their oaths of allegiance at the Court House, while residents moving out of the province had to post their intentions on the Court House door, to give their creditors a chance to collect. The Court House was the most public place to dispense forms of justice that relied on visibility, and so the pillory, stocks, and whipping post stood just outside. At night,

Old Court House _and_ First Friend's Meeting
Philad.ª
1707
Second _and_ Market St.ˢ
taken down 1837

Figure 5.1. Philadelphia's courthouse sat atop market stalls in the middle of Market Street, across the street from a Quaker meetinghouse. On election days, voters ascended the exterior stairs to cast their ballots. *Old Court House and First Friend's Meeting, Philadª, 1707, Second and Market St.ˢ, taken down 1837,* by Charles A. Poulson, Jr. [1855.] Copied from a drawing presented by John F. Watson to John McAllister. *The Library Company of Philadelphia.*

constables used the building as their base of operations, and the watchmen stored their staffs there. Provincial and municipal leaders published proclamations, ordinances, and legislation at the Court House, and new governors were presented on its steps.[13]

These Court House steps linked the indoor, formal political space with the city outside it. Inhabitants reached the courtroom by ascending one of the

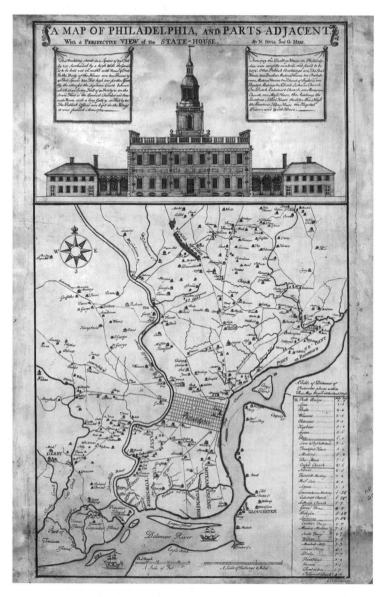

Figure 5.2. Public buildings were central to the printmakers' rendering of greater Philadelphia. The Court House is the only building visible on the city grid, and the mapmakers use it to measure distances to other localities. Meanwhile, the State House atop the print projected elegance and power to its viewers. *A Map of Philadelphia and Parts Adjacent: With a Perspective View of the State-House*, by Nicolas Scull and George Heap. Philadelphia: N. Scull et al., 1752. *Library of Congress, Geography and Map Division.*

two exterior staircases that terminated in a landing before the door. When the governor presented himself, when leaders proclaimed the coronation of a new king or other announcements, or when prominent divines preached from the Court House, they could stand at the top of these steps and speak to the people from a raised height. After the completion of the Court House, city leaders appointed an operative "to Clear the Square at the ffront of the Court House" (where there had formerly been market stalls), creating a public area in Market Street where audiences could gather. The doorway, stairs, and square helped mediate interactions between leaders and their constituents. Still, on annual election days voters had the opportunity to cross this threshold by ascending the north stairway to cast their votes at the door, and descending the south stairway.[14]

In the early 1740s, a dramatic event at the Court House door disrupted Pennsylvania's relatively calm political climate. William Allen was leading the province's proprietary faction, which supported the ruling privileges of William Penn's successors. Great Britain's war with Spain had begun in 1739, and fights were breaking out at the ballot box. The proprietary faction, hoping to strengthen Pennsylvania's wartime defenses, had unsuccessfully petitioned the Board of Trade in London to make it illegal for pacifist Quakers to hold office during wartime. They heard rumors in 1742 that the Quakers were planning to pack the election with unnaturalized Germans, while Quakers in turn suspected that the proprietary party would encourage rough sailors to drive Quaker supporters from the Court House steps on election day. On October 1, these sailors strutted around town and downed drams of rum at the Indian King tavern, threatening to "knock down the Broad Brims," kill one of the Quaker leaders, and disrupt the polls with the claim that they had "as much Right at the Election as the Dutchmen." Eventually a brawl erupted in Market Street before the Court House. While a group of Quakers hid inside the Court House and bolted the doors, the sailors broke some of the building's windows. Eventually, armed Germans and Quakers cleared the sailors from the street and reasserted control over indoor and outdoor space. In the following months, the Quakers solidified their dominance of the Assembly and attempted to punish Allen as an instigator. He did not win reelection to the Assembly for fourteen years. Nevertheless, this group of sailors and proprietary supporters had expressed their frustration at being locked out of the halls of power.[15] Though Philadelphians were usually content to remain at the bottom of the Court House steps and let their leaders govern, with sufficient provocation they might begin agitating out of doors.

By 1742, previous tumults had motivated Pennsylvania legislators to build themselves a State House. When the governor refused to sign the Assembly's paper currency bill in the 1720s during an economic recession, "turbulent Spirits" with "very little at Stake, and scarce any Thing but their Noise and Clamour to distinguish them" had presumed to "insult and menace the Members of this House," which was "to the great Terror of the Inhabitants of the City of Philadelphia in particular, to the Disturbance of the Peace." The governor reflected on this occasion that "Government is sacred; It is from God himself," and urged the suppression of such disorders.

The Assembly at the time had been meeting at the Quaker meetinghouse across the street from the Court House and in private homes. In light of the recent crowd action, the governor and some assemblymen threatened to adjourn to Chester. Instead, at the behest of Philadelphians, they began construction of the State House in the city in 1732 and finally completed additions to it and interior carvings in the mid-1750s. In the decade before the American Revolution, the State House and State House Yard would become the primary places where Philadelphians acted out indoor political conflicts and mobilized out of doors.[16]

The phrase "out of doors" originated as a household term, and the State House drew many characteristics from the everyday architecture of an eighteenth-century dwelling house. In many ways, of course, the State House was unlike any house most Americans had ever seen. At 107 by 45 feet, along with two wing buildings akin to a domestic residence's out-buildings, it was one of the three largest buildings in the colonies. It had a tower and steeple (added in the 1750s), features reserved primarily for churches and government buildings (the original design had a cupola, which sometimes adorned mansions or upper-level taverns). The State House was designed to emanate power: it projected a regularized time with its clock tower, it projected the sounds of celebration or warning with its bell, and it projected grandeur in its style and awe with its height and breadth. The inclusion of the State House elevation in Nicholas Scull and George Heap's map of 1752 (fig. 5.2) transmitted the elegance and power of its host city and province to readers far away. If the Court House was Philadelphia's center, the State House was its icon, a reminder to others of the city's cosmopolitan achievements.[17]

In spite of its uniqueness, the State House also resembled the symmetrical, graceful Georgian households of the time. Reflecting the three-bay facade that many Georgian townhouses shared, the State House had three bays of three windows. Like a fine mansion, the State House had a central hall with a grand, spacious staircase that emphasized pomp and procession and filled the visitor with awe. On either side of this great hall were major rooms for reception and business: the Assembly Room and the Supreme Court. The Philadelphia State House had a second-story long room, where it often held banquets or dancing assemblies, much like the long rooms in George Burns's tavern in New York City, the Thomas Rose house in Charleston, or the City Tavern in Philadelphia (fig. 5.3). Two second-story "private chambers" in the State House included the office of the Governor's Council and a room for the Assembly committees and library. With pilasters and keystone archways, wainscot paneling, turned balusters, trimmed doors and sash windows, a chair rail, and paneled fireplace walls, the architectural treatments resembled those of the finest houses of the Delaware Valley.[18]

Like a Georgian mansion, furthermore, the State House was located on the outskirts of Philadelphia—on Chestnut Street between Fifth Street and

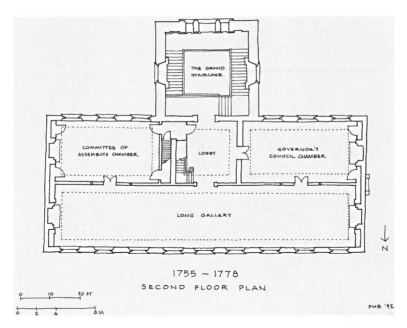

THE GRAND
STAIRCASE

COMMITTEE OF
ASSEMBLYS CHAMBER

LOBBY

GOVERNOR'S
COUNCIL CHAMBER

LONG GALLERY

N

1755 — 1778
SECOND FLOOR PLAN

0   10   20 FT

0   2   4   8 M

PHB '92

Figure 5.3. Like many large residences and taverns in colonial cities, the Philadelphia State House had a long gallery on the second floor that hosted banquets and dances. The gallery also confronted visitors to the governor and council with an intimidating approach. Second Floor Plan of the State House, 1755–78. Reproduced from "Independence Hall Historic Structures Report: Architectural Data Section," by Penelope Hartshorne Batcheler. Philadelphia, 1992. *Independence National Historical Park.*

Sixth Street. As Alexander Graydon recalled, "With the exception of here and there a straggling house, Fifth street might have been called the western extremity of the city" (fig. 5.4).[19] Henry Laurens and other urban gentlemen of the period had sought to escape the bustle and noise of the city (not to mention its tumults) by situating their houses further away: there they could cultivate gardens and ride into town for business in a carriage. The Assembly expressed similar thoughts when they voted to locate the State House on the town's edge, a compromise between the Chester site and the corner of Market Street and Third Street, where many wanted to locate the building. Like Laurens's house, the State House, too, would have green space before it, to render it "more beautiful and commodious." The Assembly forbade construction on the lot south of the State House, mandating that "the said ground shall be enclosed and remain a public open Green and Walks forever." Although the Assembly never followed through with its original vision of planting trees in this area, they did erect a wall enclosing the Yard.[20]

In many ways the designers of the State House made it much less accessible to crowds than the Court House had been. Perhaps, as the scholar Robert St. George has said of Georgian houses, it "imposed a mask of unknowability,"

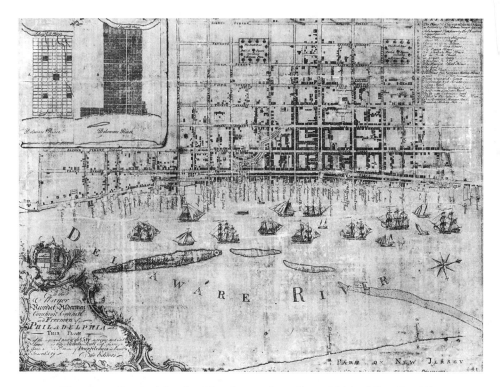

Figure 5.4. Provincial authorities chose a site on the outskirts of the city, at the corner of Fifth and Chestnut streets, for the location of the State House. *To the Mayor, Recorder, Aldermen, Common Council, and Freemen of Philadelphia This Plan of the improved part of the City surveyed and laid down by the late Nicholas Scull, Esq[r]., Surveyor General of the Province of Pennsylvania is humbly inscrib'd by the Editors,* Matthew Clarkson and Mary Biddle. Philadelphia, 1762. *The Library Company of Philadelphia.*

so as to limit access from the outside.[21] The State House was further from the marketplaces and the wharves where sailors and shoppers congregated, and the building was set back from the street rather than sitting among waves of traffic in the center of the road. The wall surrounding the State House Yard—after 1770 it was seven feet high and made of brick—was designed to discourage gatherings (fig. 5.5). A visitor could only access the

Figure 5.5. This map shows the seven-foot high brick wall that surrounded the State House Yard (now Independence Square) in Philadelphia. Ironically this wall, rather than discouraging crowds, lent even greater legitimacy to the outdoor protests that increasingly took place in the State House Yard after 1770. "State House Yard, 1770–1784," in *CAD Atlas of the Archeological and Related Drawings of Independence National Historical Park,* by Paul Y. Inashima. Vol. I. Silver Spring, MD: United States Department of the Interior, 1998. *Independence National Historical Park.*

CHESTNUT STREET

PUMP 1773

PUMP 1773

"INDIAN" SHED
CA.1739 - CA. 1785

WEST WING
1736 - 1812

PIAZZA 1736-1812

CLOCK
1751-1812

STEPS - 1732-1812

THE STATE HOUSE - 1732

TOWER
1750

PIAZZA 1736-1812

COMMITTEE
ROOM &
LIBRARY
1751-CA.1812

EAST WING
1736 - 1812

"INDIAN" SHED
CA.1739 - CA.1785

WHORTLE BERRY AND OTHER BUSHES

7' HIGH BRICK WALL : 1770-1811,1812

FOOTWAY 1785

7' HIGH BRICK WALL : 1770-1811,1812

A FEW TREES ALONG BORDER

A FEW TREES ALONG BORDER

SIXTH STREET

FIFTH STREET

TWO WILLOW TREES OVERHANGING GATE

7' HIGH BRICK WALL : 1770-1812

20' HIGH GATE

WALNUT STREET

STATE HOUSE YARD   1770-1784

SOURCES:
1. HISTORY RESEARCH FILE.
2. ARCHEOLOGICAL FIELD NOTES.
3. C.W. PEALE'S. VIEW OF STATE HOUSE. 1778.
4. GROUND PLAN OF STATE HOUSE. 1785.

20'   0   20'   40'   60'   80'   100'

Yard by walking through or around the State House on the north side, or through an elaborate central gateway with high wooden doors on the south side. By contrast, an inhabitant might pass through the area in front of the Court House every day. Nor could a person scale the walls of the State House from the outside, as one could the Court House, and achieve a feeling of temporary parity on election days (after 1766, county elections were held from nine windows of the State House).[22] Rather, as they climbed to the upper rooms of the State House to meet with the governor or legislators, visitors felt themselves dwarfed in the grand hall and large interior stairwell. The State House conveyed majesty and procession, separation and enclosure. Where listeners might gather to hear a popular preacher like Whitefield before the Court House, the State House and the Yard instead played host to elite men of the Enlightenment, peering through instruments to track the transit of Venus, taking books out of the library, or listening to lectures on anatomy.[23] The State House was built in the spirit of Anglicizing Philadelphia, to shore up its status as a growing cosmopolitan city and project an image of peaceable and orderly government.

The State House helped the governor and Assembly project the authority of the empire and province. The King's Arms hung in the Supreme Court chamber, demonstrating the extension of imperial power and justice through the vessel of the governor and other Crown appointees. The Penn family crest hung in the Assembly Room, a reminder of the proprietors who governed the entire province. Benjamin Franklin asked William Strahan for two sets of Henry Popple's 1733 *Map of the British Empire in America with the French and Spanish Settlements adjacent thereto*, "for the long Gallery and the Assembly Room in the Statehouse." The copy for the Assembly room would be on one side of the door, and Franklin sought "a Map of the whole World, or of Asia, or Africa, or Europe," for the other side; if the world maps were too small to match the size of Popple's, he asked Strahan to increase the size by affixing "some Prospects of principal Cities" on the sides. Thus, visitors to the State House were expected to link the power of their leaders to the breadth of the continent and the entire world. Governors, the Assembly, and mayors hosted banquets and balls in the State House long room to honor the king's birthday, celebrate the king's military victories, welcome the king's gubernatorial appointees, and cheer the king's decision (in 1766) to repeal the Stamp Act. In addition, the governor received diplomatic embassies from Native Americans, treating with them as sovereign powers. Just as the Court House had become the marker for tracing physical distances from Philadelphia, the State House became the marker for tracing lines of political power.[24]

Philadelphians built the State House during a period when the Quakers were tightening their powerful grip on the Assembly. The Assembly had more constituents per representative than any other British colony in North America; Quakers continued to dominate the Assembly despite their diminishing presence among the population, especially in the underrepresented west; and the party extended its reach into local offices. As a result, there were few contested elections, assemblymen accumulated a great deal of seniority in a stable House, and committee assignments favored loyal party men. Within doors, a small, tight-knit group was able to control legislative power in the province. As one of this group's enemies asked in 1764, "Where is the Benefit of our annual Elections if the same Men are to claim Power, as if by Inheritance? It is a Maxim of all Popular Governments, never to continue any sett of Men too long in Power, least they become too big for their fellow Subjects, and erect themselves into an Oligarchy, or the Tyranny of a *few*."[25] The Assembly was able to hover aloof from its constituents: the galleries were generally closed to spectators, the legislature monopolized the publication of reports on their proceedings, and its members heard fewer petitions than most other colonial legislatures.[26]

In 1736, the year after the Pennsylvania Assembly moved into the State House, legislators might have heeded the warning couched in an essay in the *Pennsylvania Gazette*, which explicitly compared government to architecture: "If the Superstructure is too heavy for the Foundation, the Building totters, though assisted by the outward Props of Art." The article argued that "the people" should have their proportionate share in the legislature, so that their collective decisions might advance "the real publick Good."[27] Indeed, many Pennsylvanians resented the Assembly's arrogation of provincial power, especially supporters of the proprietor and Presbyterians who feared Quaker hegemony. The 1742 election riot and subsequent disputes over frontier defense exposed some of the chinks in the Assembly's armor. The oligarchy retained its power within the Assembly, but it faced threats from outside its doors. City dwellers were becoming incensed at imperial policies such as Parliament's new customs duties, and ethnic groups such as the Germans and Scotch-Irish outnumbered Quakers in new counties on the frontier and clamored for equitable representation.[28]

The question of defending the province, which had created tumults in Philadelphia in 1742, arose again at the beginning of the Seven Years' War. In the aftermath of General Edward Braddock's defeat in 1755, many Pennsylvanians became frustrated with the Quaker Assembly for failing to protect the frontier. A judge had even called on conscientious Quaker legislators to resign their seats (which many did, in 1756), in a reprise of the proprietary party's petitions during the previous war. John Hambright, a Lancaster Pike tavernkeeper, led about two hundred westerners into Philadelphia on November 24, 1755, threatening to "tear the whole Members of the legislative body Limb from Limb." According to Joseph Galloway, an Assembly party stalwart, some members of the proprietary faction "dispersed amongst" Hambright's men and "maliciously endeavoured to inflame their Minds against the Assembly." The riotous westerners terrified "the more moderate and reputable Inhabitants of the City," and they achieved their goal—as the Reverend William Smith wrote, "The Assembly have been <u>pelted</u> into a military Law."[29] The governor commissioned a regiment for the city's defense in

February 1756, and they were "review'd . . . in the State-House Square, where they were drawn up under Arms, and made a fine Appearance," prefiguring the musters of the Associators during the 1770s.[30]

In the aftermath of the Seven Years' War, Pontiac's Indian uprising similarly terrified the Pennsylvania frontier. Hundreds of armed men from the town of Paxton, believing the Assembly indifferent to their plight, slaughtered some of the Indians at Conestoga and then threatened the city throughout the winter of 1763–64. The Paxton men marched toward Philadelphia in February 1764, hoping to vent their rage on Indians that were now under the Assembly's protection. On February 4, a crowd of 3,000 people gathered in the State House Yard in the "pouring rain," where Governor John Penn urged them to defend the city. That afternoon, the alarmed Philadelphians (including Quakers) assembled under arms, and on February 5, they learned that the Paxton Boys had crossed the Schuylkill River and encamped a few miles away in Germantown. As in 1742, opponents of the Assembly party had once again forced the pacifist Quakers and their supporters to take up arms before the Court House. While a delegation persuaded the Paxton Boys to disperse, the squabbles between an inactive Assembly (according to its detractors) and dissatisfied citizens had forced politics out of doors.[31]

In the aftermath of the Paxton uprising, Philadelphians were treated to an avalanche of out-of-door protests in the form of pamphlets and (new to Philadelphia) satirical engravings. With three printing houses within a block of Second and Market streets (a major center for taverns and coffeehouses, as well as the markets and courthouse), these cartoons were almost as much of a visible, frontal assault on the Court House as the sailors who were breaking windows in 1742. The schoolmaster David James Dove drew up a satirical verse and commissioned Henry Dawkins to engrave *The Paxton Expedition* (fig. 5.6), which depicted cannons and militiamen gathered before the Court House. The engraving betrays a certain annoyance with the established authority: men at the railings call for "Silence" while the governor announces, "Gentlemen the Affair is punctu[a]lly settled for it, the Gov.ʳ returns you his thanks and dismisses you." Men in the square are arming themselves or cravenly running for cover; accusing each other of lying; calling for grog to be brought into the Quaker Meeting House; and disparaging each other's ethnic and religious groups. Dove chastised the pacifist Quakers for their hypocrisy in arming themselves against fellow Pennsylvanians while refraining from swift action against frontier Indians. His print displays a chaotic, raucous romp unfolding beneath the Court House and its architectural authority.[32] The Court House, located at the center of Philadelphia life, had become the foil for various forms of out-of-doors political expression: electioneering, crowd actions, oral pronouncements, and printed satire.

Over the coming months, Presbyterians formed "a Party in Opposition" to the Quakers, and the two sides launched a flurry of pamphlets at one

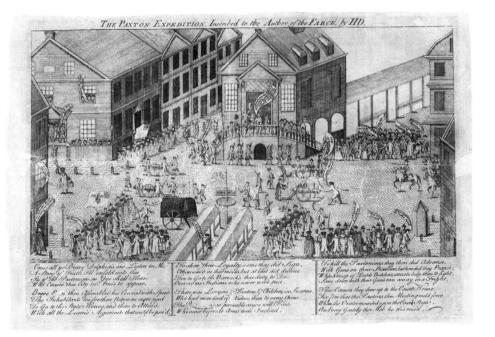

Figure 5.6. This print mocks the Quakers of Philadelphia for arming themselves against white westerners in 1764 while failing to protect the frontier from Indian raids. The Court House serves as the focus of the artist's satirical protest, just as it was the site of various crowd actions during the eighteenth century. *The Paxton Expedition, Inscribed to the Author of the Farce*, by Henry Dawkins. 1764. *I. N. Phelps Stokes Collection, Miriam and Ira D. Wallach Division of Art, Prints and Photographs, The New York Public Library, Astor, Lenox and Tilden Foundations.*

another in an attempt to influence the people out of doors. "A few design-ing men, having engrossed too much power into their hands, are pushing matters beyond all bounds," wrote Dr. John Ewing. "There are twenty-two Quakers in our Assembly, at present, who . . . never fail to contrive matters in such a manner as to afford little or no assistance to the poor distressed Frontiers." Western Pennsylvanians bridled at the Assembly party's smug complacency, and rightly complained that they did not receive propor-tional representation in the Assembly. The Assembly party, for its part, declined to address this problem. One observer wrote, "The Rage of Party Spirit has been as Violent lately in this Province as ever it was." Still, most Pennsylvanians remained "cool Spectators," much to the "Mortification" of the "Sanguine Partizans."[33]

In early 1764, the Assembly party petitioned the king for royal gov-ernment to replace the proprietary charter. The Assembly party was unhappy with proprietary government, saw itself as the champion of the people, and sought imperial intercession to change Pennsylvania's legal status.[34] Benjamin Franklin had undertaken an earlier mission to London, hoping to rally support among Englishmen. The colony's agent, Richard Jackson, was pessimistic, but offered hope that Parliament's insistence on its own constitutional authority was "too refin'd to have much general Weight, when counterpois'd by Popular Opinion." As Franklin reported to the Pennsylvania Assembly, therefore, Jackson had suggested that "before we push our Points in Parliament" they should set about "*removing the Prejudices that Art and Accident have spread among the People of this Country* against us, and obtaining for us *the good Opinion of the Bulk of Mankind without Doors.*" Jackson tried to reassure Franklin that such out-of-doors opinion was the only thing that might restrain the Ministry and the Penn family from denying the people's requests. Franklin hoped to mobilize such influence by publishing a pamphlet of Jackson's in 1759, "calculated to engage the Attention of many Readers, and at the same time efface the bad Impressions receiv'd of us." Thomas Penn, the colony's proprietor, was disdainful: "Appealing to the Publick will always displease the Administration and for that reason I shall not practice it but let them write what they please." Penn knew he could rely on his friends within doors to protect his interests.[35]

As a result, Jackson had some words of warning for Franklin and the Pennsylvania Assembly. "An Administration will probably for the future always be able to support and carry in Parliament whatever they wish to do," and "they will almost always wish to extend the Power of the Crown and themselves both mediately and immediately." Most of the principal ministers, he wrote, "wish to carry their great Points with as little Struggle and Opposition as possible." When the Ministry acted in unpopular ways, they generally did so only when the public was unconcerned with the matters at hand. Using this strategy, the Ministry could remain secure "against any evil Effects" of a "formidable Opposition" within doors, "except what may influence a Clamour without."[36] Franklin's first brush with Parliament must have left him frustrated with his inability to advance political goals out of doors in the face of entrenched interests in Parliament and at court. At the same time, he was developing an understanding of how best to harness "a Clamour without."

Given Franklin's failure, the Pennsylvania Assembly decided to bypass the Ministry and send their petition directly to the king. Having observed the proprietary faction's methods for mustering popular opinion and activity (especially during the violent clashes of 1742 and 1764), the Assembly party branched outward from the halls of power to take the fight out of doors. Galloway, an ally of Franklin's, harangued a crowd in the State House Yard in late March or early April. Franklin printed thousands of free pamphlets defending their positions, as well as 300 copies of the petition. Members of the Assembly party waited at people's houses to solicit signatures and thereby add the weight of Pennsylvania's populace to their address. They held an "open house . . . at a Tavern for all the Blackguards in Town," with "the assistance of Punch and Beer" to coax willing and unwitting signatures. By mid-May they had collected 3,500 signatures in their support, a disproportionate number of these from Philadelphia. This was a meager sampling of the province, however. Though Franklin and his allies got a taste of urban mobilization and its effectiveness, their provincewide quest to alter the legal structures of Pennsylvania's place in the empire was about to fail.[37]

This is not to say that the Assembly party somehow lacked a common touch—indeed, they retained power over the Assembly and could count on solid votes from certain areas of the province. Their enemies, however, successfully exploited fears about defending the province, religious animosity between Presbyterians and Quakers, and a general lack of understanding about the issues that arose between the Assembly and the proprietor. Presbyterians and supporters of the proprietor were unable to use these divisions to build a formal political coalition of their own, but by the end of the summer they succeeded in garnering 15,000 signatures against the solicitation of royal government. "These will at least shew," wrote Attorney General Benjamin Chew (a proprietary appointee), "that the Assembly have express'd their own Wishes only in their Application to the Crown & not the Desires of their Constituents. It is certain that the Assembly have never in all their wild Sallies engaged in a Measure so very disagreable to a great Majority of the People as this is."[38]

The lawyer John Dickinson and others lodged a protest against petitioning the king for a royal government, arguing that the colony should not take such a drastic step "without the almost universal Consent of the People." They worried that Pennsylvania was developing a reputation for "Confusion and Anarchy, through Multitudes of tumultuous and riotous Insurgents." Such tumults were especially visible in the cities, and Philadelphians wanted to think of themselves as more orderly than the people of Boston or New York. Furthermore, Philadelphians did not want to goad Parliament into stationing royal troops in their city to quell the disturbances—that was exactly how anarchy led to tyranny.[39] Dickinson believed that even though "public contests" might disrupt society, they were preferable to perfect calmness in government. When a ruling party became too complacent, such power would not easily allow limits or constraints to be placed upon it.[40] Dickinson's protests irked the Assembly party. Galloway followed Dickinson from the State House one September evening, and tried to seize Dickinson's nose and whack him with his cane. Dickinson warded off the blow, riposted with his stick, and the two grappled for a couple of minutes before bystanders broke up the fight.[41] Galloway's loss of composure out of doors revealed that Pennsylvania's facade of politeness and propriety was slipping. This was an early sign that the province's oligarchic system was weakening as well.

With tensions running high, the 1764 election proved to be "the Greatest & most Contested Election Ever Known." As a supporter of the Assembly party wrote, "to gain your Votes and Interest," both parties "profess a zealous Concern for the preservation of the Rights and Privileges of the good People of this Province." New Jersey merchant Charles Pettit described some of their methods, though he thought them ineffectual: "A number of squibs, quarters, and half sheets, were thrown among the populace on the day of election, some so copious as to aim at the general dispute, and others, more confined, to Mr. Dickinson and Mr. Galloway, with now and then a skit at the Doctor [Franklin]." Chief Justice William Allen predicted some of the same "warm work" he had been accused of fostering in 1742. The polls opened at 9 A.M. on October 1, and throughout the day the stairs of the Court House were so crowded that it took fifteen minutes for a voter to ascend them and cast his ballot. People were still voting at 3 A.M. when advocates of the "new ticket" (those opposed to the Assembly party) moved to close the polls. The Assembly party refused, bringing "a reserve of the aged and lame" to vote, and so voting continued until 6 A.M. The "new ticket men" rallied their own supporters, and the polls did not finally close until 3 P.M. on October 2. The Assembly party was perhaps too confident, however. They closed the polls too early for thirty of their supporters who would have made the difference—Franklin was defeated by eighteen votes, Galloway by seven.[42]

The Assembly party's leaders were beaten, but if the anti-Assembly confederation expected that this would halt the campaign for royal government, they were mistaken. Franklin and Galloway had been turned out of doors, but Chew observed with disgust that they still "had the entire Direction of Matters within Doors, the Measure & plan of each Days proceeding being setled by them every Evening at private Meetings & Cabals with their Friends in the house."[43] Pettit echoed these words, noting that the Assembly had voted to send Franklin as agent to London to petition the Privy Council. "The opposition given to this measure, occasioned some debate, in the course of which the new Speaker [Joseph Fox] gave some hints that a debate was needless, as the members had determined the affair without doors. The Gentlemen in the opposition, finding themselves overruled, drew up a protest in form . . . but could not get it entered on the minutes of the House.[44] In 1766, an anonymous broadside author likewise criticized Galloway for concerting measures "out of doors," based on his "factious views," and pursuing political ends "by means often utterly inconsistent with *freedom of debate*, and the good of your country."[45] While the Assembly supposedly drew its legitimacy indoors from the imprimatur of the majority of Pennsylvanians, the enemies of the Assembly party accused them of squandering that legitimacy by engaging in secret conclaves "out of doors" and thereby failing to submit their plans to the public for legislative debate.

In the weeks before this election, Franklin and Galloway, "a Set of Ambitious Tribunes," vigorously defended legislative prerogative indoors. To Dickinson's protest, Franklin replied, "Tho' Protesting may be a Practice with the Lords of Parliament, there is no Instance of it in the House of Commons, whose Proceedings are the Model follow'd by the Assemblies of America."[46] Later, when Franklin's enemies objected to his appointment as an agent to go to London, he wrote, "This Mode of *Protesting* by the Minority, with a String of Reasons against the Proceedings of the Majority of the House of Assembly, is quite new among us." Franklin wrote that the recording of such protests in the minutes would encumber public business and might give rise to "a new Form of Libelling." The need for expediting his appointment, he wrote, ought to be "as obvious to every one out of Doors as it was to those within."[47]

The election and Franklin's mission to England inspired three more prints featuring the Court House. The first, entitled *The Election a Medley, Humbly Inscribed, to Squire Lilliput Professor of Scurrillity*, supported Franklin and featured a number of satires to the tune of popular songs. It began by trumpeting the Assembly party's gentle stewardship of politics indoors over the course of the eighteenth century, then took aim at Presbyterians. Another song enjoined "traitrous Sons of Tumult" to pay attention to the "Factious" electioneering practices of the Assembly party's opponents. The verses and cartoon also lampooned Presbyterians for praying for God to sway the election and then hitting the punch bowls immediately afterward; accused the proprietor's allies of bribery, electoral fraud, and using their influence over tavern licenses to compel votes from innkeepers; and mocked their enemies' ailments and venereal diseases.[48]

In 1765, Philadelphians were engaging in the same debates over imperial policy that took place in the other port cities. Since the Assembly party was attempting to curry favor with the Ministry, they declined to mount vigorous protests against the Stamp Act as legislative houses in other colonies had done. Naturally, this left the issue to the proprietary faction, which harnessed its "indefatigable Industry," Galloway wrote, "to prevail on the People to give every Kind of Opposition to the Execution of this Law." He argued that the Stamp Act's detractors were alienating the people's affections from king, lords, and commons, while "Judges of the Courts of Justice from the first to the most Inferiour" (all of whom were the proprietor's appointees) irreverently abused Parliament "in the Presence of the attending Populace." Galloway and his allies became concerned that these actions "tend with great rapidity to create in the Minds of the Populace and weaker part of Mankind a Spirit of Riot and Rebellion, which will be hereafter Quelled with great Difficulty, if ever Quelled at all." He worried, for instance, in 1766, when William Allen accused Franklin of opposing the Stamp Act's repeal on the floor of the House of Commons, which "filled the Members as well as the People out of Doors, with . . . resentment." Galloway hoped that, by countering the screeds against the Stamp Act with his own writings, he might "at least prevent the Contagion of Rebellion from spreading irrecoverably far."[49]

When the Stamp Act's opponents found no outlet for their protest within the halls of government, they took to the streets to express their outrage at imperial policy. John Hughes, an ally of Franklin and Galloway, became the focus of antagonism when he was appointed distributor of stamps for Pennsylvania. On September 16, 1765, a crowd gathered at the London Coffee House, a block away from the Court House, to threaten the houses of Franklin, Galloway, and Hughes. At this point, Galloway realized that his written words might not be enough. Instead, "(at the Instance of Mr. [John] Hughes's Friends, and not by any order from the Government of the City) near 800 of the sober Inhabitants, posted in different Places," assembled and declared themselves "ready to prevent any Mischief that should be attempted by the Mob." This tactic "effectually intimidated" Stamp Act protesters and prevented rioting in the city.[50]

On October 5, the vessel with stamped papers arrived at Philadelphia. As Thomas Wharton, merchant, wrote, "Such confusion and disorder it created as thou never saw with Us." Hughes reported that a group of the Stamp Act's opponents meeting at the Coffee House caused muffled drums to beat through the streets and the muffled State House bell to ring. The group directed "all Enquirers to repair to the State House for Information." As a result, "Several thousand citizens gathered at the State House," wrote the clergyman Henry Muhlenberg, "where a number of leading English merchants and lawyers harangued the people and the people echoed them with their yeas and nays." The meeting sent deputies to Hughes demanding his resignation as stamp distributor, threatening "Destruction to my Person & Property if I refused to gratify them in their Demands." The newspapers reported that had Hughes not been ill, "it is impossible to say what Lengths their Rage might have carried them." Again, Hughes had supporters in the crowd, and the threats and counterthreats resulted in a compromise on October 7, which was read from the Court House steps. While Hughes agreed not to enforce the Stamp Act, which met with "three Huzza's," he did not resign his office definitively. Many declared themselves "dissatisfied" in the aftermath, a dark warning that future out-of-door action might ensue.[51]

In early November, inhabitants gathered again at the Court House, to hang Hughes in effigy, and at the State House, with new calls for his resignation. By this time many local leaders were encouraging these actions: Speaker Joseph Fox "indiscreetly intermixed with this Mob." At the same time, radical leaders such as merchant Charles Thomson realized that out-of-door activity might cut both ways, as the White Oaks who supported the Assembly party "hissed or opposed" the radicals' proposals. Galloway boasted, "we can Muster ten to their one" when it came to mobilizing force in the city streets—and he continued to use such muscle "to preserve the Peace" during celebrations of the Stamp Act's repeal. Unlike other cities, Philadelphia did not mobilize a widespread coalition to protest the Stamp Act. In spite of their recent setbacks and frustrations, the Assembly party retained their power, both within doors and without.[52]

For the rest of the 1760s, when disagreements over British customs duties inflamed cities and colonies throughout North America, Pennsylvania was generally slower to mobilize against imperial policies. The Assembly party was busy currying favor with Parliament, while the leaders of their opposition, many of them officeholders of the proprietary faction, also had little desire to offend the Ministry.[53] This anemic response was a significant contrast to the level of outrage that had been brewing out of doors, and radicals recognized that their rejection of imperial taxation would require a new party.[54] Since they could not hope to find significant support for their views in the State House, their opposition developed out of doors: in the presses, in Presbyterian churches, in the taverns, and in the streets. John Dickinson's *Letters from a Pennsylvania Farmer* series, published in the *Pennsylvania Chronicle* beginning in December 1767, was the toast of radicals throughout North America. Thomson, Dickinson, and other leaders began pushing for nonimportation at meetings of merchants in March and April of 1768. They argued that boycotts were of a piece with other forms of protest—pamphlets, petitions, and "vigorous exertion"—all of which were even more effective when they represented unity within and among urban communities. "Philander" cheered as "the spirit of liberty spreads from place to place," and predicted, "Smaller towns will ambitiously rise 'as your example fires.' Zeal in a good cause has done wonders!" Out-of-door action in Boston or New York was influencing out-of-door action elsewhere, even as Pennsylvania's Assembly attempted to remain isolated and aloof. Within doors, Parliament urged the provincial assemblies to reject the Massachusetts Circular Letter (inspired by Dickinson), ordering governors to dissolve any house that responded to such a "flagitious attempt to disturb the public peace." The Pennsylvania Assembly adjourned until September rather than consider the letter.[55]

While Thomson attempted to organize nonimportation agreements among small groups of merchants, the Philadelphia radicals also attempted to apply pressure at the State House. On July 30, 1768, "a very great number of the most respectable inhabitants of this city, and many from the country, attended at the State-House." The inhabitants learned how Parliament was reducing provincial assemblies "from being the representatives of a free people, to be the subject tools of ministerial power." The address enjoined Pennsylvanians "while yet we have representatives, [to] apply to them and instruct them to unite with our brethren in the other colonies in the common cause."[56] The Assembly party was at this time unwilling to submit petitions to king, lords, and commons. Yet radicals hoped that a show of force outside the State House might convince the Assembly otherwise. That summer, a radical author thought it "pompous" to insist that "when any contention or controversy arises between the governors and governed, the LEGISLATURE is . . . the proper tribunal for the determination of THEM, being a body of men duly authorized, in a legal capacity, to ADDRESS, redress, hear and determine the rights of the subject, and the prerogative of the crown."[57] Radicals were discovering new outlets, outside the legislature, to address the rights of the people.

A month after this State House meeting, the pseudonymous "Country Farmer" wrote a satire for the *Pennsylvania Chronicle* entitled "To our 'patriotic'

FREEMEN, the Promoters of Town-Meetings." The satire was directed mostly at Dickinson, "our City-Farmer," and Thomson, "the Town-Carter" who had manured Dickinson's illustrious political path with "filth and excrement." The satirist was bemused that "from this time forth for-ever-more, town-meetings (in imitation of the orderly republicans of Boston) shall be held to instruct our dignified servants, the assembly," despite the fact that "such meetings are unknown to the constitution of Pennsylvania." The "Country Farmer" wondered why the Assembly should be expected to obey popular committees, and believed that such a topsy-turvy arrangement was antithetical to a tranquil and unified empire. The next step, wrote the author, would be for Thomson's committee to decree that Dickinson could take "a seat, stool, or chair in the house of assembly" whether he was elected in October or not. This type of accusation touched a nerve: two years later a defender of the nonimportation agreements felt it necessary to parry "the reproach of setting up the mob for statesmen" when he addressed himself to mechanics and tradesmen as well as farmers and merchants. "The whole people, who are the public," he wrote, could best judge whether the Townshend Acts were depriving Americans of their liberty.[58] Still, many Pennsylvanians remained uncomfortable with New England–style town meetings and insisted on leaving matters of public importance to the Assembly.

Dickinson and Thomson were undaunted by the civic impasse. The merchants of Boston and New York adopted nonimportation agreements in August and urged the Philadelphians to join them. Philadelphia radicals called a meeting of the merchants and traders at the Court House on September 22, but less than a quarter of the city's dry-goods merchants attended. That day the Pennsylvania Assembly sent only a tepid protest of the Townshend Acts to the king, lords, commons, and the colony's agents. Philadelphians decided to await the results rather than embark on a nonimportation agreement. Still, the furious newspaper articles appearing that autumn motivated the merchants to send their own, cautious petition to British merchants and manufactures on November 1. The formal political channels were too slow for American radicals, especially the New York and Boston merchants whose agreements would not work without Philadelphia's cooperation. The merchants continued to meet, deciding in February to cancel orders for goods, pending an answer from London. When word arrived and the London merchants were unresponsive, Philadelphia merchants agreed to nonimportation on March 10, 1769—six months later than the merchants of New York and Boston. For a few months, Philadelphia merchants managed the nonimportation movement in committees of their own. When the *Charming Polly* arrived with a cargo of malt on July 17, the "Committee of Merchants" called a mass meeting at the State House for the following day. At that meeting a group of brewers resolved that any person who bought or unloaded the malt was an "Enemy to his Country." Noting this hint of violence, the Philadelphia Monthly

Meeting of Quakers thereafter advised its members to have nothing to do with nonimportation.[59]

Radical leaders in Philadelphia were adopting a strategy that combined small committee meetings in taverns, coffeehouses, or government buildings with larger meetings out of doors. Importers schemed to back out of the nonimportation agreement prior to a May 14 meeting, but Thomson kept the pact alive after a May 23 "Meeting of the Artificers, Manufacturers, Tradesmen, Mechanicks, and others" resolved to postpone any steps toward dissolution. "A Lover of Liberty and a Mechanic's Friend" defended the May 23 meeting against the critics who called its participants a "Rabble" by asserting the mechanics' "right to determine in a point of universal concern," since "the liberties of the people is a universal maxim in government." At a State House meeting on June 5, only four people dissented from an agreement to continue nonimportation. Joseph Fox chaired another large gathering of "the Inhabitants of this City and County" at the State House on July 14, condemning New Yorkers' exit from the nonimportation agreement. By now there was a Merchants Committee as well as a Mechanicks Committee in operation. By September 12, the merchants were impatient to break the agreements; their resolutions prompted a larger meeting of subscribers at John Davenport's tavern on September 20, where the merchants voted to end the boycott. In response, the radicals resigned in disgust from the committee and hastily organized a mass meeting at the State House on September 27 "to vindicate the Honour of this City." The merchants ignored this meeting's appeal to continue nonimportation—as their defender, "Philadelphus," argued, "some few Men are fond of arrogating to themselves a superior Degree of Discernment and Penetration, and rashly condemning their Neighbours for not being of their Sentiments." The majority of Pennsylvanians ultimately sided with the merchants, and the continental nonimportation agreements collapsed despite the wider participation of political actors out of doors.[60]

While crowds had gathered before the Court House in 1742, 1764, and 1765, radical leaders increasingly began to hold mass meetings in the State House Yard instead. In 1764 and 1765, Philadelphians had gathered in the Yard in response to the Paxton uprising, at a rally petitioning for royal government, and twice to encourage John Hughes to resign his office. On these occasions, leaders may have preferred the State House Yard to the Court House for a number of reasons. Popular activity in Market Street in front of the Court House was risky because the space was near the waterfront and open to the streets; they were places for unbridled, violent popular expression like the election riot of 1742 or the hanging of Hughes in effigy. Furthermore, after the construction of the State House, the Court House and the moribund city government had somewhat diminished in importance. The State House, by contrast, was the real source of power and order in Pennsylvania. To demonstrate in the State House Yard, despite its peripheral location, was to make one's voice heard before the most important people in the province: the jurists of the Supreme Court, assemblymen, and the Governor's Council. Furthermore, the Assembly had widened the State House Yard during the years 1769–70. The province had purchased most of the private lots in the square south of the State House by February 1769, and builders had completed the high brick wall enclosing the Yard by February 1770. The frequency of meetings in the State House Yard increased thereafter; the expansion of the Yard no doubt gave it greater capacity to accommodate large gatherings, and perhaps the enclosure of the Yard lent newfound orderliness, and therefore legitimacy, to these meetings. It was now possible for leaders to control the space in a way that they could not control Market Street. If, in the contemporary view, riots outdoors had the smallest degree of legitimacy and parliamentary proceedings indoors had the greatest, then crowd participants may have hoped that an enclosed yard adjacent to a statehouse was the next best thing to a formal petition.[61]

During this period, radical Philadelphians began agitating for greater participation in the formal political process. Now that their actions outside the State House were gaining greater recognition, they sought to puncture the boundaries between the Assembly and its constituents. An incident in 1758 signified the uphill battle that this would entail. The Assembly was outraged when a speech by one of its members inspired "a loud tumultuous Stamping of Feet, Hissing and Clapping of Hands." The Speaker ordered the doors shut and the offenders seized. The House subsequently fined the noisemakers and resolved that such disturbances were "an high Contempt to the Authority of this House, a Breach of the Privileges thereof, and destructive to the Freedom and Liberties of the Representatives of the People."[62] The inhabitants of Philadelphia petitioned the Assembly in 1764 "to be admitted to hear the Debates in the House, and thereby be informed of the true State of such Matters under the Deliberation of the Representatives of the People, as may in any wise affect the Interest and Welfare of their Constituents." The petitioners sought "a standing Order, that the Freemen of the Province shall have free Access, at all seasonable Times in the future, to inform themselves accordingly, as is the Custom of the Honourable House of Commons in *Great-Britain*, and elsewhere in his Majesty's Dominions."[63] Franklin, Hughes, and other members of an appointed committee examined the standing orders of the House of Commons, which mandated that "no Stranger" be "admitted, for whom Leave has not been expresly asked and given by the House." The committee noted that, notwithstanding the Assembly doors were left open in Virginia and Maryland, in New Jersey and New York "the Practice is, as hitherto it has been in this Province, to keep the Doors shut, except at Hearings on contested Elections, or the like, which are usually public."[64]

On October 17, 1770, after two years of frequent meetings in the State House Yard, the Assembly heard another motion "That the Doors of the Assembly Room be set open, and the Freeholders and other reputable

Inhabitants admitted at seasonable Times to hear the Debates of the House."[65] The Assembly allowed those inhabitants "qualified to elect Members of the Assembly" to hear debates "at such Times, and under such Regulations and Restrictions, as the House shall think Proper."[66] These restrictions, however, allowed the House to keep control of who could be present at debates, and when. For example, in March 1772, "A Tradesman" lambasted "the absurd and tyrannical custom of shutting the Assembly doors against you, whose interest and right it is to enter whenever you think it necessary to your security." Instead, the people "are obliged to put up with dark hints, sometimes given by a few of the Members to some of their friends." Legislators could use misleading titles and preambles such that by the time the populace could consider a law's merit, a bill would already have been passed. In October, radicals expressed their dissatisfaction with the "old corrupt Junto" of the Assembly with its "enslaving and oppressive Laws." In early 1773, Josiah Quincy of Massachusetts (where the assembly doors had been open since 1766) noted, "Their debates are not public, which is said now to be the case of only this house of commons throughout the continent. Many have been the attempts to procure an alteration in this respect but all to no purpose." Ordinary Philadelphians hoped to break down the barriers separating indoors from outdoors. They hoped to force legislators to hear their voices, rather than continuing to insulate themselves from their constituents. Still, on March 8 and October 31, 1775, the Assembly again denied entry to spectators in the midst of contentious political debates.[67]

Thus, at the beginning of 1773, the Assembly was still giving radical Philadelphians cause for complaint. Quincy noted this dissatisfaction, calling the House "a body held in great, remarkable, and general contempt, . . . singularly odious for certain provincial manœuvres too circumstantial to relate." Many Philadelphians likened the oligarchic nature of the Assembly to the corrupt House of Commons.[68] As meetings out of doors gained strength, as Americans continued to deny Parliament's right to impose internal taxes on its colonies, and as the Assembly proved unsatisfying as a protest mechanism, Philadelphia radicals increasingly began to link the Assembly and Parliament, two unresponsive legislative bodies, in their minds.

The passage of the Tea Act in 1773 inspired further outdoor meetings. "The merchants, as might be expected, first expressed their uneasiness," wrote lawyer Joseph Reed, "but in a few days it became general. Some of the principal inhabitants and merchants, called a general meeting of the people." In anticipation of the arrival of the East India Company tea, Philadelphians met at the State House on October 18. The inhabitants resolved that Parliament could not levy a tax on Americans without their consent, and that the tax "has a direct tendency to render assemblies useless," since it allowed Parliament to eclipse the legislatures' authority to support government, administer justice, and defend the colonies. "A. Z." exulted that "the appearance at the State-House this day, and the

Resolutions formed by so respectable a body of People, without one dissenting voice, will reflect much honor on the Inhabitants of Pennsylvania." The meeting appointed a committee on behalf of "the united desire of the city" to convince the appointed consignees to give up their commissions to receive the tea.[69] Thomas Wharton feared that such out-of-door political action would lead to lawlessness: "To such a pitch of zeal are some people rais'd . . . that I fear the worst."[70]

As the ship bearing the dutied tea drew closer, small committee meetings once again preceded mass meetings out of doors. A group of "principal inhabitants" unanimously agreed "to compel the master of the ship to return with his cargo."[71] When Captain Samuel Ayres of the *Polly* anchored below town on December 26, a group of Philadelphians discouraged him from coming up to town, given "the present temper of the inhabitants." Ayres was astonished to find "most of the Inhabitants of the said City collected together in a Body and with One general Voice exclaiming against his said Ship's coming up and the Tea being landed." Within hours, Ayres consulted with various men in town and ultimately agreed "to comply with the sense of the city on this occasion." The next morning, Philadelphia leaders managed to mobilize a crowd "upon an hour's notice," and when the 8,000 people that arrived at the State House could not fit indoors, "they adjourned into the Square." Joseph Reed noted the "great number of the most considerable both in rank and property," while the newspaper reported, "This meeting is allowed by all to be the most respectable, both in the numbers and in the rank of those who attended it, that has been known in this city." The meeting acknowledged the actions against tea shipments at Boston, New York, and Charleston, and ordered Captain Ayres to leave Philadelphia without unloading his cargo. The *Pennsylvania Packet* celebrated the fact that "the force of a law" that damaged British commerce and insisted on Parliament's right to tax Americans "had been effectually broken." Reed recounted these events to Lord Dartmouth, secretary of state for the American colonies, to demonstrate "how general and unanimous the opinion is" about Parliamentary taxation—in Boston, Charleston, New York, and "throughout the country."[72]

Reed also sought to convey to Dartmouth how orderly Philadelphia's out-of-door actions had been: "This city has been distinguished for its peaceable and regular demeanour, nor has it departed from it on the present occasion, as there have been no mobs, no insults to individuals, no insult to private property." Still, Reed noted that resistance to legislative action might occasion violent conflict with Great Britain as well as social upheaval: "Any further attempt to enforce this act, I am humbly of opinion, must end in blood," he wrote, adding that "the frequent appeals to the people must in time occasion a change, and we every day perceive it more and more difficult to repress the rising spirit of the people."[73] Out-of-door action might walk a fine line between a "regular demeanour" and an "end in blood"; other American cities, particularly Boston, had provided plenty of evidence of the ways in which extralegal activity could get out of control and threaten peace, property, and personal safety. Radical organizers would have to be vigilant if they wanted to maintain the province's reputation for peace and good order.[74]

In May 1774, Philadelphia learned of the provisions of the Boston Port Act, and Paul Revere rode into town on behalf of the Boston Committee of Correspondence, seeking support. During the next two months, political activity in Philadelphia accelerated. Some radical leaders "secretly concerted" measures among themselves, and some endeavored to "prepare the minds of the people" with published writings. Radicals also held a series of small committee meetings. They formed a Committee of Nineteen on May 20, which resolved to answer the letter from the Boston Committee of Correspondence. The Nineteen also petitioned Governor John Penn to call an emergency session of the Assembly that would send delegates to a Continental Congress.[75]

The broader population of Philadelphia also participated in important out-of-door activities in the weeks following Revere's visit. On June 1, shops closed, the bells of Christ Church sounded in mourning, the flags of vessels in the harbor flew at half mast, and churches filled with congregants: "Sorrow, mixed with indignation, seemed pictured in the countenances of the inhabitants, and the city wore the aspect of deep distress." Three days later was the birthday of King George III, and pharmacist Christopher Marshall noted that "scarcely, if any, notice was taken of it in this city, by way of rejoicing: not one of our bells suffered to ring and but very few colors were shown by the shipping in the harbor; no, nor not one bonfire kindled."[76]

When Governor Penn rejected the Nineteen's petition on June 7, two groups of Philadelphians soon organized meetings in the State House Yard. On June 8, a broadside was addressed "to the Manufacturers and Mechanics" of Philadelphia and its vicinity. The broadside called Philadelphia's mechanics to a meeting the next day "to manifest to the world" that they knew their rights "as *free-born* Americans." It asked them to consider a letter from New York's mechanics, to support Boston, and to undertake measures "as will most effectually tend to unite us in the common cause of our country." In response to this broadside, 1,200 mechanics gathered with John Ross as chair and agreed to correspond with New York's craftsmen. They expressed their concern "at this most alarming and critical time when American liberty is so deeply wounded, and her rights so unjustly invaded, by levying taxes on us without our consent." Parliament's actions, these artisans declared, "call aloud upon all Americans to assemble, consult, and determine firmly to pursue such measures for their own and neighbours future security." The mechanics resolved to strengthen the Nineteen's hand (they called it "the Committee of Merchants") and called for "a general meeting of all the inhabitants" to form "one grand joint Committee."[77]

This "general meeting" was scheduled for June 15 and then postponed to June 18 to give inhabitants of the countryside sufficient time to attend. Thomas Wharton wrote, "A general meeting is to be held in this city, when its not doubted, that the greatest numbers will attend that was ever known on any occasion." Prior to this general meeting, the Nineteen met at the Philosophical Society Hall, just outside the State House, on June 10 and 11 to prepare a slate for a new committee (which incorporated several mechanics) and draft resolves for the Philadelphians out of doors to approve. The Nineteen also debated the method of appointing delegates to the Continental Congress. Though a Provincial Assembly was "the most eligible Mode of appointing those Deputies," the governor had refused to convene the Assembly. Dickinson suggested bypassing the Assembly altogether by having each locality appoint delegates to a provincial convention, which would in turn choose delegates for the Continental Congress. This proved too controversial for some Pennsylvanians, and so the Nineteen worked out a compromise: the general meeting would ask Galloway (Speaker of the House since 1766) to convene the Assembly unofficially, while Philadelphia and the rural counties would "draw up Instructions" for the assemblymen at a provincial convention. Radicals threatened to undermine the authority of the Assembly, just as Americans were questioning the authority of Parliament.[78]

Dickinson and Justice Thomas Willing chaired the general meeting on June 18, a "very large and respectable meeting of the Freeholders and Freemen of the city and county of Philadelphia." The Reverend Dr. William Smith's speech demonstrated the ambivalence with which many moderate upper-class Philadelphians regarded these town meetings. On the one hand, Smith said, "Whatever *vote* is known to be now passed, upon full deliberation, and by the unanimous voice of this great city and county, will not only be *respected* through all America, but will have such a weight as the proudest Minister in England may have reason to *respect*." At the same time, Smith solicited the unity and harmony that Pennsylvanians cherished in their indoor political culture: "What I have in charge to request of you is this—that is, on any point, we should have a difference of sentiments, every person may be allowed to speak his mind *freely*, and to conclude what he has to offer, without any such outward marks of approbation or disapprobation, as *clapping or hissing*; and that if a division should be necessary (which it is hoped may not be the case this day) such division may be made in the manner desired by the *chairmen*, with all possible order and decorum."[79] Smith hoped that the hissing and clapping that had so outraged the Assembly in 1758 would not become the dominant force in this new out-of-door politics. He wanted town leaders to maintain tight control over such meetings, and he betrayed his fears that the crowd might get the better of sensible upper-class leaders.

The June 18 meeting was, in fact, a contentious one. Philadelphians were unwilling to simply approve the Nineteen's resolutions. The mass meeting resolved that the Boston Port Act was unconstitutional, that a committee of correspondence (the Committee of Forty-Three) be established, and that this committee—rather than the Assembly—would "determine what is the most proper mode of collecting the sense of this province" and of appointing delegates to the Continental Congress. These Philadelphians distrusted the Assembly and the meeting's chairmen, and sought to enact their will independently of these politicians. When the chairmen put forth their proposed slate of candidates for the Forty-Three, "This Produced murmers & enquiries" among the attendees, who asked "what right they had to dictate." Willing hastened to reassure the crowd that the nominees "were persons high in reputation," and that the chairmen "had done only what all had right to do," that is, "spoken their sentiments." He and Dickinson urged unity and harmony in the service of "our Countrys Common Good," so that "passion & heat" would not rule the meeting.[80]

Radicals took to the press to express their distrust of the Assembly. "J. R.—" believed that the freemen of Pennsylvania should elect their own committees of correspondence, which would hold a provincial convention and choose delegates for the Continental Congress. The author argued that "The whole *people* are oppressed" and that therefore "*They* must relieve themselves." Pennsylvanians could not presume that the Assembly would represent them "virtually" based on the "*supposed* or *implied* assent of the people." Such arguments against virtual representation were the same ones radicals had used against Parliament's authority to legislate for America. Politics out of doors was gaining legitimacy at the expense of representatives indoors.[81]

The progress of Pennsylvania toward republicanism and democracy was by no means linear in the years 1774–76. After the June 18 meeting, the mechanics were *still* dissatisfied, but the Forty-Three ignored their threats and complaints. Leaders did not heed out-of-door agitation indiscriminately, and people with different viewpoints on the imperial crisis still jockeyed with one another for power. The radicals who had launched the committee movement tried to strengthen their new power structures: as in South Carolina, radical representatives went into the backcountry to mobilize support. The Forty-Three avoided divisive issues so that they might maintain their fragile alliance of moderates and radicals. Meanwhile, delegates to the provincial convention began meeting on July 15 in Philadelphia's Carpenter's Hall, an indoor facility that became a symbolic meeting place for elected bodies outside the State House. The convention drew up instructions for the Assembly, gave terms for an acceptable settlement between Great Britain and her American colonies, and resolved that with regard to Parliament, "a line there must be, beyond which her authority cannot extend."[82]

The Assembly had reconvened in the State House as the convention was meeting. The legislators "*Resolved*, upon Motion, That the Committees from the several Counties of this Province, now met on public Affairs in this City, be admitted, if they chuse it, to hear the Debates of the House" on July 21. On that day, members of the provincial convention marched from Carpenter's Hall to the State House, presented the colonies' grievances, recommended measures for redress, and suggested a slate of congressional delegates.[83] There was powerful symbolism in such a march, as members of an out-of-door provincial convention forced open the doors and secrecy privileges of the Assembly to present them with the people's own instructions.

That evening an anonymous author, "The Freeman," sent a pamphlet to members of the Assembly that praised their "prudence" and defended their constitutionality and "legal authority" indoors. The elected representatives, the author wrote, "are the only persons before whom *every* grievance should come . . . in *you* we have reposed the most unlimited confidence—no body of men are to supersede you—you are the guardians of our rights— we look to you for protection against every encroachment—and now implore you to avert every innovation." By contrast, as the philosopher David Hume wrote, "All numerous assemblies however composed, are mere mob, and swayed in their debates by the least motive. . . . An absurdity strikes a member, he conveys it to his neighbours, and the whole is infected. . . . The only way of making people wise, is to keep them from uniting into large assemblies." By failing to follow this advice, Pennsylvanians were "deviating from the long known, and securely trodden paths of prudence and regularity," and "wander[ing] into the maizy labyrinths of perplexity and disorder." The convention was letting "the noise and confusion of the scene stifle the voice of wisdom." Its zealous partisans and fiery spirits were "setting up a power to controul you" and "setting up anarchy above order— it is the beginning of republicanism. . . . They are gigantic strides to set up the resolves of the populace above the law and above the constitution."[84]

The following day the Assembly decided to reassert its power. The chamber admitted the members of the provincial convention, but legislators waited until the convention men withdrew before debating their resolutions. By closing its doors, the Assembly was going back on its earlier decision to permit the convention men to hear its proceedings. This done, the Assembly rolled back the efforts of the convention and its supporters. Its members appointed a mostly moderate and conservative delegation (including Galloway) to the Continental Congress and gave them no particular instructions to wring concessions from Parliament—indeed, the delegates were "strictly charged to avoid every Thing indecent or disrespectful to the Mother State."[85] John Young would write to his aunt, "I belive the Comittees and indeed people in general are not well pleased at the Assembly's chusing the members of y.ᵉ Congress out of their own house; indeed I think it is a reflection on them that the <u>Farmer</u> [Dickinson] was not one of the number." Young believed, along with many Philadelphians, that "the proceedings of the British Parliament are tyrannical to the last degree." He apparently echoed a widespread distrust of Parliament, as well as the sitting Assembly.[86] Philadelphia was destined to play a crucial role in the imperial crisis; as Joseph Reed wrote, "The weight of influence of this Province and city" was "considerable."[87] When the Continental Congress arrived in Philadelphia, he added, "the eyes of all America are upon this city, and at this time the transactions of the Congress are indeed very important to the whole British Empire."[88]

If the radicals were denied their opportunity to see a provincial convention assume the duties of the Provincial Assembly, they at least had the satisfaction of seeing a Continental Congress challenge the authority of Parliament. The presence of the Continental Congress in Philadelphia lent strength to the radicals and their growing movement out of doors to storm the closet of the ossified and oligarchic Assembly. Galloway attempted to draw the Continental Congress within his orbit by offering them the State House. The State House was "evidently the best place," according to Connecticut delegate Silas Deane, "but as he offers, the other party oppose." This party, sympathetic to the radicals, chose the extralegal site at Carpenter's Hall for their meetings rather than the State House. Galloway wrote bitterly that this decision and the choice of Charles Thomson as secretary "were privately settled by an Interest made out of Doors." Galloway not only criticized the decisions that had been made behind his back but expressed a more general sense of affront akin to that of "A Freeman," who may have in fact been Galloway himself. The Continental Congress was the product of provincial conventions throughout the continent, led by the populace out of doors. Galloway could not tolerate this body of questionable legitimacy or its challenges to the Assembly's authority. Reed, an active member of the committee movement, on the other hand, defended Congress: "As yet there is no illegality in the meeting of a number of gentlemen from different Provinces to deliberate upon public affairs, and draw up a decent and proper representation." Congress donned a new mantle of parliamentary legitimacy as the delegates ensconced themselves in Carpenter's Hall: they would reflect "the true and real designs of Americans," or public opinion out of doors, and represent them as a body of respectable statesmen.[89]

In some ways, the first Continental Congress was no more open to public opinion than the Pennsylvania Assembly had been. Congress operated in secret, keeping its doors closed to the public. Caesar Rodney of Delaware wrote, "The Congress has injoined every member to keep a Secret till the Whole business is done, When the Whole of their proceedings Will be published to avoid needless disputations out of Doors." He added, "This is much to the disappointment of the Curious," who no doubt found such restrictions to be undemocratic. Nevertheless, Philadelphians with connections might learn of the proceedings indoors, and congressmen had no compunction about listening to opinions "out of doors among citizens, gentlemen, and persons of all denominations."[90] The members of the Continental Congress interacted with Philadelphians, especially those with a more radical bent, and helped to influence public opinion. When Congress adjourned at the end of October, they had achieved significant unity among the American colonies, agreed upon important grievances and resolutions, addressed a petition to King George III, and set nonimportation and nonexportation agreements in motion. The Continental Congress had mobilized Philadelphians, Pennsylvanians, and Americans in ways that the more cautious Assembly had not.[91]

After the departure of the Congress, the committee movement in Philadelphia and Pennsylvania continued to grow. Important events at the State House included a general meeting on November 7, 1774, the election of a new committee the following week "to manage public affairs for this City" until the sitting of the next Continental Congress, and a five-day provincial convention on January 23, 1775. Just before this last meeting, the committee canvassed "the people['s] sentiments Out of Doors." A broadside attacked the convention and its members:

> Can public Virtue by me stand,
> See Faction stalking through the Land?—
> Faction that Fiend, begot in Hell—
> In *Boston* nurs'd—here brought to dwell
> By *Congress*, who, in airy Freak,
> Conven'd to plan a *Republick?*
>
> . . . .
>
> Can Judges, fam'd for Probity,
> Sit tame Spectators by, and see
> The Laws oppugn'd by Committee—
> Who laugh at Courts, and Loyalty?[92]

In spite of such criticism, radicals managed to break the power of the last remnants of the old Assembly party. They divided the Quakers who had formerly held sway over the Assembly and largely dominated the presses. As late as March 4, Galloway exulted that he could weaken the power of the Continental Congress and destroy the unity of the American colonies by having Pennsylvania submit a splinter petition to King George III. Galloway wrote that his opponents, "despairing of success in preventing a petition to his Majesty, moved that the Doors should be thrown open, and the Mob let in upon me." Galloway managed to defeat this maneuver, but on March 8, Philadelphians learned that the king had rejected the petition of the Continental Congress. The backlash of public opinion motivated the Assembly to defeat Galloway's splinter petition, and Galloway resigned his House seat in humiliation.[93]

Though many Philadelphians inclined toward moderation, the reactions of the Crown and Parliament to American petitions continued to drive Pennsylvanians toward the radicals' way of thinking. The outbreak of fighting at Lexington and Concord accelerated this tendency. Philadelphians first heard the news on April 24 and instantly called a meeting at the State

House Yard the following day. This afternoon meeting attracted around 8,000 inhabitants to the State House Yard, where participants heard speeches, "and the Company unanimously agreed to associate, for the purpose of defending with Arms their Property, Liberty and Lives, against all Attempts to deprive them of them." In the aftermath of the battles, the State House Yard also became the site of military mobilization. On April 29, Christopher Marshall found the patriot mathematician James Cannon at the State House Yard "to help consult and regulate the forming of the militia." These Associators formed committees of their own, among officers as well as rank-and-file militiamen. For much of 1775, Philadelphians debated the funding and regulation of these groups that were mobilizing out of doors, exercising and storing artillery in the State House Yard, and parading before the Court House. These militia groups were important tools for political mobilization, giving Philadelphia men a way to display their active concern for the public good. The militia organizations, Philadelphia's Committee of Observation (which had grown out of the November 1774 election), the new Committee of Safety (established in June), and the Continental Congress (which reconvened in May 1775) provided the resistance movement of Philadelphia with a myriad of outlets for extralegal political mobilization, in addition to the radical faction of the Assembly.[94]

Marshall became involved in the committee movement when he was elected a member of the Committee of Observation (the first Committee of One Hundred) on August 16, 1775. He attended weekly committee meetings in the Philosophical Society Hall, just outside the State House, as well as subcommittee meetings in the London Coffee House, just outside the Court House, and mingled with delegates to Congress. Meanwhile, radicals made significant gains in the Assembly, dealing a rebuke to conservatives and moderates in the elections of October 1775. When the new Assembly met later that month, it found itself bombarded by petitions from various groups out of doors. On October 31, sixty-six members of the First One Hundred marched two by two to the State House and presented their grievances to the legislature. The act was reminiscent of the march of July 21, 1774, when the Assembly had ignored the convention's requests, but this time committee men successfully demanded access to politics indoors.[95]

The second Continental Congress had begun meeting on May 10, 1775, now at the State House. John Adams appreciated the increased legitimacy of this new location, even as he found himself forced to defend his aims. "It would be very curious," he wrote, "to give you an History of the out a Door Tricks for this important Evil of dividing the Colonies." Adams referred to the agitation of New England Baptists, Quakers, and landjobbers, but he might just as easily have discussed his own "out a Door Tricks" in attempting to *unite* the colonies. He and other congressmen schemed and argued out of doors in Philadelphia, often in the State House Yard. As Deane wrote, for instance, "People here, members of the Congress and others, have unhappily and erroneously thought me a schemer; this has brought on me rather more than my share of business, out doors at least, in the Committee way."[96] Once the members of the Continental Congress had settled more comfortably indoors, they were able to project their power without, using the tools of influence, gladhanding, and informal politicking that previous legislators had used.

By now, the issue of declaring independence from Great Britain had arisen in Pennsylvania. This would represent the ultimate rejection of legal authority, both from the king and Parliament. Many Pennsylvanians worried about the repercussions of independence for the legal authority of the Assembly. Pennsylvanians, who had disagreed over proprietary and royal government for over a generation, faced serious issues regarding the representation and legitimacy of its government at the imperial and provincial level. The Assembly, for its part, gave instructions to its new slate of congressional delegates on November 9, 1775: "We strictly enjoin you, that you, in Behalf of this Colony, dissent from, and utterly reject, any Propositions . . . that may cause, or lead to, a Separation from our Mother Country, or a Change of the Form of this Government." Independence caught on slowly in Pennsylvania. Nevertheless, once radicals began agitating for a separation from Great Britain, they also began to question the legitimacy of a Provincial Assembly that would thwart such a goal. In early 1776, Philadelphians had several outlets for expressing themselves and acting out of doors: a series of elections at the State House for government and committee posts in January, February, and March, as well as the discussion of the latest radical opinion pieces in the press.[97]

The most famous of these opinion pieces was Thomas Paine's *Common Sense*, published in Philadelphia on January 10, 1776. Paine drew part of his inspiration from Obadiah Hulme's *An Historical Essay on the English Constitution*, a London essay of 1771. Hulme emphasized the annual elections of the ancient Saxon government, an egalitarian principle that successive Parliaments had overturned. "It always did happen," he wrote, "and always will be the consequence, that when one class of men gains an ascendancy, in the legislative authority in any state, they make use of their power, as members of the legislative body, to promote their own interests, as individuals; and incline the laws to establish their power, and interests, at the expence of every other man in the state."[98] This indictment gave ideological ammunition to Pennsylvanians who were frustrated with the Assembly's position on independence.

Paine echoed Hulme's fear of legislative tyranny. The establishment of government, after all, began in the state of nature, out of doors: "Some convenient tree" could suffice as "a State House, under the branches of which the whole colony may assemble to deliberate on public matters." Eventually the members of this colony would have to delegate responsibilities to a legislature, but this would require vigilance and "a large and equal representation." Paine used specific examples from Pennsylvania. He pointed to the November 1775 votes on the Associators' petition, warning that if too few assemblymen had been present at the State House on a given day, two Quaker counties might have voted as an obstructionist bloc and thereby governed the entire province. He accused the Assembly of scheming "to gain an undue authority" over the province's delegates to Congress and argued that this "ought to warn the people at large, how they trust power out of their own hands." In his second example, Paine wrote that moderates had constrained the colony's delegates on November 9, 1775, with instructions that "would have dishonored a school-boy . . . after being approved by a few, a very few without doors." He was indignant that such instructions, unrepresentative of the people's interests, were passed "*in behalf of the whole colony*." Were Pennsylvanians to be aware of this, they would think their representatives "unworthy of such a trust."[99] Paine's pamphlet was most famous for influencing Americans to reject monarchical government. At the same time, he helped Pennsylvanians associate the oligarchic State House with the oligarchs of Whitehall.

Thus, the issue of independence starkly confronted Philadelphians in 1776 as the Continental Congress sat in the State House that had formerly been the Assembly's domain. A Philadelphia gentleman warned Samuel Adams in January 1776 "that he could not believe the People without Doors would follow the Congress passibus aequis [step by step], if such Measures as some called spirited, were pursued." By March, Reed believed a majority of the delegates to Congress to be in favor of independence, "but they must have a concurrence of the people, or at least a general approbation of any such material change." Leaders like Thomas McKean, during this period, were important for building bridges between radicals inside Congress and those without.[100] The debate in the press, meanwhile, continued: Provost William Smith, writing as "Cato," disparaged committee activities. When the Second One Hundred rescinded their February 28 call for a convention on March 4, he invited them to retreat out of the "back door" from whence they came without further attempting to intimidate the Assembly "in the discharge of the important trust committed to them by the voice of their country." Smith insisted that "no Committees were ever entrusted with any authority to speak the sense of the People of Pennsylvania" on the question of independence.[101] He feared—and his opponents cheered—that independence would lead to republicanism.

Around this same time, Pennsylvanians heeded Paine's advice and petitioned to loosen the oligarchic character of the Assembly by expanding its membership and granting Philadelphia and the frontier greater representation. Pennsylvanians had an opportunity to offer their voice in an expanded Assembly in a May 1 election. This was the most contentious election since 1764, and a similar incident took place on this occasion as well: just after six o'clock the sheriff closed the polls, and the resentful populace (suspecting a tactic by the moderates) forced him to open them again. Despite all the efforts of the radicals, however, Philadelphians elected three anti-independence candidates and one pro-independence candidate, by very slim margins. If radicals in Congress and in Pennsylvania had been hoping that the elections would ratify their position, they were disappointed when moderate men retained a majority in the Assembly. Moderates, on the other hand, interpreted these results as an indication that independence was not as popular out of doors as the radicals had believed. The radicals, for their part, had no choice now but to mobilize like-minded people out of doors and destroy the power of the Assembly. In the *Pennsylvania Gazette*, "Civis" wrote that "True Whigs" ought to defend the Pennsylvania charter from the "secret machinations of ambitious innovators as against the open attack of the British parliament." These "ambitious innovators" coalesced into a cabal of radicals seeking to overthrow British government as well as the provincial Assembly.[102]

The radicals moved to act before the Assembly even met. The Second One Hundred had the support of the county committees of observation, as well as the militia units. At the instigation of John Adams, Congress passed its May 10 resolution recommending that the colonies establish new governments if the present government was not "sufficient to the Exigencies of their Affairs." When Pennsylvania's moderate delegates insisted that the Assembly was indeed sufficient, on May 15 Adams added a preamble to the resolution that since the Assembly operated under oaths to the Crown, Pennsylvania should establish a new government "under the Authority of the People." The Virginia delegate Carter Braxton wrote, "It was not so understood by Congress" as a declaration of independence, "but I find those out of doors on both sides the question construe it in that manner." James Wilson, one of the moderate Pennsylvania delegates, feared that Adams's preamble, forbidding "the exercise of every kind of authority under the crown," would cause "an immediate dissolution of every kind of authority; the people will instantly be in a State of nature." In language reminiscent of Henry Laurens's, he asked, "Before we are prepared to build the new house, why should we pull down the old one, and expose ourselves to all the inclemencies of the season?" For an attorney like Wilson, used to the warmth inside the halls of power, this was a legitimate fear—but those who were limited to practicing politics "out of doors" had less to lose.[103]

That evening and the next day radicals gathered unofficially at the Philosophical Society Hall. They resolved to call a provincial convention that would supersede any activity by the Assembly, and would make their case to a mass meeting at the State House Yard on the morning of May 20. Over the next few days, radicals had two opportunities to change Philadelphians' views on independence. The first was a fast day on May 17 that Congress had scheduled months before, when Philadelphians heard their ministers' sentiments. The second was the publication of *The Alarm* on March 19. The author of *The Alarm* (possibly Thomas Paine) argued that the Assembly lacked any legitimate claim to power: either the Assembly did not exist, or it existed unconstitutionally, since its election had taken place prior to Congress's resolve for establishing new governments: "Until the authority of the Crown, by which the present House of Assembly sits, be suppressed, the House is not qualified to carry the Resolve of Congress, respecting a new government, into execution." The Assembly had further disqualified itself by imposing "unwise and impolitic instructions" on the Pennsylvania delegates not to vote for independence, by taking "oaths of allegiance to our enemy . . . as members of the House," and by their "undue influence and partial connexions." The author called this "a treasonable tendency towards dissolving the happy union of the colonies" and argued that a convention was the proper body for forming a new government, like the English convention during the Glorious Revolution of 1688. "We can no longer confide in the House of Assembly," the author wrote. "They have, by a feeble and intimidating prudence held us up as sacrifices to a bloody-minded enemy."[104]

In the week leading up to the town meeting of May 20, James Clitherall "perceived in this city that parties ran high" and that "the body of the people were for Independency." He added, "The rage of the multitude at present only vented itself in whisperings, but on a recommendation of Congress that those Colonies that did not find their present form of government sufficient for the exigency of the times, would settle a form of government for themselves, the rage of the people burst out in a protest against their present Assembly, who had instructed their Delegates not to vote for Independency." Echoing the sentiments of *The Alarm*, he wrote, "The people . . . chose governors among themselves—this nettled the gentlemen and they too late saw their behaviour had been too timorous and very impolitick."[105]

The May 20 meeting would "take the sense of the People" about the most recent Congressional steps toward independence. The printer William Bradford showed up at this meeting "notwithstanding the badness of the day," as did about 4,000 others in the State House Yard. The committee led the meeting with the merchant Daniel Roberdeau as chair. Its members accused the Pennsylvania Assembly of acting to "withdraw the province from this union of the Colonies both in council and action," by failing to instruct the province's delegates to Congress on establishing new governments. The committee further asserted that "the supineness of our government" was due to its allegiance to "old established forms." Pennsylvanians could only expect the protection of their liberty and safety under "a free government, established on '*the authority of the people*,' and having *their interest alone in view*." The attendant crowd passed the resolutions, not least (according to Clitherall) because "the people behaved in such a tyrannical manner that the least opposition was dangerous." Within sight of Philadelphia's most prominent symbol of authority, the people resolved that the present government was insufficient, that the Assembly could not legally form a new one, and that Pennsylvania would hold a convention on June 18 to form a new government. As Bradford put it, "This gives the Coup de Grace to the King's authority in this province."[106]

As a result of this meeting, "the Inhabitants of this Province" published a broadside protest against the Pennsylvania Assembly. The broadside announced Pennsylvania's intention to "hereby renounce and protest against the authority of this House," in response to the congressional resolve recommending the formation of new provincial governments. The petition lamented that the Assembly derived its chartered power from the king, and that so many of the representatives were under the influence of the proprietor through connections of patronage or "pecuniary employments." The petitioners did approve of the Assembly's radicals, who had been valiantly "struggling against a weight of opposition within doors." Yet despite this "consolation" that these members had been able to prevent even *more* reactionary stances, the petition called on the Assembly to refrain from undertaking any new legislation and to adjourn, considering themselves thereafter "Members Only of the Community at large." Henceforth, Pennsylvanians would determine the will of the people out of doors, as a community at large.[107]

As they stood in the rain that afternoon, the Philadelphians in the State House Yard probably gave little thought to the difficult hurdles of political mobilization that had brought North America to this threshold. Yet they might have pondered their urban brethren: the members of the Boston waterfront community that had united, despite their differences, to defend their rights against British officials; the New York taverngoers who had done the face-to-face work of persuading their companions to join the resistance and drawing together a network of taverngoers throughout North America; the Charleston grandees who fought a rear-guard action to maintain control over domestic relations in the midst of turmoil; the Newport congregants who bickered and reached for salvation amidst the pluralistic urban climate. Yet Philadelphians would have recognized all these incidents of political mobilization: they had met in taverns, struggled with the political ramifications of their religious affiliations, attempted to achieve cross-class alliances, and strived to maintain order amidst the urban maelstrom. The Court House and State House stood, after all, at the nexus of urban household, house of worship, public house, waterfront, marketplace, and city streets. These buildings straddled the indoor and outdoor worlds of city dwellers, and presided over connections with the Atlantic world and the countryside. Philadelphia leaders struggled to manage the indoor and outdoor political activities of city dwellers, and their success would be crucial for political mobilization.

In the aftermath of the May 20 meeting, moderates and radicals each sought to mobilize Philadelphia and the countryside to their cause. Moderates, in an attempt at countermobilization, drew up a Remonstrance defending their platform of reconciliation with Great Britain and the preservation of the Assembly's authority. The moderates garnered 6,000 signatures in the city and backcountry. The radicals, meanwhile, also set out to project their new power in the countryside. Their members journeyed throughout Philadelphia, discrediting the Assembly and rallying the militia companies—who already had grievances against the Assembly—in favor of independence and a provincial convention. As Clitherall observed, the Committee of Privates, "a body founded in faction and growing in insolence," strong-armed Philadelphians into supporting independence: "They put the question to the City Battalions under arms, and any man who dared oppose their opinion was insulted and hushed by their interruptions, cheers and hissings."[108]

By the end of May 1776, the Assembly was split by feuds and ignored by both its constituents and Congress. Philadelphians were doing little indoor legal business at all: on June 6, Reed reported, "The Courts are stopped, consequently no business done in my profession." The anti-independence bloc, now a minority, lost a vote on June 8, and so the Assembly permitted its congressional delegates to vote for independence. The following week radical assemblymen were so often absent from sessions that the House could not make a quorum. On June 14, the Assembly adjourned until August, its power broken. The radical Associators and committee members, meeting out of doors, had won. Provincial Council member James Tilghman, who had worried about the leveling tendencies of the radicals since 1766, wrung his hands: "I expect a popular Government will soon take place here and God knows what, in that Event, will become of private Property."[109]

From June 18 to June 25, a provincial conference met to approve of independence and organize a constitutional convention. They met, like the July 1774 provincial convention and the first Continental Congress, at Carpenter's Hall. They determined that Pennsylvanians would elect delegates to a state constitutional convention on July 8. Voters would enjoy a much wider franchise than they had under the 1701 constitution, but might be required to swear an oath in support of independence. Pennsylvanians had added their voices in support of independence. Radicals had channeled public opinion out of doors and destroyed the power of the Assembly. With this obstacle lifted, the Continental Congress affirmed the independence of the thirteen colonies on July 2 and approved the Declaration of Independence on July 4.[110]

Philadelphians out of doors exulted. The Second One Hundred met at Philosophical Hall on July 6 and "agreed that the Declaration of Independence be declared at the State House" on July 8. This was a day of great pageantry. The Committee of Safety marched as one to the State House Yard, "where, in the presence of a great concourse of people, the Declaration of Independence was read by John Nixon. The company declared their approbation by three repeated huzzas. The King's Arms were taken down in the Court Room, State House [at the] same time." Some went to a tavern to celebrate; the five battalions of Associators heard the Declaration read; and Philadelphians voted for representatives to the provincial convention. That night Philadelphians celebrated in traditional

urban fashion, with "bonfires, ringing bells, with other great demonstra-
tions of joy upon the unanimity and agreement of the declaration."[111]

A week later on July 15, Pennsylvania opened its constitutional convention in the State House. They completed their work by September 28. The
resulting constitution involved the framing of a government "by common
Consent, and without Voilence [sic]." As part of an enumeration of rights,
the constitution asserted that all power derived from the people; that the
community had a right to reform government; that elections would be regular, open to all taxpayers, and free of treating or bribery; and that people
were free to speak and publish their sentiments. The constitution recognized the rights of the people out of doors in a number of ways. First, "the
People have a right to Assemble together to consult for their Common good,
to instruct their representatives, and to apply to the Legislature for Redress
of Grievances by Address Petition or Remonstrance." Second, "The Doors
of the . . . General Assembly, shall be and remain open for the Admission of
all persons, who behave decently except only when the welfare of this State
may require the doors to be shut." The Assembly would publish bills *before*
debating on them and proposed amendments; and the Assembly was to
publish its votes and proceedings.[112] Thus, Pennsylvania had enshrined
many of the mechanisms of mobilization that had brought the province to
this point. The constitution gave the people freedom of expression through
the press and petitions, allowed input from the politicized masses, and
opened up avenues for out-of-door politicking.[113]

This constitution was bound to stir controversy. Using the same strategy
that radicals had been using since the Townshend duties crisis, the anti-
constitutionalists organized first in a small meeting and then led a larger
public meeting in the State House Yard. A group meeting at the Philosophical
Society Hall on October 17 expressed its displeasure vehemently. It argued
"that the people are generally and greatly dissatisfied with the said
Constitution," that such unrest had contributed to "the late increase of the
number and insolence of tories," and that "more dangerous consequences
may be expected." The group gathered "a large and respectable number of
the citizens of Philadelphia, in the State House Yard" on October 21 and 22,
about 1,500 people. McKean and Dickinson spoke against the proposed
constitution, while James Cannon, Timothy Matlack, Dr. Thomas Young,
and Colonel James Smith spoke in favor. The town meeting passed most of
the resolves, and then appointed committees "to go to each county, to carry
the proceedings and request their concurrence &c."[114] Though the anti-
constitutionalists were using what was now almost a standard method for
mobilizing public opinion in Philadelphia, "A Real Friend to the Christian
Religion" criticized this out-of-doors meeting. The writer used words that
made the radicals sound like James Galloway in 1774: these were "nasty
resolves to be swallowed by an inconsiderate multitude." The author
argued, "Men warmly inspired by popular harangues may be brought
almost to do, or assent to anything." He continued, "If a dissatisfied junto

may at any time be allowed to raise a cry against our Constitution, or Charters, and Plan of Government, and call on the populace to invest the Assembly with powers to pluck up the foundations, and to new model our Constitution, we can never have any stable Constitution or Plan of Government." He continued by disparaging the results of a meeting that had "little authority," writing, "You may be assured that, though a great number of inconsiderate men readily held up their hands, to show their consent to all your rash and hasty resolves . . . , yet there were some, that did not approve your worrying the characters of honest men."[115] This new practice of establishing a government founded on out-of-door mobilization was proving to be a tricky business.

The author's use of the word "foundation" calls to mind a common metaphor that Philadelphians often used to refer to their constitutions. In 1759, James Galloway warned that William Smith of the proprietary faction designed "To sap the Foundation of this Constitution, and raze the firm Basis on which it is established." Galloway warned that a proprietary government would be so ill conceived that it would require constant amendments, thus "endangering [sic] the *Ruin* of its Superstructure" and "securing the Building by taking away its Foundation." Rather than amend it constantly according to the vicissitudes of trade, "exposing it to a *perpetual mutability*, to be blown about by every Wind, and toss'd by every Wave," it was better to establish the charter more soundly "on the *broad capacious Rock*, on which it now lies."[116] Galloway was also wary of subjecting "the Assembly to the directions of a *fickle*, and *confused Multitude*." Ironically, Galloway had been advocating a *change* in the constitution by overthrowing the proprietary system for royal government.[117]

Philadelphians were searching for a "*Rock*," a solid foundation for a government that would serve the public good. Though the city's turbulent politics had inspired many changes since 1764, Philadelphians could still look to its enduring edifices of government. The State House (though its tower was deteriorating) and Court House continued to serve their functions as government buildings, supplemented by the Coffee House and Philosophical Hall. Furthermore, the State House Yard and Market Street continued to play host to political expression out of doors. Benjamin Rush held a public meeting at the State House on November 12 to present instructions to the newly elected Assembly. Rush disapproved of the new state constitution, but he recognized the power of the people out of doors. A few months before, he had reminded his fellow congressmen that the "majority of the people . . . will determine questions out of doors, and wherever we go contrary to their sentiments they will resent it—perhaps with arms." Divisions on the question of independence had already given rise to "Bad consequences." Philadelphians strove for order, yet they also agitated out of doors when dissatisfied.[118]

By the following spring, Philadelphians revived the ceremonial pageantry of their colonial governors. The new chief executives, President

Thomas Wharton Jr. and Vice President George Bryan of the Executive Council, headlined a procession from the State House and "were proclaimed formally at the Court House" on March 5, 1777, "in the presence of a vast concourse of people, who expressed the highest satisfaction on the occasion, by unanimous shouts of acclamation."[119] Pennsylvanians had reestablished a legal authority indoors.

During the Revolutionary era, Philadelphians embraced politics out of doors as a tool of mobilization: petitions and remonstrances; pamphlets, satires, and newspapers; secret negotiations and committee meetings; and parades, processions, and other forms of crowd action. While these tools were necessary to secure independence and reform local governments, Philadelphians also encountered the negative aspects of their republic: the unruly nature of a participatory democracy, the violent nature of mobs, and the pernicious nature of backroom deals. Nor did Philadelphia's negotiations end in 1776. Bitter struggles over the governance of Pennsylvania and America continued during and after the American Revolution. The State House would be the site for the drafting of the Articles of Confederation in 1777, the Constitution in 1787, and Pennsylvania's revised constitution in 1790.[120] The State House Yard, meanwhile, would be the site of protests over price fixing on May 25 and July 26–27, 1779, the mutiny of unpaid soldiers on June 21, 1783, and several lively—and occasionally violent—rallies and protests thereafter.[121] Ultimately, the very radicals who lamented their exclusion in the prerevolutionary years found themselves *inside* the halls of power, worrying about new threats from without doors. Always a state of nature loomed along the horizon, and Americans faced the challenge of governing their mobilized coalition. Americans continued to refine their understanding and craft new theories of popular sovereignty, consent of the governed, and representation. Revolutionary mobilization in Philadelphia and elsewhere in America had wrought new forms of indoor politics, new controversies, and important new developments in the philosophy and practice of government.

EPILOGUE

The Forgotten City

Political activity in the cities helped lead the colonists to independence, but in the process, the cities rendered themselves obsolete. As the Revolutionary War began, urban taverns and narrow streets ceased to be the focus of revolutionary politics. The committees and militia units of the countryside had become politically mobilized, and city dwellers now became minority populations within the larger movement. The war's cataclysmic events deprived the cities of their role in the nation's political development, as the seaport towns were abandoned, occupied, and immobilized. When the British armed forces descended on the shores of America, they seized the cities as essential posts for prosecuting the war against the rebellious colonists. In time the British withdrew from each of the cities, but Americans would no longer think of their seaports as centers for political mobilization; indeed, they would forget or suppress the part that the cities had played in the years of resistance.

When news of the Boston Tea Party reached London in 1774, it was clear to the British that their efforts at countermobilization had failed. The passage of the Coercive Acts set the tone for the new British policy: they would immobilize Boston until its inhabitants were willing to comply with parliamentary supremacy. The new laws and the British occupation of Boston immobilized the city in a number of ways: town meetings were limited; the people would have no voice in the selection of juries or certain government officials; the port was shut up; soldiers chopped down the Liberty Tree; and eventually many of the city's meetinghouses and some other buildings were either torn down or used as stables and barracks for the troops. Many of the city's inhabitants fled the city, while a skittish General Thomas Gage fortified Boston Neck and later restricted the number of people moving in and out of Boston. The British had aimed to stamp out the resistance that had crackled in the city for a decade and more—and they largely succeeded.[1]

Revolutionary politics fizzled in Newport, as well. The British presence presented Newporters with an uncomfortable choice: the inhabitants could either comply with the demands of visiting British ships and supply provisions for the garrison at Boston, or they could heed the rallying cry of local Patriots, who refused to assist British forces. Beginning in November 1774, Captain James Wallace of the *Rose* kept Newport in thrall by actively demonstrating his willingness to destroy local residences, which prompted mass evacuations from the city. By June 1775, the remaining inhabitants had to choose outright Loyalism, radical Patriotism, or a moderate stance that held out hope of reconciliation and made the town's preservation a priority. Newporters, under the guns of the *Rose*, were too panicked and divided to organize politically. The British had neutralized the cities' sites of political mobilization.[2]

Even as politics started to stagnate in the coastal towns, the revolutionary movement took on a life of its own in the New England countryside. Residents of the rural hinterlands took the lead in political and military mobilization. The troop presence in Boston, in addition to the other Coercive Acts, had angered people throughout the thirteen colonies. Country people gathered in town meetings and county conventions, nominated committees of correspondence, drew up resolutions of rights and grievances, signed articles of Association, and stocked up arms and gunpowder. When such provocations led to the battles of Lexington and Concord, the New England militia turned out in massive numbers to surround the British at Boston. Crowds tormented a number of country Loyalists, who fled to Boston for sanctuary. Meanwhile, the Provincial Congress of Massachusetts had convened at Salem, Concord, Cambridge, and Watertown. The center of Patriot activity had moved westward, away from the coastal seaports.[3]

The British, faced with the task of salvaging their crumbling empire, now sought to take advantage of the cities' deep harbors, public buildings, and importance as centers of commerce and communication to shelter and supply the armed forces. As they occupied New York City, Newport, Philadelphia, Savannah, and Charleston, the British hoped to mobilize the local Loyalists and reestablish colonial rule using the cities as strong points. Patriots, on the other hand, found they could no longer depend upon the cities. This situation left them with three choices: defend the cities, abandon them, or destroy them. Local leaders, understandably, begged the Continental Congress to defend American cities. This strategy unfailingly placed the Continental Army at great risk, and generally ended in disaster. The British Navy was powerful enough that it could successfully support an assault on almost any coastal position. As a result, Americans surrendered more men during the battles around New York City in 1776 and during the unsuccessful defense of Charleston in 1780 than they did during the entirety of any given year of the war.[4]

In other cases, the Patriots decided to abandon the cities. These retreats rankled many Patriots because they handed the British all the advantages of the ports. Still, the alternative was often the destruction of the Continental Army—hence, the British took Newport without firing a shot in 1776 and faced minimal opposition at Philadelphia in 1777 (though the Continental defense of the Delaware River proved more tenacious). Many Patriots would never return to these cities, which helped to diffuse the memory of the cities' political mobilization.[5]

Since the Continental Army could not defend the cities, since the British could reap great civilian and military benefit from the cities, and since Loyalists owned much of the cities' property, many radical Patriots did not hesitate to suggest burning coastal cities or allowing the British to destroy them. When the British began shelling Norfolk, Virginia, on New Year's Day, 1776, Patriot forces took the opportunity to burn the rest of the city themselves. Six days after the British occupation of New York City on September 15, 1776, a sixth of the city burned. Patriots were the likely culprits in this instance as well, though after both fires, Patriot newspapers deflected blame toward the British.[6] Patriots also considered permitting the destruction of Boston, Newport, Savannah, and possibly Philadelphia.[7] "Cities may be rebuilt," John Adams wrote, "But a Constitution of Government once changed from Freedom, can never be restored. Liberty once lost is lost forever." Colonel Rufus Putnam agreed: "What are 10: or 20 towns to the grand object[?]" A willingness to allow the destruction of cities became a badge of honor, the subsuming of self-interest beneath support for the common cause. The destruction of cities served the Patriot cause, ultimately, because British atrocities made great propaganda: every burnt town would convince more Americans to leave the brutal empire for the Patriot side.[8]

As the cities became untenable, Patriots desperately sought sanctuary inland to preserve their bid for freedom. Provincial institutions of government eluded the British with cautious retreats equivalent to the defensive, Fabian strategy of General George Washington and the Continental Army. Patriots took advantage of the fact that they were politically decentralized.[9] As Thomas Paine wrote in 1777, "In former wars, the countries followed the fate of their capitals," but this was not the case in America, where British possession of a city gave them little strategic advantage. Britain would see, the Bostonian congressman James Lovell wrote, "that we count Seaports and all the Merchandize they contain of no Value in Comparison of our Rights." General Charles Lee of Virginia cautioned Patriots against a "cursed tenderness for seaport towns." Patriots therefore evaded the enemy in the countryside and met their military, logistical, political, and economic needs without relying on the colonial urban network.[10] Provincial governments moved inland in every state where British forces occupied the coasts, and the Continental Congress met at Lancaster and York during the British occupation of Philadelphia. Mobile institutions, like the Continental Army and the peripatetic legislatures, picked up the banner of political mobilization, sapping the cities of their former prominence. Once Americans perceived that their cities were expendable, or even extraneous, they began to conceive of them differently.

Urban Americans had previously cherished their cities, but during the war many were able to give them up. How did Patriots justify their shift in sentiment? In many cases they did so by devaluing their cities. Benjamin Franklin wrote that cities were places where Americans "generally import only Luxuries and Superfluities," and if Great Britain stopped this commerce it would "contribute to our Prosperity." Ezra Stiles wrote in his diary, "It is a right[e]ous & holy thing with G[o]d to bring the Severest Calamities of this civil War upon the maritime Towns, because [they are] most abounding with Vice & Wickedness." After the burning of Charlestown (fig. E.1) and Falmouth, Abigail Adams asked, "Are we become a Sodom?" As she pondered the Lord permitting "Evil to befall a city," she wrote, "We have done Evil or our Enemies would be at peace with us. The Sin of Slavery as well as many others is not washed away." It was foolish to be too attached to cities, wrote Lovell: "We act as if Commerce and not Acres was our Foundation."[11] Over the course of the war, many Patriots came to see the countryside as worth defending, but deliberately set the cities aside as stinking dens of commerce and corruption.

Figure E.1. In 1775, during the Battle of Bunker Hill, Bostonians watched helplessly as British forces burned neighboring Charlestown. Other coastal towns shared this fate, and many Americans became refugees for want of shelter, yet radical Patriots congratulated themselves for sacrificing sinful cities in the name of liberty. *View of the Attack on Bunker's Hill, with the Burning of Charles Town, June 17, 1775,* by Millar. [London, 1783.] *Picture Collection, The Branch Libraries, The New York Public Library, Astor, Lenox, and Tilden Foundations.*

From a psychological standpoint, abandoning the cities was probably for the best. Outmatched by amphibious British forces, the Americans had garnered few laurels during their fights over seaport cities—only surrenders, retreats, and smoldering ruins. For Americans, commemoration of the stirring victories at rural Trenton, Saratoga, Cowpens, and Yorktown would yield greater satisfaction. The cities and their scenes of revolutionary action were slipping away, not just in terms of their political importance but in American memory as well.

The cities did not fare well under British occupation, and their sad fate was difficult to absorb. With the Patriots evading blockades, attacking ships, repulsing raids and forage expeditions, and retreating into the countryside, the British garrisons were sullen and frustrated. Soon after the battle of Bunker Hill, Gage complained, "I wish this Cursed place was burned," and British soldiers expressed similar frustrations about the cities they occupied. When the British occupied Philadelphia, Adams predicted, "They will hang a Mill stone about their Necks." Adams was correct: by the time the British evacuated the city in 1778, British officers were complaining, "We have possessed it, at the expence of a whole Campaign, to very little purpose." When the British were forced to withdraw from cities, they sometimes expressed regret that they had not burned these places to the ground. Weeks after the evacuation, Lieutenant Loftus Cliffe wrote, "I believe our Troops left Philadelphia extreamly dissatisfied that it was not consumed."[12] If the British stopped short of burning the occupied cities to the ground, they still did extensive damage to the urban landscape. Even with the best of intentions, an occupying army is often ham-handed, and the British army was no different. Patriots returning to the cities after the British evacuations were shocked at what had happened to private residences, churches, and public buildings. Economic hardship also plagued the cities, leading to riots over food, wages, and prices, with women, sailors, and militiamen at the forefront.[13]

Many city dwellers demonstrated questionable patriotism during the war—all had supported substantial Loyalist populations, augmented by the migration of refugees (including blacks hoping to obtain freedom) from the countryside. When the British evacuated Philadelphia in 1778 and took many Loyalists with them, Benjamin Rush wrote, "Our city has undergone some purification, but it still too much resembles the Ark which preserved not only the clean, but the unclean beasts from the effects of the deluge." Many more city dwellers selfishly pursued neutrality and trade with the British in the interest of safety and survival.[14]

In the spring of 1779, Charlestonians almost collapsed in fear and panic as Major General Augustine Prévost and the British army approached the town. Governor John Rutledge sent out a flag of truce and asked Prévost for terms. When the British general demanded surrender and oaths of loyalty to the Crown, Rutledge and the majority of his Privy Council proposed "a neutrality, during the war between Great-Britain and America," with South Carolina's allegiance to be determined by the eventual peace treaty. When Prévost demurred answering such terms, the Patriot general William Moultrie took charge of the situation and refused to surrender. With reinforcements arriving, Prévost lifted the siege, and the British postponed their capture of Charleston for another year.[15] No doubt a series of fire scares and persistent fears of slave revolts in the city had contributed to Charleston's timidity.[16]

When the war ended, the cities were in a difficult position. Their populations had undergone dramatic upheaval (see appendix 1), with Patriots fleeing during the British occupation and Loyalists fleeing when the British left. The economic effects of British blockades, commercial collapse, military appropriation and corruption, uncollected rents, and deteriorated property had been devastating. Loyalism, neutrality, and riots had poisoned the cities in many Americans' minds. The war was particularly devastating to Newport, which never recovered its economic importance or its demographic dominance.

In 1783, a mutiny exacerbated the cities' declining reputation. On June 21, 1783, a few hundred Continental soldiers protested outside the State House in Philadelphia, demanding not to be disbanded until the government had settled their accounts. The delegate Alexander Hamilton of New York favored calling up the Pennsylvania militia, but state authorities (who had jurisdiction) refused. The incident exposed the weakness of the federal government, and an indignant Congress used the mutiny as a pretext to leave Philadelphia. As they decamped for Princeton, New Jersey, congressmen reflected that Pennsylvania's interference, alcohol-fueled mob action, the Loyalist presence, and commercial influence had all made a large city like Philadelphia a threat to decentralized government and unfit as the seat of a republic. At the end of 1783, after news of the Treaty of Paris arrived, the British evacuated New York City. Americans gleefully watched the backs of the British soldiers recede into the distance, yet many Americans were turning their backs on the cities as well.[17]

The cities themselves, of course, survived. The golden age of Newport and Charleston was in the past. Merchants went looking elsewhere for these ports' principal products, the slave trade legally ended in 1807, and neither city had the resources to open new avenues for growth. In Newport, there was almost no one left to remember its revolutionary legacy after the war, and its prominence gave way to Providence. Charleston remained the state's principal port (though it never became a railroad hub), and cotton sustained the state until it exhausted the soil. Charlestonians of the early nineteenth century celebrated their local Revolutionary heroes, but became increasingly defensive about slavery (and against slave uprisings). As their economy faltered, their voices rose. By the 1840s and 1850s, their vigorous campaign of sectionalism had absorbed their revolutionary contributions. By then, neither Newport nor Charleston could look upon the Revolution and its effects with much fondness.[18]

After their postwar economic setbacks, Boston, New York City, and Philadelphia roared into the nineteenth century with new markets, new financial institutions, a cosmopolitan cultural outlook, and plenty of potential to nourish new manufacturing sectors. What the cities lost, ultimately, was their ability to feel that they were leaders in America's political mission. Provincial legislatures had acquired a taste for the relative safety of the countryside, and they sought more central locations away from the coast, amidst a westward-moving population. New York City and Philadelphia each served temporarily as the nation's capital (though New Yorkers had little use for Congress during its stay), and then the federal hub went elsewhere. By the century's end, both cities had relinquished their positions as state capitals. South Carolinians voted to move their state capital inland in 1786, and almost every other state in the nation made similar decisions in the ensuing decades. Rhode Islanders continued to rotate the seat of government. Only Boston remained the center of government, economy, and society for Massachusetts, though it often invited resentment and distrust from the countryside and the rest of the nation, a far cry from the outpouring of sympathy and support it had enjoyed in 1774. The cities would be places of economic rather than political leadership.[19]

Critiques of the cities and urban politics during the late eighteenth century arose from many sources. First, the country itself was still mostly rural: on the eve of independence, 7 or 8% of Americans lived in towns of over 2,500. By 1790, this number had fallen to 5.1% and remained below 7% until 1810. In America, city dwellers were a small minority.[20]

Second, being a city dweller was anathema to agrarian visions of the new nation's political economy. Many Americans, particularly rural southerners, challenged the mercantile interests who represented northern cities. These agrarian champions preferred to lionize the self-sufficient yeoman farmer. As republicans, they distrusted the financiers, foreign traders, courtiers, and bureaucrats that had corrupted the metropolises of Europe and would defile American cities as well. The regional divisions of the early republic helped to define party disputes over foreign policy, debt, tariffs, constitution making, and other issues—and such divisions often led to national policies that favored the rural south over the more urbanized sections of the country.[21]

Third, many Americans—especially the elite—had a strong distaste for the urban crowds, urban problems, and dependent urban poor who were thought to arise from a nation's insufficient attention to agriculture. Americans of the early republic observed the rioting, labor actions, fires, filth, diseases, crimes, irreligion, ethnic mixing, and vice that plagued the cities and saw ample proof for their prejudices. From a political standpoint, the "mobs and tumults, so naturally incident to great cities," were particularly threatening to republican government. These "mobs and tumults," though they had been crucial to political mobilization before the war, were now anathema. Many leaders of the new republic strove to limit the influence of politics out of doors. As Christopher Gadsden had written in 1778, "I am afraid we have too many amongst us who want again to be running upon every fancy to the Meetings of [the] liberty tree," which was a "disease amongst us far more dangerous" than the Loyalists had been.[22]

This anti-urban bias, combined with a suspicion of the metropolises of centralized governments, helped shape the decision to locate the national capital at a sparsely populated bend of the Potomac River rather than in an existing urban center. Those who distrusted a federal city conjured up fearsome images of its power, its privileges, and its threats to civil rights, states' rights, and slavery. Congress chose to build Washington, D.C., on the Maryland-Virginia border as a concession to the rural south and with rural, pastoral notions of classical virtue in mind. The new capital city kept urban values, urban vices, and urban commercial ventures at arm's length, and remained moribund as a city for a hundred years. The founders of the nation's capital sought to escape from cities rather than engage with their disorderly bustle and intrigue. The four Virginians among the country's first five presidents were content with this arrangement. For its first forty years, the United States would largely be a nation led by Virginia, for Virginia, and (all but) from Virginia.[23]

In the new republican government, many city dwellers had a new outlet for political action at the voting booth. Yet even a representative government could frustrate city dwellers' desire for wider political participation, and both of the national political parties that emerged in the 1790s appeared disinclined toward broad-based urban politics. The Federalist Party was the party of urban mercantile interests that detested the French Revolution and its excesses of political mobilization. Though the cities were natural rallying points for the Federalists, the party leaders' elitist attitudes kept them at arm's length from democratic mass politics. In 1791, President Washington wrote, "The tumultuous populace of large cities are ever to be dreaded." His treasury secretary, Alexander Hamilton, distrusted urban tumults as well. When arguing for the Constitution, he had expressed similar fears of "the depredations which the democratic spirit is apt to make on property." Congressman Fisher Ames of Massachusetts railed against the "self-created societies" that sprang up in American cities in the 1790s—in a republic, that sort of political mobilization was unnecessary and dangerous.[24]

Such attitudes, combined with anti-British and pro-French sentiment, drove more city dwellers into the arms of these Democratic societies (which were explicitly modeled on revolutionary organizations) and the Republican Party. The Republicans earned urban support with their canny local alliances and their promises of broader social and economic opportunity. Yet any party with Thomas Jefferson at its head was bound to have mixed feelings toward cities. Jefferson, a rural Virginia slave-owner, made little secret of his distaste for cities and his vision for an agrarian republic. "Those who labor the earth," he wrote, "are the chosen people of God," while "the mobs of great cities" were "sores" on the body politic. "The great mass of our people are agricultural," he wrote during his presidency, "and the commercial cities, though, by the command of newspapers, they make a great deal of noise, have little effect on the direction of the government." Jefferson even called city dwellers a distinct people under a "foreign influence" who were "clamorous" against the "agricultural interest" and its virtuous "country people." Jefferson and his disciple, James Madison, acknowledged a need for commercial and manufacturing centers, but they feared the actions of city people who (economically speaking) were still under the thumb of the British Empire. In Jefferson's mind, the worst institutions of countermobilization (aside from foreign states, armies, and navies) were American countinghouses, banks, and their puppet newspapers. Jeffersonian Republicans may have had electoral success in the cities, but a national story written by Republicans would not be one that celebrated the cities' role in the spirit of 1776. Jeffersonian dismissal of the cities would become painfully clear when the Embargo of 1807 and the War of 1812 disrupted urban commerce. During the Age of Andrew Jackson, Democrats with a backcountry slaveholder at their head would similarly recruit city dwellers while denigrating the cities. Following Jefferson's lead, most Americans located the nation's soul in the countryside.[25]

If the American narrative seemed to be bypassing the cities, they nonetheless remained important sites for political mobilization. The mechanisms of revolutionary mobilization—newspapers, crowd action, parades, voluntary associations, tavern toasts, and organized meetings—largely endured and helped draw together the city and countryside, though these mechanisms also developed in ways that would have rendered them unrecognizable to colonial city dwellers. The nineteenth century was to be an age of wage labor and slave labor, immigration and westward migration, manufacturing and rapid transportation, interest groups and corporations, individualism and party politics. Many of these new phenomena encouraged new mechanisms of mobilization, such as broader suffrage, workers' associations, reform movements, nationalist festivals, party conventions, and the partisan press. In other ways, the changes of the nineteenth century discouraged political mobilization by atomizing the cities and divorcing individualist striving from civic duty. Where revolutionary radicals had claimed to mobilize the people, nineteenth-century city dwellers were mobilizing money, interests, and party. Colonial conflicts had been divisive, and the resistance to Great Britain had given city dwellers (and their rural neighbors) grounds for unity, but after the Revolution new crises appeared to divide Americans much more often than they encouraged broad coalitions.[26]

The Revolution had reshaped American politics, and cities no longer served the same function in the early republic as they had in the colonial era. Postrevolutionary Americans split into partisan camps and splintered into numerous other factions and interest groups with different perspectives on local and national issues. Slavery, labor, foreign policy, race, government, taxation, vice, and immigration all continued to make the cities fertile ground for political action. Coalitions formed and disbanded, just as they had done immediately before the Revolution. Sometimes a broad urban coalition trumped narrower interests; at other times, interests fractured the cities.[27] Of course, at the end of the day, all these mobilizing city dwellers called themselves Americans—and that had been the purpose of the Revolution. American nationhood and the nation's thriving nineteenth-century political culture were the principal legacies of urban political mobilization.

As the nineteenth century progressed, the nature of urban places changed. The richest city dwellers owned most of the wealth and real estate; they were increasingly separating themselves into their own neighborhoods; they kept to themselves in elite voluntary organizations (and helped cement their position through philanthropy); and they controlled city government. The waterfronts retained their potential as hotbeds of political action, but the merchants abandoned them, and the workers who remained were politically weaker and more divided than they had been before the Revolution. As strikes became increasingly common, the urban workplace was often the forge of political protest. Taverns were still vital places for gathering and politics. Yet the loose hierarchy of colonial urban taverns was becoming more stratified, giving way to respectable upper-class hotels and pleasure gardens and rowdy, violent lower-class saloons that were the founts of working-class politics and the targets of temperance forces and local peacekeepers. Church adherence remained spotty, flexible, and pluralistic in the cities, and the variety of religious groups grew even more during the nineteenth century. Churches retained their towering (and increasingly refined) presence in the urban landscape, and they remained powerful sources of mobilization for their congregations. Differences in religious belief continued to play a role in politics, and religion infused debates over slavery, temperance, and nativism. Urban households ceased to be the main sites of production for working men, while household authority, consumption, and virtue persisted as urgent concerns, with new implications for public health and welfare. Popular protests still focused on civic buildings and the squares around them, but these spaces also changed to suit the needs of contemporaries. To encourage order and uniformity, city authorities promoted grid streetscapes, compartmentalized buildings, and courthouses dominated by increasingly professional judges and lawyers. To discourage rioting and out-of-door politics in the streets, cities introduced new prisons and municipal police forces.[28]

Americans had redrawn the boundaries of political mobilization, but some traditional hierarchies persisted. Cities were magnets for free blacks and runaways in cities north and south. In southern cities, blacks found themselves excluded from public life, yet free blacks (and sometimes slaves) engaged in crowd action or pursued their limited freedom in churches and associations, as well as the shadow landscape of the waterfront (and waterborne) community, grogshops, groceries, and illegal schools. Nevertheless, every rumor of slave disobedience or revolt resulted in even tighter restrictions for urban blacks. Emancipated from slavery in the north, blacks nevertheless faced oppression, exclusion, racism, poverty, and violence in nineteenth-century cities. Concentrated populations of urban black men and women found their own political voice in the northern cities, and developed their own sites of political mobilization, especially in churches, schools, and voluntary associations, but also in newspapers, vigilance committees, and public celebrations. As they sought inclusion, equality, and independence, black Americans understood that further political mobilization would be necessary.[29]

Women of the early republic ran up against a prevailing ideology that sought to confine them to the "separate sphere" of the household. Still, men reached out to women for support—though they sometimes co-opted their efforts. White women took their own initiative to congregate, to mobilize, and to escape the confines of the Victorian household. Politicized women took advantage of cosmopolitan cities and their churches, voluntary associations, communication networks, street culture, and print culture for their own purposes and for the public good. In addition to using these old mechanisms of revolutionary mobilization in new ways, women also helped create new sites of political action, such as the theater and the salon.[30]

After the Revolution ended, Americans never fully embraced the urban political mobilization that had preceded it. Rural Americans had numerous reasons to ignore or disclaim the cities, yet urban Americans also forgot their cities' role as cradles that had nursed the resistance to Great Britain. The Sons of Liberty began bowdlerizing the resistance movement as soon as crowds had gotten out of hand in 1765. After the war was over, Boston's Federalist leaders emphasized commemorative celebrations that were orderly, staid, compartmentalized, and hierarchical. As they mobilized the past for purposes of national unity, they robbed the Revolution of its complex, dynamic history. Occasionally city dwellers would explicitly revive and recall the political mobilization of the 1760s and 1770s by hoisting liberty poles or staging new mass meetings at Boston's Faneuil Hall or Philadelphia's State House Yard. Yet these tended to be the acts of radical groups like supporters of the French Revolution, nascent unions, and (paradoxically) both pro-slavery secessionists and the antislavery movement. Local and national leaders refused to sanction such acts—conservative elites understood the risks involved in opening the door to unfettered political mobilization. As a result, most Americans continued the process of forgetting. Developments of the nineteenth century encouraged city dwellers to withdraw into their private domains, and the growing apparatus of local, state, and national governments threatened to insulate itself from the people's input. At moments of crisis, city dwellers remembered their history of popular mobilization and resisted new encroachments on their rights, but this was often an uphill battle.[31]

City dwellers still engaged in political action, and they continued to redefine the boundaries of political mobilization. Their cities persisted as vibrant, dynamic, and cosmopolitan places that fostered diversity and innovation. Radical groups commemorated and celebrated the urban political mobilization that had nourished the American Revolution, even when leading politicians and writers declined to do so. As city builders leveled hills and paved the way for commerce, they erased substantial portions of their revolutionary landscapes. Older forms of political mobilization that had made the cities essential to the revolutionary movement likewise disappeared. The cities had changed since the days of the Stamp Act resistance and the signing of the Declaration of Independence, for better and for worse. The outbreak of the Revolutionary War diminished the cities' importance. Yet the Revolution had begun, not on Paul Revere's lonely road to Concord or amid floating chunks of ice in the Delaware River, but on the waterfront and in the streets, squares, and meeting places of the cities. These were the places that made the Revolution possible.

APPENDIX 1

Population Estimates for the Largest American Cities, 1740–83

	1740	1750	1760	1770	Prewar High	Wartime Low
Philadelphia	10,117	13,926	18,598	26,789	32,073 (1775)	16,000 (1776) to 24,000 (1778)
New York	<10,000	13,300	~15,000	21,000	~25,000 (1775)	5,000 (1776)
Boston	16,800	15,890	15,631	15,520	16,540 (1771)	3,500 (1776)
Charleston	6,300	8,200	9,700	11,500	12,800 (1776)	8,000 (1782)
Newport	6,200	>6,508	7,500	9,000	9,209 (1774)	2,300 (1776) to 5,530 (1782)

Note: Population estimates probably undercount the population of mariners, transients, laborers, servants, unmarried youths, the poor, and other people in the cities. See, for instance, Marietta and Rowe, *Troubled Experiment*, 90–93; Pencak, *War, Politics, and Revolution*, 205; Kulikoff, "Progress of Inequality," 403; Price, "American Port Towns," 137.

Sources: All Philadelphia figures are from Klepp, "Demography in Early Philadelphia," 100, 104–105. Figures for New York in 1740, 1760, and prewar are based on estimates in Nash, *Urban Crucible*, 407–9, while figures for 1750, 1770, and wartime are from Schultz, "Urban America in War and Peace," 130. Figures for Boston, 1740–50 and prewar, are from Nash, *Urban Crucible*, 407–9, while figures for 1760–70 and wartime are from Schultz, supplemented by Price, "American Port Towns," 176. Figures for Charleston, 1740–70 and prewar, are from Coclanis, *Shadow of a Dream*, 114, while the wartime figure is from "Report of a Board of General and Field Officers" to Sir Henry Clinton, April 15, 1782, in General Alexander Leslie's Letter Book, Thomas Addis Emmet Collection, New York Public Library. Figures for Newport are from Schultz, "Urban America in War and Peace," 130, and Crane, *Dependent People*, 123, 157, supplemented by Price, "American Port Towns."

APPENDIX 2

Licenses Granted for Retailing Strong Liquors in New York City, 1753–73, and the Population of New York

Table A2.1. Licenses Granted for Retailing Strong Liquors in New York City, 1753–73

Year[a]	No. of Licenses
1753	160
1754	192
1755	186
1756	–
1757	218
1758	210
1759	232
1760	273
1761	314
1762	241
1763	282[b]
1764	278[c]
1765	279[d]
1766	290[e]
1767	303
1768	325
1769	339
1770	340
1771	365
1772	396
1773	385

Notes: [a] Year begins March 25 unless otherwise noted.
[b] Includes one person who was licensed on December 13, 1763, to retail to March 25, 1764, and paid for license in 1764.
[c] Includes three persons who were licensed in October 1764 to retail to March 25, 1765, and paid for licenses in 1766.
[d] Year begins June 2, 1766.
[e] Includes two persons who paid for their licenses in 1769.

Table A2.2. Population of New York City

Year	Population
1756	13,045 with 2,046 taxables
1771	21,863 with 3,539 taxables

Sources: MCCNY, 5:369, 407, 458, 6:31, 117, 143, 180–81, 219, 259, 317, 359, 397, 7:2, 58, 93, 144, 196, 250, 329, 420, 8:21; Greene and Harrington, *American Population*, 102–3; Salinger, *Taverns and Drinking*, 185, 295 n26; Wells, *Population of the British Colonies*, 110–33.

APPENDIX 3

Newport Denominations: Meetinghouse Size, Congregants, Communicants

Denomination	Dimensions of Meetinghouse (ft.)[a]	Square Footage	No. Families 1770[b]	Est. Number Congregants[c]	Full Members[d]
First Baptist	$40^1/_2 \times 30^1/_2$ (1773: 40 × 50)	$1235^1/_4$ (2000)	40 (50)	180 (225)	18 (37)
Second Baptist	59 × 49	2891	200 (250)	900 (1125)	180 (230)
Sabbatarian Baptist	36 × 27	972	40 (39)	180 (176)	(54)
Separate Bapt. (Dawson)	30–35 × 30–35	$1056^1/_4$[e]	20	90	N/A
Quakers	80 × 45	3600	150	675	—
First Congregational	60 × 40	2400	135	608	70
Second Congregational	60 × 42	2520	130	655 [678]	75
Anglicans	70 × $45^3/_4$ (1763: 100 × $45^3/_4$)	$3202^1/_2$ (4575)	200	900	120
Moravians	39 × 49	1911	35	158	20
Jews	40 × $39^1/_2$	1580	30	135	—

Notes: [a] From Stiles, *Literary Diary*, 1:62, 388. Note that Morgan Edwards gives the following dimensions for the Baptist churches. First Baptist: 40 ft. by 30 ft.; Second Baptist: 62 ft. by 52 ft., extended in 1768 to 76 ft. by 52 ft.; Sabbatarian Baptist: 38 ft. by 26 ft. Edwards, "History of the Baptists," 323, 335, 340. James Honyman described the original length of Trinity Church as "70 foot long and 46 foot wide, beside 6 foot more for the break of the altar and 16 for the belfry, in all 92 feet in length." Hattendorf, *Semper Eadem*, 58. For different measurements, see Jackson, "Newport, R.I., Ecclesiastically."

[b] Estimates are taken from Ezra Stiles, Second Congregational Church Records, NHS, p. 122. Figures in parentheses are for 1771, and are taken from Edwards, "History of the Baptists," 324, 335–36, 340.

[c] Ezra Stiles multiplied the number of families by $4^1/_2$ to arrive at his figures of congregants. That method is used here. See Second Congregational Church Records, NHS, p. 122. Note that Stiles gave more precise figures for his own church, which are indicated in brackets: 135 families or 608 white congregants, plus 70 black congregants. It is possible that he accidentally reversed the figures for First Congregational Church and his own.

[d] Members in full communion, 1770. Estimates are taken from Second Congregational Church Records. Figures in parentheses are for 1771, from Edwards, "History of the Baptists," 324, 335–36, 340. Jews and Quakers do not take communion.

[e] Figure is approximate, determined by squaring $32^1/_2$.

APPENDIX 4

Newport Religious Leaders, 1740–83

Note: Pastors are listed with degrees held or earned while in town, and reasons for end of service, if known. Denominations are listed in the order that the congregation was organized.

First Baptist Church (Five Principle/Particular/"Free Grace")

Organized 1639, becomes Baptist in 1644

John Callender (Harvard College A.B. 1723, A.M.), 1731–48 [died]

Edward Upham (Harvard College A.B. 1734, A.M., Rhode Island College Hon. A.M. 1769), 1748–71 [left due to his unpopular support for locating Rhode Island College in Providence]

Erasmus Kelley (Philadelphia College A.B. 1769, Rhode Island College A.M. 1772), 1771–78 [settled elsewhere]

Second Baptist Church (Six Principle/General/"General Redemption")

Organized 1656

Daniel Wightman, 1736–50 [died]

Nicholas Eyres, 1750–59 [died]

Gardner Thurston, 1759–1802 [died]

Quaker Meeting (Society of Friends)

Organized 1658

New England Yearly Meeting begins in Newport, 1683

Seventh-Day Baptist Church (Sabbatarian)

Organized 1671

John Maxson, 1754–78 [died]

William Bliss, 1779–1808 [died]

First Congregational Church

Organized 1695

Nathaniel Clap (Harvard College A.B. 1690, A.M.), 1695–1746 [died]

William Vinal (Harvard College A.B. 1739, A.M.), 1746–68 [dismissed for alcoholism]

Samuel Hopkins (Yale College A.B. 1741, S.T.D. Rhode Island College, 1790), 1770–1803 [died]

Trinity Church (Church of England)

Organized ca. 1698

James Honyman, 1704–50 [died]

Jeremiah Leaming (Yale College A.B. 1745, A.M.), 1750–54 [interim pastor; settled at Norwalk, CT, in 1758]

Thomas Pollen (Oxford A.B. 1720/1, Oxford A.M. 1723/4), 1754–60 [left for Kingston, Jamaica]

Marmaduke Browne (Trinity College [Dublin] A.B. 1754), 1760–71 [died]

George Bisset (Unknown A.M. from England), 1771–79 [left with British troops]

Second Congregational Church

Organized 1728

James Searing (Yale College A.B. 1725, A.M.), 1731–55 [died]

Ezra Stiles (Yale College A.B. 1746, A.M., Harvard College Hon. A.M. 1754, University of Edinburgh S.T.D. 1765), 1755–78 [became President of Yale College]

Separate Baptist Churches

Timothy Peckom, 1742–48 [congregation dissolved]

Henry Dawson, 1770–74 [moved to New Jersey]

Moravian Church (United Brethren)

Organized 1758

Richard Utley (unknown), 1758

Thomas Yarrell (unknown), 1758–65

Frederick Smith (unknown), 1763

Albert Rudolph Russmeyer (University of Grypswald [Pomerania] A.M., 1738), 1766–83

Jewish Congregation (Congregation Nephuse Israel, later Congregation Yeshuat Israel)

Formally organized 1762, synagogue dedicated 1763

Isaac Touro, Chazzan/Cantor, 1763–76 [left when British occupied Newport]

No permanent rabbi

Sources: Weis, Colonial Clergy of New England; McLoughlin, New England Dissent, 1:11, 423; Sanford, "Entering Into Covenant"; Shipton, *Sibley's Harvard Graduates*, 4:36–39, 8:586–89, 7:150–55, 9:443–48; 10:412–15; Hattendorf, *Semper Eadem*; *Diary of Isaac Backus*, 713 n1; Bolhouse, "Moravian Church," 10–16.

ABBREVIATIONS

ADM: Admiralty
AHR: American Historical Review
APS: American Philosophical Society
BPL: Boston Public Library
CO: Colonial Office
HSP: Historical Society of Pennsylvania
JAH: Journal of American History
JCBL: John Carter Brown Library
LCP: Library Company of Philadelphia
LDC: Letters of Delegates to Congress
LOC: Library of Congress
MCCNY: Minutes of the Common Council of the City of New York
MHS: Massachusetts Historical Society
NEHGR: New England Historical and Genealogical Register
NEQ: New England Quarterly
NHS: Newport Historical Society
NYCCO: New York County Clerk's Office
NYGWPB: New-York Gazette or Weekly Post-Boy
N-YHS: New-York Historical Society
NYMCGQS: New York Mayor's Court of General Quarter Sessions
NYSC: New York Supreme Court
NYJ: New-York Journal or General Advertiser
NYWJ: New-York Weekly Journal
PBF: Papers of Benjamin Franklin
PGW: Papers of George Washington
PHL: Papers of Henry Laurens
PMHB: Pennsylvania Magazine of History and Biography

PRO: Public Record Office
RIHS: Rhode Island Historical Society
SCG: South Carolina Gazette
SCHM: South Carolina Historical Magazine
SCHS: South Carolina Historical Society
T: Treasury
TNA: The National Archives of the United Kingdom
WLCL: William L. Clements Library
WMQ: William and Mary Quarterly

NOTES

Introduction

1. Bridenbaugh, *Cities in Revolt*, 419.

2. "Diary of James Allen," 185.

3. This interpretation differs slightly from the idea that the city was a *theatrum mundi*, or "theater of the world," where preachers, paraders, and the fashion-conscious engaged in various forms of self-presentation. Sennett, *Fall of Public Man*.

4. Greene, "American Revolution: An Explanation," 63–64.

5. For a definition: "mobilization, *n.*," "mobilize, *v.*¹," *OED Online*, September 2002, Oxford University Press, July 11, 2005, http://dictionary.oed.com/cgi/entry/00312898, http://dictionary.oed.com/cgi/entry/00312900; Countryman, *People in Revolution*, 132–35. On boundaries and community formation, see Upton, "Architecture in Everyday Life," 716–18.

6. Lemisch, "Jack Tar in the Streets"; Brown, *Revolutionary Politics in Massachusetts*; Ryerson, "Political Mobilization and the American Revolution"; Maier, *From Resistance to Revolution*; Ammerman, *In the Common Cause*; Olton, *Artisans for Independence*; Isaac, "Popular Mobilization in Virginia"; Shy, *People Numerous and Armed*; Hoerder, *Crowd Action in Revolutionary Massachusetts*; Ryerson, *Revolution Is Now Begun*; Countryman, *People in Revolution*; Rosswurm, *Arms, Country and Class*. For more recent treatments, see McDonnell, "Popular Mobilization"; Linebaugh and Rediker, *Many-Headed Hydra*, chap. 7; Carp, "Fire of Liberty"; Breen, *Marketplace of Revolution*.

7. See, for instance, Zuckerman, *Peaceable Kingdoms*. This is not to say that smaller towns or rural areas were free of internal conflict; see Gross, *Minutemen and Their World*; Brown, *Revolutionary Politics in Massachusetts*; Isaac, "Popular Mobilization in Virginia"; Countryman, *People in Revolution*; McDonnell, "Popular Mobilization." Only 7 or 8% of the people in British America lived in places of 2,500 inhabitants or more, while only 4% lived in the five largest cities. McCusker and Menard, *Economy of British America*, 250.

8. The choice of these five cities neglects three regions of the British Empire in the Western Hemisphere: the regions that would become Canada, the Caribbean

and Atlantic Islands, and the Chesapeake. Kingston, Jamaica, was similar to Charleston in size, if not larger. No doubt it would provide a useful contrast with the American cities, particularly because Jamaica did not join the revolt against Great Britain. Nevertheless, the unique social, military, and political circumstances in the Caribbean were sufficiently distinct that I elected to focus on the American continent. Quebec City, with its population of 8,000 in 1760, also remained in the British Empire, yet here, too, the cultural and military situation of the cities along the St. Lawrence River was distinct from that of the cities in the thirteen colonies. The Chesapeake region, meanwhile, contained almost a third of the thirteen colonies' population. By 1775, Norfolk and Baltimore were sufficiently large urban centers that they, too, would have provided useful points of comparison. Still, these cities were smaller than Newport, neither was a political center, and both cities developed much later than the largest American cities. See sources for appendix 1; also Meinig, *Shaping of America*, 1:245, 249–50; Hornsby, *British Atlantic*; Greene, *Pursuits of Happiness*; Steffen, *Mechanics of Baltimore*; O'Shaughnessy, *Empire Divided*; Parramore, *Norfolk*; Burnard, "Economic Function of Kingston, Jamaica"; Neatby, *Quebec*; Charbonneau et al., "Population of the St. Lawrence Valley," 131.

9. See Bridenbaugh, *Cities in the Wilderness*; Bridenbaugh, *Cities in Revolt*; Butler, *Becoming America*, chap. 1; Withey, *Urban Growth*.

10. The following paragraphs draw from Bridenbaugh, *Cities in Revolt*; Tucker and Hendrickson, *Fall of the First British Empire*; Price, "American Port Towns"; Earle and Hoffman, "Staple Crops and Urban Development"; Meinig, *Shaping of America*, vol. 1; Hornsby, *British Atlantic*, chap. 5.

11. McCusker and Menard, *Economy of British America*, chap. 13; Bushman, *Refinement of America*; Breen, *Marketplace of Revolution*; Morgan, "Business Networks"; Hancock, "Wine Distribution"; Egnal and Ernst, "Economic Interpretation of the American Revolution"; see also chap. 1 of this volume, note 6.

12. Meinig, *Shaping of America*, 1:100–101, 121–22, 125–36, 140–44, 187, 190, 245, 249–50.

13. Olson, *Making the Empire Work*, 7–8, 109–14, 116, 162–64; Bridenbaugh, *Cities in Revolt*, chaps. 4–5, 9–10; Earle and Hoffman, "Staple Crops and Urban Development," 12–13.

14. Shy, *Toward Lexington*; Bridenbaugh, *Cities in Revolt*, 22–24, 60–61; Hornsby, *British Atlantic*, 191–93, 201, 214–16, 222, 229.

15. Kammen, "British and Imperial Interests," 152; Hornsby, *British Atlantic*, 27.

16. Josiah Tucker, *The True Interest of Great Britain Set Forth in Regard to the Colonies*, Tract 4 (Gloucester, 1774), 193–94, quoted in Tucker and Hendrickson, *Fall of the First British Empire*, 382.

17. Bridenbaugh, *Cities in Revolt*, 425.

18. See, for instance, Nash, *Urban Crucible*; Countryman, *People in Revolution*; Hoerder, *Crowd Action in Revolutionary Massachusetts*; Lemisch, "Jack Tar in the Streets"; Lemisch, *Jack Tar*.

19. See Young, *Beyond the American Revolution*, 3–24, 317–64.

20. Nash, *Urban Crucible*, chaps. 7–8; Breen, *Marketplace of Revolution*, xv, 38–39, 61, 127, 158, 167, 169, 201, 220.

21. Tiedemann, *Reluctant Revolutionaries*, 56–57.

22. Nash, *Urban Crucible*, chaps. 7–8.

23. Nash, *Urban Crucible*, chap. 9; Tucker and Hendrickson, *Fall of the First British Empire*, chaps. 2–3, esp. pp. 25–26.

24. The following paragraphs draw from Jensen, *Founding of a Nation*; Morgan and Morgan, *Stamp Act Crisis*; Labaree, *Boston Tea Party*.

25. Wilson, *Sense of the People*, 12.

26. Other historians have observed these developments in British and French cities; see Ozouf, *Festivals and the French Revolution*; Ozouf, "Space and Time"; Hunt, *Politics, Culture, and Class*; Colley, *Britons*; Ogborn, *Spaces of Modernity*; Rogers, *Whigs and Cities*; Wilson, *Sense of the People*.

27. Upton, "Another City," 62–63; see also Olson, *Emblems of American Community*; Markus, *Buildings and Power*. Henri Lefebvre defines three concepts of space: spatial practice (the use of space), representations of space (conceptions of space, knowledge, and ideology), and representational space (symbolisms, often linked to underground life or art); Lefebvre, *Production of Space*, 16–18, 33, 38–46. Lefebvre attaches other, specific meanings to these concepts.

28. John Adams to Jedidiah Morse, November 29, 1815, *Works of John Adams*, 10:182. James Epstein writes that "spatial practice and spatial imaginings" are useful for "understanding how political meanings are ordered, lives are lived and how alternative social worlds are imagined." Epstein, "Spatial Practices," 297; see also Upton, "Architecture in Everyday Life," 712–14, 720.

29. Warner, *Private City*, 14; Foner, *Tom Paine*, 37; Rothschild, *New York City Neighborhoods*, 83–103, 107–33, 182–83; Crane, "Uneasy Coexistence," 104; Crane, *Dependent People*, 49–52; Hornsby, *British Atlantic*, 185–87, 198–202.

30. Tiedemann, *Reluctant Revolutionaries*, 32; Olson, *Making the Empire Work*, 142–43, 156–59; Kammen, *Rope of Sand*.

31. See Crane, *Dependent People*; Crane, *Ebb Tide in New England*; Wood, *Radicalism of the American Revolution*, chaps. 3–5; Bushman, *King and People*; Norton, *Liberty's Daughters*, chap. 5; Morgan, *Slave Counterpoint*, 257–300; Olwell, *Masters, Slaves, and Subjects*, 187–219; Isaac, *Transformation of Virginia*, 70–79; Brewer, *By Birth or Consent*.

32. Bridenbaugh, *Cities in the Wilderness*, 298–300, 328, 364, 407.

33. Wood, *Radicalism of the American Revolution*, pt. 2; Carp, "Fire of Liberty," 785–87, 796–97, 813–14; Rosswurm, *Arms, Country, and Class*; Smith, "Food Rioters"; Hoerder, *Crowd Action in Revolutionary Massachusetts*.

34. Hoerder, *Crowd Action in Revolutionary Massachusetts*; Maier, *From Resistance to Revolution*.

35. Upton, "Another City," 64; Herman, "Embedded Landscapes," 43; Lefebvre, *Production of Space*, 379; Foote, *Black and White Manhattan*, 182; see also Sjoberg, *Preindustrial City*, 133–37; Radford, "Testing the Model of the Pre-Industrial City," 393–94; Hodder, *Reading the Past*, 118–46; Upton, "Architecture in Everyday Life," 714; Upton, *Holy Things and Profane*, 205–19. Scholars of religion particularly embrace these concepts of liminality, margins, thresholds, and boundaries as they relate to the establishment of bonds among a community and the potential for revolutionary change. See Turner, "Variations," esp. p. 37; Turner, *Ritual Process*, chaps. 3–4, esp. pp. 125, 128–29; Orsi, "Crossing the City Line," 3–19, 40–58.

36. See Beeman, *Varieties of Political Experience*, esp. chap. 9; Olson, "Eighteenth-Century Colonial Legislatures"; Nash, *Unknown American Revolution*; Nash, *Urban Crucible*; Waldstreicher, *In the Midst of Perpetual Fetes*, chap. 1; Pencak, Dennis, and Newman, *Riot and Revelry in Early America*; Conroy, *In Public Houses*; Thompson, *Rum Punch and Revolution*; Lemisch, *Jack Tar*; Lemisch, "Jack Tar in the Streets"; Heimert, *Religion and the American Mind*; Stout, "Religion, Communications, and Ideological Origins"; McLoughlin, "Enthusiasm for Liberty."

37. Carp, "Fire of Liberty," 785–96.

38. For a similar interpretation of the French Revolution, see Hunt, *Politics, Culture, and Class*, 12.

39. Most Loyalist studies do not focus on mobilization, but see some of the essays (including the bibliographical essay) in Calhoon, *Loyalist Perception*; also Countryman, *People in Revolution*, 148–54.

40. Greene, "Uneasy Connection."

41. Potter, *Liberty We Seek*, 59–61; Brown, *Good Americans*, 62–69, 224; Bailyn, *Ideological Origins of the American Revolution*; Calhoon, *Loyalists in Revolutionary America*.

42. *NYGWPB*, February 12, April 16, 1770; Bridenbaugh, *Cities in Revolt*, 289–91, 388–425; Nash, *Urban Crucible*, vii, 3–5, 382–84; Isaac, "Popular Mobilization in Virginia"; Brown, *Knowledge Is Power*; Waldstreicher, *In the Midst of Perpetual Fetes*, 17–52; Schlesinger, *Prelude to Independence*; Cook, "Geography and History"; Pred, "Urban Systems Development."

43. Conroy, *In Public Houses*; Thompson, *Rum Punch and Revolution*.

44. Grodzins, *Loyal and the Disloyal*, 29.

45. Schlesinger, "Biography of a Nation of Joiners," 1–16; Carp, "Fire of Liberty"; Brooke, "Ancient Lodges and Self-Created Societies," 273–359; Waldstreicher, *In the Midst of Perpetual Fetes*, 17–52; Newman, *Parades and Politics*, 28; Isaac, "Popular Mobilization in Virginia"; Bullock, "Revolutionary Transformation"; Shields, "Anglo-American Clubs"; Clark, *British Clubs and Societies*; Thompson, *Rum Punch and Revolution*, 62–63, 79, 84–88, 161–66; Salinger, *Taverns and Drinking*, 76–82.

46. Price, "American Port Towns," 140.

47. See *Peter Oliver's Origin and Progress of the American Rebellion*, 29, 41–45, 63–64, 106, 163; Baldwin, *New England Clergy*, chaps. 7–9; Akers, *Called Unto Liberty*; Akers, *Divine Politician*; Griffin, *Old Brick*; Lippy, *Seasonable Revolutionary*; Bridenbaugh, *Mitre and Sceptre*.

48. Pointer, *Protestant Pluralism*; Hutson, *Pennsylvania Politics*.

49. For the prevailing denominational conflicts, see also Clark, *Language of Liberty*.

50. See Habermas, *Structural Transformation of the Public Sphere*, 3–4; Salinger, *Taverns and Drinking*, 248 n9; Thompson, *Rum Punch and Revolution*, 7–9, 15, 17–20; Carp, "Fire of Liberty," 783.

51. Crane, *Ebb Tide in New England*, chaps. 4–5; Norton, *Liberty's Daughters*, 41, 45–50; Brewer, *By Birth or Consent*; for a good bibliography on slave law, see Hoffer, *New York Conspiracy*, 178; Breen, *Marketplace of Revolution*.

52. Bushman, *Refinement of America*, 139.

53. Morgan, *Slave Counterpoint*, 257–300; Olwell, *Masters, Slaves, and Subjects*, 187–219.

54. Morgan, "Black Life in Charleston," 188–89; Berlin, *Many Thousands Gone*, 144–45, 151–57; Edgar, *South Carolina*, 151–53.

55. Greene, *Quest for Power*; Greene, *Peripheries and Center*; Greene, *Negotiated Authorities*; Egnal, *Mighty Empire*; Newcomb, *Political Partisanship*; Bushman, *King and People*; Beeman, *Varieties of Political Experience*.

1. The Boston Waterfront as Contested Space, 1747–74

1. Revere, *British Ships Of War Landing Their Troops*.

2. Bridenbaugh, *Cities in Revolt*, 421.

3. For a similar approach, see Bourne, *Cradle of Violence*.

4. Withey, *Urban Growth*.

5. Konvitz, *Cities and the Sea*, 164–65, 178; Vickers, *Young Men and the Sea*, 132–34.

6. Carr, "Boston's Demographics," 583–84; Pencak and Crandall, "Metropolitan Boston," 57–65; Forbes, *Paul Revere*, 7; Konvitz, *Cities and the Sea*, 179–80; Bailyn, *Voyagers to the West*, 25, 283, 573–74; Villaflor and Solokoff, "Migration in Colonial America," esp. 543–44, 549–51; Burrows and Wallace, *Gotham*, 126–35, 194–95; Foote, *Black and White Manhattan*, chap. 2, p. 207; Wax, "Demand for Slave Labor"; Soderlund, "Black Importation and Migration"; Wokeck, *Trade in Strangers*; Foner, *Tom Paine*, 43–45; Morgan, "Black Life in Charleston," 188–89; Crane, *Dependent People*, 24, 51–52, 64–65; Berlin, *Many Thousands Gone*, 144–45, 155–57, 178–80, 182–83; Bridenbaugh, *Cities in Revolt*, 4, 14, 85–89, 134–36, 216, 231, 272, 322–23, 332–34, 421; Baseler, *Asylum for Mankind*, 105–13.

7. Richard Revere and Thomas Irving to Lords of Treasury, April 18, 1768, TNA: PRO T 1/465, pt. 5; Joseph Harrison and Benjamin Hallowell Jr. to Lords of Treasury, April 30, 1768, TNA: PRO T 1/465, pt. 3; Letter of John Scollay, quoted in Schlesinger, Colonial Merchants, 314. See also Andrews, "Boston Merchants"; Tyler, *Smugglers and Patriots*; Innes, *Creating the Commonwealth*, 271–300; Price, "American Port Towns," 145–49, 173, 183; Wolkins, "Boston Customs District." On merchant communities in other cities, see Jensen, *Maritime Commerce of Colonial Philadelphia*; Doerflinger, *Vigorous Spirit of Enterprise*; Crane, *Dependent People*; Harrington, *New York Merchant*; Matson, *Merchants and Empire*; Sellers, *Charleston Business*; Calhoun, Zierden, and Paysinger, "Geographic Spread of Charleston's Mercantile Community"; Nash, "Organization of Trade and Finance in the Atlantic Economy."

8. Nash, *Urban Crucible*, 64, 434 n46; see also Lemisch, "Jack Tar in the Streets"; Lemisch, *Jack Tar*; Rediker, "Motley Crew of Rebels"; Linebaugh and Rediker, *Many-Headed Hydra*; Crane, *Dependent People*, 34, 63, 69.

9. Kulikoff, "Progress of Inequality," 376–77, 385–86, 411–12; see also Smith, *Lower Sort*, 78.

10. *Boston Gazette*, November 11, 1765; see also Foner, *Tom Paine*, 21, 32–33.

11. Brown, *Knowledge Is Power*, 3–41, 82–131, 268–96, quote 129.

12. Chudacoff, *Evolution of American Urban Society*, 26.

13. Kulikoff, "Progress of Inequality," 394, 397; see also Crane, *Dependent People*, 49–51; Vickers, *Young Men and the Sea*, 132–36.

14. *Inhabitants and Estates of Boston* (formerly Thwing Database, MHS).

15. Triber, True Republican, 26–27; *Boston Gazette*, February 18, 1765, January 13, 20, August 4, 1766, March 2, 1767; Young, "George Robert Twelves Hewes," 579.

16. Fischer, *Paul Revere's Ride*, 10; Forbes, *Paul Revere*, 49–51.

17. Thwing, *Crooked and Narrow Streets*, 55, 81, 192; Day and Day, "Another Look at the Boston 'Caucus,'" 21; Wood, *Radicalism of the American Revolution*, 57–63; Brown, *Knowledge Is Power*, 34, 112–14, 123–24, 129, 277–80.

18. Rediker, *Between the Devil and the Deep Blue Sea*, 64–65; Gilje, *Liberty on the Waterfront*, 16–17; Thatcher, *Traits of the Tea Party*, 34, 58.

19. Vickers, *Farmers and Fishermen*, 140, quote 189; Earle, *Sailors*, 4; Rediker, *Between the Devil and the Deep Blue Sea*, 82, 169–204; Creighton, "American Mariners and the Rites of Manhood," 147; Vickers, "Beyond Jack Tar"; Gilje, *Liberty on the Waterfront*; Chase, "Boundaries in Time," 171.

20. Franklin, "Silence Dogood No. 13," in PBF, 1:41–42; see also *Boston Gazette*, July 9, 1764.

21. Rediker, *Between the Devil and the Deep Blue Sea*, 205–53; Bolster, "Inner Diaspora," 421–27, 433, 437; Bolster, *Black Jacks*, chaps. 1, 3; Linebaugh and Rediker, *Many-Headed Hydra*, chap. 6.

22. Tager, *Boston Riots*, chap. 3; Brunsman, "Evil Necessity."

23. Other historians have attributed seamen's collectivity to lower-class exclusion or proletarian strength. Lemisch, *Jack Tar*, 6; Lemisch, "Jack Tar in the Streets," 371–80; Labaree et al., *America and the Sea*, 106–9.

24. Adams, *A Defence of the Constitutions of Government of the United States of America*, in *Works of John Adams*, 4:392; *Boston Gazette*, March 11, 1765, March 2, 1767; Piersen, *Black Yankees*, 14–18, 43, 192 n30; Greene, *Negro in Colonial New England*, 84–88, 111–21; Morgan, "Black Life in Charleston," 196–200.

25. Fowler, *Baron of Beacon Hill*, 69; John Hancock to Nathaniel Tidmarsh, MS Am 727, BPL.

26. Memorial of Owen Richards, April 11, 1768, TNA: PRO T 1/465, pt. 6.

27. See Wood, *Radicalism of the American Revolution*, 63–92; Brown, *Knowledge Is Power*, 24–25.

28. Although one scholar has questioned the accuracy of the 1771 tax valuation list, the small number of Bostonians who owned "superficial feet of wharf" is apparent from the lists: 28% of the 252,914 feet of listed wharfage is unaccounted for due to missing records (including John Rowe, Esq., owner of Rowe's Wharf), and Long Wharf accounted for 20% of total Boston wharfage; only forty-eight men were taxed as owners of the remainder of the wharfage. On average, these men possessed real estate worth about £36, and thirty of them had merchandise worth an average of £755. Half the men owned slaves, a third owned vessels, and many owned livestock, warehouses, distilleries, and tanneries. Pruitt, *Massachusetts Tax Valuation List of 1771*; Warden, "Inequality and Instability."

29. See entries for William Clough, John Preston, Nathaniel Wales, Peter Roberts, Benjamin Gooding, Silas Atkins, Robert Robins, Fortesque Vernon, William Pain, Jonathan Brown, Clement Collins, Bartholomew Rand, John Coffin, James Richardson, Thomas Amory, John Hooton, David Spear, John Ruddock, and John Ballard in *Inhabitants and Estates of Boston*.

30. Warden, *Boston*, 68; *Boston Pier*, 3–7; *Reports of the Record Commissioners of the City of Boston*, 16:89.

31. *Letters and Diary of John Rowe*, 6, 128, 158, 159, 186, 238, 267.

32. *Boston Gazette*, September 3, 1764; November 5, 1764.

33. The evidence here is spotty, but see transactions in *Inhabitants and Estates of Boston*.

34. Towner, "Indentures of Boston's Poor Apprentices," 417 n1, 424–26, 435–68; Earle, *Sailors*, 24–25, 43–45, 50; Rediker, *Between the Devil and the Deep Blue Sea*, 84–86; Rediker, "Anglo-American Seaman as Collective Worker," 259–61; Labaree et al., *America and the Sea*, 106, 108–9; Gilje, *Liberty on the Waterfront*, 27–32; Thatcher, *Traits of the Tea Party*, 39–40, 49; Brown, *Knowledge Is Power*, 122–23; Nash, "Up from the Bottom in Franklin's Philadelphia," 57–83; Vickers, *Young Men and the Sea*, chap. 4.

35. Tyler, *Smugglers and Patriots*, 7–13, 258–77; *Boston Gazette*, April 30, May 28, 1764; Baker, *Boston Marine Society*, 302–9, 316–69.

36. Tyler, *Smugglers and Patriots*, 56, 62–63, 258–77, 285 n17; Pierce, introduction to *Letters and Diary of John Rowe*, 36–37.

37. Drake, *Old Boston Taverns*, 45–50; Warden, *Boston*, 156–58; Forbes, *Paul Revere*, 118–21; Day and Day, "Another Look at the Boston 'Caucus,'" 31–33.

38. Petitions of Joseph Ingersoll [July 17, 1764], Joseph Coolidge [July 9, 1765], Jonathan Tarbox [September 30, 1767], Edward Blanchard [July 12, 1769], to the . . . Court of General Sessions of the Peace . . . for the County of Suffolk, and the Gentlemen the Selectmen of Boston, Misc. Bound MSS, 1763–73, MHS; Conroy, *In Public Houses*, esp. 129–31, 255, 257–58; Linebaugh and Rediker, *Many-Headed Hydra*, 181–83. For relationships among seamen and tavernkeepers, see also Lemisch, *Jack Tar*, 57–60.

39. *Boston Gazette*, April 30 (Burton and Butler), May 21 (Shehane), November 12 (waterfront theft), 1764, June 9 (Regan), 1766; see also Waldstreicher, *Runaway America*, chap. 1; Waldstreicher, "Reading the Runaways"; Lemisch, *Jack Tar*, chap. 3; Linebaugh and Rediker, *Many-Headed Hydra*, chap. 6; Foote, *Black and White Manhattan*, 189–99; Quimby, *Apprenticeship in Colonial Philadelphia*, chap. 5; Salinger, *Labor and Indentured Servants in Pennsylvania*, 101–9, 112–13, 133; Smith, "Runaway Slaves"; Crane, *Dependent People*, 79–80; Wood, *Black Majority*, chap. 9; Morgan, "Black Life in Charleston," 214–17.

40. Young, *Shoemaker and the Tea Party*, 56–57.

41. Young, "Women of Boston," 192–93; *Boston Gazette*, June 6, 1763, May 19, 1766; Boyle, "Boyle's Journal," 84:154.

42. Brigham et al., "Captain-Lieutenant John Larrabee"; Pencak, *War, Politics, and Revolution*, 119–22, 136, 217–19, 222–23; Nicolson, *Francis Bernard*, 124–26, 137–38, 226; Nicolson, "Nathaniel Coffin and the Loyalist Interpretation"; Nicolson, "Massachusetts Friends of Government"; Maier, *From Resistance to Revolution*, 31, 61–63, 139–42, 151–54, 278–79; Bailyn, *Ordeal of Thomas Hutchinson*; Morgan and Morgan, *Stamp Act Crisis*, chap. 12; Calhoon, *Loyalists in Revolutionary America*, chaps. 4, 20, 24; Potter, *Liberty We Seek*, 17, 24, 27–30, 64–65, 73–74.

43. Wood, *Radicalism of the American Revolution*, 61–63, 74–75, 77–92; Brown, *Knowledge Is Power*, 24.

44. Wroth, "Massachusetts Vice-Admiralty Court," 38–45, 48–49, 63 n37, 65 n62; Ubbelohde, *Vice-Admiralty Courts*, 5, 9–13, 16, 20–21; Rediker, *Between the Devil and the Deep Blue Sea*, 140, 140 n69, 119–21, 212–13, 240–41, 312–16; Barrow, *Trade and Empire*, 60–64, 88, 128, 154, 167; William Bollan to Board of Trade, February 26, 1742/43, in Swift, *Historical Manuscripts*, 1:4–6.

45. Barrow, *Trade and Empire*, 76–77; Joseph Harrison and Benjamin Hallowell Jr. to Lords of Treasury, April 30, 1768, TNA: PRO T 1/465, pt. 3.

46. Barrow, *Trade and Empire*, 143; *Boston Gazette*, January 2, 1764; Bollan to Board of Trade, in Swift, *Historical Manuscripts*, 1:3–8.

47. Bollan to Board of Trade, in Swift, *Historical Manuscripts*, 1:5, 8; Thomas Hancock to Captain Simon Gross, April 12, 1742, quoted in Baxter, *House of Hancock*, 85–86, 86 n25; *Peter Oliver's Origin and Progress of the American Rebellion*, 46–48; Schlesinger, *Colonial Merchants*, 42–49; Jensen, *Maritime Commerce of Colonial Philadelphia*, chap. 10; Crane, *Dependent People*, chaps. 8–9.

48. Brunsman, "Evil Necessity," chaps. 1–2, 4; Pencak, *War, Politics, and Revolution*, 124, 185–90; Lax and Pencak, "Knowles Riot," 166–68, 170–80; Hoerder, *Crowd Action in Revolutionary Massachusetts*, 61.

49. *Journals of the House of Representatives of Massachusetts*, 20:84, 99.

50. Lax and Pencak, "Knowles Riot," 179–82; Brunsman, "Evil Necessity," chap. 4; Rediker, *Between the Devil and the Deep Blue Sea*, 77–115, 205–53; Rediker, "Motley Crew of Rebels," 157–68.

51. Lax and Pencak, "Knowles Riot," 183–94; William Shirley to Lords of Trade, December 1, 1747, in *Correspondence of William Shirley*, 1:412–19, quote 416; Lemisch, "Jack Tar in the Streets," 387, 391.

52. Proclamation of William Shirley, November 21, 1747, and William Shirley to Lords of Trade, December 1, 1747, in *Correspondence of William Shirley*, 1:410, 418; *Reports of the Record Commissioners of the City of Boston*, 14:127; [Boston] *Independent Advertiser*, February 8, 1748; Lax and Pencak, "Knowles Riot," 194–210, 214.

53. Earle, "Boston, Vanguard," 161–69; Nash, *Urban Crucible*, 235–36, 241–46; Boyle, "Boyle's Journal," 84:164; *Letters and Diary of John Rowe*, 74, 78; Pencak, *War, Politics, and Revolution*, 190; Tyler, *Smugglers and Patriots*, 25–63, 72; Pencak and Crandall, "Metropolitan Boston," 71–73, 78–79.

54. Barrow, *Trade and Empire*, 178–84; Tyler, *Smugglers and Patriots*, chap. 1; Gould, *Persistence of Empire*, 55–57, 68–69; 108–9; Smith, *Writs of Assistance Case*; Morgan and Morgan, *Stamp Act Crisis*, 38–43; Hoerder, *Crowd Action in Revolutionary Massachusetts*, 86–87; Hutchinson, *History of the Province of Massachusetts*, 3:92–93; *Letters and Diary of John Rowe*, 64; "Shearjashue Squeezum," *Boston Gazette*, August 27, 1764, March 18, 1765. On the choice of the term "Black Act," see Thompson, *Whigs and Hunters*.

55. Alexander Colville to Admiralty, August 8, 1765, TNA: PRO ADM 1/482; *Massachusetts Gazette*, May 17, 1764, quoted in Morgan and Morgan, *Stamp Act Crisis*, 46–47; see also Frese, "Smuggling, the Navy, and the Customs Service."

56. Stout, "Manning the Royal Navy," 179; Charles Leslie to Charles Antrobus, December 18, 1764, TNA: PRO ADM 1/482; Colville to Admiralty, February 16, 1765, TNA: PRO ADM 1/482; Lemisch, *Jack Tar*, chap. 2; Tyler, *Smugglers and Patriots*, 264–65; Linebaugh and Rediker, *Many-Headed Hydra*, 218; Brunsman, "Evil Necessity," chap. 5; Skemp, "Newport's Stamp Act Rioters," 55–56.

57. Colville to Admiralty, November 9, 1764, August 8, 1765, TNA: PRO ADM 1/482.

58. Morgan and Morgan, *Stamp Act Crisis*, 159–61, 234–36, 244–45; Hoerder, *Crowd Action in Revolutionary Massachusetts*, 92–97; Zobel, *Boston Massacre*, 37–38; Tager, *Boston Riots*, 41–51; Maier, *From Resistance to Revolution*, 85–86, 307; *Boston Gazette*, April 30, 1764.

59. Francis Bernard to Lord Halifax, August 15, 1765, Sparks MSS, Harvard Houghton Library, 4.4.141; Hoerder, *Crowd Action in Revolutionary Massachusetts*, 97–102, 120; Morgan and Morgan, *Stamp Act Crisis*, chap. 8; Zobel, *Boston Massacre*, 29–36; *Boston Gazette*, August 19, 1765.

60. Hoerder, *Crowd Action in Revolutionary Massachusetts*, 104–10.

61. Morgan and Morgan, *Stamp Act Crisis*, chap. 9; Skemp, "Newport's Stamp Act Rioters"; Lemisch, *Jack Tar*, chap. 4, esp. pp. 84, 90–91, 101–3; Linebaugh and Rediker, *Many-Headed Hydra*, 229–30.

62. "Speech of Governor Bernard, to the Council and House of Representatives, September 25, 1765," in Bradford, *Speeches of the Governors of Massachusetts*, 41–42.

63. "Answer of the House of Representatives, to the Governor's Speech, October 23, 1765," in Bradford, *Speeches of the Governors of Massachusetts*,

44–45, 47; *Boston Gazette*, September 23, 1765; Maier, "Charleston Mob," 176; Olton, *Artisans for Independence*, 38–39; Hutson, "Investigation of the Inarticulate"; Lemisch and Alexander, "White Oaks."

64. *Boston Gazette*, September 16, 1765, March 3, May 19, 1766; McCrady, *History of South Carolina under the Royal Government*, 569–71; *Massachusetts Gazette and Boston News-Letter*, March 24, 1768; Hutchinson, *History of the Province of Massachusetts*, 3:160–64, 188.

65. Boyle, "Boyle's Journal," 84:253; see also Dickerson, *Navigation Acts*, 212–19; Smith, "Charles Paxton."

66. Breen, *Marketplace of Revolution*, chap. 7; Jensen, *Founding of a Nation*, chaps. 9–10.

67. Hulton, *Letters of a Loyalist Lady*, 8; Joseph Harrison to Lord Rockingham, June 17, 1768, in Watson, "Joseph Harrison," 588; Boyle, "Boyle's Journal," 84:253.

68. Harrison to Rockingham, in Watson, "Joseph Harrison," 588–89; *Massachusetts Gazette and Boston News-Letter*, March 24, 1768; Hulton, *Letters of a Loyalist Lady*, 11; Francis Bernard to Lord Shelburne, March 19, 21, 1768, Sparks MSS, Harvard Houghton Library, 10.2.74, 78; Bernard to Lord Barrington, March 4, 1768, *Barrington-Bernard Correspondence*, 147–50; *Letters and Diary of John Rowe*, 150; Hutchinson, *History of the Province of Massachusetts*, 3:188; Hoerder, *Crowd Action in Revolutionary Massachusetts*, 146, 156–57. For similar acts in other cities, see Schlesinger, *Colonial Merchants*, 101; Jensen, *Maritime Commerce of Colonial Philadelphia*, 149–52.

69. Charles Paxton to Lord George Townshend, May 18, 1768, in "Letters of Charles Paxton," 349.

70. Wolkins, "Daniel Malcolm and the Writs of Assistance," 14, 26–84; Baker, *Boston Marine Society*, 331, 338; *Reports of the Record Commissioners of the City of Boston*, 23:29. The spelling of Malcom's last name varied.

71. Bernard to Shelburne, March 21, 1768, Sparks MSS, Harvard Houghton Library, 10.2.78; Hutchinson, *History of the Province of Massachusetts*, 3:188; Commissioners of Customs to Lords of Treasury, March 28, 1768, Treasury 1/465, pt. 6; Hoerder, *Crowd Action in Revolutionary Massachusetts*, 156–57.

72. Dickerson, "John Hancock"; Hutchinson, *History of the Province of Massachusetts*, 3:188–89.

73. Memorial of Owen Richards, April 11, 1768, TNA: PRO T 1/465, pt. 6; Baker, *Boston Marine Society*, 338–40; Allan, *John Hancock*, 102–4; Hoerder, *Crowd Action in Revolutionary Massachusetts*, 164.

74. *Boston Gazette*, June 20, 1768; *Boston Post-Boy and Advertiser*, June 20, 1768; Hutchinson, *History of the Province of Massachusetts*, 3:191; Hoerder, *Crowd Action in Revolutionary Massachusetts*, 165–66; Zobel, *Boston Massacre*, 72–74; Wolkins, "Seizure," 249–50; Thomas Hutchinson to Richard Jackson, June 16, 1768, in Wolkins, "Seizure," 282–83.

75. *Boston Gazette*, June 20, 1768; *Boston Post-Boy and Advertiser*, June 20, 1768; Joshua Henshaw Jr. to William Henshaw, June 15, 1768, NEHGR; Wolkins, "Seizure," 250–55, 281–84; *Peter Oliver's Origin and Progress of the American Rebellion*, 69; Joseph Harrison to Lord Rockingham, June 17, 1768, in Watson, "Joseph Harrison," 589–92; Hutchinson, *History of the Province of Massachusetts*, 3:189–91; Dickerson, "John Hancock," 517–30, 536 n37; Dickerson, *Navigation Acts*, 231–50; Hoerder, *Crowd Action in Revolutionary Massachusetts*, 166–68; Zobel, *Boston Massacre*, 74–76; Boyle, "Boyle's Journal," 84:254–55.

76. Joshua Henshaw Jr. to William Henshaw, NEHGR, 403; see also Board of Commissioners to Samuel Hood, June 15,1768, TNA: PRO ADM 1/483; Francis Bernard, Thomas Hutchinson, Andrew Oliver and Robert Auchmuty to Henry Hulton, William Burch, Charles Paxton and John Robinson, December 22, 1768, in Wolkins, "Seizure," 279–80.

77. Hulton, *Letters of a Loyalist Lady*, 11–17; Carp, "Fire of Liberty."

78. Hulton, *Letters of a Loyalist Lady*, 11–17; Bernard to Barrington, July 20, 1768, *Barrington-Bernard Correspondence*, 167; Bernard to John Corner, July 4, 1768, TNA: PRO ADM 1/483; *Peter Oliver's Origin and Progress of the American Rebellion*, 70.

79. *Letters and Diary of John Rowe*, 181; *Rex v. Corbet*, case 56, in *Legal Papers of John Adams*, 2:276–335; John Adams to Jedediah Morse, January 20, 1816, in *Works of John Adams*, 10: 204–10; John Adams to William Tudor, December 30, 1816, in *Works of John Adams*, 2:224–26; Hutchinson, *History of the Province of Massachusetts*, 3:231–33; Boyle, "Boyle's Journal," 84:258–59; Dickerson, *Boston under Military Rule*, 3, 23, 51, 90, 94–95, 104–5, 110–12; Hoerder, *Crowd Action in Revolutionary Massachusetts*, 199–200; Zobel, *Boston Massacre*, 113–31; Stout, "Manning the Royal Navy," 182–83; Brunsman, "Evil Necessity," chap. 5.

80. *Massachusetts Gazette [Boston Evening-Post]*, June 20, 1768.

81. Hoerder, *Crowd Action in Revolutionary Massachusetts*, 175–76, 199–200, 241–42; Lemisch, "Jack Tar in the Streets," 379–80, 387.

82. Francis Bernard to Lord Shelburne, March 21, 1768, Sparks MSS, Harvard Houghton Library, 10.2.78–79; Boyle, "Boyle's Journal," 84:255, 260; Hoerder, *Crowd Action in Revolutionary Massachusetts*, 204–8; Tyler, *Smugglers and Patriots*, 112–21, 127–32, 136–38, 167–69; Hulton, *Letters of a Loyalist Lady*, 26–27; Nash, *Urban Crucible*, 360–61.

83. *Reports of the Record Commissioners of the City of Boston*, 16:289, 297–98; 18:16–17; Breen, *Marketplace of Revolution*, 254–67; Andrews, "Boston Merchants," 223–25.

84. Tyler, *Smugglers and Patriots*, 136–69; Hoerder, *Crowd Action in Revolutionary Massachusetts*, 161–62, 198–99, 212–14; Young, "Women of Boston," 195–96.

85. Journal of Transactions in Boston, New England Papers, Sparks MSS, Harvard Houghton Library, 10.3.55–56; Hulton, *Letters of a Loyalist Lady*, 26–27.

86. *Reports of the Record Commissioners of the City of Boston*, 18:13, 20; Nash, Urban Crucible, 362.

87. Tyler, *Smugglers and Patriots*, chaps. 3–4; Labaree, *Boston Tea Party*, chaps. 2–3.

88. Lemisch, *Jack Tar*, chap. 5; Boyer, "Lobster Backs," 294–308.

89. Boyle, "Boyle's Journal," 84:256; Shy, *Toward Lexington*, 303–17; Dickerson, *Boston under Military Rule*, 21; Forbes, *Paul Revere*, 141–42; Zobel, *Boston Massacre*, 104, 107–12, 134–44, 164–79, 182–83; Hoerder, *Crowd Action in Revolutionary Massachusetts*, 177–84, 190–96; "A complaint from the town dock watch," 9; *Peter Oliver's Origin and Progress of the American Rebellion*, 88–89.

90. Zobel, *Boston Massacre*, 184–210; Hoerder, *Crowd Action in Revolutionary Massachusetts*, 224–33, 240–43; *Rex v. Weems*, case 64, in *Legal Papers of John Adams*, 3:266; Thatcher, *Traits of the Tea Party*, 103–23; *Peter Oliver's Origin and Progress of the American Rebellion*, 89–91; Hulton, *Letters of a Loyalist Lady*, 26–28;

Thomas Gage to the Earl of Hillsborough, April 10, 1770, in Davies, *Documents of the American Revolution*, 2:70–73.

91. Thomas Young to Hugh Hughes, September 15, 1770, Misc. Bound MSS, 1763–73, MHS; Zobel, *Boston Massacre*, 238–40.

92. There is some evidence that the Boston incidents were more vicious than tarrings and featherings elsewhere in North America. Irvin, "Tar, Feathers, and the Enemies of American Liberties"; Young, "English Plebeian Culture" 185–86, 189–94, 205; *Peter Oliver's Origin and Progress of the American Rebellion*, 93–94, 98; Boyle, "Boyle's Journal," 84:265; Memorials of Owen Richards, Josiah King, and Joshua Dutton, May 21, 1770, New England Papers, Sparks MSS, Harvard Houghton Library, 10.4.1; Memorials of John Woart, Robert Hallowell and William Sheaffe, May 21, 1770, New England Papers, Sparks MSS, Harvard Houghton Library, 10.4.2; Hoerder, *Crowd Action in Revolutionary Massachusetts*, 241, 268–69; Zobel, *Boston Massacre*, 159–61, 233; Hulton, *Letters of a Loyalist Lady*, 26–28, 70–72; Thatcher, *Traits of the Tea Party*, 124–33; Thomas Newell, Diary for 1773 to the End of 1774, January 25, 1774, BPL.

93. William Bull to Board of Trade, November 3, 1765, quoted in McDonough, *Gadsden and Laurens*, 72; and in Walsh, *Charleston's Sons of Liberty*, 36–37; William Bull to earl of Hillsborough, November 30, 1770, in Davies, *Documents of the American Revolution*, 2:274.

94. Linebaugh and Rediker, *Many-Headed Hydra*, 218–19; Maier, *From Resistance to Revolution*, 6–8, 10–15; Hoerder, *Crowd Action in Revolutionary Massachusetts*, 188–90, 209, 222, 268; Irvin, "Tar, Feathers, and the Enemies of American Liberties"; Brunsman, "Evil Necessity," chap. 5; Tyler, *Smugglers and Patriots*, 157; Schlesinger, *Colonial Merchants*, 246–52, 262–67.

95. For background, see Labaree, *Boston Tea Party*, 85–103, 110–13, 135–36; Drake, *Tea Leaves*, 5–23.

96. Pigou & Booth to James & Drinker, October 4, 1773, Drinker Papers, 1739–79, HSP, quoted in Labaree, *Boston Tea Party*, 91.

97. Labaree, *Boston Tea Party*, 88–105, 109–18, 152–60; Tyler, *Smugglers and Patriots*, 186–203; Drake, *Tea Leaves*, 23, 26–38, 210, 223, 282–91; Hulton, *Letters of a Loyalist Lady*, 64–65; Rogers, "Charleston Tea Party"; Tiedemann, *Reluctant Revolutionaries*, 175–83; Ryerson, *Revolution Is Now Begun*, 33–38.

98. Labaree, *Boston Tea Party*, 118–38, 145; Drake, *Tea Leaves*, 38–58, 96–97, 104, 320–31; Hoerder, *Crowd Action in Revolutionary Massachusetts*, 255–61; Hulton, *Letters of a Loyalist Lady*, 69–70; *Peter Oliver's Origin and Progress of the American Rebellion*, 102.

99. Rediker, "Anglo-American Seaman as Collective Worker," 258, 264–67; Labaree, *Boston Tea Party*, 138–45; Drake, *Tea Leaves*, 58–81, 92–97, 103, 109–10, 116, 119, 124, 137, 141–45, 162, 166–67, 336; Hoerder, *Crowd Action in Revolutionary Massachusetts*, 262–64; *Inhabitants and Estates of Boston*; *Peter Oliver's Origin and Progress of the American Rebellion*, 102–3.

100. Brown, *Revolutionary Politics in Massachusetts*; Schlesinger, "Liberty Tree," 448–50; Young, "Liberty Tree," esp. 347, 351, 362, 384 n39.

101. Gross, *Minutemen and Their World*, 42–46; Bushman, "Massachusetts Farmers," 77–79; Labaree, *Boston Tea Party*, 124, 138; Warden, *Boston*, 296.

102. John Adams to Benjamin Rush, May 21, 1807, in *Works of John Adams*, 9:597–98; Conroy, *In Public Houses*, 276; see also Brown, *Knowledge Is Power*, 65–81, 132–59, 187–89, 245–53.

103. Boyle, "Boyle's Journal," 84:374; Warden, *Boston*, 288–91.

104. "An Association, Signed by 89 Members of the Late House of Burgesses," May 27, 1774, in *Papers of Thomas Jefferson*, 1:107–8; see also Reid, *Constitutional History: Rights*, 33.

105. Boyle, "Boyle's Journal," 84:374.

106. Newell Diary, June 14, August 4, 1774, BPL; Boyle, "Boyle's Journal," 84:374–81.

107. Hulton, *Letters of a Loyalist Lady*, 73–74; Newell Diary, June 15, 1774, BPL.

108. Boyle, "Boyle's Journal," 84:377; George Washington to George William Fairfax, June 10–15, 1774, *PGW: Colonial Series*, 10:96.

109. Gross, *Minutemen and Their World*, 9–10, quote 61; Earle, "Boston, Vanguard," 157–58, 165, 169–71; Patterson, *Political Parties in Revolutionary Massachusetts*, 74–90, chap. 4.

110. Bushman, "Massachusetts Farmers"; Bailyn, *Ideological Origins of the American Revolution*, 94–95, 99–143; Rediker, "Motley Crew of Rebels," 172.

2. Orderly and Disorderly Mobilization in the Taverns of New York City

1. John Case to James Rivington, January 7, 1775, *Rivington's New York Gazetteer*, January 12, 1775; "A Friend to Constitutional Liberty," "To the PUB-LIC," *NYJ*, February 2, 1775; see also Maier, *Old Revolutionaries*, 73; Ranlet, *New York Loyalists*, 49, 184–85.

2. Two recent works address the taverns as sites of political mobilization: Conroy, *In Public Houses*; and Thompson, *Rum Punch and Revolution*. Both of these works, while groundbreaking and useful, largely explain tavern culture in their chosen geographic locations. Conroy describes the taverns of colonial Massachusetts as places of opposition to a dominant Puritan culture that did not exist in New York. Nor did New York's taverns precisely resemble those of Philadelphia. New York never fully embraced price ceilings on the sale of drinks, and so by the eve of the Revolution—when Thompson observes increasing class stratification among Philadelphia's taverns—New York taverngoers had long been accustomed to the loose ranking of taverns. For treatments of New York taverns, see Bayles, *Old Taverns of New York*; Rice, *Early American Taverns*.

3. McCusker, *Rum and the American Revolution*, 1:433, 441–44, 468–79, 2:563; see also Rorabaugh, *Alcoholic Republic*, 8–10, 225–26, 232–33; Owen, *Narrative of American Voyages*, 33; Kalm, *Travels into North America*, 131; Salinger, *Taverns and Drinking*, 3, 128; Bridenbaugh, *Cities in Revolt*, 106–7, 296; Koeppel, *Water for Gotham*, 28–34.

4. Hamilton, *Gentleman's Progress*, 193; see also "An Essay on Bumpers," *NYG-WPB*, December 19, 1748; Jaher, *Urban Establishment*, 167; Klein, "Cultural Tyros," 113; Rothschild, *New York City Neighborhoods*, 43; MCCNY, 7:57, 211, 269, 440, 8:98, 103; Copy of a Resolution of the Common Council, September 15, 1775, New York City Misc. MSS, Box 11, N-YHS; New York City Inquisitions, New York City Misc. MSS, Boxes 9–11, N-YHS; Charles Nicoll Ledger, 1758–74, N-YHS; Kammen, *Colonial New York*, 1, 56, 63–64, 154–55.

5. Alexander Mackraby to Sir Philip Francis, March 5, June 4 (quote), 13, 1768, "Philadelphia Society," 279, 282 (quote), 283.

6. Hamilton, *Gentleman's Progress*, 89, 185; M'Robert, *Tour Through Part of the North Provinces of America*, 9–10; various entries in "Letter Book of John Watts."

7. William Gordon to Chief Justice William Allen, March 9, 1754, HSP, quoted in Harrington, *New York Merchant*, 201.

8. Smith, *History of the Province of New-York*, 1:227; John Watts to Samuel Carter, March 27, 1762, to Thomas Astin, April 10, 1762, to Gedney Clarke, May 18, 1762, to Philip Gibbs, April 5, 1764, to John Collins, July 30, 1765, in "Letter Book of John Watts," 30, 42, 55, 236–37, 362.

9. Rothschild, *New York City Neighborhoods*, 66–67, 69–74, 80.

10. Crowley, "Alcoholic License."

11. Honyman, *Colonial Panorama*, 27; see also Birket, *Some Cursory Remarks*, 43–44.

12. Bushman, *Refinement of America*, 161–62.

13. Graydon, *Memoirs*, 82.

14. Singleton, *Social New York under the Georges*, 303–8; Valentine, *History of the City of New York*, 281–82; *Colonial Laws of New York*, 5:532; *NYWJ*, November 7, 1748; Mackraby to Francis, June 4, 1768, "Philadelphia Society," 282–83.

15. Hamilton, *Gentleman's Progress*, 89, 176, 179; Honyman, *Colonial Panorama*, 29; John Watts to Gedney Clarke, November 5, 1762, in "Letter Book of John Watts," 95, "Montresor Journals," 363; Lydon, *Pirates, Privateers, and Profits*, 225–32, 245–46.

16. Ogborn, *Spaces of Modernity*, 209–10.

17. Hodges, *New York City Cartmen*, 46–47, 182.

18. *NYWJ*, April 26, 1740; Lydon, *Pirates, Privateers, and Profits*, 185–87, 198, 220–21; Lemisch, *Jack Tar*, 57–59; Nash, *Urban Crucible*, 165–67, 236–40; Thompson, *Rum Punch and Revolution*, 80.

19. Lydon, *Pirates, Privateers, and Profits*, 245.

20. Salinger, *Taverns and Drinking*, 8–18.

21. John Watts to James Napier, June 1, 1765, "Letter Book of John Watts," 355.

22. Dickerson, *Navigation Acts*, 175–79, 184–86; Harrington, *New York Merchant*, 200–201, 318–22, 331–32.

23. *Colonial Laws of New York*, 1:789, 2:768–87, 3:828–29; MCCNY, 3:80–81; Ogborn, *Spaces of Modernity*, chap. 5; Brewer, *Sinews of Power*; "B." [William Livingston], No. 2, "Remarks on the Excise; and the Farming it, shewn to be injurious to the Province," December 7, 1752, and No. 25, "Remarks on the Excise, resumed," May 17, 1753, in Klein, *Independent Reflector*, 61–68, 228–34; see also Kalm, *Travels into North America*, 136.

24. *Colonial Laws of New York*, 3:951–57, 4:1–8, 191–98, 5:500–510; MCCNY, 1:80–81, 100–101, 137, 183–84, 301, 5:215.

25. John Watts to General Robert Monckton, January 23, 1765, "Letter Book of John Watts," 326–27; MCCNY, 4:207, 314.

26. Greenberg, *Crime and Law Enforcement*, 38–39; Salinger, *Taverns and Drinking*, 128. For examples of theft in taverns, see *New-York Gazette* (Weyman), September 7, 1767; *NYJ*, September 3, 1767; see also *New-York Gazette* (Weyman), March 5, 1764.

27. *NYJ*, October 30, 1766 (misdated as October 23), February 12, 1767, December 14, 1769, September 23, 1773; *NYGWPB*, June 27, 1765, March 28, 1768; *New-York Chronicle*, November 13, 1769.

28. Mary Anderson vs. Dr. Harding et al., court pleadings, reel 5, NYMCGQS pleadings, reel 48, K-460, NYCCO; King vs. John Lawrence et al., brief, court pleadings, reel 48, K-501, NYCCO; King vs. John Lawrence et al., July 1755, NYSC pleadings, reel 49, K-650, NYCCO; King vs. Elizabeth Anderson,

August 1754, NYSC pleadings, reel 49, K-638, NYCCO; King vs. [Elizabeth] Anderson, affidavit of John French, July 1754, reel 51, K-1022, NYCCO; *NYG-WPB*, March 21, March 28, 1757; King vs. Thomas Martin and Edward Groomes, April 1765, presentment, reel 50, K-788, NYCCO; King vs. Thomas Martin and Edward Groomes, April 1765, indictment, reel 50, K-797, NYCCO; Cadwallader Colden to William Pitt, December 4, 1760, "Colden Letter Books," 1:43–44; King vs. John Dalton, January 1765, NYSC, John Tabor Kempe Papers, N-YHS; *NYGWPB*, October 22, 1767.

29. *Colonial Laws of New York*, 3:194–95; 5:621–24.

30. King vs. Samuel Connor, April 1775, NYSC pleadings, reel 50, K-869, NYCCO; King vs. Mary Clarke, August 1769, NYMCGQS pleadings, reel 48, K-523, NYCCO; King vs. Robert Mitchner, October 1769, [filed under King vs. Mary Daily], John Tabor Kempe Papers, N-YHS; King vs. eight different persons, [n.d.], John Tabor Kempe Papers, N-YHS.

31. King vs. eight different persons, [n.d.], John Tabor Kempe Papers, N-YHS; King vs. Henry Smith, February 1749, NYMCGQS pleadings, reel 51, K-997, NYCCO; "Burghers and Freemen," 166; King vs. Edward McCoy, May 1768, NYMCGQS pleadings, reel 48, K-483, NYCCO; King vs. Peter Hampton, August 1752, NYMCGQS pleadings, reel 51, K-999, NYCCO; King vs. John Dowers, October 1767, NYSC, John Tabor Kempe Papers, N-YHS; King vs. Sarah wife of Edward Dyllon, July 1774, NYSC pleadings, reel 50, K-856, NYCCO; Grand jury presentment against Catherine O'Neal for keeping a disorderly house, 1767, New York Legal MSS, N-YHS; King vs. Anthony O'Neal, January 1762, NYSC pleadings, reel 49, K-744, NYCCO; King vs. Mary Cavenagh, Court of Oyer and Terminer [n.d.], John Tabor Kempe Papers, N-YHS; King vs. Elizabeth Kelsey, January 1775, NYSC pleadings, reel 47, K-250, NYCCO; King vs. Catherine Carroe, October 1767, NYSC, John Tabor Kempe Papers, N-YHS; King vs. Mary Connor, October 1767, NYSC, John Tabor Kempe Papers, N-YHS; King vs. Barberie Myer, October 1773, NYSC pleadings, reel 47, K-247, NYCCO; King vs. Hester Campbell, October 1773, NYSC pleadings, reel 48, K-380, NYCCO; Greenberg, *Crime and Law Enforcement*, 58, 67–68.

32. King vs. William Powers, February 1769, NYMCGQS pleadings, reel 48, K-460, NYCCO; King vs. Catherine O'Neal, October 1766, NYSC pleadings, reel 47, K-249, NYCCO; King vs. eight different persons, [n.d.], John Tabor Kempe Papers, N-YHS; Greenberg, *Crime and Law Enforcement*, 50–53, 57–59, 138, 140, 142; Salinger, *Taverns and Drinking*, 163.

33. Greenberg, *Crime and Law Enforcement*, 89, 91–92, 96–98, 198–99; *NYG-WPB*, November 5, 1767.

34. *Colonial Laws of New York*, 2:952–55, 3:166, 194–95, 460–62, 756–59, 4:490.

35. *MCCNY*, 134–35.

36. Lender and Martin, *Drinking in America*, 21–29; Mancall, *Deadly Medicine*, esp. chaps. 4–5.

37. *Colonial Laws of New York*, 2:679–83; *MCCNY*, 1:2, 25, 139, 223–24, 276–77; Salinger, *Taverns and Drinking*, 24–38, 101–2, 130–36, 228–30, 237; Foote, *Black and White Manhattan*, 203–4.

38. Hodges, *Root and Branch*, 91–99; Davis, *Rumor of Revolt*; Lepore, *New York Burning*; Hoffer, *New York Conspiracy*; Wilder, *In the Company of Black Men*, 22–26; Linebaugh and Rediker, *Many-Headed Hydra*, chap. 6; *NYWJ*, June 29, 1741; Foote, *Black and White Manhattan*, 163, 166–68, 171–72, 183; Zabin, "Places of Exchange."

39. Hodges, *Root and Branch*, 15–16, 48–50, 67, 88–89, 95–96.

40. King vs. Catherine O'Neal, October 1766, NYSC pleadings, reel 47, K-249, NYCCO; see also King vs. Henry Smith.

41. The King vs. Cornelius Edison, John Crawford, John Brown, and Eneas a Mulatto Slave, October 1771, NYSC pleadings, reel 47, K-274, NYCCO; "Burghers and Freemen," 182.

42. See Linebaugh and Rediker, *Many-Headed Hydra*, chap. 7.

43. M'Robert, *Tour Through Part of the North Provinces of America*, 3, 5; see also *New-York Mercury*, July 23, 1753, October 6, 1760; *NYGWPB*, June 4, 1767; *New-York Gazette* (Weyman), September 7, 1767; Salinger, *Taverns and Drinking*, 23–24, 47, 220–26; Thompson, *Rum Punch and Revolution*, 89–90; Clark, *British Clubs and Societies*, 198–204; Smith, *History of the Province of New-York*, 1:226–27; Hamilton, *Gentleman's Progress*, 89; Zabin, "Places of Exchange," chap. 5. The tavern was also a place for flouting gender conventions; see *Contrast*, Evans #11223; Hamilton, *Gentleman's Progress*, 84; Graydon, *Memoirs*, 52; Salinger, *Taverns and Drinking*, 231–32.

44. Hamilton, *Gentleman's Progress*, 42–43, quote 87, 186; John Case to James Rivington, January 7, 1775, *Rivington's New York Gazetteer*, January 12, 1775.

45. Kann, *Republic of Men*, chap. 3.

46. Graydon, *Memoirs*, 82.

47. Graydon, *Memoirs*, 93.

48. "Peaceable" to John Peter Zenger, February 2, 1740/41, *NYWJ*, May 11, 1741; see also *NYGWPB*, November 12, 1767.

49. James Murray to Sir John St. Clair, December 18, 1765, James Murray to [Mrs. Moreland], August 9, 1764, Dickinson Papers, Logan Papers, HSP, 40:58, 59.

50. Hamilton, *Gentleman's Progress*, 82, 88, 174; "Peaceable" to John Peter Zenger, February 2, 1740/41, *NYWJ*, May 11, 1741; "Alcanor," *New-York Chronicle*, July 13, 1769.

51. Hamilton, *Gentleman's Progress*, 179.

52. Smith, *History of the Province of New-York*, 1:227.

53. *Diary of John Adams*, 2:104–5, 109 (quote), 110; see also Mackraby to Francis, June 13, 1768, "Philadelphia Society," 283.

54. *Diary of John Adams*, 2:109.

55. Hamilton, *Gentleman's Progress*, 185–86.

56. Bushman, *Refinement of America*, 185–86; Zabin, "Places of Exchange," chap. 5.

57. Shields, *Civil Tongues and Polite Letters*.

58. Graydon, *Memoirs*, 93; Smith, *History of the Province of New-York*, 1:226; Hamilton, *Gentleman's Progress*, 88; John Watts to Robert Porter, June 7, 1763, "Letter Book of John Watts," 144.

59. "Alcanor," *New-York Chronicle*, July 13, 1769; Clark, *British Clubs and Societies*, 225–27; Conroy, *In Public Houses*, 266; Thompson, *Rum Punch and Revolution*, 97–99.

60. Graydon, *Memoirs*, 93; "A. B.," "Reflections on immoderate Drinking," *NYWJ*, June 19, 1749.

61. Hamilton, *Gentleman's Progress*, 43.

62. Hamilton, *Gentleman's Progress*, 88.

63. See Conroy, *In Public Houses*, 2.

64. Lang, *History of Freemasonry in New York*, 25–39; Clark, *British Clubs and Societies*, 302–4, 390.

65. Crèvecoeur, "Reflections on the Manners of y' Americans," in *More Letters from the American Farmer*, 102.

66. "An Essay on Bumpers," *NYGWPB*, December 19, 1748; "To the Author of the Essay on Bumpers," *NYGWPB*, December 20, 1748; "Hezekiah Broadbrim," "To the Author of the Sayings . . . Concerning Bumpers," *NYWJ*, January 2, 1748/9; Shields, *Civil Tongues and Polite Letters*, 26–27.

67. "Z. Q.," "A Discription of the Inhabitants, and Customs of the Province of Drinkallia," *NYWJ*, June 5, 1749.

68. Hamilton, *Gentleman's Progress*, 45–47, 80–83.

69. Thompson, *Rum Punch and Revolution*, 116–23.

70. Smith, *Historical Memoirs*, 1:91, 107.

71. Shields, *Civil Tongues and Polite Letters*, 31–33.

72. William Livingston to Chauncey Whittelsey, August 23, 1744, Letter Book, 1744–45, Sedgwick Papers, MHS, quoted in Klein, *Independent Reflector*, 410 n3; Jones, *History of New York*, 1:3–4; William Livingston to Noah Welles, November 27, 1746, January 27, 1747, Johnson Family Papers, Yale University; Charles Nicoll Account Book, 1768–75, N-YHS; William Smith to William Smith Johnson, May 25, 1749, Johnson Papers, Connecticut Historical Society, quoted in Upton, *Loyal Whig*, 19; *Contrast*, Evans #11223.

73. Lender and Martin, *Drinking in America*, 34–35; "X. and Z." [John Morin Scott and William Livingston], in No. 3, "The Abuses of the Road, and City-Watch," December 14, 1752, in Klein, *Independent Reflector*, 73; "Shadrech Plebianus" [William Peartree Smith], March 17, 1753, in No. 29, "Of the Extravagance of our Funerals," June 14, 1753, in Klein, *Independent Reflector*, 259–60, 447; "T. T." [William Livingston], in No. 48, "Of the Waste of Life," October 25, 1753, in Klein, *Independent Reflector*, 404–8, 410 n5.

74. "And-per se-and" to John Peter Zenger, *NYWJ*, February 13, 1748/9; "A Brother Philosopher," "To the Sage Philosophers . . . ," *NYWJ*, February 27, 1748/9; Klein, "Cultural Tyros," 116.

75. "Scotus Ferrarius," "To Mr. S—th Clerk and Tachygraphist of a Society, said to be instituted for the Promotion of useful Knowledge," March 28, 1749, in *NYWJ* (supplement), April 3, 1749.

76. Haley, "Voluntary Organizations," 98–99; Keep, *History of the New York Society Library*, 138, 148, 151, 171, 175; Moot Club, N-YHS; *New-York Gazette and the Weekly Mercury*, July 1, 1771, January 3, 1774; *NYJ*, March 28, 1776; "Social Club of New York," 467; *New-York Chronicle*, September 14, 1769.

77. Hume quoted in Ogborn, *Spaces of Modernity*, 89–90; Clark, *British Clubs and Societies*, 94, 98–100, 141–93, 229–30, 388–406.

78. Clark, *British Clubs and Societies*, 5.

79. Haley, "Voluntary Organizations," 45–47, 91–92; Moot Club, N-YHS.

80. Smith, *Historical Memoirs*, 1:80; Clark, *British Clubs and Societies*, 204–8.

81. "X.," "To the Author of the several Rhapsodies . . . ," *NYWJ*, March 20, 1748/9.

82. Crèvecoeur, "Manners of y' Americans," in *More Letters from the American Farmer*, 102–3; see also Thompson, *Rum Punch and Revolution*, 143.

83. Quoted in Countryman, *People in Revolution*, 58; "Z." [William Livingston], in No. 32, "Of Elections, and Election-Jobbers," July 5, 1753, in Klein, *Independent Reflector*, 278–84; see also Crèvecoeur, "Manners of y' Americans," in *More Letters from the American Farmer*, 102–3; *Diary of John Adams*, 1:96; Varga, "Election Procedures," 264–66, 268, 271; Conroy, *In Public Houses*, 247–48, 250–51; Thompson, *Rum Punch and Revolution*, 134–41; Dinkin, *Voting in*

Provincial America, 98–99, 102–6; McDonough, *Gadsden and Laurens*, 101; *Newport Mercury*, June 23, 1764; Beeman, *Varieties of Political Experience*, 77, 314 n25.

84. "J.W., a Squinter on Public Affairs," *Mode of Elections Considered*, Evans #11517; see also "Bibibus," *Tooth-Full of Advice*, Evans #10833; "Occasionalist," *To the Freeholders, and Freemen, of the City of New-York*, Evans #11017; "Publicola," *To the Public*, Evans #11829.

85. Hamilton, *Gentleman's Progress*, 88; Tully, *Forming American Politics*, chap. 6, quote p. 243; see also *Watchman, No.2*, Evans #11916; George Clinton to the Duke of Bedford, June 28, 1749, in O'Callaghan, *Documents Relative to the Colonial History of the State of New-York*, 6:513–14.

86. Smith, *History of the Province of New-York*, 2:244–45.

87. "Believer in Politicks," *Political Creed for the Day*, Evans #11047; see also Tully, *Forming American Politics*, 174, 485 n50.

88. Tully, *Forming American Politics*, 244.

89. Conroy, *In Public Houses*, 242–49.

90. *NYGWPB*, December 5, 1765.

91. Clark, *British Clubs and Societies*, 175–82, 403–4.

92. "Willem Johonas Von Dore Manadus," *To the Freeholders and Freemen of the City*, Evans #11040.

93. Jones, *History of New York*, 1:25; Lydon, *Pirates, Privateers, and Profits*, 267.

94. Maier, *Old Revolutionaries*, 51–52, 59.

95. Leake, *Life of John Lamb*, 9; Tiedemann, *Reluctant Revolutionaries*, 168–70; Maier, *From Resistance to Revolution*, 95–96, 303, 312 n24; *New-York Gazette and Weekly Mercury*, June 19, 1769.

96. Willett, *Willett Families*, 1:111–13; Bailey, "Willett Family"; Wager, *Marinus Willett*, 3; Willett, *Narrative of Marinus Willett*, 29–30; Tiedemann, *Reluctant Revolutionaries*, 218.

97. Tiedemann, *Reluctant Revolutionaries*, 72.

98. Petition of George Spencer [November 26, 1761], "Colden Papers," 6:89–99, quotes 93.

99. *New-York Gazette* (Weyman), January 30, 1764.

100. *New-York Gazette* (Weyman), March 5, 1764.

101. Tiedemann, *Reluctant Revolutionaries*, 64.

102. Zacharias Hood to Cadwallader Colden, September 16, 1765, "Colden Papers," 7:77–78; David Colden to Zacharias Hood, September 16, 1765, "Colden Letter Books," 2:33; Weslager, *Stamp Act Congress*, 112–15; Ketchum, *Divided Loyalties*, 97, 122–24; Maier, *From Resistance to Revolution*, 53–69; Tiedemann, *Reluctant Revolutionaries*, 62–73, 79; Becker, *Political Parties in New York*, 41.

103. The following paragraphs are based on Robert R. Livingston to Robert Monckton, November 8, 1765, "Aspinwall Papers," 559–67; E. Carther to unknown, November 2, 1765, in *New York City during the American Revolution*, 41–49, quote 42; *NYGWPB*, September 12, 1765; *New-York Mercury*, November 7, 1765; "Montresor Journals," 336–38; Tiedemann, *Reluctant Revolutionaries*, 1–3, 70, 74–78; "Colden Papers," 7:56–72, 84–95, 98–101; Cadwallader Colden to Henry Seymour Conway, November 5, 1765, "Colden Letter Books," 2:54–56. Carther described himself as "in high spirits full of Old Madeira" during the days of rioting.

104. Ogborn, *Spaces of Modernity*, 118–19, 142–48, 150–55.

105. Cadwallader Colden to Major Thomas James, December 11, 1765, "Colden Letter Books," 2:64–65; "Montresor Journals," 369–70; Stokes, *Iconography*, 4:786, 6:627.

106. See also Robert R. Livingston to Robert Monckton, November 8, 1765, "Aspinwall Papers," 566; Tiedemann, *Reluctant Revolutionaries*, 86–87; Maier, *From Resistance to Revolution*, xv, 21–26.

107. "Cethegus," *New-York Chronicle*, May 8, 15, June 29, 1769.

108. Conroy, *In Public Houses*, 254.

109. "Colden Papers," 7:84–85, 91; Colden, *Conduct of Cadwallader Colden*, 460; "Montresor Journals," 344–46, 355, 358, 362; *New-York Mercury*, February 17, 1766; "Belinda," "A Letter from a Young Lady in Town to her Friend in the Country," *A Patriotic Advertisement*, Shipton and Mooney #41576.

110. Joseph Allicocke to [John Lamb], November 21, 1765, John Lamb Papers, N-YHS; *New-York Mercury*, December 2, 9, 23, 1765, January 13, 1766; NYG-WPB, January 9, 1766; Tiedemann, *Reluctant Revolutionaries*, 73–98.

111. Cadwallader Colden to Henry Seymour Conway, September 23, 1765, "Colden Letter Books," 2:35; Tiedemann, *Reluctant Revolutionaries*, 74, 94–96; Maier, *From Resistance to Revolution*, 78–82, 94–96; Morgan and Morgan, *Stamp Act Crisis*, 258–60.

112. "A Son of Liberty," *NYGWPB*, December 26, 1765, February 20, 1766; "Montresor Journals," 348–50, 355, quote 357; Champagne, "Military Association of the Sons of Liberty"; Carp, "Fire of Liberty," 796, 811–14, 817.

113. "Montresor Journals," 349, 351.

114. *New-York Mercury*, February 17, 1766.

115. John Stranger to the Duke of Blenheim, October 9, 1770, Blenheim Papers, vol. 572, British Library Additional MSS, #61672, f. 114.

116. *New-York Mercury*, May 26, 1766; "Montresor Journals," 368, 370–71; O'Shaughnessy, *Empire Divided*, 92.

117. *NYJ*, March 17, 24, 1768.

118. Conroy, *In Public Houses*, 266; Waldstreicher, *In the Midst of Perpetual Fetes*, 17, 20, 26.

119. "Montresor Journals," 347.

120. *New-York Gazette* (Weyman), February 13, 1766 (supplement).

121. *NYJ*, March 16, 23, 1769.

122. "Semper Idem" to John Holt, *NYJ*, March 1, 1770.

123. Haley, "Voluntary Organizations," 55–56.

124. "Montresor Journals," 56–62, 66, 68.

125. John Watts to Thomas Astin, January 1, 1762, to Francis Clarke, January 2, 1762, to Gedney Clarke Jr., January 16, 1762, to Isaac Barré, February 28, 1762, "Letter Book of John Watts," 3, 6, 10. See also Mackraby to Francis, March 5, 9, 1768, "Philadelphia Society," 279, 281.

126. Jesse Lemisch, "Jack Tar in the Streets," 381.

127. "Montresor Journals," 346.

128. Shy, *Toward Lexington*, 176–77.

129. John Watts to James Napier, June 1, 1765, "Letter Book of John Watts," 26.

130. Chatham quoted in Tucker and Hendrickson, *Fall of the First British Empire*, 235; "Montresor Journals," 353, 374; Mackraby to Francis, March 5, 1768, "Philadelphia Society," 280; Shy, *Toward Lexington*, 232, 252–53; Tiedemann, *Reluctant Revolutionaries*, 90–91, 108–14, 117–24, 136–45, 184–85; see also [John Watts to General Robert Monckton], September 12, 1766, January 23, 1768, Chalmers Papers, New York, New York Public Library, 2:15, 18.

131. Kann, *Republic of Men*, 55–56, 69–71; *NYJ*, September 3, 1767; *New-York Gazette* (Weyman), September 7, 1767.

132. Zobel, *Boston Massacre*; Hoerder, *Crowd Action in Revolutionary Massachusetts*; Conroy, *In Public Houses*, 251.

133. Graydon, *Memoirs*, 51–54, quote 54; see also Shy, *Toward Lexington*, 253; Thompson, *Rum Punch and Revolution*, 56–60.

134. *NYJ*, November 6, 13, 1766; see also *New-York Gazette* (Weyman), November 17, 1766. The law against serving soldiers was renewed in 1768; *MCCNY*, 6:44–45, 7:195.

135. Tiedemann, *Reluctant Revolutionaries*, 85, 109; *NYJ*, October 23, 1766; *New-York Gazette* (Weyman), October 27, 1766. See also King vs. Thomas Lee, February 1771, NYMCGQS pleadings, reel 51, K-1033, NYCCO; *NYGWPB*, June 25, 1767; *NYJ*, February 4, 1768, August 31, 1769.

136. King vs. William Jones, February 1769, NYMCGQS pleadings, reel 48, K-515, NYCCO; King vs. John Campbell, February 1769, NYMCGQS pleadings, reel 48, K-469, NYCCO; King vs. Thomas Dunn and Jane Dunn, August 1770, NYMCGQS pleadings, reel 48, K-519, NYCCO; King vs. Mary Clarke, August 1769, NYMCGQS pleadings, reel 48, K-523, NYCCO.

137. "Montresor Journals," 341, 356–57, 368.

138. The symbol had counterparts in other cities; for instance, the liberty trees and poles in Boston, Charleston, and Newport, and the statue of William Pitt in Charleston. Pencak, "Play as Prelude to Revolution," 132–33, 136–37, 140, 142, 145; McDonough, *Gadsden and Laurens*, 76–77, 121, 101, 106, 112–15, 180, 190, 294 n59; Schlesinger, "Liberty Tree"; Young, "Liberty Tree," esp. 347–51, 384 n39.

139. "Montresor Journals," 382–84; *NYJ* (supplement), March 26, 1767; Tiedemann, *Reluctant Revolutionaries*, 110–12.

140. *NYJ*, November 17, 1768; Tiedemann, *Reluctant Revolutionaries*, 129–33.

141. "At this alarming Crisis," Evans #11379; *NYJ*, January 18, March 1 (supplement), 1770; *NYGWPB*, February 5, 1770; Leake, *Life of John Lamb*, 54–55; Tiedemann, *Reluctant Revolutionaries*, 151.

142. *MCCNY*, 7:203–4; *To the Sons of Liberty in this City*, Evans #11891; *New-York Gazette and Weekly Mercury*, February 5, 1770; *NYJ*, February 8, 1770; Tiedemann, *Reluctant Revolutionaries*, 143–53.

143. Jones, *History of New York*, 1:27–28; *NYJ*, February 15, March 22, 29, April 12, 1770; *NYGWPB*, February 19, March 26, April 2, 1770. For similar rituals in Boston and Charleston, see Conroy, *In Public Houses*, 265; McDonough, *Gadsden and Laurens*, 121.

144. *NYGWPB*, February 5, 1770; *NYJ*, February 8, 1770.

145. *NYJ*, February 15, March 29, 1770; Leake, *Life of John Lamb*, 62–63.

146. Smith, *Historical Memoirs*, 1:102–3, 211; Tiedemann, *Reluctant Revolutionaries*, 168; Jones, *History of New York*, 1:82.

147. "Alcanor," *New-York Chronicle*, July 13, 1769.

148. Smith, *Historical Memoirs*, 1:145.

149. Smith, *Historical Memoirs*, 1:156–57.

150. Smith, *Historical Memoirs*, 1:163.

151. Tiedemann, *Reluctant Revolutionaries*, 182–83.

152. Alexander McDougall, "Political memorandums relative to the Conduct of the Citizens on the Boston Port Bill," May 14–22, 1774, Alexander McDougall Papers, N-YHS; *NYJ*, May 19, 26, 1774; Tiedemann, *Reluctant Revolutionaries*, 186–88.

153. Alexander McDougall, "Political memorandums relative to the Conduct of the Citizens on the Boston Port Bill," May 14–22, 1774, Alexander McDougall

Papers, N-YHS; *NYJ*, May 19, 26, 1774; *New-York Gazette and Weekly Mercury*, May 23, July 25, 1774; Tiedemann, *Reluctant Revolutionaries*, 188–97.

154. Force, *American Archives*, 4th ser., 6:1151–57, 1166, 1775.

155. Smith, *Historical Memoirs*, 1:208, 211.

156. Hamilton, *Gentleman's Progress*, 79; see also George Clinton to the Duke of Bedford, June 28, 1749, in O'Callaghan, *Documents Relative to the Colonial History of the State of New-York*, 6:513–14.

157. Jones, *History of New York*, 1:233.

158. Conroy, *In Public Houses*, 270–71; see also the discussion of Loyalist tavern clubs in *Diary of Christopher Marshall*, 80. For an example of a different political climate just on the other side of the East River, see Tiedemann, "Communities in the Revolution"; Tiedemann, "Revolution Foiled."

159. Josiah Martin to Samuel Martin, June 8, August 7, 1767, British Library Additional MSS #41361; "A Friend to Order," *To the Publick*, Evans #14513; "A Sober Citizen," *To the Inhabitants of the City and County of New-York*, Evans #15110; see also Conroy, *In Public Houses*, 272; Tiedemann, *Reluctant Revolutionaries*, 206, 228.

160. Smith, *Historical Memoirs*, 1:163.

161. John Watts to [General Robert Monckton?], May 30, 1774, Chalmers Papers, New York, New York Public Library, 2:22.

162. Jones, *History of New York*, 1:59–60.

163. Jones, *History of New York*, 1:64, 568; Tiedemann, *Reluctant Revolutionaries*, 246.

164. "Bellisarius" to James Rivington, February 12, 1775, in *Rivington's New-York Gazetteer, or Weekly Advertiser*, March 9, 1775.

165. *Diary of John Adams*, 2:106–7.

166. [William] Goddard to John Lamb, March 23, 1774, John Lamb Papers, N-YHS.

167. Paul Revere to John Lamb, March 28, 1774, John Lamb Papers, N-YHS.

168. *New-York Gazette and Weekly Mercury*, October 3, 1774; Honyman, *Colonial Panorama*, 68; see also Maier, *Old Revolutionaries*, 72; *To the Inhabitants of the City and County of New-York*, Evans #14505; Jacobus Van Zandt et al., *To the Publick*, Evans #14514; *[New York] Constitutional Gazette*, January 24, 1776.

169. Honyman, *Colonial Panorama*, 29.

170. Honyman, *Colonial Panorama*, 67.

171. Honyman, *Colonial Panorama*, 31.

172. "Colonel Marinus Willett's Narrative," *New York City during the American Revolution*, 57, 61.

173. Maier, *Old Revolutionaries*, 74.

174. *Advertisement*, Evans #11778; Tavern keeper's license book, New York City Mayor's Office, 1756–66, N-YHS.

175. Alexander McDougall, "Political memorandums relative to the Conduct of the Citizens on the Boston Port Bill," May 28, 1774, Alexander McDougall Papers, N-YHS.

176. "Colonel Marinus Willett's Narrative," *New York City during the American Revolution*, 53–65; Willett, *Narrative of Marinus Willett*, 29–31; Tiedemann, *Reluctant Revolutionaries*, 231–32.

177. Tiedemann, *Reluctant Revolutionaries*, 222.

178. Smith, *Historical Memoirs*, 1:222–23.

179. Smith, *Historical Memoirs*, 1:228c–228d.

180. Graydon, *Memoirs*, 163.

181. Honyman, *Colonial Panorama*, 29.

182. Conroy, *In Public Houses*, 275–98; Clark, *British Clubs and Societies*, 399; Breen, "Horses and Gentlemen"; Isaac, *Transformation of Virginia*, 80–90, 94–114, 253–54, 317.

183. Tiedemann, *Reluctant Revolutionaries*, 8–9.

184. *[New York] Constitutional Gazette*, March 27, June 5, 1776; "Social Club of New York," 467; *New-York Chronicle*, September 14, 1769; Gilje, *Road to Mobocracy*; Clark, *British Clubs and Societies*, 248–50, 349, 396, 412, 482; Salinger, *Taverns and Drinking*, 246.

185. Maier, *Old Revolutionaries*, 17–20, 28–30; Fischer, *Paul Revere's Ride*, 19–20, 51, 79; Walsh, *Charleston's Sons of Liberty*; Rosswurm, *Arms, Country, and Class*, 37–38. For a different view of class cooperation, see Thompson, *Rum Punch and Revolution*, esp. 141–44, 161–63, 167–70.

3. The Religious Landscape of Newport

1. Smith, *Historical Memoirs*, 1:247; Lovejoy, *Religious Enthusiasm*, 222–23.

2. For this debate over the link between midcentury revivals or the "First Great Awakening" and the American Revolution, see Heimert, *Religion and the American Mind*; McLoughlin, "Enthusiasm for Liberty," 47–73; Nash, *Urban Crucible*, 342–44; Stout, "Religion, Communications, and Ideological Origins"; Morgan, review of *Religion and the American Mind*; Butler, "Enthusiasm Described and Decried," 319–21; Cooper, "Enthusiasts or Democrats?"; Noll, "American Revolution and Protestant Evangelicalism."

3. Butler, *Awash in a Sea of Faith*, 113–16; Bushman, *Refinement of America*, 169–80.

4. See Hall, *Contested Boundaries*, esp. 5–7, 9–10, 14–15, 29–30; Kidd, *Protestant Interest*; Jacobsen, *Unprov'd Experiment*, 115–19.

5. Hattendorf, *Semper Eadem*, 21–58, 100–102, quote 58; Stiles, *Literary Diary*, 1:62; Downing and Scully, *Architectural Heritage of Newport*, 54–57; Stachiw, *Early Architecture and Landscapes of the Narragansett Basin*, vol. 1.

6. Steiner, "New England Anglicanism," 128.

7. Crane, *Dependent People*, 52, 59.

8. Bell, *Imperial Origins of the King's Church*.

9. Stiles, *Literary Diary*, 1:62; Channing, *Early Recollections*, 72.

10. Sarah Osborn to Joseph Fish, May 16, 1762; Osborn to Fish, June 2, 1763; Sarah Osborn to Mary Noice [Noyes], July 13, 1764, Sarah Osborn Letters, American Antiquarian Society.

11. Dinkin, "Seating the Meetinghouse in Early Massachusetts."

12. Crawford, *Seasons of Grace*, chaps. 8, 11; Lambert, *Inventing the "Great Awakening*," chap. 5; Brown, *Knowledge Is Power*, chap. 3; Bell, *Imperial Origins of the King's Church*, chap. 11; Rhoden, *Revolutionary Anglicanism*, chap. 3.

13. Stiles, *Literary Diary*, 1:62.

14. Stiles, *Literary Diary*, 1:62, 388; Records of the First Baptist Church, NHS; Crane, *Dependent People*, 131.

15. Stiles, *Literary Diary*, 1:81, 199.

16. Guild, *Early History of Brown University*, 7–22; "Seventh-Day Baptist Church at Newport," 37–38; McLoughlin, *New England Dissent*, 1:281, 506–7; Papers of Hezekiah Smith, LOC; *Diary of Isaac Backus*, 2:589, 646, 693, 717, 795, 844, 907, 931, 943, 956.

17. Downing, "History of the Friends Meeting House"; Bullock, "Friends Meeting House," 25–50; James, *Colonial Rhode Island*, quote 216.

18. Stiles, *Literary Diary*, 1:496.

19. Worrall, *Quakers in the Colonial Northeast*.

20. Bolhouse, "Moravian Church," 10–12; Stiles, *Literary Diary*, 1:29, 81, quote 103, 121, 166, 213, 220, 225, 247, 323–26, 365, 438; Hamilton, *John Ettwein*, 71, 98–99, 243, 254–55.

21. Lewis, "Touro Synagogue"; Schless, "Peter Harrison."

22. Sanford, "Entering Into Covenant," 17, 26–34, 47.

23. Morgan, *Gentle Puritan*, 180–91; Second Congregational Church Records, NHS, pp. 129–30.

24. William Vinal to Ezra Stiles, January 31, 1766, Washburn Papers, MHS, vol. 14, p. 16.

25. Second Congregational Church Records, NHS, p. 122.

26. Marmaduke Browne to the Society for Propagation of the Gospel, February 29, 1764, Papers of the United Society for Propagation of the Gospel, Rhodes House; quoted in Hattendorf, *Semper Eadem*, 102.

27. Hamilton, *Gentleman's Progress*, 157; Daniels, *Dissent and Conformity*, 108–14.

28. Hamilton, *Gentleman's Progress*, 20; Pointer, *Protestant Pluralism*, ix, 1–7; McLoughlin, *New England Dissent*, 1:126, 423; Whitehill, *Boston*, 22–46; Woodmason, "A Report on Religion . . ." (1765), in *Carolina Backcountry*, 73–74.

29. Olson, "Question of Religious Diversity," 108.

30. See Owen, *Narrative of American Voyages*, 27, 31, 40–41, 51; Hamilton, *Gentleman's Progress*, 45, 109–10, 139, 150, 180, 190–91.

31. Crane, *Dependent People*, 59, 130; Hopkins, *Life and Character of Susanna Anthony*, 31–35; Stiles, *Literary Diary*, 1:33–34, 61, 91, 252–53; Pointer, *Protestant Pluralism*, 35–36.

32. Franklin, *Autobiography*, 89–90, 119–20, 138, 248; Hamilton, *Gentleman's Progress*, 24, 85; Stiles, *Literary Diary*, 1:166; Shipton, *Sibley's Harvard Graduates*, 9:360–65.

33. Sarah Rogers to the Baptist Church in Newport under the Pastoral Care of Rev.'d Erasmus Kelly, read November 30, 1773, Records of the First Baptist Church, NHS, pp. 56–57.

34. Stiles, *Literary Diary*, 1:416, 644; Elton, "Notes to the Memoir of John Callender," 40–43.

35. Stiles, *Literary Diary*, 1:326.

36. Crane, "Religion and Rebellion," 74–79.

37. Arnold, *Vital Record of Rhode Island*, 4:20, 7:12, 53; Stiles, *Itineraries*, 12–13; Mason, *Annals of Trinity Church*, 1:127; Trinity Parish Records, 1786–1861, index at NHS; Stiles, *Literary Diary*, 1:555; Maier, *From Resistance to Revolution*, 310; Crane, *Dependent People*, 132; Phelps, "Solomon Southwick," MS, JCBL, pp. 3–5, 8, 34, 52 n36; Stiles, *Literary Diary*, 1:532; "RESOLVES of a certain Patriotic Committee in a neighbouring Colony, March 5, 1775," *Rivington's New-York Gazetteer*, March 30, 1775. See also Cook, "Jeffry Watson's Diary," 83–84, 98–102.

38. Stiles, *Itineraries*, 105; Bridenbaugh, *Cities in Revolt*, 155; Pointer, *Protestant Pluralism*, 38–40; Hall, *Contested Boundaries*, 30–32, 35–36.

39. *Diary of Isaac Backus*, 2:588.

40. Shipton, *Sibley's Harvard Graduates*, 4:36–39; Second Congregational Church Newport, Correspondence, RIHS.

41. Stiles, *Literary Diary*, 1:62.

42. Shipton, *Sibley's Harvard Graduates*, 10:412–15.

43. Second Baptist Church, Newport, RIHS; McLoughlin, *New England Dissent*, 1:363 n8, 423; Stiles, *Literary Diary*, 1:18–19, 40–41, 43, 47, 90, 101–2, 106, 168, 170–71, 247, 334; *Diary of Isaac Backus*, 2:712–13, 877–78; Henry Dawson to Nicholas Brown, June 23, 1772; Nicholas Brown to Henry Dawson, July 4, 1772, Brown Papers, JCBL.

44. Stiles, *Literary Diary*, 1:5–7, 87–88, 99–100, 261–68, 426, 455, 534–35, 578–81; Chyet, *Lopez of Newport*, 34.

45. Morgan, *Gentle Puritan*, 207–9; Stiles, *Literary Diary*, 1:289–92, 296, 416–17, 424; Joseph Fish to Ezra Stiles, November 23, December 7, 1772; Ezra Stiles to Joseph Fish, December 11, 1772, microfilm, MHS, orig. in Ezra Stiles Papers, Yale University.

46. Stiles, *Literary Diary*, 1:179–81, 299–302, 385–86; Brooke, "Sectarian Religion"; Butler, *Awash in a Sea of Faith*, 88.

47. Butler, *Awash in a Sea of Faith*, chap. 3; Seeman, *Pious Persuasions*, chap. 4.

48. Crane, *Dependent People*, esp. 11–37.

49. Crane, *Dependent People*, 25–29; Withey, *Urban Growth*, 128.

50. Crane, *Dependent People*, 63–92.

51. Lovejoy, *Rhode Island Politics*, 29; see also Stiles, *Literary Diary*, 1:298. James, *Colonial Rhode Island*, 300, writes that religious affiliation helped to determine political affiliation in these local disputes.

52. Samuel Ward quoted in Lovejoy, *Rhode Island Politics*, 66.

53. Hattendorf, *Semper Eadem*, 66.

54. Shipton, *Sibley's Harvard Graduates*, 10:412–15.

55. McLoughlin, *New England Dissent*, 1:317, 499–500; *Boston Gazette*, February 9, 1748, quoted in Shipton, *Sibley's Harvard Graduates*, 9:154–55; Edward Upham, Ministerial Records, April 25, 1771, American Antiquarian Society.

56. Hopkins, *Inquiry into the Nature of True Holiness*, 31–32; see also Breitenbach, "Unregenerate Doings."

57. Mason, *Annals of Redwood Library*; Stiles, *Literary Diary*, 1:166 n1; "Hand-in-Hand Fire-Club," Shipton and Mooney #40558.

58. Stiles, *Literary Diary*, 1:323–24. The Philadelphians were Dr. Richard Peters, Provost William Smith, and Jacob Duché; Duché and the Moravian Bishop Augustus Gottlieb Spangenburg had apparently hit it off on a voyage to England years before.

59. Stiles, *Literary Diary*, 1:96; for the variety of pallbearers that attended another funeral for an Anglican clergyman, see Stiles, *Literary Diary*, 1:201.

60. Quoted in Chyet, *Lopez of Newport*, 195; see also Pencak, *Jews and Gentiles*, chap. 3.

61. Moses Brown to Obadiah Brown and Co., October 14, 1761, George Benson to Nicholas Brown, September 25, 1775, Brown Papers, JCBL.

62. Jacob Rodriguez Rivera to Nicholas Brown, June 12, 1775, Brown Papers, JCBL; see also Pencak, *Jews and Gentiles*, 41, 51, 92, 265.

63. Hattendorf, *Semper Eadem*, 66.

64. Ezra Stiles, Compositions, "The Religious State of the Colony of Rhode Island," MS, 1774?, Holmes Papers, Holmes Family Papers, Quincy, Wendell, Holmes, and Upham Papers (microfilm), MHS.

65. Stiles, *Literary Diary*, 1:166 n1; Morgan, *Gentle Puritan*, 217–18.

66. Stiles, *Literary Diary*, 1:96; Stiles, "Religious State of the Colony of Rhode Island," MHS.

67. Stiles, *Literary Diary*, 1:323–24, 363.

68. Stiles, *Discourse on Christian Union*, 28, 51.

69. Stiles, *Discourse on Christian Union*, 8.

70. Stiles, *Discourse on Christian Union*, 27–28.

71. Stiles, *Discourse on Christian Union*, 36, 109–23.

72. Stiles, *Discourse on Christian Union*, 96–100.

73. Ezra Stiles, "The Religious State of the Colony of Rhode Island," MHS; McLoughlin, *New England Dissent*, 1:3–25.

74. McLoughlin, *New England Dissent* 1:491–500; Herbst, "Charter for a Proposed College."

75. Bronson, *History of Brown University*, 13–27.

76. Guild, *Early History of Brown University*, 124–26; Nicholas Brown to Nathan Spears, February 15, 1770, Brown Papers, JCBL.

77. "A. Z.," *Providence Gazette*, March 2, 1771.

78. Stiles, *Literary Diary*, 1:109–10; Lovejoy, *Rhode Island Politics*, 148.

79. Stiles, *Literary Diary*, 1:173.

80. Chyet, *Lopez of Newport*, 35–38; Stiles, *Itineraries*, 52–53; Crane, "Uneasy Coexistence," 105–7; Pencak, *Jews and Gentiles*, 100–103.

81. Pointer, *Protestant Pluralism*, chap. 3; Tiedemann, *Reluctant Revolutionaries*, 21–25, 34–36, 127, 132–36, 183, 191–92, 206–9, 226–29, 245, 265; Olson, "New York Assembly"; Hutson, *Pennsylvania Politics*, 95–103, 153–56, 160–61, 207–13, 238–39; Ryerson, *Revolution Is Now Begun*, esp. 74–75, 187–89; Doerflinger, *Vigorous Spirit of Enterprise*, 185–88, 195; Tully, *Forming American Politics*, 423–25.

82. "Journal of a French Traveller in the Colonies," 75.

83. Committee of the Sons of Liberty of Newport to the Committee of the Sons of Liberty of Providence, April 4, 1766, RIHS, p. 12:67; Second Congregational Church Records, NHS, p. 137; Maier, *From Resistance to Revolution*, 309–10.

84. Lovejoy, *Rhode Island Politics*, 100–113; Stiles quoted in Crane, *Dependent People*, 128.

85. John Bours, Christmas Sermons, RIHS. Thomas R. Bours apparently presented these unattributed sermons, collected by his grandfather John Bours (a senior warden at Trinity Church), to a Rev. Hale in 1848. They are dated and described as having been preached at Newport. Given the Bours provenance and the fact that these are Christmas sermons, the conclusion that they were read at Trinity Church is difficult to avoid. See also Rhoden, *Revolutionary Anglicanism*, chap. 4.

86. Butler, *Awash in a Sea of Faith*, 196.

87. See, for instance, George Benson to Nicholas Brown, May 24, 1779, Brown Papers, JCBL; Pointer, *Protestant Pluralism*, 76–77.

88. See Reid-Maroney, *Philadelphia's Enlightenment*; Gladwell, *Tipping Point*, 30–59.

89. Ezra Stiles to Jonathan Trumbull, May 6, 1771, Marchant Papers, RIHS.

90. Ezra Stiles to Richard Price, May 6, 1771, Marchant Papers, RIHS.

91. See Marchant Papers, RIHS. Marchant also carried letters from future Loyalists such as Joseph Wanton and Thomas Hutchinson.

92. Henry Marchant to Richard Price, November 21, 1772, Henry Marchant Journal and Letter Book, 16–17, NHS; see also Cole, "Henry Marchant's Journal"; Lovejoy, "Henry Marchant and the Mistress of the World."

93. *Peter Oliver's Origin and Progress of the American Rebellion*, 29, 41–45, 63–64, 106, 163; Baldwin, *New England Clergy*, chaps. 7–9; Lovejoy, *Rhode Island Politics*, 142–47; Crane, *Dependent People*, 116–19.

94. Stiles, *Literary Diary*, 1:344–45; see also Ditz, "Mercantile Representations of Failure," 74–79.

95. [Isaac Hunt], *A Looking-Glass for Presbyterians, or A Brief Examination of their Loyalty, Merit* . . . (Philadelphia, 1764), 9, quoted in Ireland, "Ethnic-Religious Dimension of Pennsylvania Politics," 425.

96. "Journal of a French Traveller in the Colonies," 75.

97. Stiles, *Literary Diary*, 1:78, 168–70; McLoughlin, *New England Dissent*, 1:576–78.

98. John Collins to Samuel Ward, January 4, 1774, Ward Family Papers, RIHS.

99. Samuel Ward to John Collins, January 17, 1774, in *Correspondence of Samuel Ward*, 24–25.

100. Stiles, *Literary Diary*, 1:7, 474; Second Congregational Church Records, NHS, p. 128.

101. Stiles, *Literary Diary*, 1:472–75, quote 473; see also the excellent discussion of this meeting in McLoughlin, *New England Dissent*, 1:558–64.

102. For this and the following paragraph, see Stiles, *Literary Diary*, 1:492–96.

103. Cogliano, *No King, No Popery*, esp. 17–18, 34–35, 43, 46–52; Hanson, *Necessary Virtue*, esp. 11–13.

104. Stiles, *Literary Diary*, 1:490–91.

105. For this and the following paragraph, see "RESOLVES of a certain Patriotic Committee in a neighbouring Colony, March 5, 1775," *Rivington's New-York Gazetteer*, March 30, 1775; Stiles, *Literary Diary*, 1:530–33.

106. Nathanael Greene to Colonel Ephraim Bowen, June 21, 1779; Nathanael Greene to John Collins, August 18, 1779; Jacob Greene to Nathanael Greene, August 27, 1779; Collins to Nathanael Greene, September 7, 1779; Nathanael Greene to Collins, September 17, 1779; Collins to Nathanael Greene, October 29, 1779, *Papers of Nathanael Greene*, 4:173–74, 326–27, 339–41, 367–70, 391–93, 518–19. While serving in Congress, Collins may have observed the way in which a Calvinist faction had taken over the Pennsylvania General Assembly and then proceeded to protect their power by exacting loyalty oaths, replacing the College of Philadelphia with the University of Pennsylvania, and favoring a constitution favorable to their interests. Ireland, "Ethnic-Religious Dimension of Pennsylvania Politics," 423–48.

107. George Benson to Nicholas Brown, July 1?, 1780, Brown Papers, JCBL; see also McLoughlin, *New England Dissent*, 1:591–659.

108. Sanford, "Entering Into Covenant," 47; "Ebenezer David" and "John Tanner," *Seventh Day Baptist Memorial* 3 (July 1854), 102–5; Stiles, *Literary Diary*, 2:28.

109. Stiles, *Literary Diary*, 2:29; McLoughlin, *New England Dissent*, 1:585.

110. Stiles listed Thurston and Kelly as residents of Newport at the end of 1776 and gave neither of them stars as Loyalists. Stiles, *Literary Diary*, 2:28–29, 131–32.

111. Channing reported that during the postrevolutionary period, "Baptists had no fellowship with Congregationalists, because of their unbelief in the validity of infant baptism." Channing, *Early Recollections*, 75.

112. Stiles, *Literary Diary*, 2:133; Rhode Island Monthly Meeting, Friends Records, 1773–90, NHS, pp. 101–3.

113. Stiles, *Literary Diary*, 1:559, 591, 2:27–28.

114. Stiles, *Literary Diary*, 2:36.

115. The verse was Luke 2:13–14: "And suddenly there was with the angel a multitude of the heavenly host praising God, and saying, Glory to God in the highest, and on earth peace, good will toward men." Bours, Christmas Sermons, RIHS.

116. Stiles, *Literary Diary*, 2:132, 134; George H. Richardson, "Loyalists Property Confiscated" in "Occupations," MS scrapbook, NHS, p. 65; Rhoden, *Revolutionary Anglicanism*, 89; Mason, *Annals of Trinity Church*, 1:51; Smith, *Civil and Military List of Rhode Island*, 395.

117. Stiles, *Literary Diary*, 1:491, 591, 2:28, 132.

118. Jews heard a sermon from the visiting Rabbi Chaim Carigal on May 28, 1773, that railed against tyranny. On the Congressional fast day of 1775, the visiting Rabbi Samuel Cohen gave a sermon on Numbers 25:11–12. In that passage God withholds his destructive wrath from the Israelites when he notes Phinehas's zealous execution of a heretic and his wife; Pencak, *Jews and Gentiles*, 97–98; 103–9; Stiles, *Literary Diary*, 1:591.

119. Thomas Vernon to J. R. Esq. [John Robinson?], June 27, 1770, Vernon Papers, NHS; John Collins to Samuel Ward, January 4, 1774, Ward Family Papers, RIHS; *Correspondence of Samuel Ward*, 24; Thomas Young to John Lamb, October 4, 1774, John Lamb Papers, N-YHS.

120. "Hays Was a Patriot," 126.

121. See Phillips, *Cousins' Wars*, 170–77; Clark, *Language of Liberty*, 363–81.

122. *Newport Mercury*, June 20, 27, 1768; Stiles, *Itineraries*, 14.

123. Stiles, *Literary Diary*, 1:8–9, 53, 106, 107, 237.

124. Ulrich, *Age of Homespun*, 178, 181, 183; *Peter Oliver's Origin and Progress of the American Rebellion*, 64; see also Ulrich, "'Daughters of Liberty,'" 211–28; Crane, "Religion and Rebellion," 81–83.

125. Second Congregational Church Records, NHS, p. 165; Roll of Members of the First Baptist Church in Newport, Rhode Island, NHS; Juster, *Disorderly Women*, 44; Brown and Hall, "Family Strategies and Religious Practice."

126. Stiles, *Literary Diary*, 1:145–47; Crane, *Ebb Tide in New England*, 72–74, 78–79.

127. Committee Book, [First] Congregational Church, 1743–99, NHS.

128. Kujawa, "Precarious Season at the Throne of Grace," 216; Kujawa, "Great Awakening of Sarah Osborn"; Sarah Osborn to Joseph Fish, August 7, 1754, Osborn to Fish, February 17, 1760, Osborn to Fish, July 20, 1761, Osborn to Fish, April 28, 1768, Sarah Osborn Letters, American Antiquarian Society.

129. Conforti, *Samuel Hopkins*, 97–106; Samuel Hopkins to Sarah Osborn, August 27, 1769, Simon Gratz Collection, LOC; Stiles, *Literary Diary*, 1:42–46, quote 1:44; Kujawa, "Path of Duty Plain"; Crane, *Ebb Tide in New England*, 77.

130. [Osborn], *Nature, Certainty and Evidence of True Christianity*, 3, 8.

131. Hopkins, *Memoirs of the Life of Sarah Osborn*, 51.

132. Grimsted, "Anglo-American Racism and Phillis Wheatley," 379–80; Kujawa, "Great Awakening of Sarah Osborn," 150.

133. Sarah Osborn to the Reverend Joseph Fish, February 28–March 7, 1767; reprinted in Norton, "My Resting Reaping Times," 523.

134. Osborn to Fish, in Norton, "My Resting Reaping Times," 525.

135. Hopkins, *Life and Character of Susanna Anthony*, 35, 87.

136. Although there is no evidence that the Moravians converted any blacks in Newport during this period, see Thorp, "Chattel with a Soul."

137. Hattendorf, *Semper Eadem*, 55, 60, 77, 80.

138. Thomas Pollen to Bray Associates, July 6, 1755, Marmaduke Browne to John Waring, November 29, 1762, Browne to Waring, November 6, 1764, Bray Associates, Rhodes House, quoted in Hattendorf, *Semper Eadem*, 95, 98, 109; see also pp. 110, 118–20.

139. "An Epistle of tender Love and Advice to the Negroes at Newport and other Parts of New-England," MS, JCBL; Worrall, *Quakers in the Colonial Northeast*, 184–85; James, *People among Peoples*, 111–14, 238.

140. Stiles, *Literary Diary*, 1:95, 97, 247–48, 329, 355; see also Saillant, *Black Puritan*, 129–33.

141. Stiles discoursed on John 17:3, Rom. 3:22–25 ("the righteousness of God . . . is by faith of Jesus Christ unto all and upon all them that believe: for there is no difference: For all have sinned . . ."), Ephes. 1:5–7, Luke 14:16–18, 2 Cor. 5:20–21, and Rom. 3:24–26; in New Haven he discoursed on John 2:1–3, Luke 14:22, 1 Peter 1:17, and Rev 7:9–10 (wherein a multiracial crowd stands before the Lamb); of these, almost none carry any hint of mandating obedience and inequality (except perhaps the verse from Peter). Greene, *Negro in Colonial New England*, 287; Piersen, *Black Yankees*, 56–57, 198 n31; Stiles, *Literary Diary*, 1:39, 91, 104, 213–14, 355, 415, 3:78, 82, 102, 104.

142. Second Congregational Church Records, NHS, p. 118.

143. Luke 14:22; Papers of Hezekiah Smith, LOC.

144. [Hopkins], *Dialogue, Concerning Slavery*, 12.

145. Stiles, *Literary Diary*, 1:213, 3:82. Greene, *Negro in Colonial New England*, 287, and Piersen, *Black Yankees*, 56, interpret this meeting and the use of this biblical passage as having a "particular message of passivity preached especially to slaves." On the contrary, the servant stands for Jesus and his apostles and is quite active in this parable, while the wealthy guests of Pharisees attempt to excuse themselves from eating bread in the kingdom of God. Furthermore, ministers preached this parable to whites as well as blacks.

146. Stiles, *Literary Diary*, 1:213–14; Berlin, *Many Thousands Gone*, 189, 436–37 n32, drawing on this statistic and on Piersen, *Black Yankees*, argues that there were few black converts and that most slaves viewed Christianity with suspicion, hostility, opposition, and contempt as "the religion of the owning class"; see also Greene, *Negro in Colonial New England*, 269; Bonomi, *Under the Cope of Heaven*, 124–25.

147. Stiles may have dickered with the numbers in order to make his own ratio seem roughly equivalent to those of the neighboring churches. Marmaduke Browne reported in 1766 that 6% of his 120 communicants were black. Second Congregational Church Records, NHS, pp. 122–23; Greene, *Negro in Colonial New England*, 273.

148. Second Congregational Church Records, NHS, pp. 61–62, 73, 168–70; Stiles, *Literary Diary*, 1:412–13, 441, 447, 521, 525, 534, 542, 572, 2:272; Records of the First Baptist Church, NHS, pp. 17, 57; "Seventh Day Baptist Church at Newport," 77, 82, 84–85, 89; Sanford, "Entering into Covenant," 46.

149. In addition to sources cited in note 148, see Olivas, "Partial Revival."

150. Mason, *Reminiscences of Newport*, 106.

151. Sanford, "Entering into Covenant," 32.

152. Mason, *Annals of Trinity Church*, 1:155.

153. Channing, *Early Recollections*, 105.

154. Stiles, *Literary Diary*, 1:340; see also Sarah (Richardson) Robinson to Thomas Richardson, February 27, 1770, Robinson Family Papers, Haverford College Library; reprinted in Jonathan Wren, "The Robinson and Richardson Families of Newport and Philadelphia," MS, 1989, NHS.

155. Samuel Hopkins to Stephen West, June 23, 1780, American Colonial Clergy, Gratz MSS, HSP.

156. Worrall, *Quakers in the Colonial Northeast*, 152–65; James, *People among Peoples*, 229; Davis, *Problem of Slavery*, chap. 5, pp. 275–76, 293–99, 469, 537–38; Bradley, *Slavery, Propaganda, and the American Revolution*, chaps. 5–6.

157. Conforti, *Samuel Hopkins*, chap. 8.

158. Samuel Hopkins to Moses Brown, April 29, 1784, Moses Brown Papers, RIHS.

159. Hopkins, *Dialogue, Concerning Slavery*, 62–63.

160. For a more caustic view of Hopkins and his allies, see Saillant, *Black Puritan*, p. 20, chap. 3.

161. [Hopkins], "A Narrative of the rise & progress of a proposal and attempt to send the gospel to Guinea, by educating, and sending two negroes there to attempt to christianize their brethren," American Colonial Clergy, Gratz MSS, HSP; Kujawa, "Path of Duty Plain," 80–84; Kujawa, "Precarious Season," 37, 128, 261–68; Akers, "Our Modern Egyptians"; Levernier, "Phillis Wheatley and the New England Clergy"; Grimsted, "Anglo-American Racism," esp. 370–94; Willard, "Wheatley's Turns of Praise"; Crane, *Ebb Tide in New England*, 53–55, 97; Juster, *Disorderly Women*, 72, 208; Conforti, *Samuel Hopkins*, 141; Saillant, *Black Puritan*; Stiles, *Literary Diary*, 1:363; Valeri, "New Divinity and the American Revolution"; Davis, *Problem of Slavery*; Bradley, *Slavery, Propaganda, and the American Revolution*, chaps. 5–7.

162. Hatch, *Democratization of American Christianity*; Butler, *Awash in a Sea of Faith*, 247–52, 280–82; Cott, *Bonds of Womanhood*.

163. Rhoden, *Revolutionary Anglicanism*, 88, 91, 117–18; Brown, *Knowledge Is Power*, chap. 3.

4. *The Revolutionary Movement in Charleston's Domestic Spaces*

1. Henry Laurens to Jonas Baird, August 16, 1776, *PHL*, 11:246.

2. Berlin, *Many Thousands Gone*, 290–324; Olwell, *Masters, Slaves, and Subjects*, 221–70; Frey, *Water from the Rock*, 108–42; Walsh, *Charleston's Sons of Liberty*; Klein, *Unification of a Slave State*; Lambert, *South Carolina Loyalists*; Kierner, *Beyond the Household*; Nobles, "Class Act," 301.

3. Herman, *Town House*, chap. 1.

4. Glover, *All Our Relations*; Kierner, "Hospitality, Sociability, and Gender"; for a definition of "household," see Fox-Genovese, *Within the Plantation Household*, 31–32, 82–92.

5. Zierden and Herman, "Charleston Townhouses," 205; Goldfield, *Cotton Fields and Skyscrapers*, 17–18; Crowley, *Invention of Comfort*, 102–5. Fox-Genovese ignores urban households, pointing to the rural character of the South and the decline of Charleston during the nineteenth century. I support her contention that southern households drew their characteristics from the rural slave society of the South, but argue that these patterns can provide a useful framework for interpreting urban households as well. See Fox-Genovese, *Within the Plantation Household*, 70–81.

6. For contemporary population estimates, see William Bull to the Earl of Hillsborough, November 30, 1770, in Merrens, *Colonial Scene*, 262; see also Morgan, "Black Life in Charleston," 188–89; Berlin, *Many Thousands Gone*, 144–45, 151–57; Edgar, *South Carolina*, 151–53.

7. McCusker and Menard, *Economy of British America*, 184–85; Lewis, "Metropolis and Backcountry"; Goldfield, *Cotton Fields and Skyscrapers*, 17–21, 24–26.

8. *SCG*, November 20, 27, December 25, 1740; Moses Lopez to Aaron Lopez, May 3, 1764, in Tobias, "Charles Town in 1764," 67–68; Bridenbaugh, *Cities in Revolt*, 18–19, 227–28, 336–37; Bridenbaugh, *Myths and Realities*, 76–77.

9. Breen, *Marketplace of Revolution*; Breen, "'Baubles of Britain'"; Waterhouse, *New World Gentry*, 92–96; Rogers, *Charleston in the Age of the Pinckneys*, 81–83; Smith and Smith, *Dwelling Houses of Charleston*, 183; McInnis, *In Pursuit of Refinement*; Hurst and Prown, *Southern Furniture*, esp. 23–33, 83–85, 282–84, 308–10, 359, 382.

10. Governor James Glen to Lords Commissioners for Trade and Plantations, March 1751, in Merrens, *Colonial Scene*, 189–91; see also "Charleston, S.C., in 1774 as Described by an English Traveller," in Merrens, *Colonial Scene*, 281. For the location of other Charleston merchants and craftsmen, see Calhoun, Zierden, and Paysinger, "Geographic Spread of Charleston's Mercantile Community"; see also Zierden and Herman, "Charleston Townhouses," 204.

11. Henry Laurens to Thomas Osborne, February 8, 1763, *PHL*, 3:241.

12. Hall, "Nefarious Wretches," 154; Rogers, *Charleston in the Age of the Pinckneys*, 26–30, 86–88.

13. *SCG*, May 9, 1768, June 21, 1772.

14. Jones, "1780 Siege of Charleston," 71; "Charleston, S.C., in 1774 as Described by an English Traveller," in Merrens, *Colonial Scene*, 286; see also Crowley, *Invention of Comfort*, 232–34.

15. Jones, "1780 Siege of Charleston," 71; see also Smith and Smith, *Dwelling Houses of Charleston*; "Journal of Ebenezer Hazard," 183.

16. "Charleston, S.C., in 1774 as Described by an English Traveller," in Merrens, *Colonial Scene*, 282–83; see also Coclanis, "Sociology of Architecture in Colonial Charleston," 610–14.

17. *SCG*, October 13, 1766, October 8, 1772; see also Henry Laurens to John Laurens, December 19, 1774, *PHL*, 10:8–9; for the names of fire-masters listed as elite merchants, compare the *SCG* announcements with Calhoun, Zierden, and Paysinger, "Geographic Spread of Charleston's Mercantile Community," 188, 207–11.

18. Peter Manigault to Mary Lee, n.d. [1765], in "Letterbook of Peter Manigault," 88–89.

19. Bridenbaugh, *Cities in Revolt*, 232, 236–37; see also Foner, *Tom Paine*, 23.

20. Since the Laurens house was demolished in 1916, architectural historians have not devoted much time to its analysis. Nevertheless, accounts of a lightning strike in 1771, a description by Laurens's biographer, photographs in the possession of descendants, and other documentary evidence can help us reconstruct some of the house's characteristics; *PHL*, 4:9n; Henry Laurens to Robert Deans, December 2, 1763, *PHL*, 4:65; Henry Laurens to John Ettwein, March 13, 1764, *PHL*, 4:209; see also Gillespie, *Martha Laurens Ramsay*, 24–26.

21. Henry Laurens to William Keith, [June 1764], *PHL*, 4:297.

22. Herman, *Town House*, chap. 2; Morgan, *Slave Counterpoint*, 257–300; Olwell, *Masters, Slaves, and Subjects*, 187–219; Isaac, *Transformation of Virginia*; 70–79; Pearson, "Planters Full of Money"; Weir, "Harmony We Were Famous For"; Beeman, *Varieties of Political Experience*, chap. 5; Shammas, *Household Government*, chap. 2; Gillespie, *Martha Laurens Ramsay*, 17, 70.

23. Henry Laurens to James Laurens, April 15, 1774, *PHL*, 9:408. This passage paraphrases 1 Kings 4:25, 2 Kings 18:31, Isa. 36:16, and Mic. 4:3–4; generations of Anglo-American gentlemen had echoed these idyllic sentiments,

laying out their own gardens as an expression of the ideal landscape of peace, prosperity, retirement, comfort, virtue, and order. See Brown, "Eighteenth-Century Virginia Plantation Gardens," 125 n1, 125–26, 154–55, 159–62.

24. Henry Laurens to Benjamin Addison, May 26, 1768, *PHL*, 5:702; see also Henry Laurens to John Augustus Shubart, December 31, 1763, *PHL*, 4:116; "Journal of Ebenezer Hazard," 183. Laurens was prescient about his motives, since he removed to London for three years for the sake of his sons' education, and to Philadelphia and Europe during the Revolutionary War for business with the Continental Congress.

25. Henry Laurens to James Laurens, April 15, 1774, *PHL*, 9:408; Drayton, *Nature's Government*, 59–67.

26. Henry Laurens to Joseph Brown, August 19, 1765, *PHL*, 4:664.

27. Henry Laurens to John Ettwein, March 13, 1764, *PHL*, 4:209; Henry Laurens to Lachlan McIntosh, August 15, 1764, *PHL*, 4:368.

28. Henry Laurens to Lachlan McIntosh, August 15, 1764, *PHL*, 4:368; Henry Laurens to John Rutherford, February 7, 1764, *PHL*, 4:162.

29. Pelatiah Webster, "Journal of a Voiage [sic] from Philadelphia to Charlestown in So. Carolina, begun May 15, 1765," in Merrens, *Colonial Scene*, 221–24; "Journal of Josiah Quincy," 442–51; Waterhouse, *New World Gentry*, 92–96; Rogers, *Charleston in the Age of the Pinckneys*, 81–83; Brown, *Good Wives, Nasty Wenches*, 267–72.

30. "John Tobler's Description of South Carolina," 144.

31. *SCG*, October 31, 1765.

32. Henry Laurens to Joseph Brown, October 11, 1765, *PHL*, 5:25.

33. Christopher Gadsden to James Pearson, February 13, 1766, in "Two Letters by Christopher Gadsden," 173.

34. Henry Laurens to Joseph Brown, October 28, 1765, *PHL*, 5:29–32; Henry Laurens to James Grant, November 1, 1765, *PHL*, 5:37–40; see also Maier, *From Resistance to Revolution*, 66–67.

35. St. George, *Conversing by Signs*, 206–8, 242–95; Morgan and Morgan, *Stamp Act Crisis*, 163–68, 187–91, 250–51, 314–18; Carp, "Fire of Liberty," 798.

36. *SCG*, October 31, 1765.

37. Pencak and Crandall, "Metropolitan Boston"; Brobeck, "Proprietary Gentry," 425–26.

38. For interactions in Charleston's public spaces, see Olwell, *Masters, Slaves, and Subjects*, 17–19; on courthouses, see Dayton, *Women Before the Bar*; for an overview of the ways in which power is practiced within architectural spaces, see Dovey, *Framing Places*.

39. See Henry Laurens to Isaac King, March 15, 1764, *PHL*, 4:211; Crowley, *Invention of Comfort*, 122–30; Leith, "After the Chinese Taste"; Breen, *Marketplace of Revolution*.

40. For two accounts, see "Newspaper Account" from *SCG*, November 28, 1771, and James Laurens to John Laurens, December 5, 1771, both in *PHL*, 8:61–62, 80–84.

41. Henry Laurens to James Laurens, December 26, 1771, *PHL*, 8:123–25.

42. Breen, *Marketplace of Revolution*, chap. 6.

43. *SCG*, February 2, March 23, June 1, 29, July 6, 13, 1769; December 27, 1770; Breen, *Marketplace of Revolution*, chap. 7.

44. Henry Laurens, *Extracts from the Proceedings of the High Court of Vice-Admiralty . . .* (1769), reprinted in *PHL*, 6:370.

45. Egerton Leigh, *The Man Unmasked* (1769), reprinted in *PHL*, 6:489, 528.

46. The two men later quarreled over domestic matters when Leigh impregnated his own sister-in-law—Leigh's wife and her sister were Laurens's nieces. See Henry Laurens, *Appendix to the Extracts from the Proceedings of the High Court of Vice-Admiralty in Charlestown, South-Carolina, &c.* (1769), reprinted in *PHL*, 7:57, 99–100; McDonough, *Gadsden and Laurens*, 23–25, 94–98; Gillespie, *Martha Laurens Ramsay*, chap. 3.

47. "Journal of Ebenezer Hazard," 186.

48. Glen to Lords of Trade, in Merrens, *Colonial Scene*, 180; Breen, *Marketplace of Revolution*, chap. 5.

49. David Ramsay, quoted by William Henry Drayton in Olwell, *Masters, Slaves, and Subjects*, 39–40.

50. Olwell, *Masters, Slaves, and Subjects*, 41–43 (quote 42), 145–58, 166–78, chap. 5; White and White, "Slave Clothing"; Bullock, "Tom Bell," esp. 233, 238–40; "Journal of Ebenezer Hazard," 190; "The Stranger," *SCG*, September 24, 1772; "The Presentments of the Grand Jurors for the District of Charles-Town," *SCG*, May 24, 1773, June 3, 1774; see also Williams, "Regimentation of Blacks"; Baumgarten, *What Clothes Reveal*, 136–37.

51. "Pro Gege et Rege" [Christopher Gadsden], "To the Planters, Mechanicks and Freeholders of the province of South Caroline, no ways concerned in the importation of British manufactures," *SCG*, June 22, 1769; Gibson, "Costume and Fashion in Charleston," 225–32; Baumgarten, *What Clothes Reveal*, 96.

52. Breen, *Marketplace of Revolution*, 271–75.

53. Fryer, "Mind of Eliza Pinckney"; Kross, "Mansions, Men, Women"; Kierner, "Hospitality, Sociability, and Gender"; Kilbride, "Early National Gentry"; Gillespie, *Martha Laurens Ramsay*, chap. 3; see also "Journal of Josiah Quincy," 442–51; Charles B. Cochran to Mary Cochran, December 24, 1778, Mary Cochran to Charles B. Cochran, July 16, 1781, Bacot-Huger Collection, Cochran Family letters, 1752–82, Typescripts, SCHS; Sarah Gibbes to John Gibbes, August 13, 1783, September 16, 1783, Gibbes-Gilchrist Collection, SCHS; Robert Raper to James Crokatt, March 2, 1763, September 2, 1763, Robert Raper Letterbook, SCHS; Peter Manigault to Thomas Gadsden, June 18, 1764, in "Letterbook of Peter Manigault," 83–84.

54. Hartigan-O'Connor, "Measure of the Market," 322–27; see also Wulf, *Not All Wives*, 181–84.

55. "Pro Gege et Rege" [Gadsden], "To the Planters," *SCG*, June 22, 1769; see also Breen, *Marketplace of Revolution*, 175–82.

56. "Pro Libertate et Lege," *SCG*, July 13, 1769; Wulf, *Not All Wives*, 184–87.

57. "Margery Distaff—Conditionally," *SCG*, October 5, 1769.

58. David Ramsay, "A Sermon on Tea," in "David Ramsay," 181; Breen, *Marketplace of Revolution*, chap. 8; Rogers, "Charleston Tea Party."

59. James Laurens to John Laurens, December 5, 1771, *PHL*, 8:82.

60. The Husband of the Planter's Wife [William Tennent] to the Ladies of South Carolina, in "Writings of the Reverend William Tennent," 136–37 [this letter also appeared in *South Carolina Gazette and Country Journal*, August 2, 1774]; see also Roth, "Tea-Drinking in Eighteenth-Century America."

61. Henry Laurens to John Laurens, June 8, 1775, *PHL*, 10:168; Kierner, *Beyond the Household*, 80–81.

62. Norton, *Liberty's Daughters*, 166–70; Nash, *Unknown American Revolution*, 133–46; Breen, *Marketplace of Revolution*, 279–89, 312–14.

63. Abigail Adams to John Adams, March 31, 1776, John Adams to Abigail Adams, April 14, 1776, Abigail Adams to John Adams, May 7, 1776, *Adams*

Family Correspondence, 1:370, 382, 402; see also Crane, "Political Dialogue"; Smith, "Food Rioters"; Brown, "Antiauthoritarianism and Freedom," 84; Crane, *Ebb Tide in New England,* chap. 6.

64. Henry Laurens to John Laurens, January 22, 1775, *PHL,* 10:40; see also Gilje, *Road to Mobocracy,* 5.

65. Woodmason, "The Remonstrance," in *Carolina Backcountry,* 221, 239; Nadelhaft, *Disorders of War,* 12–21; Klein, *Unification of a Slave State,* chap. 2.

66. Gadsden to Pearson, "Two Letters by Christopher Gadsden," 172.

67. Edgar, *South Carolina,* 222–24; see also Wallace and Burrows, *Gotham,* 203; references to rural uprisings in chap. 5 of this volume.

68. Henry Laurens to John Laurens, January 22, 1775, *PHL,* 10:39–40.

69. These three joined Camden area merchant Joseph Kershaw and Prince Frederick County Cherokee fighter Colonel Richard Richardson; see Nadelhaft, *Disorders of War,* 20; Brinsfield, *Religion and Politics in Colonial South Carolina,* 92–103.

70. Klein, *Unification of a Slave State,* esp. 2–8, 110–14,150–52, 257, 271–76.

71. "Journal of Josiah Quincy," 454.

72. Walsh, *Charleston's Sons of Liberty,* chaps. 2–3, pp. 24–25, 109–10, quote p. 67; Hart, "Constructing a New World"; Nadelhaft, *Disorders of War,* 98–99, 121; Villers, "Smythe Horses Affair"; see also Nash, *Urban Crucible*; Olton, *Artisans for Independence.*

73. Henry Laurens to Thomas Fletchall, July 14, 1775, *PHL,* 10:214.

74. "Journal of Ebenezer Hazard," 190.

75. Henry Laurens to John Knight, December 24, 1764, *PHL,* 4:556.

76. Morgan, "Black Life in Charleston," 214–15; Waldstreicher, "Reading the Runaways," esp. 249–55; Smith, "Runaway Slaves," esp. 214–27; Nash and Soderlund, *Freedom by Degrees,* esp. 26–32, 76–77, 94–95; Hodges, *Root and Branch,* esp. 130–33, 139–61; Van Buskirk, *Generous Enemies,* chap. 5; Withey, *Urban Growth,* 73–76; Frey, *Water from the Rock,* 120.

77. Jones, "1780 Siege of Charleston," 71–72.

78. Morgan, *Slave Counterpoint,* 95–101; Berlin, *Many Thousands Gone,* 144–45, 152–57; McCusker and Menard, *Economy of British America,* 181–82.

79. Herman, "Slave and Servant Housing in Charleston"; Herman, "Embedded Landscapes," 45–48, 52–54; Herman, *Town House,* chap. 4; Haney, "In Complete Order," 25–27; Upton, "White and Black Landscapes," 357–69.

80. "Charleston, S.C., in 1774 as Described by an English Traveller," in Merrens, *Colonial Scene,* 283; Morgan, "Black Life in Charleston," 189, 189 n5.

81. Capt. Martin, "A Description of Charles Town in 1769," in Merrens, *Colonial Scene,* 230.

82. Quoted in Morgan, "Black Life in Charleston," 187; Olwell, *Masters, Slaves, and Subjects,* 141–80.

83. Nadelhaft, *Disorders of War,* 99, 102; Lepore, *New York Burning*; Davis, "Emancipation Rhetoric"; Breen, "Making History."

84. Henry Laurens to James Laurens, June 7, 1775, *PHL,* 10:163.

85. *SCG,* September 3, 1753; reprinted in *PHL,* 1:242; see also Waldstreicher, "Reading the Runaways," 258–61.

86. Henry Laurens to George Dick, June 1764, *PHL,* 4:299.

87. See also "The Stranger," *SCG,* September 17, 24, 1772.

88. Henry Laurens to John Laurens, August 14, 1776, *PHL,* 11:223–25.

89. "Journal of Josiah Quincy," 457; Olwell, *Masters, Slaves, and Subjects,* chap. 2.

90. "The Stranger," *SCG,* September 17, 24, 1772.

91. Nash, *Unknown American Revolution*, 118–28,151–57.

92. "Journal of Josiah Quincy," 456; Henry Laurens to John Lewis Gervais, January 29, 1766, *PHL*, 5:53–54; Wood, "Liberty Is Sweet," 155–59, 166–68, quote 166; Christopher Gadsden to Samuel Adams, May 23, 1774, in *Writings of Christopher Gadsden*, 93; Frey, *Water from the Rock*, 64–65; see also "The Presentments of the Grand Jurors for the District of Charles-Town," *SCG*, May 24, 1773; Olwell, *Masters, Slaves, and Subjects*, 187–219, 229–43; Olwell, "Domestick Enemies"; Nash, *Forging Freedom*, 44–46.

93. Henry Laurens to John Laurens, August 20, 1775, *PHL*, 10:321–23; Weir, *Colonial South Carolina*, 200–203; Morgan, "Black Life in Charleston," 213; Bull, *Oligarchs in Charleston*, 238–39; see also Hodges, *Root and Branch*, 136–37.

94. Greene, "Slavery or Independence," 268–89; Christopher Gadsden to Samuel Adams, June 5, 1774, in *Writings of Christopher Gadsden*, 95.

95. "Robert Smith's 1775 Humiliation Sermon," 13, 17–18.

96. Henry Laurens to James Laurens, April 15, 1774, *PHL*, 9:408.

97. Williams, *St. Michael's, Charleston*, 30–39; Weir, "Who Shall Rule at Home."

98. Henry Laurens to John Laurens, August 14, 1776, *PHL*, 11:228.

99. Gadsden to Adams, May 23, 1774, in *Writings of Christopher Gadsden*, 94; [William Henry Drayton,] "A Letter from 'Freeman' of South Carolina to the Deputies of North America . . . ," in Gibbes, *Documentary History of the American Revolution*, 1:37; Snapp, "William Henry Drayton," 653. For Drayton, whose father had married the sixteen-year-old Rebecca Perry against his son's will, this familial analogy was particularly poignant.

100. Henry Laurens to Jonas Baird, August 16, 1776, *PHL*, 11:247.

101. Henry Laurens to Robert Deans, February 6, 1775, *PHL*, 10:53.

102. Henry Laurens to Jonas Baird, August 16, 1776, *PHL*, 11:247.

103. Bull, *Oligarchs in Charleston*, 241; Henry Laurens to John Laurens, June 18, 1775, *PHL*, 10:184; Henry Laurens to John Laurens, June 23, 1775, *PHL*, 10:194–95; Sellers, *Charleston Business*, 131, 144, 211–12; Rogers, *Charleston in the Age of the Pinckneys*, 30, 38, 69–70; Dixon, "Miles Brewton House"; McInnis, "Idea of Grandeur"; "Journal of Josiah Quincy," 444; Smith and Smith, *Dwelling Houses of Charleston*, 93–103, 105–10.

104. Gouverneur Morris to [John] Penn, May 20, 1774, in Jensen, *English Historical Documents*, 9:862; Wood, *Radicalism of the American Revolution*, quote 136–37, 160–61; see also Brown, *Knowledge Is Power*, 105.

105. Shammas, *Household Government*, 65.

106. See Shammas, *Household Government*, 65–66; *Letters of Eliza Wilkinson*, 17; Norton, *Liberty's Daughters*; Kerber, *Women of the Republic*; Kierner, *Beyond the Household*; Lyons, *Sex among the Rabble*; Kilbride, "Early National Gentry"; Walsh, *Charleston's Sons of Liberty*, 81–87, 111–24, 136; Olwell, *Masters, Slaves, and Subjects*, 243–83; McCowen, *British Occupation of Charleston*, chap. 5; Frey, *Water from the Rock*, 108–42.

107. Nadelhaft, *Disorders of War*, 4–5, 8–11; Weir, "Harmony We Were Famous For"; Klein, *Unification of a Slave State*, 84–86; Glover, *All Our Relations*, 140–45.

5. *Philadelphia Politics, In and Out of Doors, 1742–76*

1. Ferling, *Leap in the Dark*, 158, 164; William Bradford, Memorandum Book and Register, HSP, May 8–9, 20, 1776, f. 11–12, 23; *Diary of Christopher Marshall*, 69–73.

2. Zaret, *Origins of Democratic Culture*, 7, 44, 212–13, chaps. 3–6; Hill, *Nation of Change and Novelty*, 46–47; Cogswell, "Underground Verse"; Underdown, *Revel, Riot, and Rebellion*, 121.

3. Hume, *History of England*, 5:296, 372; Zaret, *Origins of Democratic Culture*, quote 212, also chaps. 7–8; Sharp, "Popular Political Opinion in England," 13–14; Harris, "Understanding Popular Politics."

4. Ryerson, "Portrait of a Colonial Oligarchy"; Foord, *His Majesty's Opposition*; Brewer, *Party Ideology*, 6, 8; Dickinson, *Politics of the People*; Harris, *Politics of the Excluded*, 1–29; Wilson, *Sense of the People*, 4, 19.

5. Henry St. John Bolingbroke to Sir Robert Walpole, *Dissertation on Parties*, Letter 13, para. 5.

6. See Heath, *Chronicle of the Late Intestine War*, 414; Zaret, *Origins of Democratic Culture*, 260–61.

7. See Hume, *Treatise on Human Nature*, xiv; Henry Laurens to John Laurens, August 20, 1775, *PHL*, 10:321–23.

8. Harris, "Problem of 'Popular Political Culture,'" 45; Underdown, *Revel, Riot, and Rebellion*, 3.

9. See also Morgan, *Inventing the People*, esp. chap. 9.

10. For English examples, see "J. D.," *Word Without-Doors*; Underdown, *Revel, Riot, and Rebellion*; Harris, *London Crowds*; Harris, "Parties and the People"; Rudé, *Crowd in History*; Rudé, *Ideology and Popular Protest*; Thompson, "Patrician Society, Plebeian Culture"; Rogers, *Whigs and Cities*; Rogers, *Crowds, Culture, and Politics*, esp. 7–12; Dickinson, *Politics of the People*; Wilson, *Sense of the People*; Black, *Politics of Britain*, chap. 5; for American examples, see "Americanus" to the printers, *Pennsylvania Gazette*, August 25, 1779; James Pemberton to Benjamin Franklin, May 1, 1766, *PBF*, 13:260; Benjamin Rush to John Adams, August 19, 1779, *Letters of Benjamin Rush*, 1:239; Wood, *Creation of the American Republic*, esp. 319–28; Maier, *From Resistance to Revolution*; Hoerder, *Crowd Action in Revolutionary Massachusetts*; Dinkin, *Voting in Provincial America*; Shaw, *American Patriots*; Countryman, *People in Revolution*; Young, "English Plebeian Culture"; Smith, "Food Rioters"; Waldstreicher, *In the Midst of Perpetual Fetes*; Newman, *Parades and Politics*; Pencak, Dennis, and Newman, *Riot and Revelry*; Irvin, "Tar, Feathers, and the Enemies of American Liberties"; Schlesinger, *Prelude to Independence*; Lucas, *Portents of Rebellion*; Warner, *Letters of the Republic*; Conroy, *In Public Houses*; Breen, "Making History"; Thompson, *Rum Punch and Revolution*; Grasso, *Speaking Aristocracy*.

11. Goodsell, *Social Meaning of Civic Space*, 10–13, defines "civic space" for later periods of history.

12. *Minutes of the Provincial Council of Pennsylvania*, 2:424–27; Jackson, *Market Street*, 21; Mackiewicz, "Philadelphia Flourishing," 425–37; Watson, *Annals of Philadelphia*, 295, 299–300; Eberlein and Hubbard, *Portrait of a Colonial City*, 16–17.

13. *Minutes of the Provincial Council of Pennsylvania*, 3:409, 414, 440; Mackiewicz, "Philadelphia Flourishing," 411–15, 417–18, 434–37; Jackson, *Market Street*, 21; Snyder, *City of Independence*, 76; "Order of the Mayor and Aldermen Concerning the Constabulary and Watch" [July 7, 1752], *PBF*, 4:328; see also McNamara, *From Tavern to Courthouse*, 14–20, 30–32.

14. Significantly, the stairs had been demolished by the end of the Revolution, destroying this connection between the street and the courtroom. Common Council Minutes, July 15, 1719, Minutes of the Common Council of the City of Philadelphia, quoted in Mackiewicz, "Philadelphia Flourishing," 432; Jackson, *Market Street*, 22–23; Watson, *Annals of Philadelphia*, 296–97, 299.

15. Cohen, "Philadelphia Election Riot"; Parsons, "Bloody Election"; see also "A, B, C, D, &c.," *To the Freeholders and other Electors*, Evans #9854.

16. MacKinney, *Votes and Proceedings*, 3:1910–12, 1939–40, 2154–56; Nash, *Urban Crucible*, 153–55; Mackiewicz, "Philadelphia Flourishing," 437–40.

17. Platt et al., "Historic Structures Report," chap. 2, sec. 1; Snyder, *City of Independence*, 35–41.

18. Bushman, *Refinement of America*, 112–20, 160–61; Thompson, *Rum Punch and Revolution*, 150–51; Platt et al., "Historic Structures Report," chap. 2, sec. 1, pp. 37–39; Batcheler, "Independence Hall Historic Structures Report," pt. 2, pp. 4–8; Dorman, "Furnishing Plan."

19. Graydon, *Memoirs*, 44; Mires, *Independence Hall*, 6; Toogood, "Independence Square," 3–9.

20. MacKinney, *Votes and Proceedings*, 3:2163, 6:5342–43, 5484, 7:6561; *Statutes at Large of Pennsylvania*, 6:223–26; 7:207–8; Toogood, "Independence Square"; Etting, *Old State House*, 11–15; Mackiewicz, "Philadelphia Flourishing," 445; Bushman, *Refinement in America*, 127–31; Bridenbaugh, *Cities in the Wilderness*, 306–7.

21. St. George, *Conversing by Signs*, 270.

22. Toogood, "Independence Square," 9–14, 22–26; *Statutes at Large of Pennsylvania*, 7:39; Westcott, *History of Philadelphia*, 2:325; *Diary of Jacob Hiltzheimer*, 22.

23. Eberlein and Hubbard, *Diary of Independence Hall*, 106, 119–24; Toogood, "Independence Square," 27–32; Mires, *Independence Hall*, 11–12.

24. Benjamin Franklin to William Strahan, May 22, 1746, November 28, 1747, *PBF*, 3:77, 214; Eberlein and Hubbard, *Diary of Independence Hall*, 79, 81, 82–90, 94–95, 116–18, 128–30; Thomas Wharton to Benjamin Franklin, May 22, 1766, *PBF*, 13:282; Toogood, "Independence Square," 18–19, 19 n35; Dorman, "Furnishing Plan," pt. D, p. 4; William Logan [to John Smith?], March 17, 1764, Smith MSS, LCP, 5:130.

25. Ryerson, "Portrait of a Colonial Oligarchy," 106–35, quote 107; "To the Freeholders and Electors," *Pennsylvania Journal* (supplement), September 27, 1764; Tully, *Forming American Politics*, 369–70.

26. Tully, *Forming American Politics*, 366, 379; Olson, "Colonial Legislatures," 554–58, 564.

27. *Pennsylvania Gazette*, April 1, 1736.

28. Ryerson, "Portrait of a Colonial Oligarchy," 133–34.

29. Hutson, *Pennsylvania Politics*, quote 25; Robert Hunter Morris to Thomas Penn, November 28, 1755, *PBF*, 6:279–84; [Galloway], *True and Impartial State*, 143; William Smith to Thomas Penn, November 27, 1755, Thomas Penn Papers, HSP.

30. *Pennsylvania Journal*, March 4, 1756; Toogood, "Independence Square," 17. These musters illustrated a wider trend of excluding women from politics; see Wulf, *Not All Wives*, chap. 6.

31. *Journals of Henry Melchior Muhlenberg*, 2:18–22; "Journal Kept by Samuel Foulke," 69; Hutson, *Pennsylvania Politics*, 84–113; Dunbar, *Paxton Papers*; Hindle, "March of the Paxton Boys." For the use of the term "Assembly party," see Newcomb, *Political Partisanship*, 141.

32. Richardson, "Birth of Political Caricature," 71, 76; Olson, "Pamphlet War," 31, 35; Dawkins, *Paxton Expedition*, Evans #9627.

33. [Charles Pettit to Joseph Reed], May 2, 1764, Joseph Reed Papers, N-YHS, 1:19; Dr. John Ewing to Joseph Reed, 1764, *Life and Correspondence of Joseph*

Reed, 1:34; Tully, *Forming American Politics*, 182–90; Hutson, *Pennsylvania Politics*, 94–113.

34. Hutson, *Pennsylvania Politics*.

35. Richard Jackson to Benjamin Franklin, "Private Sentiments and Advice on Pensilvania Affairs," [April 24, 1758?], *PBF*, 8:26–27; Benjamin Franklin to Thomas Leech and Assembly Committee of Correspondence, June 10, 1758, *PBF*, 8:89; Thomas Penn to Richard Peters, May 13, 1758, Penn Papers, HSP, quoted in *PBF*, 8:89 n3.

36. Jackson to Franklin, [April 24, 1758], *PBF* 8:26.

37. [Charles Pettit to Joseph Reed], May 4, 1764 [in letter dated May 2, 1764], Joseph Reed Papers, N-YHS, 1:19; "To the Freeholders and Electors," *Pennsylvania Journal* (supplement), September 27, 1764; John Penn to Thomas Penn, May 5, 1764, Thomas Penn Papers, HSP; Hutson, *Pennsylvania Politics*, 124–29, 132–33.

38. Hutson, *Pennsylvania Politics*, 148–56, 162–68; William Smith, "Preface," *A Speech, Delivered in the House of Assembly of the Province of Pennsylvania, by John Dickinson, Esq., May 24, 1764*, in *Writings of John Dickinson*, 12–13; Benjamin Chew to Thomas Penn, September 25, 1764, Correspondence and General Papers, Box 4, Chew Family Papers, HSP.

39. *Pennsylvania Journal*, July 19, 1764; *Pennsylvania Gazette*, July 26, 1764.

40. Dickinson, *Speech, Delivered in the House of Assembly*, in *Writings of John Dickinson*, 33–34.

41. Charles Pettit to Joseph Reed, September 21, 1764, Joseph Reed Papers, N-YHS, 1:37.

42. William Logan to John Smith, [October 2, 1764], [October 4, 1764], Smith MSS, 5:255–56; "A, B, C, D, &c.," *To the Freeholders and other Electors*, Evans #9854; Charles Pettit to Joseph Reed, November 3, 1764, *Life and Correspondence of Joseph Reed*, 1:36–37; William Allen to D. Barclay and Sons, September 25, 1764, in Lewis Burd Walker, "Extracts from Chief Justice William Allen's Letter Book," Burd Papers, HSP, p. 56; Hutson, *Pennsylvania Politics*, 175–76.

43. *Counter-Medly*, Evans #9943; Benjamin Chew to Thomas Penn, November [5], 1764, Correspondence and General Papers, Box 4, Chew Family Papers, HSP; see also Hutson, *Pennsylvania Politics*, 179.

44. Charles Pettit to Joseph Reed, November 3, 1764, *Life and Correspondence of Joseph Reed*, 1:37; see also Hutson, *Pennsylvania Politics*, 179 n2; [Smith], *To the Freeholders and Electors*, Evans #9915.

45. *Six Arguments Against Chusing Joseph Galloway*, Evans #10494.

46. Benjamin Chew to Thomas Penn, September 25, 1764, Correspondence and General Papers, Box 4, Chew Family Papers, HSP; Franklin, "Preface," *The Speech of Joseph Galloway . . . in Answer to the Speech of John Dickinson* (1764), in *PBF*, 11:307–8.

47. Franklin, *Remarks on a Late Protest Against the Appointment of Mr. Franklin an Agent for this Province* (Philadelphia, November 5, 1764), in *PBF*, 11:430, 437–38.

48. *Election a Medley*, Evans #9650; see also *Election Humbly Inscrib'd*, Evans #9963.

49. Joseph Galloway to Benjamin Franklin, [July] 18, 1765, January 13, [1766], June 16, 1766, *PBF*, 12:217–19, 13:36–37, 317; Hutson, *Pennsylvania Politics*, 192–95.

50. [Samuel Wharton] to Benjamin Franklin, October 13, 1765, *PBF*, 12:315; Joseph Galloway to Benjamin Franklin, September 20, 1765, *PBF*, 12:270.

51. Thomas Wharton to Benjamin Franklin, October 5, 1765, *PBF*, 12:291; John Hughes to John Penn, October 8, 1765, John Hughes Papers, APS; *Pennsylvania Gazette*, October 10, 1765; *Journals of Henry Melchior Muhlenberg*, 2:273; *Pennsylvania Journal*, October 10, 1765, September 4, 1766 (supplement); Morgan and Morgan, *Stamp Act Crisis*, 314–18; Hutson, *Pennsylvania Politics*, 195–97.

52. Joseph Galloway to William Franklin, November 14, 1765, *PBF*, 12:372–74; Joseph Galloway to Benjamin Franklin, June 7, 1766, *PBF*, 13:294; Hutson, *Pennsylvania Politics*, 198–99; *Maryland Gazette*, May 29, 1766; Thomas Penn to Benjamin Chew, [April 1, 1766], Correspondence and General Papers, Box 2, Chew Family Papers, HSP; Thomas Wharton to Benjamin Franklin, May 22, 1766, *PBF*, 13:282; Joseph Galloway to Benjamin Franklin, May 23, 1766, *PBF*, 13:284–85.

53. Hutson, *Pennsylvania Politics*, 199–203, 210–15.

54. For changing uses of the term "radical," see Ryerson, *Revolution Is Now Begun*, 3 n9, 25 n4, 39 n2, 89 n2, 122 n20, 151 n7, 207 n2.

55. MacKinney, *Votes and Proceedings*, 7:6271–81; *Pennsylvania Gazette*, March 31, April 6, 1768; Thomas Wharton to Benjamin Franklin, March 29, 1768, *PBF*, 15:91–92; "Philander," *Pennsylvania Gazette*, May 12, 1768; *Pennsylvania Chronicle*, July 25, August 1, 1768; "C. D.," "Answers to 15 Queries," July 29, 1768, in *Pennsylvania Gazette*, August 4, 1768; Brunhouse, "Effect of the Townshend Acts"; Hutson, *Pennsylvania Politics*, 226–27; Ryerson, *Revolution Is Now Begun*, 22–23, 28; *Writings of John Dickinson*, 409–10.

56. *Pennsylvania Chronicle*, August 1, 8, 1768; *Pennsylvania Gazette*, August 4, 11, 1768.

57. "C. D.," "Answers to 15 Queries," July 29, 1768, in *Pennsylvania Gazette*, August 4, 1768.

58. *Pennsylvania Chronicle*, August 22, 1768; "Nestor," "To the Public," *Pennsylvania Journal*, July 12, 1770.

59. *Pennsylvania Gazette*, September 22, 1768, July 20, 1769; Protest of James Henderson, July 21, 1769, Papers Pertaining to the Shipment of Tea, HSP, p. 6; *Writings of John Dickinson*, 435–36; Schlesinger, *Colonial Merchants*, 126–32, 191–94; see also "Extract of a Third Letter from the same Place [London]," January 24, 1769, *Pennsylvania Gazette*, April 6, 1769.

60. *The Tradesmen, Artificers, and other Inhabitants*, Evans #11897; *Inhabitants of the City of New-York*, Evans #11817; *Diary of Jacob Hiltzheimer*, 22; *Many respectable Freeholders and Inhabitants*, Evans #11879; "Lover of Liberty," *To the Free and Patriotic Inhabitants*, Evans #11882; *Pennsylvania Gazette*, May 24, June 7, September 20, 27, October 4, 1770; "Philadelphus," "To the Public," *Pennsylvania Gazette*, October 11, 1770; *Pennsylvania Journal*, July 5, 12, 19, 1770; Schlesinger, *Colonial Merchants*, 218–20, 227, 229–32; Brunhouse, "Effect of the Townshend Acts," 372–73; Breen, *Marketplace of Revolution*, chap. 7. On artisan participation in Philadelphia politics, see Olton, *Artisans for Independence*; Schultz, *Republic of Labor*; Foner, *Tom Paine*, 56–66, 108, 185–87; Nash, *Urban Crucible*, 376–82.

61. Toogood, "Independence Square," 24–25; Diamondstone, "Philadelphia's Municipal Corporation."

62. MacKinney, *Votes and Proceedings*, 6:4715–21.

63. MacKinney, *Votes and Proceedings*, 6:5557–58.

64. "Pennsylvania Committee: Report," March 6, 1764, *PBF*, 11:92.

65. MacKinney, *Votes and Proceedings*, 7:6587. Pole, *Political Representation*, 278, implies that this represented a permanent change in Assembly policy.

66. MacKinney, *Votes and Proceedings*, 7:6589.

67. "A Tradesman," *A Tradesman's Address to His Countrymen*, Evans #12583; *Assembly*, Evans #12387; "Journal of Josiah Quincy," 476; Pencak, *War, Politics, and Revolution*, 192; Nash, *Urban Crucible*, 377, 528 n111; MacKinney, *Votes and Proceedings*, 8:7202–3, 7333–44.

68. "Journal of Josiah Quincy," 476.

69. Joseph Reed to the Earl of Dartmouth, December 22, 1773, *Life and Correspondence of Joseph Reed*, 1:52; *Inhabitants of Pennsylvania*, Evans #12940; *Pennsylvania Journal*, October 20, 1773; *Pennsylvania Packet*, January 3, 1774.

70. Thomas Wharton to Samuel Wharton, November 30, 1773, "Letter-Books of Thomas Wharton," 319.

71. Joseph Reed to the Earl of Dartmouth, December 22, 1773, *Life and Correspondence of Joseph Reed*, 1:52.

72. Deposition of Samuel Ayres, December 27, 1773, Papers Pertaining to the Shipment of Tea, HSP, p. 11; Joseph Reed to the Earl of Dartmouth, December 27, 1773, *Life and Correspondence of Joseph Reed*, 1:54–55; *Monday Morning . . . Tea-Ship Being Arrived*, Evans #12944; *Pennsylvania Packet*, January 3, 1774.

73. Joseph Reed to the Earl of Dartmouth, December 27, 1773, *Life and Correspondence of Joseph Reed*, 1:55.

74. For examples of violence in Philadelphia, see *Diary of Christopher Marshall*, 76–77; Ryerson, *Revolution Is Now Begun*, 131–33; Rosswurm, *Arms, Country, and Class*, 46–48; Maier, *From Resistance to Revolution*, 8, 10, 194.

75. Ryerson, *Revolution Is Now Begun*, chap. 3; Thomson, "Early Days of the Revolution," 412–13; Thomas Wharton to Thomas Walpole, May 31, June 10, 1774, "Letter-Books of Thomas Wharton," 337, 432–33.

76. *Pennsylvania Journal*, June 8, 1774; *Diary of Christopher Marshall*, 5–6.

77. *To the Manufacturers and Mechanics*, Evans #13664; *Diary of Christopher Marshall*, 7; *Pennsylvania Journal*, June 15, 1774; Force, *American Archives*, 4th ser., 1:405–6; Nash, *Urban Crucible*, 37.

78. Thomas Wharton [to Thomas Walpole], June 10, 1774, "Letter-Books of Thomas Wharton," 432; *At a Meeting at the Philosophical Society's Hall*, Evans #13534; Ryerson, *Revolution Is Now Begun*, 47–50; Joseph Reed to the Earl of Dartmouth, June 10, 1774, *Life and Correspondence of Joseph Reed*, 1:69; Thomas Wharton [to Samuel Wharton], July 5, 1774, "Letter-Books of Thomas Wharton," 436–37.

79. *Pennsylvania Packet*, June 20, 1774.

80. *Pennsylvania Packet*, June 20, 1774; "Muster Rolls and Papers relating to the Associators and Militia of the County of Lancaster," in Egle, *Pennsylvania in the War of the Revolution*, 13:277–80; *Diary of Christopher Marshall*, 7; Ryerson, *Revolution Is Now Begun*, 50–52; An Acco.'t of what pass'd in the State House Yard 18.'th June 1774, Papers Pertaining to the Shipment of Tea, HSP, p. 13; *Diary of Jacob Hiltzheimer*, 31.

81. "J. R.—," *Pennsylvania Journal*, June 22, 1774.

82. The Mechanics to John Dickinson, June 27, 1774, John Dickinson Papers, R. R. Logan Collection, LCP, Box 6, Folder 4; *Diary of Christopher Marshall*, 8; [Dickinson], *Essay on the Constitutional Power of Great-Britain*, Evans #13247, p. 34; see also pp. 12–13, 35–41; Ryerson, *Revolution Is Now Begun*, 52–60.

83. MacKinney, *Votes and Proceedings*, 8:7091; *Diary of Christopher Marshall*, 8.

84. Force, *American Archives*, 4th ser., 1:607–8; "A Freeman," *To the Representatives of the Province of Pennsylvania*, Shipton and Mooney #42720.

85. MacKinney, *Votes and Proceedings*, 8:7091, 7097–100; *Diary of Christopher Marshall*, 8.

86. John Young to [Elizabeth Græme] Ferguson, August 10, 1774, Misc MSS, Berks and Montgomery Counties, HSP.

87. Joseph Reed to the Earl of Dartmouth, July 25, 1774, *Life and Correspondence of Joseph Reed*, 1:70.

88. Joseph Reed to the Earl of Dartmouth, September 25, 1774, *Life and Correspondence of Joseph Reed*, 1:80.

89. Silas Deane to Elizabeth Deane, [September 3, 1774], "Deane Papers," 1:15; Joseph Galloway to William Franklin, September 5, 1774, *LDC*, 1:27; Joseph Reed to the Earl of Dartmouth, July 25, 1774, *Life and Correspondence of Joseph Reed*, 1:71.

90. Caesar Rodney to Thomas Rodney, September 12, 1774, *LDC*, 1:66–67; John Adams to Moses Gill, June 10, 1775, *LDC*, 1:466; Thomas Wharton to [Thomas Walpole], September 23, 1774, "Letter-Books of Thomas Wharton," 446; see also *LDC*, 1:67; John Adams to Richard Cranch, September 18, 1774, *LDC*, 1:81.

91. Ryerson, *Revolution Is Now Begun*, 93–94.

92. *Diary of Christopher Marshall*, 10–13; *Pennsylvania Gazette*, November 9, 1774, February 1, 1775; *Freeholders and Other Electors*, Evans #13537; Thomas Wharton to Joseph Wharton, January 18, 1775, Thomas Wharton Sr., Letterbook, HSP; *Address of Liberty, To the Buckskins of Pennsylvania*, Evans #13790.

93. Joseph Galloway to William Franklin, March 26, 1775, quoted in Ryerson, *Revolution Is Now Begun*, 108; see also pp. 91–93, 103–12.

94. *Pennsylvania Gazette*, April 26, 1775; *Diary of Christopher Marshall*, 17, 21, 23, 29, 33, 60; William Bradford, Memorandum Book and Register, HSP, May 23, 28, 30, 1776, f. 25, 30, 32; *Papers of Charles Willson Peale*, 1:167, 172; Ryerson, *Revolution Is Now Begun*, 124–28, 133–35; Rosswurm, *Arms, Country, and Class*, chap. 2.

95. *Diary of Christopher Marshall*, 23, 37, 39–50; Ryerson, *Revolution Is Now Begun*, 128–41.

96. John Adams to James Warren, October 1775, *LDC*, 2:282; Silas Deane to Elizabeth Deane, June 18, 1775, "Deane Papers," 1:61–62; *Diary of John Adams*, 2:178, 181; 3:318, 322, 329.

97. MacKinney, *Votes and Proceedings*, 8:7353; *Diary of Christopher Marshall*, 58, 60–61; "A Lover of Order," "To the Members of the House of Assembly," *Pennsylvania Journal*, November 22, 1775; "Independent Whig," "To the Printers," *Pennsylvania Journal*, November 29, 1775, "A Continental Farmer," "To the Members of the House of Assembly," *Pennsylvania Journal*, December 6, 1775; Ryerson, *Revolution Is Now Begun*, 149–53.

98. Rosswurm, *Arms, Country, and Class*, 86–89, quote 87–88.

99. *Writings of Thomas Paine*, 1:5–6, 37–38; see also Bailyn, *Ideological Origins of the American Revolution*, 286, 288–90.

100. Samuel Adams to James Warren, January 7, 1776, *LDC*, 3:52; Joseph Reed to Charles Pettit, March 1776, *Life and Correspondence of Joseph Reed*, 1:183; Rowe, *Thomas McKean*, 72.

101. "Cato," "To the People of Pennsylvania, Letter III," *Pennsylvania Gazette*, March 20, 1776; Ryerson, *Revolution Is Now Begun*, 158–59, 166–74.

102. See Hawke, *Midst of a Revolution*, chap. 1; "Civis," "To the Freeholders and Electors of the City of PHILADELPHIA," *Pennsylvania Gazette*, May 1, 1776; William Bradford, Memorandum Book and Register, HSP, May 1–2, 1776, f. 4–5; *Diary of Christopher Marshall*, 67–68; Rosswurm, *Arms, Country, and Class*, 92–93; Ryerson, *Revolution Is Now Begun*, 162–63, 171–74.

103. *Journals of the Continental Congress*, 4:342, 357–58; Carter Braxton to Landon Carter, May 17, 1776, *LDC*, 4:19; *Diary of John Adams*, 3:382–86; Hawke, *Midst of*

a *Revolution*, 119–26; Rosswurm, *Arms, Country, and Class*, 94–95. For an alternate interpretation of Wilson's remarks, see Hall, *Philosophy of James Wilson*, 99–100.

104. *Diary of Christopher Marshall*, 71–72; *Committee Chamber, Philadelphia*, Evans #15014; *Alarm*, Evans #14642; Hawke, *Midst of a Revolution*, 133–35.

105. "Diary of Dr. James Clitherall," 469–70.

106. William Bradford, Memorandum Book and Register, HSP, May 20, 1776, f. 23; "Diary of Dr. James Clitherall," 470; *Pennsylvania Packet*, June 17, 1776.

107. *Protest of divers of the Inhabitants . . . to . . . the Representatives of . . . Pennsylvania*, Evans #15016.

108. "Diary of Dr. James Clitherall," 471; *Diary of Christopher Marshall*, 73, 77; *Pennsylvania Packet*, June 17, 1776; Hawke, *Midst of a Revolution*, chap. 7.

109. Joseph Reed to Esther Reed, June 6, 1776, *Life and Correspondence of Joseph Reed*, 1:190; James Tilghman to Julianna Penn, June 10, 1776, Misc. MS collection, APS; James Tilghman to Mr. Anderson, September 10, 1766, Misc. MS collection, APS; Ryerson, *Revolution Is Now Begun*, 219–28.

110. *Proceedings of the Provincial Conference of Committees*, Evans #14974; *Extracts from the proceedings of the Provincial Conference*, Evans #14975; Ryerson, *Revolution Is Now Begun*, 228–38.

111. *Diary of Christopher Marshall*, 80, 82–83. For previous celebrations, see Caesar Rodney to Thomas Rodney, September 12, 1774, *LDC*, 1:67; Edward Burd to Jasper Yeates, May 7, 1775, Yeates Papers, HSP; *Diary of Christopher Marshall*, 60.

112. Thayer, *Pennsylvania Politics*, 211–27; see also Selsam, *Pennsylvania Constitution*.

113. Nash, *Urban Crucible*, 380.

114. *Pennsylvania Packet*, October 22, October 29, 1776; *Diary of Christopher Marshall*, 98–99.

115. "A Real Friend to the Christian Religion," "To the Printer," *Pennsylvania Packet*, October 29, 1776; see also *Pennsylvania Packet*, November 5, 1776.

116. [Galloway], *True and Impartial State*, 8–11.

117. [Galloway], *True and Impartial State*, 29.

118. Benjamin Rush's notes for a speech in Congress, [August 1, 1776], *LDC*, 4:600.

119. *Diary of Christopher Marshall*, 102–3; Richard Bache to Benjamin Franklin, March 10, 1777, *PBF*, 23:455–56; *Pennsylvania Gazette*, March 5, 12, 1777; Selsam, *Pennsylvania Constitution*, 228–30; Ebelein and Hubbard, *Diary of Independence Hall*, 213–14. On the opening of the city courts, see *Pennsylvania Gazette*, July 30, 1777; on processions, see McNamara, *From Tavern to Courthouse*, 58–63.

120. See Wood, *Creation of the American Republic*; Brunhouse, *Counter-Revolution*.

121. Rosswurm, *Arms, Country, and Class*, 179–81, 189–91; Eberlein and Hubbard, *Diary of Independence Hall*, 248–56, 293–99, 348–50; Mires, *Independence Hall*, 24, 35–37, 83–86, 92–93, 97, 100, 123, 170, 207; Bowling, "Philadelphia Mutiny"; see also Smith, "Attack on Fort Wilson"; Rosswurm, *Arms, Country, and Class*, chap. 7; Smith, *James Wilson*, 264–66; Hall, *Philosophy of James Wilson*, 22, 63, 127–28; Schultz, *Republic of Labor*, chap. 2.

Epilogue

1. Warden, *Boston*, chaps. 14–15; Young, *Shoemaker and the Tea Party*, 118; Frothingham, *History of the Siege of Boston*, 5–17, 37–40, 93–96, 234–38, 282, 327–28; Alden, *General Gage in America*, 255–56; *Journals of the Continental*

Congress, 2:151; Thomas Gage to the Earl of Dartmouth, May 13, 1775, in *Correspondence of General Thomas Gage*, 1:397–98; *Massachusetts Spy*, May 3, 1775; N. Taylor to Thomas Flucker, January 16, 1776, CO 5/40, TNA: PRO, f. 130–31; Akers, "Samuel Cooper's Sermon," 127.

2. Roelker and Collins, "Patrol of Narragansett Bay"; Stiles, *Literary Diary*, 1:539–40, 546, 589, 610–11, 620–31, 643; *Newport Mercury*, October 9, 1775; Richard Smith, diary, [January 5, 1776], *LDC*; *Journals of the Continental Congress*, 4:35–36; see also Bliven, *Under the Guns*.

3. Patterson, *Political Parties*, esp. chap. 4; Brown, *Revolutionary Politics in Massachusetts*, chap. 9; Gross, *Minutemen and Their World*.

4. For casualty statistics, see Peckham, *Toll of Independence*, 22–26, 70, 130; on New York, see Schecter, *Battle for New York*; Burrows and Wallace, *Gotham*, chap. 15; on Charleston, see Borick, *Gallant Defense*, esp. chap. 13.

5. On Newport, see Account of Andrew Snape Hamond's part in the American Revolution, 1775–77, 1783–85, MSS 680, Tracy W. McGregor Library of American History, Special Collections, University of Virginia Library; James Campbell to the Earl of Loudon, November 29 to December 7, 1776, Loudon Papers, Huntington Library; on Philadelphia, see Jackson, *With the British Army in Philadelphia*, chaps. 1–4; on outmigration and memory, see Young, *Shoemaker and the Tea Party*, 121–22.

6. Carp, "Night the Yankees Burned Broadway."

7. On Boston, see Belknap, "Journal of My Tour," 82–83; *Journals of the Continental Congress*, 3:444–45; John Hancock to George Washington, December 22, 1775, *PGW: Revolutionary Series*, 2:589–90; on Newport, see William Ellery to Henry Marchant, November 6, 1775, Marchant Papers, RIHS; Stiles, *Literary Diary*, 1:626–31; on Savannah, see John Graham, Lewis Johnston, and John Stuart to Sir James Wright, March 2, 1776, Clinton Papers, WLCL, 14:20; Andrews, *History of the War with America*, 3:167–68; Lawrence, *Storm over Savannah*, chap. 10; on Philadelphia, see Smith, *Historical Memoirs*, 2:58, 122.

8. John Adams to Abigail Adams, July 7, 1775, in *Adams Family Correspondence*, 1:241; Rufus Putnam to George Washington, September 3, 1776, in *PGW: Revolutionary Series*, 6:211; see also Benjamin Franklin to William Franklin: Journal of Negotiations in London, March 22, 1775, Benjamin Franklin to Jonathan Shipley, July 7, 1775, Franklin and Lafayette's List of Prints to Illustrate British Cruelties [*c*. May, 1779], Franklin to Edward Bridgen, October 2, 1779, Franklin to David Hartley, February 2, 1780, in *PBF*, 21:584, 22:95, 29:590–91, 30:429–31, 31:437–39; Abigail Adams to John Adams, June 18, 1775, in *Adams Family Correspondence*, 1:222–23; John Page to Thomas Jefferson, November 11, 1775, in *Papers of Thomas Jefferson*, 1:258–59; George Washington to Joseph Reed, January 31, 1776, in Force, *American Archives*, 4th ser., 4:899–900; Robert Morris to Robert Herries, February 15, 1776, *LDC*; *Journals of the Provincial Congress . . . of New-York*, 1:266; *Journals of the Continental Congress*, 7:276–79, 8:565.

9. Royster, *Revolutionary People at War*, 113.

10. *Writings of Thomas Paine*, 1:68; James Lovell to Oliver Wendell, May 3, [1775], in Upham, "Occupation of Boston," 172; Charles Lee to Richard Henry Lee, December 12, 1775, in "Lee Papers," 1:228; Mackesy, *War for America*, 35; Meinig, *Shaping of America*, 1:376, 380–85; see also Benjamin Franklin to Jonathan Shipley, September 13, 1775, *PBF*, 22:199.

11. Benjamin Franklin to Jonathan Shipley, July 7, 1775, *PBF*, 22:95; Stiles, *Literary Diary*, 1:624; Abigail Adams to John Adams, October 25, 1775, in

Adams Family Correspondence, 1:313; James Lovell to Oliver Wendell, May 3, [1775], in Upham, "Occupation of Boston," 172; see also John Adams to Abigail Adams, June 2, June 14, August 23, 1777, in *Adams Family Correspondence*, 2:253–54, 262, 326.

12. General Thomas Gage to Lord Viscount Barrrington, June 26, 1775, in *Correspondence of General Thomas Gage*, 2:686–87; John Adams to Abigail Adams, June 4, 1777, in *Adams Family Correspondence*, 2:262; *Diary of Frederick Mackenzie*, 1:297–98; Loftus Cliffe to [Charles Totten], July 5, 1778, Loftus Cliffe Papers, WLCL; see also Lieutenant William Feilding to Basil Feilding, sixth Earl of Denbigh, April 28, 1776, in Balderston and Syrett, *Lost War*, 76–77; *Journal of Ambrose Serle*, 300–302; "Letters of Robert Biddulph," 101; Kwasny, *Washington's Partisan War*; Mackesy, *War for America*, 65–66, 97–102, 150–51, 154–57, 172–73, 185–86, 198 n2, 220–21, 254–56, 269–71, 405–10.

13. On Boston, see Carr, *After the Siege*, chap. 1; Frothingham, *History of the Siege of Boston*, 327–28; on New York City, see Barck, *New York City*, chaps. 4, 8; Burrows and Wallace, *Gotham*, 249–55, 266; on Newport, see Crane, *Dependent People*, epilogue; Withey, *Urban Growth*, chap. 5; on Philadelphia, see Jackson, *With the British Army in Philadelphia*, esp. chap. 16; on British depredations, see Conway, "Great Mischief"; Conway, "To Subdue America"; on rioting, see Rosswurm, *Arms, Country, and Class*, chaps. 5–7; Schultz, *Republic of Labor*, 51–68; Foner, *Tom Paine*, chap. 5; Smith, "Food Rioters"; Walsh, *Charleston's Sons of Liberty*, 77–87, 100–105.

14. Benjamin Rush to Abigail Adams, August 15, 1778, in *Adams Family Correspondence*, 3:74; see also Lambert, *South Carolina Loyalists*, esp. chaps. 11, 14; McCowen, *British Occupation of Charleston*; Van Buskirk, *Generous Enemies*; Barck, *New York City*, chaps. 5–6, 9; Burrows and Wallace, *Gotham*, 245–49; Hodges, *Root and Branch*, chap. 4; Jackson, *With the British Army in Philadelphia*, esp. chaps. 8, 11, 14; Doerflinger, *Vigorous Spirit of Enterprise*, 218–23; Irvin, "Streets of Philadelphia," 22–32; Schultz, *Republic of Labor*, 48–51.

15. Haw, "Broken Compact"; Moultrie, *Memoirs of the American Revolution*, 1:402–35; Borick, *Gallant Defense*, chap. 1; Godbold and Woody, *Christopher Gadsden*, 192–95.

16. John Wells Jr. to Henry Laurens, January 23, 1778, *PHL*, 12:332–35; Hart, "Memorandum," 393–97; Kennett, "Charleston in 1778," 109; "Journal of Ebenezer Hazard," 181–83; Henry Laurens to John Laurens, March 1, 1778, Henry Laurens to John Lewis Gervais, March 11, 1778, Henry Laurens to John Laurens, June 7, 1778, *LDC*; *South-Carolina and American General Gazette*, January 29, February 5, 1778; *Pennsylvania Gazette*, May 23, 1778; Stoney, "Great Fire of 1778," 23–26; Olwell, *Masters, Slaves, and Subjects*, 228–43.

17. Bowling, "Philadelphia Mutiny"; Bowling, *Creation of Washington*, chap. 1.

18. Crane, *Dependent People*, epilogue; Withey, *Urban Growth*, chap. 6, conclusion; Coclanis, *Shadow of a Dream*; Goldfield, *Cotton Fields and Skyscrapers*, 76–78; McInnis, *Politics of Taste*, esp. chap. 5; Travers, "Paradox of 'Nationalist' Festivals."

19. Aggarwala, "Seat of Empire"; Doerflinger, *Vigorous Spirit of Enterprise*, chaps. 7–8; Burrows and Wallace, *Gotham*, esp. 306, 354; Spaulding, *New York in the Critical Period*, 113, 163; Zagarri, "Representation and the Removal of State Capitals"; Zagarri, *Politics of Size*, chap. 1; Thomas Jefferson, Notes concerning a Bill for the Removal of the Seat of Government of Virginia, [November 11, 1776?], *Papers of Thomas Jefferson*, 1:602–3; Formisano, *Transformation of Political Culture*, 150, 160–61; Onuf, *Jefferson's Empire*, 121–29;

Meinig, *Shaping of America*, 1:400–403; Waldstreicher, *In the Midst of Perpetual Fetes*, 251–62.

20. McCusker and Menard, *Economy of British America*, 250.

21. Cress, "Whither Columbia"; Bowling, *Creation of Washington*; McCoy, *Elusive Republic*; see also Olton, *Artisans for Independence*, chaps. 8–9; Foner, *Tom Paine*, chap. 6; Burrows and Wallace, *Gotham*, 300–302.

22. Cress, "Whither Columbia," quote 592; Walsh, *Charleston's Sons of Liberty*, quote 87, see also chap. 5; McCoy, *Elusive Republic*; Bowling, *Creation of Washington*; Gilje, *Road to Mobocracy*; Burrows and Wallace, *Gotham*, esp. pp. 266–70, 322–25, 350–52, 413–14, chaps. 23–25, 29–33, 35–37.

23. Elkins and McKitrick, *Age of Federalism*, chap. 4; Cress, "Whither Columbia"; Bowling, *Creation of Washington*.

24. George Washington to the Marquis de Lafayette, July 28, 1791, *PGW: Presidential Series*, 8:378; Hamilton quoted in Young, *Democratic Republicans*, 59; Ames quoted in Elkins and McKitrick, *Age of Federalism*, 486; see also Morgan, *Inventing the People*; Gilje, *Road to Mobocracy*, 71, 103–4, 107; Rock, *Artisans of the New Republic*, esp. chaps. 1–2; Kerber, *Federalists in Dissent*, esp. chap. 6.

25. Jefferson, *Notes on the State of Virginia*, 197; Onuf, *Jefferson's Empire*, 69–72, 90–93, quote 204 n57, 224 n37; Thomas Jefferson to Thomas Mann Randolph Jr., May 6, 1793, in *Papers of Thomas Jefferson*, 25:668; Elkins and McKitrick, *Age of Federalism*, chap. 5; Berg, *Remembered Gate*, chap. 2; Murrin, "Great Inversion"; Link, *Democratic-Republican Societies*; Young, *Democratic Republicans*; Young, "Mechanics and the Jeffersonians"; Rock, *Artisans of the New Republic*, chap. 3, pp. 123, 176, 280; Miller, *Philadelphia*; Koschnik, "Political Conflict and Public Contest"; Shankman, "Malcontents and Tertium Quids"; Shankman, *Crucible of American Democracy*; Kornblith, "Artisan Federalism"; Bender, *Toward an Urban Vision*, 3; McCoy, *Elusive Republic*; Aggarwala, "Seat of Empire," chap. 5; White and White, *Intellectual Versus the City*, esp. chap. 2.

26. Gilje, "Rise of Capitalism"; Nash, "Social Evolution"; Salinger, *Labor and Indentured Servants in Pennsylvania*, epilogue; Ryan, *Civic Wars*; Neem, "Freedom of Association"; Bridges, *City in the Republic*; Appleby, *Inheriting the Revolution*; Gunn, *Decline of Authority*; Greenberg, *Cause for Alarm*; Waldstreicher, *In the Midst of Perpetual Fetes*; Newman, *Parades and Politics*; Travers, *Celebrating the Fourth*; Davis, *Parades and Power*; Brooke, "Ancient Lodges and Self-Created Societies"; Koschnik, "Democratic Societies of Philadelphia"; Bullock, *Revolutionary Brotherhood*, esp. chap. 8; Pasley, *Tyranny of Printers*; Rock, *Artisans of the New Republic*; Wilentz, *Chants Democratic*; Gilje, *Road to Mobocracy*, esp. chap. 8.

27. Ryan, *Civic Wars*; Teaford, *Municipal Revolution*; see, for example, Young, *Democratic Republicans*, 100–102, 201–2, 405–7, 495.

28. Nash, "Social Evolution"; Ryan, *Civic Wars*; McInnis, *Politics of Taste*; Bushman, *Refinement of America*; Burrows and Wallace, *Gotham*; Gilje, *Road to Mobocracy*; Wilentz, *Chants Democratic*, esp. 53–54, 77–87; Stott, *Workers in the Metropolis*; Rosenberg, *Religion and the Rise of the American City*; on the elite, see Pessen, *Riches, Class, and Power*; Jaher, "Politics of the Boston Brahmins"; Jaher, *Urban Establishment*, chaps. 2–4; but see also Gough, "Philadelphia Economic Elite"; Kornblith and Murrin, "Making and Unmaking"; on the waterfront and workplace, see Gilje, *Liberty on the Waterfront*; Laurie, *Working People of Philadelphia*; Schultz, *Republic of Labor*; on taverns, see Thompson, *Rum Punch*

and Revolution, epilogue; Salinger, *Taverns and Drinking*, conclusion; Kaplan, "New York City Tavern Violence"; but see also Shankman, "Malcontents and Tertium Quids," 57–58; on churches, see Bilhartz, *Urban Religion*; Appleby, *Inheriting the Revolution*, chap. 7; Butler, *Awash in a Sea of Faith*, chap. 9; Laurie, *Working People of Philadelphia;* on households, see Stansell, *City of Women*, esp. 11, 22, 30–37, 41–42, 63–68, 92–94, 163–64, 187–88, chap. 10; Lyons, *Sex among the Rabble*; Blackmar, *Manhattan for Rent*; Herman, *Town House*; McCoy, *Elusive Republic;* on public spaces, see Upton, "Another City"; Mires, *Independence Hall*, esp. 60; McNamara, *From Tavern to Courthouse*, chap. 4; Davis, *Parades and Power*, esp. 30–36.

29. Wade, *Slavery in the Cities*; Powers, *Black Charlestonians*, chaps. 1–2; McInnis, *Politics of Taste*, esp. chaps. 3, 6, 8; Egerton, *Gabriel's Rebellion*; Nash, *Forging Freedom*; Horton and Horton, *Black Bostonians*; Curry, *Free Black in Urban America*; Bolster, *Black Jacks*; Newman, "Protest in Black and White"; Perlman, "Organizations of the Free Negro"; White, *Somewhat More Independent*; Hodges, *Root and Branch*, chaps. 5–8; Gilje, *Road to Mobocracy*, chap. 6; Waldstreicher, *In the Midst of Perpetual Fetes*, esp. chap. 6.

30. Crane, *Ebb Tide in New England*, 96–97, chap. 6; Cott, *Bonds of Womanhood*; Zagarri, "Women and Party Conflict"; Lebsock, *Free Women of Petersburg*, chap. 7; Branson, *These Fiery Frenchified Dames*; Waldstreicher, *In the Midst of Perpetual Fetes*, esp. 232–41; Berg, *Remembered Gate*; Boylan, *Origins of Women's Activism*; Stansell, *City of Women*; Ryan, *Women in Public*.

31. Young, *Shoemaker and the Tea Party*, pt. 2; Young, "Mechanics and Jeffersonians," 276; Schoenbachler, "Republicanism in the Age of Democratic Revolution," 243, 256–57; Newman, *Parades and Politics*, 94, 123–26, 129–30, 144, 148, 172–76; Gilje, *Road to Mobocracy*, 110; Mires, *Independence Hall*, esp. 28–29, 120–21; Carp, "Nations of American Rebels"; Teaford, *Municipal Revolution*; Ryan, *Civic Wars*.

BIBLIOGRAPHY

Manuscripts

American Antiquarian Society
    Sarah Osborn Letters.
    Edward Upham, Ministerial Records.
American Philosophical Society Library
    John Hughes Papers.
    Miscellaneous Manuscripts Collection.
Boston Public Library
    John Hancock, Miscellaneous letters.
    Thomas Newell, Diary for 1773 to the End of 1774.
British Library
    Additional Manuscripts, #41361.
    Blenheim Papers, Additional Manuscripts, #61672.
Historical Society of Pennsylvania
    American Colonial Clergy, Gratz Manuscripts.
    William Bradford Papers.
    Burd Papers.
    Chew Family Papers.
    Logan Papers.
    Miscellaneous Manuscripts, 1693–1869, Berks and Montgomery Counties.
    Papers Pertaining to the Shipment of Tea, etc., Philadelphia, 1769–73.
    Thomas Penn Papers.
    Thomas Wharton Sr., Letterbook, 1773–84.
    Yeates Papers.
Houghton Library, Harvard University
    Francis Bernard Papers, 1758–79. Sparks Manuscripts.
    New England Papers, 1765–70. Sparks Manuscripts.
Huntington Library
    Hastings Collection.
    Loudon Papers.

    Miscellaneous Manuscripts.

    Richard Pope's Book.

    Thomas Young Letters.

John Carter Brown Library

    Brown Papers.

    "An Epistle of tender Love and Advice to the Negroes at Newport and other Parts of New-England."

    Phelps, C. Deirdre. "Solomon Southwick (1731–97), Patriotic Printer of Rhode Island." MS, 1983. Revised, 2001.

Library Company of Philadelphia (stored at Historical Society of Pennsylvania)

    John Dickinson Papers, R. R. Logan Collection.

    Smith Manuscripts.

Library of Congress. Manuscript Division

    Simon Gratz Collection.

    Hezekiah Smith Papers.

Massachusetts Historical Society

    Miscellaneous Bound Manuscripts, 1763–73.

    Quincy, Wendell, Holmes & Upham Papers.

    Ezra Stiles Papers. Microfilm from Yale University.

    Thwing Database.

    Washburn Papers.

The National Archives of the United Kingdom: Public Record Office

    Admiralty 1/482. LOC transcripts.

    Admiralty 1/483. LOC transcripts.

    Colonial Office 5/40.

    Treasury 1/465. LOC transcripts.

Newport Historical Society

    First Baptist Church Records and Roll of Members.

    [First] Congregational Church Committee Book, 1743–99.

    Henry Marchant Journal and Letter Book.

    Rhode Island Monthly Meeting, Friends Records, 1773–90.

    Richardson, George H. "Occupations." Scrapbook.

    Second Congregational Church Records and Correspondence.

    Trinity Parish Records index, 1786–1861.

    Vernon Papers.

    Wren, Jonathan. "The Robinson and Richardson Families of Newport and Philadelphia." 1989.

New York County Clerk's Office

    New York Mayor's Court of General Quarter Sessions pleadings.

    New York Supreme Court pleadings.

        Presentments, Affadavits, Indictments.

New-York Historical Society

    John Tabor Kempe Papers.

    Lamb Papers.

    McDougall Papers.

    Moot Club.

    New York City Miscellaneous Manuscripts.

    New York Legal Manuscripts.

    Charles Nicoll Ledger, 1758–74.

    Quinn Collection.

    Joseph Reed Papers.

Tavern keeper's license book, New York City Mayor's Office, 1756–66.
New York Public Library
  Chalmers Papers.
  Thomas Addis Emmet Collection.
Rhode Island Historical Society
  John Bours, Christmas Sermons.
  Moses Brown Papers.
  Marchant Papers.
  Rhode Island Historical Society Manuscripts.
  Second Baptist Church Records.
  Ward Family Papers.
South Carolina Historical Society
  Cochran Family letters, 1752–82. Bacot-Huger Collection.
  Gibbes-Gilchrist Collection.
  Robert Raper Letterbook.
University of Virginia Library
  Andrew Snape Hamond Papers
William L. Clements Library, University of Michigan
  Loftus Cliffe Papers.
  Clinton Papers.
Yale University Library
  Johnson Family Papers.

Newspapers

[Annapolis] Maryland Gazette, 1766.

Boston Evening Post, 1768.

Boston Gazette, 1763–68.

[Boston] Independent Advertiser, 1748–49.

Boston News-Letter, 1768.

Boston Post-Boy and Advertiser, 1768.

[Charleston] South-Carolina and American General Gazette, 1778.

[Charleston] South Carolina Gazette, 1740, 1765–70, 1772–74.

[Charleston] South Carolina Gazette and Country Journal, 1774.

Newport Mercury, 1764, 1768, 1775–76.

New-York Chronicle, 1769.

[New York] Constitutional Gazette, 1775–76.

New-York Gazette (William Weyman), 1764, 1766–67.

New-York Gazette and the Weekly Mercury, 1769–71, 1774, 1776–77.

New-York Gazette or Weekly Post-Boy, 1748, 1750, 1757, 1765–68, 1770.

New-York Journal or General Advertiser, 1766–70, 1773–76.

New-York Mercury, 1753, 1760, 1765–66.

New-York Weekly Journal, 1740–41, 1748–49.

[Philadelphia] Dunlap's Pennsylvania Packet or the General Advertiser, 1774, 1776.

[Philadelphia] *Pennsylvania Chronicle*, 1768.

[Philadelphia] *Pennsylvania Gazette*, 1736–37, 1751, 1755, 1763–65, 1768–71, 1774–80.

[Philadelphia] *Pennsylvania Journal and the Weekly Advertiser*, 1756, 1764–66, 1770, 1773–76.

Providence Gazette, 1771.

Rivington's New York Gazetteer, 1775.

[Worcester] *Massachusetts Spy, or American Oracle of Liberty*, 1775.

Published Works

Wherever possible, primary sources are listed under the heading of the principal author (e.g., "Adams, John" for *Legal Papers of John Adams*).

"A, B, C, D, &c." *To the Freeholders and other Electors for the City and County of Philadelphia, and Counties of Chester and Bucks.* Philadelphia, 1764. Evans #9854.

Adams Family Correspondence. Edited by L. H. Butterfield, et al. 7 vols. Cambridge, MA: Harvard University Press, Belknap Press, 1963–2005.

Adams, John. *Diary and Autobiography of John Adams.* Edited by L. H. Butterfield, et al. 4 vols. Cambridge, MA: Harvard University Press, Belknap Press, 1961. Reprint, New York: Atheneum, 1964.

——. *Legal Papers of John Adams.* Edited by L. Kinvin Wroth and Hiller B. Zobel. 3 vols. Cambridge, MA: Harvard University Press, Belknap Press, 1965.

——. *The Works of John Adams, Second President of the United States: with a Life of the Author.* Edited by Charles Francis Adams. 10 vols. Boston: Little, Brown, and Co., 1850–56. Reprint, New York: AMS Press, 1971.

The Address of Liberty, To the Buckskins of Pennsylvania, on hearing of the intended Provincial Congress. Philadelphia, January 7, 1775. Evans #13790.

Advertisement. New York, January 5, 1770. Evans #11778.

Aggarwala, Rohit Thomas. "Seat of Empire: New York, Philadelphia, and the Emergence of an American Metropolis, 1776–1837." Ph.D. diss., Columbia University, 2002.

Akers, Charles W. *Called Unto Liberty: A Life of Jonathan Mayhew, 1720–1766.* Cambridge, MA: Harvard University Press, 1964.

——. *The Divine Politician: Samuel Cooper and the American Revolution in Boston.* Boston: Northeastern University Press, 1982.

——. "'Our Modern Egyptians': Phillis Wheatley and the Whig Campaign Against Slavery in Revolutionary Boston." *Journal of Negro History* 60, no. 3 (July 1975): 397–410.

——, ed. "'A Place for my People Israel': Samuel Cooper's Sermon of 7 April 1776." *NEHGR* 132 (April 1978): 123–29.

——. "Religion and the American Revolution: Samuel Cooper and the Brattle Street Church." *WMQ*, 3rd ser., 35, no. 3 (July 1978): 477–98.

The Alarm. Philadelphia, 1776. Evans #14642.

Alden, John Richard. *General Gage in America: Being Principally a History of His Role in the American Revolution.* Baton Rouge: Louisiana State University Press, 1948.

Allan, Herbert S. *John Hancock: Patriot in Purple.* New York: Macmillan Co., 1948.

Allen, James. "Diary of James Allen, Esq., of Philadelphia, Counsellor-at-Law, 1770–1778." *PMHB* 9, no. 2 (1885): 176–96.

Ammerman, David. *In the Common Cause: American Response to the Coercive Acts of 1774.* Charlottesville: University Press of Virginia, 1974.

Anderson, George P. "Ebenezer Mackintosh: Stamp Act Rioter and Patriot." *Publications of the Colonial Society of Massachusetts* 26 (1924–26): 15–64.

———. "A Note on Ebenezer Mackintosh." *Publications of the Colonial Society of Massachusetts* 26 (1924–26): 348–61.

Andrews, Charles McLean. "The Boston Merchants and the Non-Importation Movement." *Publications of the Colonial Society of Massachusetts* 19 (1918): 159–259.

Andrews, John. *History of the War with America, France, Spain, and Holland . . . .* 4 vols. London, 1785–86.

Appleby, Joyce. *Inheriting the Revolution: The First Generation of Americans.* Cambridge, MA: Harvard University Press, Belknap Press, 2000.

Arnold, James N., ed. *Vital Record of Rhode Island, 1636–1850.* Vols. 4, 7. Providence, RI: Narragansett Historical Publishing Company, 1893, 1895.

"The Aspinwall Papers," pt. 2. *Collections of the Massachusetts Historical Society.* 4th ser. Vol. 10 (1871).

Assembly . . . . Philadelphia, October 1, 1772. Evans #12387.

At a Meeting at the Philosophical Society's Hall on Friday, June 10th . . . . Philadelphia, June 13?, 1774. Evans #13534.

"At this alarming Crisis . . . ." New York, July 7, 1769. Evans #11379.

Backus, Isaac. *The Diary of Isaac Backus.* Edited by William G. McLoughlin. 3 vols. Providence, RI: Brown University Press, 1979.

Bailey, Rosalie Fellows. "Willett Family of Flushing, Long Island." *New York Genealogical and Biographical Record* 80 (1949): 1–9, 83–95, 156–64.

Bailyn, Bernard. *The Ideological Origins of the American Revolution.* Enlarged edition. Cambridge, MA: Harvard University Press, Belknap Press, 1992.

———. *The Ordeal of Thomas Hutchinson.* Cambridge, MA: Harvard University Press, Belknap Press, 1974.

———. *Voyagers to the West: A Passage in the Peopling of America on the Eve of the Revolution.* With Barbara DeWolfe. New York: Alfred A. Knopf, 1986.

Baker, William A. *A History of the Boston Marine Society, 1742–1981.* 2nd ed. Worcester, MA: Commonwealth Press, 1982.

Balderston, Marion, and David Syrett, eds. *The Lost War: Letters from British Officers during the American Revolution.* New York: Horizon Press, 1975.

Baldwin, Alice M. *The New England Clergy and the American Revolution.* Durham, NC: Duke University Press, 1928.

Barck, Oscar Theodore. *New York City during the War for Independence with Special Reference to the Period of British Occupation.* Port Washington, NY: Ira J. Friedman, 1931.

The Barrington-Bernard Correspondence and Illustrative Matter, 1760–1770. Edited by Edward Channing and Archibald Cary Coolidge. Cambridge, MA: Harvard University Press, 1912.

Barrow, Thomas C. *Trade and Empire: The British Customs Service in Colonial America, 1660–1775.* Cambridge, MA: Harvard University Press, 1967.

Baseler, Marilyn C. *"Asylum for Mankind": America, 1607–1800.* Ithaca, NY: Cornell University Press, 1998.

Batcheler, Penelope Hartshorne. "Independence Hall Historic Structures Report: Architectural Data Section." Philadelphia, 1992. Independence National Historical Park.

Baumgarten, Linda. *What Clothes Reveal: The Language of Clothing in Colonial and Federal America: The Colonial Williamsburg Collection.* Williamsburg, VA: Colonial Williamsburg Foundation, 2002.

Baxter, W. T. *The House of Hancock: Business in Boston, 1724–1775.* Cambridge, MA: Harvard University Press, 1945.

Bayles, W. Harrison. *Old Taverns of New York.* New York: Frank Allaben Genealogical Company, 1915.

Becker, Carl Lotus. *The History of Political Parties in the Province of New York, 1760–1776.* Madison: University of Wisconsin Press, 1968.

Beeman, Richard R. *The Varieties of Political Experience in Eighteenth-Century America.* Philadelphia: University of Pennsylvania Press, 2004.

"A Believer in Politicks." *A Political Creed for the Day.* New York, 1768. Evans #11047.

"Belinda." "A Letter from a Young Lady in Town to her Friend in the Country." *A Patriotic Advertisement.* New York, October 31, 1765. Shipton and Mooney #41576.

Belknap, Jeremy. "Journal of My Tour to the Camp, and the Observations I Made There." *Proceedings of the Massachusetts Historical Society,* 1st ser., no. 4 (June 1858): 77–86.

Bell, James B. *The Imperial Origins of the King's Church in Early America, 1607–1783.* New York: Palgrave Macmillan, 2004.

Bender, Thomas. *Toward an Urban Vision: Ideas and Institutions in Nineteenth-Century America.* Lexington: University Press of Kentucky, 1975.

Berg, Barbara J. *The Remembered Gate: Origins of American Feminism: The Woman and the City, 1800–1860.* New York: Oxford University Press, 1978.

Berlin, Ira. *Many Thousands Gone: The First Two Centuries of Slavery in North America.* Cambridge, MA: Harvard University Press, Belknap Press, 1998.

"Bibibus." *A Tooth-Full of Advice.* New York, 1768. Evans #10833.

Biddulph, Robert. "Letters of Robert Biddulph, 1779–1783." Edited by Violet Biddulph. *AHR* 29, no. 1 (October 1923): 87–109.

Bilhartz, Terry D. *Urban Religion and the Second Great Awakening: Church and Society in Early National Baltimore.* Rutherford, Madison, and Teaneck, NJ: Fairleigh Dickinson University Press, 1986.

Birket, James. *Some Cursory Remarks Made by James Birket in his voyage to North America, 1750–1751.* New Haven, CT: Yale University Press, 1916.

Black, Jeremy. *The Politics of Britain, 1688–1800.* Manchester, England: Manchester University Press, 1993.

Blackmar, Elizabeth. *Manhattan for Rent, 1785–1850.* Ithaca, NY: Cornell University Press, 1989.

Bliven, Bruce, Jr. *Under the Guns: New York, 1775–1776.* New York: Harper and Row, 1972.

Bolhouse, G. E. "The Moravian Church in Newport." *Newport History* 52, no. 1 (winter 1979): 10–16.

Bolingbroke, Henry St. John, to Sir Robert Walpole. *Dissertation on Parties,* Letter 13. 1733–34. Online. Available: http://www.ecn.bris.ac.uk/het/bolingbroke/parties.htm. June 14, 2006.

Bolster, W. Jeffrey. *Black Jacks: African American Seamen in the Age of Sail.* Cambridge, MA: Harvard University Press, 1997.

———. "An Inner Diaspora: Black Sailors Making Selves." In Hoffman, Sobel, and Teute, *Through a Glass Darkly*, 419–48.

Bonomi, Patricia U. *Under the Cope of Heaven: Religion, Society, and Politics in Colonial America*. New York: Oxford University Press, 1986.

Borick, Carl P. *A Gallant Defense: The Siege of Charleston, 1780*. Columbia: University of South Carolina Press, 2003.

Borsay, Peter. *The English Urban Renaissance: Culture and Society in the Provincial Town, 1660–1770*. Oxford: Oxford University Press, Clarendon Press, 1989.

Boston Pier, or Long Wharf: Incorporated by the Province of Massachusetts Bay, July 14, 1772. Boston: W. W. Clapp, 1825.

Bourne, Russell. *Cradle of Violence: How Boston's Waterfront Mobs Ignited the American Revolution*. Hoboken, NJ: John Wiley and Sons, 2006.

Bowling, Kenneth R. *The Creation of Washington, D.C.: The Idea and Location of the American Capital*. Fairfax, VA: George Mason University Press, 1991.

———. "New Light on the Philadelphia Mutiny of 1783: Federal-State Confrontation at the Close of the War for Independence." *PMHB* 101, no. 4 (October 1977): 419–50.

Boyer, Lee R. "'Lobster Backs, Liberty Boys and Laborers in the Streets': New York's Golden Hill and Nassau Street Riots." *New-York Historical Society Quarterly* 57 (1973): 281–308.

Boylan, Anne M. *The Origins of Women's Activism: New York and Boston: 1797–1840*. Chapel Hill: University of North Carolina Press, 2002.

Boyle, John. "Boyle's Journal of Occurrences in Boston." *NEHGR* 84 (1930): 142–71, 248–72, 357–82; 85 (January and April 1931): 5–28, 117–33.

Bradford, Alden, ed. *Speeches of the Governors of Massachusetts, 1765–1775: The Answers of the House of Representatives Thereto*. New York: Da Capo Press, 1971.

Bradley, Patricia. *Slavery, Propaganda, and the American Revolution*. Jackson: University Press of Mississippi, 1998.

Branson, Susan. *These Fiery Frenchified Dames: Women and Political Culture in Early National Philadelphia*. Philadelphia: University of Pennsylvania Press, 2001.

Breen, T. H. "'Baubles of Britain': The American and Consumer Revolutions of the Eighteenth Century." In *Of Consuming Interests: The Style of Life in the Eighteenth Century*, edited by Cary Carson, Ronald Hoffman, and Peter J. Albert, 444–82. Charlottesville: University Press of Virginia, 1994.

———. "Horses and Gentlemen: The Cultural Significance of Gambling among the Gentry of Virginia." *WMQ*, 3rd ser., 34, no. 2 (April 1977): 239–57.

———. "Making History: The Force of Public Opinion and the Last Years of Slavery in Revolutionary Massachusetts." In Hoffman, Sobel, and Teute, *Through a Glass Darkly*, 67–95.

———. *The Marketplace of Revolution: How Consumer Politics Shaped American Independence*. Oxford: Oxford University Press, 2004.

Breitenbach, William. "Unregenerate Doings: Selflessness and Selfishness in New Divinity Theology." *American Quarterly* 34, no. 5 (1982): 479–502.

Brewer, Holly. *By Birth or Consent: Children, Law, and the Anglo-American Revolution in Authority*. Chapel Hill: University of North Carolina Press, 2005.

Brewer, John. *Party Ideology and Popular Politics at the Accession of George III*. Cambridge: Cambridge University Press, 1976.

———. *The Sinews of Power: War, Money and the English State, 1688–1783*. London: Unwin Hyman, 1989.

Bridenbaugh, Carl. *Cities in Revolt: Urban Life in America, 1743–1776*. New York: Alfred A. Knopf, 1955. Reprint, New York: Oxford University Press, 1971.

——. *Cities in the Wilderness: The First Century of Urban Life in America, 1625–1742*. New York: Ronald Press Co., 1938. Reprint, New York: Oxford University Press, 1971.

——. *Mitre and Sceptre: Transatlantic Faiths, Ideas, Personalities, and Politics, 1689–1775*. New York: Oxford University Press, 1962.

——. *Myths and Realities: Societies of the Colonial South*. New York: Atheneum, 1965.

Bridges, Amy. *A City in the Republic: Antebellum New York and the Origins of Machine Politics*. Cambridge: Cambridge University Press, 1984.

Brigham, David R., Laura K. Mills, and Philip A. Klausmeyer. "*Captain-Lieutenant John Larrabee*, about 1750, by Joseph Badger." *Early American Paintings in the Worcester Art Museum*. 2000. Online. Available: http://www.worcesterart.org/Collection/Early_American/Artists/badger/John_Larrabee/painting.html. October 6, 2005.

Brinsfield, John Wesley. *Religion and Politics in Colonial South Carolina*. Easley, SC: Southern Historical Press, 1983.

Brobeck, Stephen. "Revolutionary Change in Colonial Philadelphia: The Brief Life of the Proprietary Gentry." *WMQ*, 3rd. ser., 33, 3 (July 1976): 410–34.

Bronson, Walter C. *The History of Brown University, 1764–1914*. Boston: Merrymount Press, 1914.

Brooke, John L. "Ancient Lodges and Self-Created Societies: Voluntary Association and the Public Sphere in the Early Republic." In Hoffman and Albert, *Launching the "Extended Republic,"* 273–359.

——. "'The True Spiritual Seed': Sectarian Religion and the Persistence of the Occult in Eighteenth-Century New England." In *Wonders of the Invisible World: 1600–1900*, edited by Peter Benes, 107–26, vol. 17 of *The Dublin Seminar for New England Folklife, Annual Proceedings, 1992*. Boston: Boston University, 1995.

Brown, Anne S., and David D. Hall. "Family Strategies and Religious Practice: Baptism and the Lord's Supper in Early New England." In *Lived Religion in America: Toward a History of Practice*, edited by David D. Hall, 41–68. Princeton, NJ: Princeton University Press, 1997.

Brown, C. Allan. "Eighteenth-Century Virginia Plantation Gardens: Translating an Ancient Idyll." In *Regional Garden Design in the United States*, edited by Therese O'Malley and Marc Treib, 125–62. Washington, DC: Dumbarton Oaks Research Library and Collection, 1995.

Brown, Kathleen M. "Antiauthoritarianism and Freedom in Early America." *JAH* 85, no. 1 (June 1998): 77–85.

——. *Good Wives, Nasty Wenches, and Anxious Patriarchs: Gender, Race, and Power in Colonial Virginia*. Chapel Hill: University of North Carolina Press, 1996.

Brown, Richard D. *Knowledge Is Power: The Diffusion of Information in Early America, 1700–1865*. New York: Oxford University Press, 1989.

——. *Revolutionary Politics in Massachusetts: The Boston Committee of Correspondence and the Towns, 1772–1774*. Cambridge, MA: Harvard University Press, 1970.

Brown, Wallace. *The Good Americans: The Loyalists in the American Revolution*. New York: William Morrow and Co., 1969.

Brunhouse, Robert Levere. *The Counter-Revolution in Pennsylvania, 1776–1790*. Philadelphia: Pennsylvania Historical Commission, 1942.

———. "The Effect of the Townshend Acts in Pennsylvania." *PMHB* 54, no. 4 (October 1930): 355–73.

Brunsman, Denver Alexander. "The Evil Necessity: British Naval Impressment in the Eighteenth-Century Atlantic World." Ph.D. diss., Princeton University, 2004.

Bull, Kinloch, Jr. *The Oligarchs in Colonial and Revolutionary Charleston: Lieutenant Governor William Bull II and His Family.* Columbia: University of South Carolina Press, 1991.

Bullock, Orin M., Jr. "The Friends Meeting House, 1699–1922: An Architectural Research Report." *Newport History* 42, no. 2 (spring 1969): 25–57.

Bullock, Stephen C. "A Mumper among the Gentle: Tom Bell, Colonial Confidence Man." *WMQ*, 3rd ser., 55, no. 2 (April 1998): 231–58.

———. *Revolutionary Brotherhood: Freemasonry and the Transformation of the American Social Order, 1730–1840.* Chapel Hill: University of North Carolina Press, 1996.

———. "The Revolutionary Transformation of American Freemasonry, 1752–1792." *WMQ*, 3rd ser., 47, no. 3 (July 1990): 347–69.

"The Burghers of New Amsterdam and the Freemen of New York, 1675–1866." *Collections of the New-York Historical Society* 18 (1885).

Burnard, Trevor. "'The Grand Mart of the Island': The Economic Function of Kingston, Jamaica in the Mid-Eighteenth Century." In *Jamaica in Slavery and Freedom: History, Heritage, and Culture,* edited by Kathleen E. A. Monteith and Glen Richards, 225–41. Kingston, Jamaica: University of the West Indies Press, 2002.

Burrows, Edwin G., and Mike Wallace. *Gotham: A History of New York City to 1898.* New York: Oxford University Press, 1999.

Bushman, Richard L. *King and People in Provincial Massachusetts.* Chapel Hill: University of North Carolina Press, 1985.

———. "Massachusetts Farmers and the Revolution." In *Society, Freedom, and Conscience,* edited by Richard M. Jellison, 77–124. New York: W. W. Norton and Co., 1976.

———. *The Refinement of America: Persons, Houses, Cities.* New York: Alfred A. Knopf, 1992. Reprint, New York: Random House, Vintage Books, 1993.

Butler, Jon. *Awash in a Sea of Faith: Christianizing the American People.* Cambridge, MA: Harvard University Press, 1990.

———. *Becoming America: The Revolution before 1776.* Cambridge, MA: Harvard University Press, 2000.

———. "Enthusiasm Described and Decried: The Great Awakening as Interpretative Fiction." *JAH* 69, no. 2 (September 1982): 305–25.

Calhoon, Robert McCluer. *The Loyalist Perception and Other Essays.* Columbia: University of South Carolina Press, 1989.

———. *The Loyalists in Revolutionary America, 1760–1781.* New York: Harcourt Brace Jovanovich, 1973.

Calhoun, Jeanne A., Martha A. Zierden, and Elizabeth A. Paysinger. "The Geographic Spread of Charleston's Mercantile Community, 1732–1767." *SCHM* 86 (July 1985): 182–220.

Cappon, Lester J., ed. *Atlas of Early American History.* Princeton, NJ: Princeton University Press, 1976.

Carp, Benjamin L. "Fire of Liberty: Firefighters, Urban Voluntary Culture, and the Revolutionary Movement." *WMQ*, 3rd ser., 58, no. 4 (October 2001): 781–818.

———. "Nations of American Rebels: Understanding Nationalism in Revolutionary North America and the Civil War South." *Civil War History* 48, no. 1 (March 2002): 5–33.

———. "The Night the Yankees Burned Broadway: The New York City Fire of 1776." *Early American Studies* 4, no. 2 (fall 2006): 471–511.

Carr, Jacqueline Barbara. *After the Siege: A Social History of Boston, 1775–1800.* Boston: Northeastern University Press, 2005.

———. "A Change 'As Remarkable as the Revolution Itself': Boston's Demographics, 1780–1800." *NEQ* 73, no. 4 (December 2000): 584–602.

Champagne, Roger. "The Military Association of the Sons of Liberty." *New-York Historical Society Quarterly* 41, no. 3 (July 1957): 338–50.

Channing, George C. *Early Recollections of Newport, R.I., 1793–1811.* Cambridge, MA: John Wilson and Son, 1868.

Charbonneau, Hubert, Bertrand Desjardins, Jacques Légaré, and Hubert Denis. "The Population of the St. Lawrence Valley, 1608–1760." In *A Population History of North America*, edited by Michael R. Haines and Richard H. Steckel, 99–142. Cambridge: Cambridge University Press, 2000.

Chase, Jeanne. "Boundaries in Time: Cities and the Problem of Scale in Early American History." *Reviews in American History* 18, no. 2 (June 1990): 165–76.

Chudacoff, Howard P. *The Evolution of American Urban Society.* Englewood Cliffs, NJ: Random House, Prentice-Hall, 1975.

Chyet, Stanley F. *Lopez of Newport: Colonial American Merchant Prince.* Detroit, MI: Wayne State University Press, 1970.

Clark, J. C. D. *The Language of Liberty, 1660–1832: Political Discourse and Social Dynamics in the Anglo-American World.* Cambridge: Cambridge University Press, 1994.

Clark, Peter. *British Clubs and Societies, 1580–1800: The Origins of an Associational World.* Oxford: Oxford University Press, Clarendon Press, 2000.

Clitherall, James. "Extracts from the Diary of Dr. James Clitherall, 1776." *PMHB* 22, no. 4 (1898): 468–74.

Coclanis, Peter A. *The Shadow of a Dream: Economic Life and Death in the South Carolina Low Country, 1670–1920.* New York: Oxford University Press, 1989.

———. "The Sociology of Architecture in Colonial Charleston: Pattern and Process in an Eighteenth-Century Southern City." *Journal of Social History* 18, no. 4 (summer 1985): 607–23.

Cogliano, Francis D. *No King, No Popery: Anti-Catholicism in Revolutionary New England.* Westport, CT: Greenwood Press, 1995.

Cogswell, Thomas. "Underground Verse and the Transformation of Early Stuart Political Culture." In *Political Culture and Cultural Politics in Early Modern England: Essays Presented to David Underdown*, edited by Susan D. Amussen and Mark A. Kishlansky, 277–300. Manchester, England: Manchester University Press, 1995.

Cohen, Norman S. "The Philadelphia Election Riot of 1742." *PMHB* 92, no. 3 (July 1968): 306–19.

Colden, Cadwallader. "The Colden Letter Books." Vols. 1–2. *Collections of the New-York Historical Society.* Vols. 9–10 (1876–77).

———. *The Conduct of Cadwallader Colden, Esquire, Late Lieutenant-Governor of New York: Relating to The Judges Commissions, Appeals to the King, and the Stamp-Duty.* 1767. In *Collections of the New-York Historical Society*, 10 (1877): 429–67.

———. "The Letters and Papers of Cadwallader Colden." Vols. 6–7. *Collections of the New-York Historical Society*. Vols. 55–56 (1922–23).

Cole, John N. "Henry Marchant's Journal, 1771–1772." *Rhode Island History* 57, no. 2 (May 1999): 30–55.

Colley, Linda. *Britons: Forging the Nation, 1707–1837*. New Haven, CT: Yale University Press, 1992.

The Colonial Laws of New York from the Year 1664 to the Revolution. 5 vols. Albany, NY: James B. Lyon, 1894.

Committee Chamber, Philadelphia. Philadelphia, May 18, 1776. Evans #15014.

"A complaint from the town dock watch against the officers of the regiments." *Proceedings of the Massachusetts Historical Society* 20 (1882–83): 9–10.

Conforti, Joseph A. *Samuel Hopkins and the New Divinity Movement: Calvinism, the Congregational Ministry, and Reform in New England Between the Great Awakenings*. Grand Rapids, MI: Christian University Press, 1981.

Conroy, David W. *In Public Houses: Drink and the Revolution of Authority in Colonial Massachusetts*. Chapel Hill: University of North Carolina Press, 1995.

A Contrast. New York, 1769. Evans #11223.

Conway, Stephen. "'The Great Mischief Complain'd of': Reflections on the Misconduct of British Soldiers in the Revolutionary War." *WMQ*, 3rd ser., 47, no. 3 (July 1990): 370–90.

———. "To Subdue America: British Army Officers and the Conduct of the Revolutionary War." *WMQ*, 3rd ser., 43, no. 3 (July 1986): 381–407.

Cook, Edward M., Jr. "Geography and History: Spatial Approaches to Early American History." *Historical Methods* 13 (winter 1980): 19–28.

———. "Jeffry Watson's Diary, 1740–1784: Family, Community, Religion and Politics in Colonial Rhode Island." *Rhode Island History* 43, no. 3 (August 1984): 79–116.

Cooper, James F., Jr. "Enthusiasts or Democrats? Separatism, Church Government, and the Great Awakening in Massachusetts." *NEQ* 65, no. 2 (June 1992): 265–83.

Cott, Nancy F. *The Bonds of Womanhood: "Women's Sphere" in New England, 1780–1835*. New Haven, CT: Yale University Press, 1977.

The Counter-Medly, being a proper Answer to all the Dunces of the Medly and their Abbettors. Philadelphia, 1765. Evans #9943.

Countryman, Edward. *A People in Revolution: The American Revolution and Political Society in New York, 1760–1790*. Baltimore: Johns Hopkins University Press, 1981.

Crane, Elaine Forman. *A Dependent People: Newport, Rhode Island in the Revolutionary Era*. 1954. Paperback ed. New York: Fordham University Press, 1992.

———. *Ebb Tide in New England: Women, Seaports, and Social Change, 1630–1800*. Boston: Northeastern University Press, 1998.

———. "Political Dialogue and the Spring of Abigail's Discontent." *WMQ*, 3rd ser., 56, no. 4 (October 1999): 745–74.

———. "Religion and Rebellion: Women of Faith in the American War for Independence." In *Religion in a Revolutionary Age*, edited by Ronald Hoffman and Peter J. Albert, 52–86. Charlottesville: University Press of Virginia, 1994.

———. "Uneasy Coexistence: Religious Tensions in Eighteenth Century Newport." *Newport History* 53, no. 3 (summer 1980): 101–11.

Crawford, Michael J. *Seasons of Grace: Colonial New England's Revival Tradition in Its British Context*. New York: Oxford University Press, 1991.

Creighton, Margaret S. "American Mariners and the Rites of Manhood, 1830–1870." In *Jack Tar in History: Essays in the History of Maritime Life and Labour*, edited by Colin Howell and Richard J. Twomey, 143–63. Fredericton, NB: Acadiensis Press, 1991.

Cress, Lawrence Delbert. "Whither Columbia? Congressional Residence and the Politics of the New Nation, 1776 to 1787." *WMQ*, 3rd ser., 32, no. 4 (October 1975): 581–600.

Crèvecoeur, J. Hector St. John de. *More Letters from the American Farmer: An Edition of the Essays in English Left Unpublished by Crèvecoeur*. Edited by Dennis D. Moore. Athens: University of Georgia Press, 1995.

Crowley, John E. "Alcoholic License." Review of *Taverns and Drinking in Early America*, by Sharon V. Salinger. *Common-place* 4, no. 1 (October 2003). Online. Available: http://www.common-place.org/vol-04/no-01/reviews/crowley.shtml. November 14, 2006.

———. *The Invention of Comfort: Sensibilities and Design in Early Modern Britain and Early America*. Baltimore: Johns Hopkins University Press, 2001.

Curry, Leonard P. *The Free Black in Urban America, 1800–1850: The Shadow of the Dream*. Chicago: University of Chicago Press, 1981.

Daniels, Bruce C. *Dissent and Conformity on Narragansett Bay: The Colonial Rhode Island Town*. Middletown, CT: Wesleyan University Press, 1983.

Davies, K. G., ed. *Documents of the American Revolution, 1770–1783 (Colonial Office Series)*. 21 vols. Dublin: Irish Academic Press, 1972–81.

Davis, David Brion. *The Problem of Slavery in the Age of Revolution, 1770–1823*. Rev. ed. New York: Oxford University Press, 1999.

Davis, Susan G. *Parades and Power: Street Theatre in Nineteenth-Century Philadelphia*. Philadelphia: Temple University Press, 1986.

Davis, Thomas J. "Emancipation Rhetoric, Natural Rights, and Revolutionary New England: A Note on Four Black Petitions in Massachusetts, 1773–1777." *NEQ* 62, no. 2 (June 1989): 248–63.

———. *A Rumor of Revolt: The "Great Negro Plot" in Colonial New York*. New York: Free Press, Macmillan, 1985.

Dawkins, Henry. *The Paxton Expedition*. Philadelphia, 1764. Evans #9627.

Day, Alan, and Katherine Day. "Another Look at the Boston 'Caucus.'" *Journal of American Studies* 5 (1971): 19–42.

Dayton, Cornelia Hughes. *Women before the Bar: Gender, Law, and Society in Connecticut, 1639–1789*. Chapel Hill: University of North Carolina Press, 1995.

Deane, Silas. "The Deane Papers." Vol. 1. *Collections of the New-York Historical Society*. Vol. 19 (1886).

Diamondstone, Judith M. "Philadelphia's Municipal Corporation, 1701–1776." *PMHB* 90, no. 2 (April 1966): 183–201.

Dickerson, Oliver Morton, ed. *Boston under Military Rule, 1768–1769 as Revealed in a Journal of the Times*. Boston: Mount Vernon Press, 1936. Reprint, New York: Da Capo Press, 1970.

———. "John Hancock: Notorious Smuggler or Near Victim of British Revenue Racketeers?" *Mississippi Valley Historical Review* 32, no. 4 (March 1946): 517–40.

———. *The Navigation Acts and the American Revolution*. Philadelphia: University of Pennsylvania Press, 1951.

Dickinson, H. T. *The Politics of the People in Eighteenth-Century Britain*. New York: St. Martin's Press, 1995.

Dickinson, John. *An Essay on the Constitutional Power of Great-Britain over the Colonies in America; with the Resolves of the Committee for the Province of Pennsylvania, and Their Instructions to Their Representatives in Assembly.* Philadelphia, 1774. Evans #13247.

———. *The Writings of John Dickinson . . . . Political Writings, 1764–1774.* Edited by Paul Leicester Ford. Memoirs of the Historical Society of Pennsylvania, 14. Philadelphia, 1895.

Dinkin, Robert J. "Seating the Meetinghouse in Early Massachusetts." In St. George, *Material Life in America*, 407–18.

———. *Voting in Provincial America: A Study of Elections in the Thirteen Colonies, 1689–1776.* Westport, CT: Greenwood Press, 1977.

Ditz, Toby L. "Shipwrecked; or, Masculinity Imperiled: Mercantile Representations of Failure and the Gendered Self in Eighteenth-Century Philadelphia." *JAH* 81, no. 1 (June 1994): 51–80.

Dixon, Caroline Wyche. "The Miles Brewton House: Ezra Waite's Architectural Book and Other Possible Design Sources." *SCHM* 82 (April 1981): 118–42.

Doerflinger, Thomas M. *A Vigorous Spirit of Enterprise: Merchants and Economic Development in Revolutionary Philadelphia.* Chapel Hill: University of North Carolina Press, 1986.

Dorman, Charles G. "Furnishing Plan (Parts D. through F.) for the Second Floor of Independence Hall." Philadelphia, 1971. Independence National Historical Park.

Dovey, Kim. *Framing Places: Mediating Power in Built Form.* London: Routledge, 1999.

Downing, Antoinette F. "History of the Friends Meeting House in Newport, Rhode Island." *Newport History* 41, no. 4 (fall 1968): 137–67.

Downing, Antoinette F., and Vincent J. Scully Jr. *The Architectural Heritage of Newport Rhode Island, 1640–1915.* 2nd ed. New York: Clarkson N. Potter, 1967.

Drake, Francis S., ed. *Tea Leaves: Being a Collection of Letters and Documents relating to the Shipment of TEA to the American Colonies in the year 1773, by the East Indian Tea Company . . . .* Boston: A. O. Crane, 1884.

Drake, Samuel Adams. *Old Boston Taverns and Tavern Clubs.* Rev. ed., with additions by Walter K. Watkins. Boston: W. A. Butterfield, 1917.

Drayton, Richard. *Nature's Government: Science, Imperial Britain, and the "Improvement" of the World.* New Haven, CT: Yale University Press, 2000.

Dunbar, John R., ed. *The Paxton Papers.* The Hague: Martinus Nijhoff, 1957.

Earle, Carville. "Boston, Vanguard of the American Revolution." In *Geographical Inquiry and American Historical Problems*, 153–72. Stanford, CA: Stanford University Press, 1992.

Earle, Carville, and Ronald Hoffman. "Staple Crops and Urban Development in the Eighteenth-Century South." *Perspectives in American History* 10 (1976): 7–78.

Earle, Peter. *Sailors: English Merchant Seamen, 1650–1775.* London: Random House, Methunen, 1998.

"Ebenezer David." *Seventh Day Baptist Memorial* 3 (July 1854): 102–4.

Eberlein, Harold Donaldson, and Cortlandt Van Dyke Hubbard. *Diary of Independence Hall.* Philadelphia: J. B. Lippincott Co., 1948.

———. *Portrait of a Colonial City: Philadelphia, 1670–1838.* Philadelphia: J. B. Lippincott Co., 1939.

Edgar, Walter. *Partisans and Redcoats: The Southern Conflict That Turned the Tide of the American Revolution.* New York: William Morrow, HarperCollins, 2001.

Edgar, Walter. *South Carolina: A History*. Columbia: University of South Carolina Press, 1998.

Edwards, Morgan. "Materials for a History of the Baptists in Rhode Island." *Collections of the Rhode Island Historical Society* 6 (1867): 301–70.

Egerton, Douglas R. *Gabriel's Rebellion: The Virginia Slave Conspiracies of 1800 and 1802*. Chapel Hill: University of North Carolina Press, 1993.

Egle, William H., ed. *Pennsylvania in the War of the Revolution: Associated Battalions and Militia*. Vol. 13 of *Pennsylvania Archives*, 2nd ser. Harrisburg, PA: E. K. Meyers, 1887.

Egnal, Marc. *A Mighty Empire: The Origins of the American Revolution*. Ithaca, NY: Cornell University Press, 1988.

Egnal, Marc, and Joseph A. Ernst. "An Economic Interpretation of the American Revolution." *WMQ*, 3rd. ser., 29, no. 1 (January 1972): 3–32.

The Election a Medley, Humbly Inscribed, to Squire Lilliput Professor of Scurrillity. Philadelphia, 1764. Evans #9650.

The Election Humbly Inscrib'd, to the Saturday-Nights Club, in Lodge Alley. Philadelphia, 1765. Evans #9963.

Elkins, Stanley, and Eric McKitrick. *The Age of Federalism*. New York: Oxford University Press, 1993.

Elton, Romeo. "Notes to the Memoir of John Callender." *Collections of the Rhode Island Historical Society* 4 (1838): 27–44.

Epstein, James. "Spatial Practices/Democratic Vistas." *Social History* 24, no. 3 (October 1999): 294–310.

Etting, Frank M. *An Historical Account of The Old State House of Pennsylvania, Now Known as the Hall of Independence*. Boston: James R. Osgood and Co., 1876.

Extracts from the proceedings of the Provincial Conference of Committees for the Province of Pennsylvania. Philadelphia, 1776. Evans #14975.

Ferling, John. *A Leap in the Dark: The Struggle to Create the American Republic*. New York: Oxford University Press, 2003.

Fischer, David Hackett. *Paul Revere's Ride*. New York: Oxford University Press, 1994.

Foner, Eric. *Tom Paine and Revolutionary America*. New York: Oxford University Press, 1976.

Foord, Archibald S. *His Majesty's Opposition, 1714–1830*. Westport, CT: Greenwood Press, 1964.

Foote, Thelma Wills. *Black and White Manhattan: The History of Racial Formation in Colonial New York City*. New York: Oxford University Press, 2004.

Forbes, Esther. *Paul Revere and the World He Lived In*. Boston: Houghton Mifflin Co., 1942.

Force, Peter, ed. *American Archives: Fourth Series, Containing a Documentary History of the English Colonies in North America from the King's Message to Parliament of March 7, 1774, to the Declaration of Independence by the United States*. 6 vols. Washington, DC: M. St. Clair Clarke and Peter Force, 1837–46.

Formisano, Ronald P. *The Transformation of Political Culture: Massachusetts Parties, 1790s—1840s*. New York: Oxford University Press, 1983.

Foulke, Samuel. "Fragments of a Journal Kept by Samuel Foulke, of Bucks County." Edited by Howard M. Jenkins. *PMHB* 5, no. 1 (1889): 60–73.

Fowler, William M., Jr. *The Baron of Beacon Hill: A Biography of John Hancock*. Boston: Houghton Mifflin Co., 1980.

———. "The Business of War: Boston as a Navy Base, 1776–1783." *American Neptune* 42 (1982): 25–35.

Fox-Genovese, Elizabeth. *Within the Plantation Household: Black and White Women of the Old South*. Chapel Hill: University of North Carolina Press, 1988.

Franklin, Benjamin. *The Autobiography and Other Writings*. Edited by Kenneth Silverman. Penguin Classics. New York: Penguin Books, 1986.

——. *The Papers of Benjamin Franklin*. 37 vols. Edited by Leonard W. Labaree, et al. New Haven, CT: Yale University Press, 1959–2003.

The Freeholders and Other Electors . . . . Philadelphia, November 11, 1774. Evans #13537.

"A Freeman." *To the Representatives of the Province of Pennsylvania, now met in this City*. Philadelphia, July 21, 1774. Shipton and Mooney #42720.

Frese, Joseph R. "Smuggling, the Navy, and the Customs Service, 1763–1772." In "Seafaring in Colonial Massachusetts." Special issue, *Publications of the Colonial Society of Massachusetts* 52 (1980): 199–212.

Frey, Sylvia R. *Water from the Rock: Black Resistance in a Revolutionary Age*. Princeton, NJ: Princeton University Press, 1991.

"A Friend to Order." *To the Publick*. New York, March 22, 1775. Evans #14513.

Frothingham, Richard, Jr. *History of the Siege of Boston, and of the Battles of Lexington, Concord, and Bunker Hill*. 2nd ed. Boston: Charles C. Little and James Brown, 1851.

Fryer, Darcy R. "The Mind of Eliza Pinckney: An Eighteenth-Century Woman's Construction of Herself." *SCHM* 99, no. 3 (July 1998): 215–37.

Gadsden, Christopher. "Two Letters by Christopher Gadsden, February 1766." Edited by Robert M. Weir. *SCHM* 75, no. 3 (July 1974): 169–76.

——. *The Writings of Christopher Gadsden, 1746–1805*. Edited by Richard Walsh. Columbia: University of South Carolina Press, 1966.

Gage, Thomas. *The Correspondence of General Thomas Gage*. Edited by Clarence Edwin Carter. 2 vols. New Haven, CT: Yale University Press, 1931, 1933.

[Galloway, James.] *A True and Impartial State of the Province of Pennsylvania*. Philadelphia: W. Dunlap, 1759. Evans #8349.

Gibbes, Robert W., ed. *Documentary History of the American Revolution*, 3 vols. New York: D. Appleton and Co., 1853–57.

Gibson, Gail. "Costume and Fashion in Charleston, 1769–1782." *SCHM* 82, no. 3 (July 1981): 225–47.

Gilje, Paul A. *Liberty on the Waterfront: American Maritime Culture in the Age of Revolution*. Philadelphia: University of Pennsylvania Press, 2004.

——. "The Rise of Capitalism in the Early Republic." *Journal of the Early Republic* 16, no. 2 (summer 1996): 159–81.

——. *The Road to Mobocracy: Popular Disorder in New York City, 1763–1784*. Chapel Hill: University of North Carolina Press, 1987.

Gillespie, Joanna Bowen. *The Life and Times of Martha Laurens Ramsay, 1759–1811*. Columbia: University of South Carolina Press, 2001.

Gladwell, Malcolm. *The Tipping Point: How Little Things Can Make a Big Difference*. Boston: Little, Brown, and Co., 2000.

Glover, Lorri. *All Our Relations: Blood Ties and Emotional Bonds among the Early South Carolina Gentry*. Baltimore: Johns Hopkins University Press, 2000.

Godbold, E. Stanly, Jr., and Robert H. Woody. *Christopher Gadsden and the American Revolution*. Knoxville: University of Tennessee Press, 1982.

Goldfield, David R. *Cotton Fields and Skyscrapers: Southern City and Region, 1607–1980*. Baton Rouge: Louisiana State University Press, 1982.

Goodsell, Charles T. *The Social Meaning of Civic Space: Studying Political Authority through Architecture*. Lawrence: University Press of Kansas, 1988.

Gough, Robert J. "The Philadelphia Economic Elite at the End of the Eighteenth Century." In *Shaping a National Culture: The Philadelphia Experience, 1750–1800*, edited by Catherine E. Hutchins, 15–43. Winterthur, DE: Henry Francis du Pont Winterthur Museum, 1994.

Gould, Eliga H. *The Persistence of Empire: British Political Culture in the Age of the American Revolution*. Chapel Hill: University of North Carolina Press, 2000.

Grasso, Christopher. *A Speaking Aristocracy: Transforming Public Discourse in Eighteenth-Century Connecticut*. Chapel Hill: University of North Carolina Press, 1999.

Graydon, Alexander. *Memoirs of His Own Time, with Reminiscences of the Men and Events of the Revolution*. Edited by John Stockton Littell. Philadelphia: Lindsay and Blakiston, 1846.

Greenberg, Amy S. *Cause for Alarm: The Volunteer Fire Department in the Nineteenth-Century City*. Princeton, NJ: Princeton University Press, 1998.

Greenberg, Douglas. *Crime and Law Enforcement in the Colony of New York, 1691–1776*. Ithaca, NY: Cornell University Press, 1974.

Greene, Evarts B., and Virginia D. Harrington. *American Population before the Federal Census of 1790*. New York: Columbia University Press, 1932.

Greene, Jack P. "The American Revolution: An Explanation." In *Understanding the American Revolution: Issues and Actors*, 48–71. Charlottesville: University Press of Virginia, 1995.

——. *Negotiated Authorities: Essays in Colonial Political and Constitutional History*. Charlottesville: University Press of Virginia, 1994.

——. *Peripheries and Center: Constitutional Development in the Extended Polities of the British Empire and the United States, 1607–1788*. Athens: University of Georgia Press, 1986.

——. *Pursuits of Happiness: The Social Development of Early Modern British Colonies and the Formation of American Culture*. Chapel Hill: University of North Carolina Press, 1988.

——. *The Quest for Power: The Lower Houses of Assembly in the Southern Royal Colonies, 1689–1776*. Chapel Hill: University of North Carolina Press, 1963.

——. "'Slavery or Independence': Some Reflections on the Relationship among Liberty, Black Bondage, and Equality in Revolutionary South Carolina." In *Imperatives, Behaviors and Identities: Essays in Early American Cultural History*, 268–89. Charlottesville: University Press of Virginia, 1992.

——. "An Uneasy Connection: An Analysis of the Preconditions of the American Revolution." In *Essays on the American Revolution*, edited by Stephen G. Kurtz and James H. Hutson, 32–80. Chapel Hill: University of North Carolina, 1973.

Greene, Jack P., Rosemary Brana-Shute, and Randy J. Sparks, eds. *Money, Trade, and Power: The Evolution of Colonial South Carolina's Plantation Society*. Columbia: University of South Carolina Press, 2001.

Greene, Lorenzo Johnston. *The Negro in Colonial New England, 1620–1776*. New York: Columbia University Press, 1942. Reprint, Port Washington, NY: Kennikat Press, 1966.

Greene, Nathanael. *The Papers of Nathanael Greene*. Edited by Richard K. Showman, et al. 11 vols. Chapel Hill: University of North Carolina Press, 1976–2000.

Griffin, Edward M. *Old Brick: Charles Chauncy of Boston, 1705–1787*. Minneapolis: University of Minnesota Press, 1980.

Grimsted, David. "Anglo-American Racism and Phillis Wheatley's 'Sable Veil,' 'Length'ned Chain,' and 'Knitted Heart.'" In Hoffman and Albert, *Women in the Age of the American Revolution*, 338–444.

Grodzins, Morton. *The Loyal and the Disloyal: Social Boundaries of Patriotism and Treason*. Chicago: University of Chicago Press, 1956.

Gross, Robert A. *The Minutemen and Their World*. New York: Hill and Wang, 1976.

Guild, Reuben Aldridge. *Early History of Brown University, Including the Life, Times, and Correspondence of President Manning, 1756–1791*. Providence, RI: Snow and Farnham, 1897.

Gunn, L. Ray. *The Decline of Authority: Public Economic Policy and Political Development in New York, 1800–1860*. Ithaca, NY: Cornell University Press, 1988.

Habermas, Jürgen. *The Structural Transformation of the Public Sphere: An Inquiry into a Category of Bourgeois Society*. Translated by Thomas Burger, with the assistance of Frederick Lawrence. Cambridge, MA: MIT Press, 1991.

Haley, Jacquetta Mae. "Voluntary Organizations in Pre-Revolutionary New York City, 1750–1776." Ph.D. diss., State University of New York at Binghamton, 1976.

Hall, John A. "'Nefarious Wretches, Insidious Villains, and Evil-Minded Persons': Urban Crime Reported in Charleston's *City Gazette*, in 1788." *SCHM* 88, no. 3 (July 1987): 151–68.

Hall, Mark David. *The Political and Legal Philosophy of James Wilson, 1742–1798*. Columbia: University of Missouri Press, 1997.

Hall, Timothy D. *Contested Boundaries: Itinerancy and the Reshaping of the Colonial American Religious World*. Durham, NC: Duke University Press, 1994.

Hamilton, Alexander. *Gentleman's Progress: The Itinerarium of Dr. Alexander Hamilton. 1744*. Edited by Carl Bridenbaugh. Chapel Hill: University of North Carolina Press, 1948. Reprint, Pittsburgh: University of Pittsburgh Press, 1992.

Hamilton, Kenneth Gardiner. *John Ettwein and the Moravian Church during the Revolutionary Period*. Bethlehem, PA: Times Publishing Co., 1940.

Hancock, David. "'A Revolution in the Trade': Wine Distribution and the Development of the Infrastructure of the Atlantic Market Economy, 1703–1807." In McCusker and Morgan, *Early Modern Atlantic Economy*, 105–53.

"The Hand-in-Hand Fire-Club." Newport, RI, 1750. Shipton and Mooney #40558.

Haney, Gina. "In Complete Order: Social Control and Architectural Organization In the Charleston Back Lot." Master's thesis, University of Virginia, 1996.

Hanson, Charles P. *Necessary Virtue: The Pragmatic Origins of Religious Liberty in New England*. Charlottesville: University Press of Virginia, 1998.

Harrington, Virginia D. *The New York Merchant on the Eve of the Revolution*. New York: Columbia University Press, 1935. Reprint, Gloucester, MA: Peter Smith, 1964.

Harris, Tim. *London Crowds in the Reign of Charles II: Propaganda and Politics from the Restoration until the Exclusion Crisis*. Cambridge: Cambridge University Press, 1987.

———. "The Parties and the People: The Press, the Crowd and Politics 'Out-of-doors' in Restoration England." In *The Reigns of Charles II and James VII and*

II, edited by Lionel K. J. Glassey, 125–51. New York: St. Martin's Press, 1997.

——, ed. *The Politics of the Excluded, c. 1500–1800*. New York: Palgrave, 2001.

——. "The Problem of 'Popular Political Culture' in Seventeenth-Century London." *History of European Ideas* 10, no. 1 (1989): 43–58.

Harris, Tim. "Understanding Popular Politics in Restoration Britain." In *A Nation Transformed: England after the Restoration*, edited by Alan Houston and Steve Pincus, 125–53. Cambridge: Cambridge University Press, 2001.

Hart, Emma. "Constructing a New World: Charleston's Artisans and the Transformation of the South Carolina Lowcountry, 1700–1800." Ph.D. diss., Johns Hopkins University, 2001.

Hart, Oliver. "A Memorandum containing Some of the Most Remarkable Occurrences in Providence . . ." City of Charleston *Yearbook* (1896): 378–401.

Hartigan-O'Connor, Ellen L. "The Measure of the Market: Women's Economic Lives in Charleston, SC, and Newport, RI, 1750–1820." Ph.D. diss., University of Michigan, 2003.

Hatch, Nathan O. *The Democratization of American Christianity*. New Haven, CT: Yale University Press, 1989.

Hattendorf, John B. *Semper Eadem: A History of Trinity Church in Newport, 1698–2000*. Newport, RI: Trinity Church, 2001.

Haw, James. "A Broken Compact: Insecurity, Union, and the Proposed Surrender of Charleston, 1779." *SCHM* 96, no. 1 (January 1995): 30–53.

Hawke, David. *In the Midst of a Revolution*. Philadelphia: University of Pennsylvania Press, 1961.

"Hays Was a Patriot." *Rhode Island Jewish Historical Notes* 4 (November 1964): 126.

Hazard, Ebenezer. "A View of Coastal South Carolina in 1778: The Journal of Ebenezer Hazard." Edited by H. Roy Merrens. *SCHM* 73, no. 4 (October 1972): 177–93.

Heath, James. *A Chronicle of the Late Intestine War in the Three Kingdoms of England, Scotland, and Ireland*. 2nd ed. London: Thomas Basset, 1676.

Heimert, Alan. *Religion and the American Mind from the Great Awakening to the Revolution*. Cambridge, MA: Harvard University Press, 1966.

Henshaw, Joshua, Jr., to William Henshaw, June 15, 1768. *NEHGR* 22 (1868): 402–3.

Herbst, Jurgen. "The Charter for a Proposed College in Newport, Rhode Island: A Chapter in the History of Eighteenth-Century Higher Education in America." *Newport History* 49, no. 2 (spring 1976): 25–49.

Herman, Bernard L. "The Embedded Landscapes of the Charleston Single House, 1780–1820." In *Exploring Everyday Landscapes*, Perspectives in Vernacular Architecture 7, edited by Annmarie Adams and Sally McMurry, 41–57. Knoxville: University of Tennessee Press, 1997.

——. "Slave and Servant Housing in Charleston, 1770–1820." *Historical Archaeology* 33, no. 3 (1999): 88–101.

——. *Town House: Architecture and Material Life in the Early American City, 1780–1830*. Chapel Hill: University of North Carolina Press, 2005.

Hill, Christopher. *A Nation of Change and Novelty: Radical Politics, Religion, and Literature in Seventeenth-Century England*. New York: Routledge, 1990.

Hiltzheimer, Jacob. *Extracts from the Diary of Jacob Hiltzheimer of Philadelphia, 1765–1798*. Edited by Jacob Cox Parsons. Philadelphia: Wm. F. Fell and Co., 1893.

Hindle, Brooke. "The March of the Paxton Boys." *WMQ*, 3rd ser., 3, no. 4 (October 1946): 461–86.

Hodder, Ian. *Reading the Past: Current Approaches to Interpretation in Archaeology*. Cambridge: Cambridge University Press, 1986.

Hodges, Graham Russell. *New York City Cartmen, 1667–1850*. New York: New York University Press, 1986.

——. *Root and Branch: African Americans in New York and East Jersey, 1613–1863*. Chapel Hill: University of North Carolina Press, 1999.

Hoerder, Dirk. *Crowd Action in Revolutionary Massachusetts, 1765–1780*. New York: Academic Press, 1977.

Hoffer, Peter Charles. *The Great New York Conspiracy of 1741: Slavery, Crime, and Colonial Law*. Lawrence: University Press of Kansas, 2003.

Hoffman, Ronald, and Peter J. Albert, eds. *Launching the "Extended Republic": The Federalist Era*. Charlottesville: University Press of Virginia, 1996

——. *The Transforming Hand of Revolution: Reconsidering the American Revolution as a Social Movement*. Charlottesville: University Press of Virginia, 1996.

——. *Women in the Age of the American Revolution*. Charlottesville: University Press of Virginia, 1989.

Hoffman, Ronald, Michael Sobel, and Fredrika J. Teute, eds. *Through a Glass Darkly: Reflections on Personal Identity in America*. Chapel Hill: University of North Carolina Press, 1997.

Honyman, Robert. *Colonial Panorama, 1775: Dr. Robert Honyman's Journal for March and April*. Edited by Philip Padelford. San Marino, CA: Huntington Library, 1939.

Hopkins, Samuel. *A Dialogue, Concerning the Slavery of the Africans*. Norwich, CT, 1776. Evans #14804.

——. *An Inquiry into the Nature of True Holiness*. Newport, RI, 1773. Evans #12811.

——. *The Life and Character of Miss Susanna Anthony*. Hartford, CT, 1799. Evans #35635.

——. *Memoirs of the Life of Mrs. Sarah Osborn*. Worcester, MA, 1799. Evans #35636.

Hornsby, Stephen J. *British Atlantic, American Frontier: Spaces of Power in Early Modern British America*. Hanover, NH: University Press of New England, 2005.

Horton, James Oliver, and Lois E. Horton. *Black Bostonians: Family Life and Community Struggle in the Antebellum North*. Rev. ed. New York: Holmes and Meier, 1999.

Hulton, Ann. *Letters of a Loyalist Lady: Being the letters of Ann Hulton, sister of Henry Hulton, Commissioner of Customs at Boston, 1767–1776*. Cambridge, MA: Harvard University Press, 1927.

Hume, David. *The History of England, from the Invasion of Julius Caesar to the Revolution in 1688*. 6 vols. London, 1778.

——. *A Treatise on Human Nature*. Edited by L. A. Selby-Bigge. 2nd ed. New York: Oxford University Press, Clarendon Press, 1978.

Hunt, Lynn. *Politics, Culture, and Class in the French Revolution*. Berkeley and Los Angeles: University of California Press, 1984.

Hurst, Ronald L., and Jonathan Prown. *Southern Furniture, 1680–1830: The Colonial Williamsburg Collection*. New York: Colonial Williamsburg Foundation and Harry N. Abrams, 1997.

Hutchinson, Thomas. *History of the Province of Massachusetts Bay*. Vol. 3. London: John Murray, 1828.

Hutson, James H. "An Investigation of the Inarticulate: Philadelphia's White Oaks." *WMQ*, 3rd ser., 28, no. 1 (January 1971): 3–25.

———. *Pennsylvania Politics, 1746–1770: The Movement for Royal Government and Its Consequences*. Princeton, NJ: Princeton University Press, 1972.

Inhabitants and Estates of the Town of Boston, 1630–1800 and Annie Haven Thwing, *The Crooked and Narrow Streets of Boston, 1630–1822*. CD-ROM, Boston: New England Genealogical Society and Massachusetts Historical Society, 2001.

Inhabitants of Pennsylvania . . . . Philadelphia, October 13, 1773. Evans #12940.

The Inhabitants of the City of New-York . . . . Philadelphia, July 12, 1770. Evans #11817.

Innes, Stephen. *Creating the Commonwealth: The Economic Culture of Puritan New England*. New York: W. W. Norton and Co., 1995.

Ireland, Owen S. "The Ethnic-Religious Dimension of Pennsylvania Politics, 1778–1779." *WMQ*, 3rd ser., 30, no. 3 (July 1973): 423–48.

Irvin, Benjamin H. "The Streets of Philadelphia: Crowds, Congress, and the Political Culture of Revolution, 1774–1783." *PMHB* 129, no. 1 (January 2005): 7–44.

———. "Tar, Feathers, and the Enemies of American Liberties, 1768–1776." *NEQ* 76, no. 2 (June 2003): 197–238.

Isaac, Rhys. "Dramatizing the Ideology of Revolution: Popular Mobilization in Virginia, 1774–1776." *WMQ*, 3rd ser., 33, no. 3 (July 1976): 357–85.

———. *The Transformation of Virginia, 1740–1790*. Chapel Hill: University of North Carolina Press, 1982. Reprint, New York: W. W. Norton and Co., 1988.

"J. D." *A Word Without-Doors Concerning the Bill for Succession*. 1670? Wing D48.

"J. W., a Squinter on Public Affairs." *The Mode of Elections Considered*. New York, December 29, 1769. Evans #11517.

Jackson, Henry. "Newport, R. I., Ecclesiastically." In *The Newport Directory*, compiled by William H. Boyd, 106–14. Newport, RI: Charles E. Hammett, 1856.

Jackson, John W. *With the British Army in Philadelphia, 1777–1778*. San Rafael, CA: Presidio Press, 1979.

Jackson, Joseph. *Market Street, Philadelphia: The Most Historic Highway in America, Its Merchants and Its Story*. Philadelphia: Joseph Jackson, 1918.

Jacobsen, Douglas G. *An Unprov'd Experiment: Religious Pluralism in Colonial New Jersey*. Brooklyn, NY: Carlson Publishing, 1991.

Jaher, Frederic Cople. "The Politics of the Boston Brahmins, 1800–1860." In *Boston, 1700–1980: The Evolution of Urban Politics*, edited by Ronald P. Formisano and Constance K. Burns, 59–86. Westport, CT: Greenwood Press, 1984.

———. *The Urban Establishment: Upper Strata in Boston, New York, Charleston, Chicago, and Los Angeles*. Urbana and Chicago: University of Illinois Press, 1982.

James, Sydney V. *Colonial Rhode Island: A History*. New York: Charles Scribner's Sons, 1975.

———. *A People among Peoples: Quaker Benevolence in Eighteenth-Century America*. Cambridge, MA: Harvard University Press, 1963.

Jefferson, Thomas. *Notes on the State of Virginia: by Thomas Jefferson*. Edited by David Waldstreicher. Boston and New York: Bedford/St. Martin's, 2002.

———. *The Papers of Thomas Jefferson*. Edited by Julian P. Boyd, et al. Vols. 1, 10, 25. Princeton, NJ: Princeton University Press, 1950, 1954, 1992.

Jensen, Arthur L. *The Maritime Commerce of Colonial Philadelphia*. Madison: State Historical Society of Wisconsin, 1963.

Jensen, Merrill, ed. *English Historical Documents*. Vol. 9, *American Colonial Documents to 1776*. London: Eyre and Spottiswoode, 1955.

———. *The Founding of a Nation: A History of the American Revolution, 1763–1776*. New York: Oxford University Press, 1968.

"John Tanner." *Seventh Day Baptist Memorial* 3 (July 1854): 104–11.

Jones, George Fenwick, ed. "The 1780 Siege of Charleston as Experienced by a Hessian Officer." *SCHM* 88, nos. 1–2 (January and April 1987): 23–33, 63–75.

Jones, Thomas. *History of New York during the Revolutionary War . . . .* Edited by Edward Floyd de Lancey. 2 vols. New York: Trow's, 1879.

"Journal of a French Traveller in the Colonies, 1765, II," *AHR* 27, no. 1 (October 1921): 70–89.

Journals of the Continental Congress, 1774–1789. Edited by Worthington Chauncey Ford, et al. 34 vols. Washington, DC: Government Printing Office, 1904–37. Online. Available: http://hdl.loc.gov/loc.law/amlaw.lwjc. November 6, 2006.

Journals of the House of Representatives of Massachusetts. Vol. 20. Reprint, Boston: Massachusetts Historical Society, 1945.

Journals of the Provincial Congress, Provincial Convention, Committee of Safety and Council of Safety of the State of New-York, 1775–1777. Vol. 1. Albany: Thurlow Weed, 1842.

Juster, Susan. *Disorderly Women: Sexual Politics and Evangelicalism in Revolutionary New England*. Ithaca, NY: Cornell University Press, 1994.

Kalm, Peter. *Travels into North America*. Translated by John Reinhold Forster. Barre, MA: Imprint Society, 1972.

Kammen, Michael G. "British and Imperial Interests in the Age of the American Revolution." In *Anglo-American Political Relations, 1675–1775*, edited by Alison Gilbert Olson and Richard Maxwell Brown, 140–54. New Brunswick, NJ: Rutgers University Press, 1970.

———. *Colonial New York: A History*. New York: Charles Scribner's Sons, 1975.

———. *A Rope of Sand: The Colonial Agents, British Politics, and the American Revolution*. Ithaca, NY: Cornell University Press, 1968.

Kann, Mark E. *A Republic of Men: The American Founders, Gendered Language, and Patriarchal Politics*. New York: New York University Press, 1998.

Kaplan, Michael. "New York City Tavern Violence and the Creation of a Working-Class Male Identity." *Journal of the Early Republic* 15, no. 4 (winter 1995): 591–617.

Keep, Austin Baxter. *History of the New York Society Library*. New York: De Vinne Press, 1908.

Kennett, Lee, ed. "Charleston in 1778: A French Intelligence Report." *SCHM* 66, no. 2 (April 1965): 109–11.

Kerber, Linda K. *Federalists in Dissent: Imagery and Ideology in Jeffersonian America*. Ithaca, NY: Cornell University Press, 1970.

———. *Women of the Republic: Intellect and Ideology in Revolutionary America*. Chapel Hill: University of North Carolina Press, 1980.

Ketchum, Richard M. *Divided Loyalties: How the American Revolution Came to New York*. New York: Henry Holt and Co., 2002.

Kidd, Thomas S. *The Protestant Interest: New England after Puritanism*. New Haven: Yale University Press, 2004.

Kierner, Cynthia A. *Beyond the Household: Women's Place in the Early South, 1700–1835*. Ithaca, NY: Cornell University Press, 1998.

——. "Hospitality, Sociability, and Gender in the Southern Colonies." *Journal of Southern History* 62, no. 3 (August 1996): 449–80.

Kilbride, Daniel. "Cultivation, Conservatism, and the Early National Gentry: The Manigault Family and Their Circle." *Journal of the Early Republic* 19, no. 2 (summer 1999): 221–56.

Klein, Milton M. "The Cultural Tyros of Colonial New York." In *The Politics of Diversity: Essays in the History of Colonial New York*, 110–23. Port Washington, NY: Kennikat Press, 1974.

——, ed. *The Independent Reflector or Weekly Essays on Sundry Important Subjects More Particularly Adapted to the Province of New York*. Cambridge, MA: Harvard University Press, Belknap Press, 1963.

Klein, Rachel N. *Unification of a Slave State: The Rise of the Planter Class in the South Carolina Backcountry, 1760–1808*. Chapel Hill: University of North Carolina Press, 1990.

Klepp, Susan E. "Demography in Early Philadelphia, 1690–1860." *Proceedings of the American Philosophical Society* 133, no. 2 (June 1989): 85–111.

Koeppel, Gerard T. *Water for Gotham: A History*. Princeton, NJ: Princeton University Press, 2000.

Konvitz, Josef W. *Cities and the Sea: Port City Planning in Early Modern Europe*. Baltimore: Johns Hopkins University Press, 1978.

Kornblith, Gary J. "Artisan Federalism: New England Mechanics and the Political Economy of the 1790s." In Hoffman and Albert, *Launching the "Extended Republic,"* 249–72.

Kornblith, Gary J., and John M. Murrin. "The Making and Unmaking of an American Ruling Class." In Young, *Beyond the American Revolution*, 27–79.

Koschnik, Albrecht. "The Democratic Societies of Philadelphia and the Limits of the American Public Sphere, circa 1793–1795." *WMQ*, 3rd. ser., 58, no. 3 (July 2001): 615–36.

——. "Political Conflict and Public Contest: Rituals of National Celebration in Philadelphia, 1788–1815." *PMHB* 118, no. 3 (July 1994): 209–48.

Kross, Jessica. "Mansions, Men, Women, and the Creation of Multiple Publics in Eighteenth-Century British North America." *Journal of Social History* 33, no. 2 (winter 1999): 385–408.

Kujawa, Sheryl Anne. "The Great Awakening of Sarah Osborn and the Female Society of the First Congregational Church in Newport." *Newport History* 65, no. 4 (fall 1994): 133–53.

——. "'The Path of Duty Plain': Samuel Hopkins, Sarah Osborn, and Revolutionary Newport." *Rhode Island History* 58, no. 3 (August 2000): 74–89.

——. "'A Precarious Season at the Throne of Grace': Sarah Haggar Wheaten Osborn, 1714–1796." Ph.D. diss., Boston College, 1993.

Kulikoff, Allan. "The Progress of Inequality in Revolutionary Boston." *WMQ*, 3rd ser., 28, no. 3 (July 1971): 375–412.

Kwasny, Mark V. *Washington's Partisan War, 1775–1783*. Kent, OH: Kent State University Press, 1996.

Labaree, Benjamin Woods. *The Boston Tea Party*. New York: Oxford University Press, 1964.

Labaree, Benjamin Woods, et al., eds. *America and the Sea: A Maritime History*. Mystic, CT: Mystic Seaport Museum, 1998.

Lambert, Frank. *Inventing the "Great Awakening."* Princeton, NJ: Princeton University Press, 1999.

Lambert, Robert Stansbury. *South Carolina Loyalists in the American Revolution.* Columbia: University of South Carolina Press, 1987.

Lang, Ossian. *History of Freemasonry in the State of New York.* Albany, NY, and New York: Hamilton Printing Co., 1922.

Laurens, Henry. *The Papers of Henry Laurens.* Edited by David R. Chesnutt. 16 vols. Columbia: University of South Carolina Press, 1968–2002.

Laurie, Bruce. *Working People of Philadelphia, 1800–1850.* Philadelphia: Temple University Press, 1980.

Lawrence, Alexander A. *Storm over Savannah: The Story of Count d'Estaing and the Siege of the Town in 1779.* Athens: University of Georgia Press, 1951.

Lax, John, and William Pencak. "The Knowles Riot and the Crisis of the 1740's in Massachusetts." *Perspectives in American History* 10 (1976): 162–214.

Leake, Isaac Q. *Memoir of the Life and Times of General John Lamb.* Albany, NY: Joel Munsell, 1850. Reprint, New York: Da Capo Press, 1971.

Lebsock, Suzanne. *The Free Women of Petersburg: Status and Culture in a Southern Town, 1784–1860.* New York: W. W. Norton and Co., 1984.

Lee, Charles. "The Lee Papers." Vol. 1. *Collections of the New-York Historical Society.* Vol. 4 (1871).

Lefebvre, Henri. *The Production of Space.* Translated by Donald Nicholson-Smith. Oxford and Cambridge: Blackwell, 1991.

Leith, Robert A. "'After the Chinese Taste': Chinese Export Porcelain and Chinoiserie Decoration in Eighteenth-Century Charleston." *Historical Archaeology* 33, no. 3 (1999): 48–61.

Lemisch, Jesse. "Jack Tar in the Streets: Merchant Seamen in the Politics of Revolutionary America." *WMQ*, 3rd ser., 25, no. 3 (July 1968): 371–407.

———. *Jack Tar vs. John Bull: The Role of New York's Seamen in Precipitating the Revolution.* New York and London: Garland Publishing, 1997.

Lemisch, Jesse, and John K. Alexander. "The White Oaks, Jack Tar, and the Concept of the 'Inarticulate.'" *WMQ*, 3rd ser., 29, no. 1 (January 1972): 109–42.

Lender, Mark Edward, and James Kirby Martin. *Drinking in America: A History.* New York: Free Press, 1982.

Lepore, Jill. *New York Burning: Liberty, Slavery, and Conspiracy in Eighteenth-Century Manhattan.* New York: Alfred A. Knopf, 2005.

Letters of Delegates to Congress, 1774–1789. Edited by Paul H. Smith. 25 vols. Washington, DC: Government Printing Office, 1976–2000. CD-ROM, Summerfield, Florida: Historical Database, 1998. Online. Available: http://hdl.loc.gov/loc.law/amlaw.lwdg. November 6, 2006.

Levernier, James A. "Phillis Wheatley and the New England Clergy." *Early American Literature* 26, no. 1 (1991): 21–38.

Lewis, Kenneth E. "The Metropolis and the Backcountry: The Making of a Colonial Landscape on the South Carolina Frontier." *Historical Archaeology* 33, no. 3 (1999): 3–13.

Lewis, Theodore. "Touro Synagogue: National Historic Site." *Newport History* 48, no. 3 (summer 1975): 281–320.

Linebaugh, Peter, and Marcus Rediker. *The Many-Headed Hydra: Sailors, Slaves, Commoners, and the Hidden History of the Revolutionary Atlantic.* Boston: Beacon Press, 2000.

Link, Eugene Perry. *Democratic-Republican Societies, 1790–1800.* New York: Columbia University Press, 1942.

Lippy, Charles H. *Seasonable Revolutionary: The Mind of Charles Chauncy.* Chicago: Nelson-Hall, 1981.

Lovejoy, David S. "Henry Marchant and the Mistress of the World." *WMQ,* 3rd ser., 12, no. 3 (July 1955): 375–98.

Lovejoy, David S. *Religious Enthusiasm in the New World: Heresy to Revolution.* Cambridge, MA: Harvard University Press, 1985.

———. *Rhode Island Politics and the American Revolution, 1760–1776.* Providence, RI: Brown University Press, 1958.

"A Lover of Liberty and a Mechanic's Friend." *To the Free and Patriotic Inhabitants of the City of Philad. and Province of Pennsylvania.* Philadelphia, May 31, 1770. Evans #11882.

Lucas, Stephen E. *Portents of Rebellion: Rhetoric and Revolution in Philadelphia, 1765–1776.* Philadelphia: Temple University Press, 1976.

Lydon, James G. *Pirates, Privateers, and Profits.* Upper Saddle River, NJ: Gregg Press, 1970.

Lyons, Clare A. *Sex among the Rabble: An Intimate History of Gender and Power in the Age of Revolution, Philadelphia, 1730–1830.* Chapel Hill: University of North Carolina Press, 2006.

Mackenzie, Frederick. *Diary of Frederick Mackenzie: Giving a Daily Narrative of His Military Service as an Officer of the Regiment of Royal Welch Fusiliers during the Years 1775–1781 in Massachusetts Rhode Island and New York.* 2 vols. Cambridge, MA: Harvard University Press, 1930.

Mackesy, Piers. *The War for America, 1775–1783.* Cambridge, MA: Harvard University Press, 1964.

Mackiewicz, Susan. "Philadelphia Flourishing: The Material World of Philadelphia, 1682–1760." Ph.D. diss., University of Delaware, 1988.

MacKinney, Gertrude, ed. *Votes and Proceedings of the House of Representatives of the Province of Pennsylvania.* Vols. 3, 6–8 of *Pennsylvania Archives,* 2nd ser. Harrisburg, PA, 1931–35.

Maier, Pauline. "The Charleston Mob and the Evolution of Popular Politics in Revolutionary South Carolina." *Perspectives in American History* 4 (1970).

———. *From Resistance to Revolution: Colonial Radicals and the Development of American Opposition to Britain, 1765–1776.* New York: Alfred A. Knopf, 1972. Reprint, New York: Vintage Books, 1974.

———. *The Old Revolutionaries: Political Lives in the Age of Samuel Adams.* New York: Alfred A. Knopf, 1980.

Mancall, Peter C. *Deadly Medicine: Indians and Alcohol in Early America.* Ithaca, NY: Cornell University Press, 1995.

Manigault, Peter. "The Letterbook of Peter Manigault, 1763–1773." Edited by Maurice A. Crouse. *SCHM* 70, 2–3 (April and July 1969): 79–96, 177–95.

Many respectable Freeholders and Inhabitants. Philadelphia, September 27, 1770. Evans #11879.

Marietta, Jack D., and G. S. Rowe. *Troubled Experiment: Crime and Justice in Pennsylvania, 1682–1800.* Philadelphia: University of Pennsylvania Press, 2006.

Markus, Thomas A. *Buildings and Power: Freedom and Control in the Origin of Modern Building Types.* London: Routledge, 1993.

Marshall, Christopher. *Extracts from the Diary of Christopher Marshall kept in Philadelphia and Lancaster, during the American Revolution, 1774–1781.* Edited by William Duane. Albany, NY: Joel Munsell, 1877. Reprint, New York: New York Times and Arno Press, 1969.

Mason, George Champlin. *Annals of the Redwood Library and Athenæum.* Newport, RI: Redwood Library, 1891.

——. *Annals of Trinity Church, Newport, Rhode Island, 1698–1821.* Vol. 1. Philadelphia: Evans Printing House, 1890.

——. *Reminiscences of Newport.* Newport, RI: Charles E. Hammett Jr., 1884.

Matson, Cathy. *Merchants and Empire: Trading in Colonial New York.* Baltimore: Johns Hopkins University Press, 1998.

Mattern, David B. *Benjamin Lincoln and the American Revolution.* Columbia: University of South Carolina Press, 1995.

McCowen, George Smith, Jr. *The British Occupation of Charleston, 1780–82.* Columbia: University of South Carolina Press, 1972.

McCoy, Drew R. *The Elusive Republic: Political Economy in Jeffersonian America.* New York: W. W. Norton and Co., 1980.

McCrady, Edward. *The History of South Carolina under the Royal Government, 1719–1776.* Reprint, New York: Russell and Russell, 1969.

McCusker, John J. *Rum and the American Revolution: The Rum Trade and the Balance of Payments of the Thirteen Continental Colonies.* 2 vols. New York: Garland Publishing, 1989.

McCusker, John J., and Russell R. Menard. *The Economy of British America, 1607–1789.* Chapel Hill: University of North Carolina Press, 1985.

McCusker, John J., and Kenneth Morgan, eds. *The Early Modern Atlantic Economy.* Cambridge: Cambridge University Press, 2000.

McDonnell, Michael A. "Popular Mobilization and Political Culture in Revolutionary Virginia: The Failure of the Minutemen and the Revolution from Below." *JAH* 85, no. 3 (December 1998): 946–81.

McDonough, Daniel J. *Christopher Gadsden and Henry Laurens: The Parallel Lives of Two American Patriots.* Sellinsgrove, PA: Susquehanna University Press, 2000.

McInnis, Maurie D. "'An Idea of Grandeur': Furnishing the Classical Interior in Charleston, 1815–1840." *Historical Archaeology* 33, no. 3 (1999): 32–47.

——. *In Pursuit of Refinement: Charlestonians Abroad, 1740–1860.* In collaboration with Angela D. Mack. Columbia: University of South Carolina Press, 1999.

——. *The Politics of Taste in Antebellum Charleston.* Chapel Hill: University of North Carolina Press, 2005.

McLoughlin, William G. "'Enthusiasm for Liberty': The Great Awakening as the Key to the Revolution." In *Preachers and Politicians: Two Essays on the Origins of the American Revolution,* edited by Jack P. Greene and William G. McLoughlin, 47–73. Worcester, MA: American Antiquarian Society, 1977.

——. *New England Dissent, 1630–1833: The Baptists and the Separation of Church and State.* 2 vols. Cambridge, MA: Harvard University Press, 1971.

McNamara, Martha J. *From Tavern to Courthouse: Architecture and Ritual in American Law, 1658–1860.* Baltimore: Johns Hopkins University Press, 2004.

Meinig, D. W. *The Shaping of America: A Geographical Perspective on 500 Years of History.* Vol. 1, *Atlantic America, 1492–1800.* New Haven, CT: Yale University Press, 1986.

Merrens, H. Roy, ed. *The Colonial South Carolina Scene: Contemporary Views, 1697–1774.* Columbia: University of South Carolina Press, 1977.

Miller, Richard G. *Philadelphia—The Federalist City: A Study of Urban Politics, 1789–1801*. Port Washington, NY: Kennikat Press, 1976.

Minutes of the Common Council of the City of New York, 1675–1776. 8 vols. New York: Dodd, Mead and Company, 1905.

Minutes of the Provincial Council of Pennsylvania. Vols. 2, 3. Harrisburg, PA: Theophilus Penn, 1840.

Mires, Charlene. *Independence Hall in American Memory*. Philadelphia: University of Pennsylvania Press, 2002.

Monday Morning, December 27, 1773. The Tea-Ship Being Arrived . . . . Philadelphia, December 27, 1773. Evans #12944.

"Montresor Journals." Edited by G. D. Scull. *Collections of the New-York Historical Society*. Vol. 14 (1881).

Morgan, Edmund S. *The Gentle Puritan: A Life of Ezra Stiles, 1727–1795*. New York: W. W. Norton and Co., 1962.

———. *Inventing the People: The Rise of Popular Sovereignty in England and America*. New York: W. W. Norton and Co., 1988.

———. Review of *Religion and the American Mind from the Great Awakening to the Revolution*, by Alan Heimert. *WMQ*, 3rd ser., 24, no. 3 (July 1967): 454–59.

Morgan, Edmund S., and Helen M. Morgan. *The Stamp Act Crisis: Prologue to Revolution*. Rev. ed. New York: Collier Books, 1962.

Morgan, Kenneth. "Business Networks in the British Export Trade to North America, 1750–1800." In McCusker and Morgan, *Early Modern Atlantic Economy*, 36–62.

Morgan, Philip D. "Black Life in Eighteenth-Century Charleston." *Perspectives in American History* 1 (1984): 187–232.

———. *Slave Counterpoint: Black Culture in the Eighteenth-Century Chesapeake and Lowcountry*. Chapel Hill: University of North Carolina Press, 1998.

Moultrie, William. *Memoirs of the American Revolution . . . .* 2 vols. New York: David Longworth, 1802.

M'Robert, Patrick. *A Tour Through Part of the North Provinces of America: Being, A Series of Letters wrote on the Spot, in the Years 1774 and 1775 . . . .* Edited by Carl Bridenbaugh. *PMHB* 59, no. 2 (April 1935): 134–80. Reprint. N.p., n.d.

Muhlenberg, Henry Melchior. *The Journals of Henry Melchior Muhlenberg*. Translated by Theodore G. Tappert and John W. Doberstein. Vol. 2. Philadelphia: Muhlenberg Press, 1945.

Murrin, John M. "The Great Inversion, or Court versus Country: A Comparison of the Revolution Settlements in England (1688–1721) and America (1776–1816)." In *Three British Revolutions: 1641, 1688, 1776*, edited by J. G. A. Pocock, 368–453. Princeton, NJ: Princeton University Press, 1980.

Nadelhaft, Jerome J. *The Disorders of War: The Revolution in South Carolina*. Orono: University of Maine at Orono Press, 1981.

Nash, Gary B. *Forging Freedom: The Formation of Philadelphia's Black Community, 1720–1840*. Cambridge, MA: Harvard University Press, 1988.

———. "The Social Evolution of Preindustrial American Cities, 1700–1820: Reflections and New Directions." *Journal of Urban History* 13, no. 2 (February 1987): 115–45.

———. *The Unknown American Revolution: The Unruly Birth of Democracy and the Struggle to Create America*. New York: Viking, 2005.

———. "Up from the Bottom in Franklin's Philadelphia." *Past and Present* 77, no. 1 (November 1977): 57–83.

———. *The Urban Crucible: Social Change, Political Consciousness, and the Origins of the American Revolution*. Cambridge, MA: Harvard University Press, 1979.

Nash, Gary B., and Jean R. Soderlund. *Freedom by Degrees: Emancipation in Pennsylvania and Its Aftermath*. New York: Oxford University Press, 1991.

Nash, R. C. "The Organization of Trade and Finance in the Atlantic Economy: Britain and South Carolina, 1670–1775." In Greene, Brana-Shute, and Sparks, *Money, Trade, and Power*, 74–107.

Neatby, Hilda. *Quebec: The Revolutionary Age, 1760–1791*. Toronto: McClelland and Stewart, 1966.

Neem, Johann N. "Freedom of Association in the Early Republic: The Republican Party, the Whiskey Rebellion, and the Philadelphia and New York Cordwainers' Cases," *PMHB* 127, no. 3 (July 2003), 259–90.

New York City during the American Revolution . . . from the Manuscripts in the Possession of the Mercantile Library Association of New York City. New York: Charles F. Allen, 1861.

Newcomb, Benjamin H. *Political Partisanship in the American Middle Colonies, 1700–1776*. Baton Rouge: Louisiana State University Press, 1995.

Newman, Richard. "Protest in Black and White: The Formation of an African American Political Community during the Early Republic." In Pasley, Robertson, and Waldstreicher, *Beyond the Founders*, 180–204.

Newman, Simon P. *Parades and Politics of the Street: Festive Culture in the Early Republic*. Philadelphia: University of Pennsylvania Press, 1997.

Nicolson, Colin. "Governor Francis Bernard, the Massachusetts Friends of Government, and the Advent of the Revolution." *Proceedings of the Massachusetts Historical Society* 103 (1991): 24–113.

———. *The "Infamas Govener": Francis Bernard and the Origins of the American Revolution*. Boston: Northeastern University Press, 2000.

———. "'McIntosh, Otis & Adams are our demagogues': Nathaniel Coffin and the Loyalist Interpretation of the Origins of the American Revolution." *Proceedings of the Massachusetts Historical Society* 108 (1996): 73–114.

Nobles, Gregory. "A Class Act: Redefining Deference in Early American History." *Early American Studies* 3, no. 2 (fall 2005): 286–302.

Noll, Mark A. "The American Revolution and Protestant Evangelicalism." *Journal of Interdisciplinary History* 23, no. 3 (1993): 615–38.

Norton, Mary Beth. *Liberty's Daughters: The Revolutionary Experience of American Women, 1750–1800*. Boston: Little, Brown, and Co., 1980. Reprint, Ithaca, NY: Cornell University Press, 1996.

———. "'My Resting Reaping Times': Sarah Osborn's Defense of Her 'Unfeminine' Activities, 1767." *Signs: Journal of Women in Culture and Society* 2, no. 2 (winter 1976): 515–29.

O'Callaghan, E. B., ed. *Documents Relative to the Colonial History of the State of New-York . . . .* Vols. 3, 6. Albany, NY: Weed, Parsons and Co., 1850, 1855.

"The Occasionalist." *To the Freeholders, and Freemen, of the City of New-York . . . .* New York, 1768. Evans #11017.

Ogborn, Miles. *Spaces of Modernity: London's Geographies, 1680–1780*. New York: Guilford Press, 1998.

Olivas, J. Richard. "Partial Revival: The Limits of the Great Awakening in Boston, Massachusetts, 1740–1742." In *Inequality in Early America*, edited by Carla Gardina Pestana and Sharon V. Salinger, 67–86. Hanover, NH: University Press of New England, 1999.

Oliver, Peter. *Peter Oliver's Origin and Progress of the American Rebellion: A Tory View*. Edited by Douglass Adair and John A. Schutz. San Marino, CA: Huntington Library, 1961. Reprint, Stanford, CA: Stanford University Press, 1967.

Olson, Alison G. "Eighteenth-Century Colonial Legislatures and Their Constituents." *JAH* 79, no. 2 (September 1992): 543–67.

———. *Making the Empire Work: London and American Interest Groups, 1690–1790*. Cambridge, MA: Harvard University Press, 1992.

Olson, Alison G. "The Pamphlet War over the Paxton Boys." *PMHB* 123, no. 1/2 (January/April 1999): 31–55.

———. "Rhode Island, Massachusetts, and the Question of Religious Diversity in Colonial New England." *NEQ* 65, no. 1 (March 1992): 93–116.

Olson, James S. "The New York Assembly, the Politics of Religion, and the Origins of the American Revolution, 1768–1771." *Historical Magazine of the Protestant Episcopal Church* 43, no. 1 (1974): 21–28.

Olson, Lester C. *Emblems of American Community in the Revolutionary Era: A Study in Rhetorical Iconology*. Washington, DC: Smithsonian Institution Press, 1991.

Olton, Charles S. *Artisans for Independence: Philadelphia Mechanics and the American Revolution*. Syracuse, NY: Syracuse University Press, 1975.

Olwell, Robert A. "'Domestick Enemies': Slavery and Political Independence in South Carolina, May 1775–March 1776." *Journal of Southern History* 55, no. 1 (February 1989): 21–48.

———. *Masters, Slaves, and Subjects: The Culture of Power in the South Carolina Low Country, 1740–1790*. Ithaca, NY: Cornell University Press, 1998.

Onuf, Peter S. *Jefferson's Empire: The Language of American Nationhood*. Charlottesville: University Press of Virginia, 2000.

Orsi, Robert A. "Introduction: Crossing the City Line." In *Gods of the City: Religion and the American Urban Landscape*, edited by Robert A. Orsi, 1–78. Bloomington and Indianapolis: Indiana University Press, 1999.

Osborn, Sarah. *The Nature, Certainty and Evidence of True Christianity*. Boston, 1755. Evans #7523.

O'Shaughnessy, Andrew Jackson. *An Empire Divided: The American Revolution and the British Caribbean*. Philadelphia: University of Pennsylvania Press, 2000.

Owen, William. *Narrative of American Voyages and Travels of Captain William Owen . . . , 1766–1771*. Edited by Victor Hugo Paltsits. New York: New York Public Library, 1942.

Ozouf, Mona. *Festivals and the French Revolution*. Translated by Alan Sheridan. Cambridge, MA: Harvard University Press, 1988.

———. "Space and Time in the Festivals of the French Revolution." *Comparative Studies in Society and History* 17, no. 3 (July 1975): 372–84.

Paine, Thomas. *The Complete Writings of Thomas Paine*. Edited by Philip S. Foner. Vol. 1. New York: Citadel Press, 1945.

Parramore, Thomas C. *Norfolk: The First Four Centuries*. With Peter C. Stewart and Tommy L. Bogger. Charlottesville: University Press of Virginia, 1994.

Parsons, William T. "The Bloody Election of 1742." *Pennsylvania History* 36, no. 3 (July 1969): 290–306.

Pasley, Jeffrey L. *The Tyranny of Printers: Newspaper Politics in the Early American Republic*. Charlottesville: University of Virginia Press, 2001.

Pasley, Jeffrey L., Andrew W. Robertson, and David Waldstreicher. *Beyond the Founders: New Approaches to the Political History of the Early American Republic*. Chapel Hill: University of North Carolina Press, 2004.

Patterson, Stephen E. *Political Parties in Revolutionary Massachusetts.* Madison: University of Wisconsin Press, 1973.

Paxton, Charles. "Letters of Charles Paxton." Edited by George Gregerson Wolkins. *Proceedings of the Massachusetts Historical Society* 56 (1922–23): 343–52.

Peale, Charles Willson. *The Selected Papers of Charles Willson Peale and His Family.* Edited by Lillian B. Miller. Vol. 1, *Charles Willson Peale: Artist in Revolutionary America, 1735–1791.* New Haven, CT: Yale University Press, 1983.

Pearson, Edward. "'Planters Full of Money': The Self-Fashioning of the Eighteenth-Century South Carolina Elite." In Greene, Brana-Shute, and Sparks, *Money, Trade, and Power,* 299–321.

Peckham, Howard H., ed. *The Toll of Independence: Engagements and Battle Casualties of the American Revolution.* Chicago: University of Chicago Press, 1974.

Pencak, William. *Jews and Gentiles in Early America, 1654–1800.* Ann Arbor: University of Michigan Press, 2005.

———. "Play as Prelude to Revolution: Boston, 1765–1776." In Pencak, Dennis, and Newman, *Riot and Revelry in Early America,* 125–55.

———. *War, Politics, and Revolution in Provincial Massachusetts.* Boston: Northeastern University Press, 1981.

Pencak, William, and Ralph J. Crandall. "Metropolitan Boston before the American Revolution: An Urban Interpretation of the Imperial Crisis." *Proceedings of the Bostonian Society, 1977–1983* (1985): 57–79.

Pencak, William, Matthew Dennis, and Simon P. Newman, eds. *Riot and Revelry in Early America.* University Park: Pennsylvania State University Press, 2002.

Perlman, Daniel. "Organizations of the Free Negro in New York City, 1800–1860." *Journal of Negro History* 56, no. 3 (July 1971): 181–97.

Pessen, Edward. *Riches, Class, and Power before the Civil War.* Lexington, MA: D. C. Heath and Co., 1973.

"Philadelphia Society before the Revolution." *PMHB* 11, nos. 3–4 (1887): 276–87, 491–94.

Phillips, Kevin. *The Cousins' Wars: Religion, Politics, and the Triumph of Anglo-America.* New York: Basic Books, 1999.

Pierce, Edward Lillie. Introduction to *Letters and Diary of John Rowe, Boston Merchant, 1759–1762, 1764–1779,* by John Rowe. Edited by Anne Rowe Cunningham. Boston: W. B. Clarke Co., 1903.

Piersen, William D. *Black Yankees: The Development of an Afro-American Subculture in Eighteenth-Century New England.* Amherst: University of Massachusetts Press, 1988.

Platt, John D. R., et al. "Historic Structures Report, Part II on Independence Hall." Philadelphia, 1962. Independence National Historical Park.

Pointer, Richard W. *Protestant Pluralism and the New York Experience: A Study of Eighteenth-Century Religious Diversity.* Bloomington and Indianapolis: Indiana University Press, 1988.

Pole, J. R. *Political Representation in England and the Origins of the American Republic.* New York: St. Martin's Press, 1966.

Potter, Janice. *The Liberty We Seek: Loyalist Ideology in Colonial New York and Massachusetts.* Cambridge, MA: Harvard University Press, 1983.

Powers, Bernard E., Jr. *Black Charlestonians: A Social History, 1822–1885.* Fayetteville: University of Arkansas Press, 1994.

Pred, Allan R. "Urban Systems Development and the Long-Distance Flow of Information Through Preelectronic U.S. Newspapers." *Economic Geography* 47, no. 4 (October 1971): 498–524.

Price, Jacob M. "Economic Function and the Growth of American Port Towns in the Eighteenth Century." *Perspectives in American History* 8 (1974): 121–86.

Proceedings of the Provincial Conference of Committees, of the Province of Pennsylvania, Held at the Carpenter's Hall. Philadelphia, 1776. Evans #14974.

The Protest of divers of the Inhabitants of this Province, in behalf of themselves and others to the Honorable the Representatives of the Province of Pennsylvania. Philadelphia, May 20, 1776. Evans #15016.

Pruitt, Bettye Hobbs, ed. *Massachusetts Tax Valuation List of 1771.* Boston: G. K. Hall and Co., 1978.

"Publicola." *To the Public.* New York, January 9, 1770. Evans #11829.

Quimby, Ian M. G. *Apprenticeship in Colonial Philadelphia.* New York: Garland Publishing, 1985.

Quincy, Josiah, Jr. "Journal of Josiah Quincy, Junior, 1773." Edited by Mark Antony De Wolfe Howe. *Proceedings of the Massachusetts Historical Society* 49 (June 1916): 424–81.

Radford, John P. "Testing the Model of the Pre-Industrial City: The Case of Ante-Bellum Charleston, South Carolina." *Transactions of the Institute of British Geographers,* new ser., 4, no. 3 (1979): 392–410.

Ramsay, David. "David Ramsay, 1749–1815: Selections from His Writings." Edited by Robert L. Brunhouse. American Philosophical Society *Transactions* 55 (1965): part 4.

Ranlet, Philip. *The New York Loyalists.* Knoxville: University of Tennessee Press, 1986.

Rediker, Marcus. "The Anglo-American Seaman as Collective Worker, 1700–1750." In *Work and Labor in Early America,* edited by Stephen Innes, 252–86. Chapel Hill: University of North Carolina Press, 1988.

——. *Between the Devil and the Deep Blue Sea: Merchant Seamen, Pirates, and the Anglo-American Maritime World, 1700–1750.* Cambridge: Cambridge University Press, 1987.

——. "A Motley Crew of Rebels: Sailors, Slaves, and the Coming of the American Revolution." In Hoffman and Albert, *Transforming Hand of Revolution,* 155–98.

Reed, Joseph. *Life and Correspondence of Joseph Reed.* Edited by William B. Reed. Vol. 1. Philadelphia: Lindsay and Blakiston, 1847.

Reid, John Phillip. *Constitutional History of the American Revolution: The Authority of Rights.* Madison, WI: University of Wisconsin Press, 1986.

Reid-Maroney, Nina. *Philadelphia's Enlightenment, 1740–1800: Kingdom of Christ, Empire of Reason.* Westport, CT: Greenwood Press, 2001.

Reports of the Record Commissioners of the City of Boston. Vols. 14, 16, 18, 19, 20, 23, 25. Boston: Rockwell and Churchill, 1886–94.

Revere, Paul. *A View of Part of the Town of Boston in New-England and British Ships of War Landing Their Troops, 1768.* Boston, 1770.

Rhoden, Nancy L. *Revolutionary Anglicanism: The Colonial Church of England Clergy during the American Revolution.* New York: New York University Press, 1999.

Rice, Kym S. *Early American Taverns: For the Entertainment of Friends and Strangers.* Chicago: Regenery Gateway, 1983.

Richardson, E. P. "The Birth of Political Caricature." In *Philadelphia Printmaking: American Prints before 1860,* edited by Robert F. Looney, 71–89. West Chester, PA: Tinicum Press, 1976.

Rock, Howard B. *Artisans of the New Republic: The Tradesmen of New York City in the Age of Jefferson.* New York: New York University Press, 1984.

Roelker, W. G., and Clarkson A. Collins III. "The Patrol of Narragansett Bay, 1774–1776, by H. M. S. *Rose,* Captain James Wallace." *Rhode Island History* 7, no. 1 (January 1948): 12–19; 7, no. 3 (July 1948): 90–95; 8, nos. 2–3 (April and July 1949): 45–63, 77–83; 9, nos. 1–2 (January and April 1950): 11–23, 52–58.

Rogers, George C., Jr. *Charleston in the Age of the Pinckneys.* Norman: University of Oklahoma Press, 1969.

——. "The Charleston Tea Party: The Significance of December 3, 1773." *SCHM* 75, no. 3 (July 1974): 153–68.

Rogers, Nicholas. *Crowds, Culture, and Politics in Georgian Britain.* Oxford: Oxford University Press, Clarendon Press, 1998.

——. *Whigs and Cities: Popular Politics in the Age of Walpole and Pitt.* Oxford: Oxford University Press, Clarendon Press, 1989.

Rorabaugh, W. J. *The Alcoholic Republic: An American Tradition.* New York: Oxford University Press, 1979.

Rosenberg, Carroll Smith. *Religion and the Rise of the American City: The New York City Mission Movement, 1812–1870.* Ithaca, NY: Cornell University Press, 1971.

Rosswurm, Steven. *Arms, Country, and Class: The Philadelphia Militia and "Lower Sort" during the American Revolution, 1775–1783.* New Brunswick, NJ: Rutgers University Press, 1987.

Roth, Rodris. "Tea-Drinking in Eighteenth-Century America: Its Etiquette and Equipage." In St. George, *Material Life in America,* 439–62.

Rothschild, Nan A. *New York City Neighborhoods: The Eighteenth Century.* San Diego, CA: Academic Press, 1990.

Rowe, G. S. *Thomas McKean: The Shaping of American Republicanism.* Boulder: Colorado Associated University Press, 1978.

Rowe, John. *Letters and Diary of John Rowe, Boston Merchant, 1759–1762, 1764–1779.* Edited by Anne Rowe Cunningham. Boston: W. B. Clarke Co., 1903.

Royster, Charles. *A Revolutionary People at War: The Continental Army and American Character, 1775–1783.* Chapel Hill: University of North Carolina Press, 1979.

Rudé, George. *The Crowd in History: A Study of Popular Disturbances in France and England, 1730–1848.* Rev. ed. London: John Wiley and Sons, 1964. Reprint, London: Lawrence and Wishart, 1981.

——. *Ideology and Popular Protest.* New York: Pantheon Books, 1980.

Rush, Benjamin. *Letters of Benjamin Rush.* Edited by L. H. Butterfield. Vol. 1. Princeton, NJ: Princeton University Press, 1951.

Ryan, Mary P. *Civic Wars: Democracy and Public Life in the American City during the Nineteenth Century.* Berkeley and Los Angeles: University of California Press, 1997.

——. *Women in Public: Between Banners and Ballots, 1825–1880.* Baltimore: Johns Hopkins University Press, 1990.

Ryerson, Richard Alan. "Political Mobilization and the American Revolution: The Resistance Movement in Philadelphia, 1765–1775." *WMQ,* 3rd ser., 31, no. 4 (October 1974): 565–88.

——. "Portrait of a Colonial Oligarchy: The Quaker Elite in the Pennsylvania Assembly, 1729–1776." In *Power and Status: Officeholding in Colonial*

America, edited by Bruce C. Daniels, 106–35. Middletown, CT: Wesleyan University Press, 1986.

——. *The Revolution Is Now Begun: The Radical Committees of Philadelphia, 1765–1776*. Philadelphia: University of Pennsylvania Press, 1978.

Saillant, John. *Black Puritan, Black Republican: The Life and Thought of Lemuel Haynes, 1753–1833*. Oxford: Oxford University Press, 2003.

St. George, Robert Blair. *Conversing by Signs: Poetics of Implication in Colonial New England Culture*. Chapel Hill: University of North Carolina Press, 1998.

——, ed. *Material Life in America, 1600–1860*. Boston: Northeastern University Press, 1988.

Salinger, Sharon V. *Taverns and Drinking in Early America*. Baltimore: Johns Hopkins University Press, 2002.

——. *"To Serve Well and Faithfully": Labor and Indentured Servants in Pennsylvania, 1682–1800*. Cambridge: Cambridge University Press, 1987.

Sanford, Don A. "Entering Into Covenant: The History of Seventh Day Baptists in Newport." *Newport History* 66, no. 1 (winter 1994): 1–48.

Schecter, Barnet. *The Battle for New York: The City at the Heart of the American Revolution*. New York: Penguin, 2002.

Schlesinger, Arthur Meier. "Biography of a Nation of Joiners." *AHR* 50, no. 1 (October 1944): 1–25.

——. *The Colonial Merchants and the American Revolution, 1763–1776*. New York: Columbia University Press, 1918.

——. "Liberty Tree: A Genealogy." *NEQ* 25, no. 4 (December 1952): 435–58.

——. *Prelude to Independence: The Newspaper War on Britain, 1764–1776*. New York: Alfred A. Knopf, 1957. Reprint, Westport, CT: Greenwood Press, 1979.

Schless, Nancy Halverson. "Peter Harrison, the Touro Synagogue, and the Wren City Church." *Winterthur Portfolio* 8 (1973): 187–200.

Schoenbachler, Matthew. "Republicanism in the Age of Democratic Revolution: The Democratic-Republican Societies of the 1790s." *Journal of the Early Republic* 18, no. 2 (summer 1998): 237–61.

Schultz, Ronald. *The Republic of Labor: Philadelphia Artisans and the Politics of Class, 1720–1830*. New York: Oxford University Press, 1993.

Schultz, Stanley K. "The Growth of Urban America in War and Peace, 1740–1810." In *The American Revolution: Changing Perspectives*, edited by William M. Fowler Jr. and Wallace Coyle, 123–48. Boston: Northeastern University Press, 1979.

Seeman, Erik R. *Pious Persuasions: Laity and Clergy in Eighteenth-Century New England*. Baltimore: Johns Hopkins University Press, 1999.

Sellers, Leila. *Charleston Business on the Eve of the American Revolution*. Chapel Hill: University of North Carolina Press, 1934. Reprint, New York: Arno Press, 1970.

Selsam, J. Paul. *The Pennsylvania Constitution of 1776: A Study in Revolutionary Democracy*. New York: Da Capo Press, 1971.

Sennett, Richard. *The Fall of Public Man*. New York: W. W. Norton and Co., 1974.

Serle, Ambrose. *The American Journal of Ambrose Serle, Secretary to Lord Howe, 1776–1778*. Edited by Edward H. Tatum, Jr. San Marino, CA: Huntington Library, 1940.

"The Seventh-Day Baptist Church at Newport, R.I." *The Seventh Day Baptist Memorial* 2 (January and April 1853): 25–38, 71–95.

Shammas, Carole. *A History of Household Government in America*. Charlottesville: University of Virginia Press, 2002.

Shankman, Andrew. *Crucible of American Democracy: The Struggle to Fuse Egalitarianism and Capitalism in Jeffersonian Pennsylvania*. Lawrence: University Press of Kansas, 2004.

——. "Malcontents and Tertium Quids: The Battle to Define Democracy in Jeffersonian Philadelphia." *Journal of the Early Republic* 19, no. 1 (spring 1999): 43–72.

Sharp, Buchanan. "Popular Political Opinion in England, 1660–1685." *History of European Ideas* 10, no. 1 (1989): 13–29.

Shaw, Peter. *American Patriots and the Rituals of Revolution*. Cambridge, MA: Harvard University Press, 1981.

Shields, David S. "Anglo-American Clubs: Their Wit, Their Heterodoxy, Their Sedition." *WMQ* 3rd ser., 51, no. 2 (April 1994): 293–304.

——. *Civil Tongues and Polite Letters in British America*. Chapel Hill: University of North Carolina Press, 1997.

Shipton, Clifford K., ed. *Sibley's Harvard Graduates*. Vols. 4, 9, 10. Cambridge, MA: Harvard University Press, 1933, 1956. Boston: Massachusetts Historical Society, 1958.

Shirley, William. *Correspondence of William Shirley, Governor of Massachusetts and Military Commander in America, 1731–1760*. Edited by Charles H. Lincoln. 2 vols. New York: Macmillan, 1912.

Shy, John. *A People Numerous and Armed: Reflections on the Military Struggle for American Independence*. Rev. ed. Ann Arbor: University of Michigan Press, 1990.

——. *Toward Lexington: The Role of the British Army in the Coming of the Revolution*. Princeton, NJ: Princeton University Press, 1965.

Singleton, Esther. *Social New York under the Georges, 1714–1776: Houses, Streets and Country Homes, with Chapters on Fashions, Furniture, China, Plate and Manners*. 1902. Reprint, New York: Benjamin Blom, 1968.

Six Arguments Against Chusing Joseph Galloway an Assemblyman at the Ensuing Election. Philadelphia, 1766. Evans #10494.

Sjoberg, Gideon. *The Preindustrial City: Past and Present*. New York: Free Press, 1960.

Skemp, Sheila. "Newport's Stamp Act Rioters: Another Look." *Rhode Island History* 47, no. 2 (May 1989): 41–59.

Smith, Alice R. Huger, and D. E. Huger Smith, *The Dwelling Houses of Charleston, South Carolina*. Philadelphia: J. B. Lippincott Co., 1917.

Smith, Barbara Clark. "Food Rioters and the American Revolution." *WMQ*, 3rd ser., 51, no. 1 (January 1994): 3–38.

Smith, Billy G. *The "Lower Sort": Philadelphia's Laboring People, 1750–1800*. Ithaca, NY: Cornell University Press, 1990.

——. "Runaway Slaves in the Mid-Atlantic Region during the Revolutionary Era." In Hoffman and Albert, *Transforming Hand of Revolution*, 199–230.

Smith, Charles Page. *James Wilson: Founding Father, 1742–1798*. Chapel Hill: University of North Carolina Press, 1956.

——. "The Attack on Fort Wilson." *PMHB* 78, no. 2 (April 1954): 177–88.

Smith, Joseph Jencks, comp. *Civil and Military List of Rhode Island, 1647–1800: A List of All Officers Elected by the General Assembly from the Organization of the Legislative Government of the Colony to 1800*. Providence, RI: Preston and Rounds Co., 1900.

Smith, Maurice H. "Charles Paxton, Founding Stepfather." *Proceedings of the Massachusetts Historical Society* 94 (1982): 15–36.

———. *The Writs of Assistance Case*. Berkeley and Los Angeles: University of California Press, 1978.

Smith, Robert. "A Declaration of Dependence: Robert Smith's 1775 Humiliation Sermon." Edited by C. P. Seabrook Wilkinson. *SCHM* 100, no. 3 (July 1999): 221–40.

[Smith, William.] *To the Freeholders and Electors of the Province of Pennsylvania*. Philadelphia, September 28, 1765. Evans #9915.

Smith, William, Jr. *Historical Memoirs . . . of William Smith: Historian of the Province of New York, Member of the Governor's Council and Last Chief Justice of that Province under the Crown Chief Justice of Quebec*. Edited by William H. W. Sabine. 2 vols. New York: Colburn and Tegg, 1956–58.

———. *The History of the Province of New-York*. Edited by Michael Kammen. 2 vols. Cambridge, MA: Harvard University Press, Belknap Press, 1972.

Snapp, J. Russell. "William Henry Drayton: The Making of a Conservative Revolutionary." *Journal of Southern History* 57, no. 4 (November 1991): 637–58.

Snyder, Martin P. *City of Independence: Views of Philadelphia before 1800*. New York: Praeger Publishers, 1975.

"A Sober Citizen." *To the Inhabitants of the City and County of New-York*. New York, April 16, 1776. Evans #15110.

"The Social Club of New York." *American Historical Record* 1, no. 10 (October 1872): 467.

Soderlund, Jean R. "Black Importation and Migration into Southeastern Pennsylvania, 1682–1810." *Proceedings of the American Philosophical Society* 133, no. 2 (June 1989): 144–53.

Spaulding, E. Wilder. *New York in the Critical Period, 1783–1789*. Port Washington, NY: Ira J. Friedman, 1963.

Stachiw, Myron O., ed. *The Early Architecture and Landscapes of the Narragansett Basin*. Vol. 1, *Newport*. N.p.: Vernacular Architecture Forum, 2001.

Stansell, Christine. *City of Women: Sex and Class in New York, 1789–1860*. New York: Alfred A. Knopf, 1986.

Statutes at Large of Pennsylvania from 1682–1801. Compiled by James T. Mitchell and Henry Flanders. Vols. 6, 7. Harrisburg, PA: Wm Stanley Ray, 1900.

Steffen, Charles G. *The Mechanics of Baltimore: Workers and Politics in the Age of Revolution, 1763–1812*. Urbana: University of Illinois Press, 1984.

Steiner, Bruce E. "New England Anglicanism: A Genteel Faith?" *WMQ*, 3rd ser., 27, no. 1 (January 1970): 122–35.

Stiles, Ezra. *A Discourse on the Christian Union*. Boston, 1761. Evans #9018.

———. *Extracts from the Itineraries and other Miscellanies of Ezra Stiles, D.D., LL.D., 1755–1794, with a Selection from His Correspondence*. Edited by Franklin Bowditch Dexter. New Haven, CT: Yale University Press, 1916.

———. *The Literary Diary of Ezra Stiles, D.D., LL.D., President of Yale College*. Edited by Franklin Bowditch Dexter. 3 vols. New York: Charles Scribner's Sons, 1901.

Stokes, I. N. Phelps. *The Iconography of Manhattan Island, 1408–1909*. 6 vols. New York: Robert H. Dodd, 1922.

Stoney, Samuel G. "The Great Fire of 1778 Seen through Contemporary Letters." *SCHM* 64, no. 1 (January 1963): 23–26.

Stott, Richard B. *Workers in the Metropolis: Class, Ethnicity, and Youth in Antebellum New York City*. Ithaca, NY: Cornell University Press, 1990.

Stout, Harry S. "Religion, Communications, and the Ideological Origins of the American Revolution." *WMQ*, 3rd ser., 34, no. 4 (October 1977): 519–41.

Stout, Neil R. "Manning the Royal Navy in North America, 1763–1775." *American Neptune* 23 (1963): 174–85.

Swift, Lindsay, ed. *Historical Manuscripts in the Public Library of the City of Boston*. Nos. 1–5. Boston: Boston Public Library, 1900–1904.

Tager, Jack. *Boston Riots: Three Centuries of Social Violence*. Boston: Northeastern University Press, 2001.

Teaford, Jon C. *The Municipal Revolution in America: Origins of Modern Urban Government, 1650–1825*. Chicago: University of Chicago Press, 1975.

Tennent, William. "Writings of the Reverend William Tennent, 1740–1777." Edited by Newton B. Jones. *SCHM* 61, nos. 3–4 (July and October 1960): 129–45, 189–209.

Thatcher, Benjamin Bussey. *Traits of the Tea Party: Being a Memoir of George R. T. Hewes . . . .* New York: Harper and Brothers, 1835.

Thayer, Theodore. *Pennsylvania Politics and the Growth of Democracy, 1740–1776*. Harrisburg, PA: Pennsylvania Historical and Museum Commission, 1953.

Thompson, E. P. "Patrician Society, Plebeian Culture." *Journal of Social History* 7, no. 4 (summer 1974): 382–405.

——. *Whigs and Hunters: The Origin of the Black Act*. New York: Pantheon Books, 1975.

Thompson, Peter. *Rum Punch and Revolution: Taverngoing and Public Life in Eighteenth-Century Philadelphia*. Philadelphia: University of Pennsylvania Press, 1999.

Thomson, Charles. "Early Days of the Revolution in Philadelphia: Charles Thomson's Account of the Opposition to the Boston Port Bill." *PMHB* 2, no. 4 (1878): 411–23.

Thorp, Daniel B. "Chattel with a Soul: The Autobiography of a Moravian Slave." *PMHB* 112, no. 3 (July 1988): 433–51.

Thwing, Annie Haven. *The Crooked and Narrow Streets of the Town of Boston, 1630–1822*. Boston: Marshall Jones Co., 1920.

Tiedemann, Joseph S. "Communities in the Midst of the American Revolution: Queens County, New York, 1774–1775." *Journal of Social History* 18, no. 1 (fall 1984): 57–78.

——. *Reluctant Revolutionaries: New York City and the Road to Independence, 1763–1776*. Ithaca, NY: Cornell University Press, 1997.

——. "A Revolution Foiled: Queens County, New York, 1775–1776." *JAH* 75, no. 2 (September 1988): 417–44.

Tilly, Charles. *Popular Contention in Great Britain, 1758–1834*. Cambridge, MA: Harvard University Press, 1995.

To the Inhabitants of the City and County of New-York. New York, April 13, 1775. Evans #14505.

To the Manufacturers and Mechanics of Philadelphia, the Northern Liberties, and District of Southwark. Philadelphia, June 8, 1774. Evans #13664.

To the Sons of Liberty in this City. New York, February 3, 1770. Evans #11891.

Tobias, Thomas J., ed. "Charles Town in 1764." *SCHM* 67, no. 2 (April 1966): 63–74.

Tobler, John. "John Tobler's Description of South Carolina, 1753." Translated by Walter L. Robbins. *SCHM* 71, no. 3 (July 1970): 141–61.

Toogood, Anna Coxe. "Cultural Landscape Report, Independence Square: Historical Narrative." Revised copy. Philadelphia, 1998. Independence National Historical Park.

Towner, Lawrence W. "The Indentures of Boston's Poor Apprentices, 1734–1865." *Publications of the Colonial Society of Massachusetts* 43 (1966): 417–68.

"A Tradesman." *A Tradesman's Address to His Countrymen*. Philadelphia, March 2, 1772. Evans #12583.

The Tradesmen, Artificers, and other Inhabitants. . . . Philadelphia, May 22, 1770. Evans #11897.

Travers, Len. *Celebrating the Fourth: Independence Day and the Rites of Nationalism in the Early Republic*. Amherst: University of Massachusetts Press, 1997.

———. "The Paradox of 'Nationalist' Festivals: The Case of Palmetto Day in Antebellum Charleston." In Pencak, Dennis, and Newman, *Riot and Revelry*, 273–95.

Triber, Jayne E. *A True Republican: The Life of Paul Revere*. Amherst: University of Massachusetts Press, 1998.

Tucker, Robert W., and David C. Hendrickson. *The Fall of the First British Empire: Origins of the War of American Independence*. Baltimore: Johns Hopkins University Press, 1982.

Tully, Alan. *Forming American Politics: Ideals, Interests, and Institutions in Colonial New York and Pennsylvania*. Baltimore: Johns Hopkins University Press, 1994.

Turner, Victor. *The Ritual Process: Structure and Anti-Structure*. Chicago: Aldine, 1969.

———. "Variations on a Theme of Liminality." In *Secular Ritual*, edited by Sally F. Moore and Barbara G. Myerhoff, 36–52. Amsterdam: Van Gorcum, Assen, 1977.

Tyler, John W. *Smugglers and Patriots: Boston Merchants and the Advent of the American Revolution*. Boston: Northeastern University Press, 1986.

Ubbelohde, Carl. *The Vice-Admiralty Courts and the American Revolution*. Chapel Hill: University of North Carolina Press, 1960.

Ulrich, Laurel Thatcher. *The Age of Homespun: Objects and Stories in the Creation of an American Myth*. New York: Alfred A. Knopf, 2001.

———. "'Daughters of Liberty': Religious Women in Revolutionary New England." In Hoffman and Albert, *Women in the Age of the American Revolution*, 211–43.

Underdown, David. *Revel, Riot, and Rebellion: Popular Politics and Culture in England, 1603–1660*. Oxford: Oxford University Press, 1985.

Upham, William P., ed. "Extracts from Letters Written at the Time of the Occupation of Boston by the British, 1775–1776." *Historical Collections of the Essex Institute* 13 (July 1876): 153–236.

Upton, Dell. "Another City: The Urban Cultural Landscape in the Early Republic." In *Everyday Life in the Early Republic*, edited by Catherine E. Hutchins, 61–117. Winterthur, DE: Henry Francis du Pont Winterthur Museum, 1994.

———. "Architecture in Everyday Life." *New Literary History* 33, no. 4 (autumn 2002): 707–23.

———. *Holy Things and Profane: Anglican Parish Churches in Colonial Virginia*. New York: Architectural History Foundation and Cambridge, MA: MIT Press, 1986. Paperback ed. New Haven, CT: Yale University Press, 1997.

———. "White and Black Landscapes in Eighteenth-Century Virginia." In St. George, *Material Life in America*, 357–69.

Upton, L. F. S. *The Loyal Whig: William Smith of New York and Quebec*. Toronto: University of Toronto Press, 1969.

Valentine, David T. *History of the City of New York*. New York: G. P. Putnam and Co., 1853.

Valeri, Mark. "The New Divinity and the American Revolution." *WMQ*, 3rd ser., 46, no. 4 (October 1989): 741–69.

Van Buskirk, Judith L. *Generous Enemies: Patriots and Loyalists in Revolutionary New York*. Philadelphia: University of Pennsylvania Press, 2002.

Van Zandt, Jacobus, et al. *To the Publick*. New York, March 24, 1775. Evans #14514.

Varga, Nicholas. "Election Procedures and Practices in Colonial New York." *New York History* 41, no. 3 (July 1960): 249–77.

Vickers, Daniel. "Beyond Jack Tar." *WMQ*, 3rd ser., 50, no. 2 (April 1993): 418–24.

———. *Farmers and Fishermen: Two Centuries of Work in Essex County, Massachusetts, 1630–1850*. Chapel Hill: University of North Carolina Press, 1994.

———. *Young Men and the Sea: Yankee Seafarers in the Age of Sail*. With Vince Walsh. New Haven, CT: Yale University Press, 2005.

Villaflor, Georgia C., and Kenneth L. Solokoff. "Migration in Colonial America: Evidence from the Militia Muster Rolls." *Social Science History* 6, no. 4 (autumn 1982): 539–70.

Villers, David H. "The Smythe Horses Affair and the Association." *SCHM* 70, no. 3 (July 1969): 137–58.

Wade, Richard C. *Slavery in the Cities: The South, 1820–1860*. New York: Oxford University Press, 1964.

Wager, Daniel E. *Col. Marinus Willett: The Hero of Mohawk Valley*. Utica, NY: Utica Herald Publishing Co., 1891.

Waldstreicher, David. *In the Midst of Perpetual Fetes: The Making of American Nationalism, 1776–1820*. Chapel Hill: University of North Carolina Press, 1997.

———. "Reading the Runaways: Self-Fashioning, Print Culture, and Confidence in Slavery in the Eighteenth-Century Mid-Atlantic." *WMQ*, 3rd. ser., 56, no. 2 (April 1999): 243–72.

———. *Runaway America: Benjamin Franklin, Slavery, and the American Revolution*. New York: Hill and Wang, 2004.

Wallace, David Duncan. *The Life of Henry Laurens*. New York and London: G. P. Putnam's Sons, Knickerbocker Press, 1915.

Walsh, Richard. *Charleston's Sons of Liberty: A Study of the Artisans, 1763–1789*. Columbia: University of South Carolina Press, 1959.

Ward, Samuel. *Correspondence of Governor Samuel Ward, May 1775–March 1776*. Edited by Bernhard Knollenberg. Providence, RI: Roger Williams Press, 1952.

Warden, G. B. *Boston, 1689–1776*. Boston: Little, Brown, and Co., 1970.

———. "The Caucus and Democracy in Colonial Boston." *NEQ* 43, no. 1 (March 1970): 19–45.

———. "Inequality and Instability in Eighteenth-Century Boston: A Reappraisal." *Journal of Interdisciplinary History* 6, no. 4 (spring 1976): 585–620.

Warner, Michael. *The Letters of the Republic: Publication and the Public Sphere in Eighteenth-Century America*. Cambridge, MA: Harvard University Press, 1990.

Warner, Sam Bass, Jr. *The Private City: Philadelphia in Three Periods of Its Growth*. Philadelphia: University of Pennsylvania Press, 1968.

Washington, George. *George Washington Papers at the Library of Congress*. Manuscript Division, Library of Congress. 1998–2000. Online. Available: http://memory.loc.gov/ammem/gwhtml/gwhome.html. November 5, 2006.

Washington, George. *The Papers of George Washington: Colonial Series*. Edited by W. W. Abbot and Dorothy Twohig. Vol. 10. Charlottesville: University Press of Virginia, 1995.

——. *The Papers of George Washington: Presidential Series*. Edited by Mark A. Mastromarino. Vol. 8. Charlottesville: University Press of Virginia, 1999.

——. *Papers of George Washington: Revolutionary War Series*. Edited by Philander D. Chase, et al. 15 vols. Charlottesville: University Press of Virginia, 1985–2006.

The Watchman, No. 2. New York, February 17, 1770. Evans #11916.

Waterhouse, Richard. *A New World Gentry: The Making of a Merchant and Planter Class in South Carolina, 1670–1770*. New York: Garland Publishing, 1989.

Watson, D. H., ed. "Joseph Harrison and the *Liberty* Incident." *WMQ*, 3rd ser., 20, no. 4 (October 1963): 585–95.

Watson, John F. *Annals of Philadelphia, Being a Collection of Memoirs, Anecdotes and Incidents of the City and Its Inhabitants . . . .* Philadelphia, Uriah Hunt, 1830.

Watts, John. "Letter Book of John Watts, Merchant and Councillor of New York, January 1, 1762–December 22, 1765." Edited by Dorothy C. Barck. *Collections of the New-York Historical Society*. Vol. 61 (1928).

Wax, Darold D. "The Demand for Slave Labor in Colonial Pennsylvania." *Pennsylvania History* 34, no. 4 (October 1967): 331–45.

Weir, Robert M. *Colonial South Carolina: A History*. Millwood, NY: KTO Press, 1983.

——. "'The Harmony We Were Famous For': An Interpretation of Pre-Revolutionary South Carolina Politics." *WMQ*, 3rd ser., 26, no. 4 (October 1969): 473–501.

——. "Who Shall Rule at Home: The American Revolution as a Crisis of Legitimacy for the Colonial Elite." *Journal of Interdisciplinary History* 6, no. 4 (spring 1976): 679–700.

Weis, Frederick Lewis. *The Colonial Clergy and the Colonial Churches of New England*. Lancaster, MA, 1936. Reprint, Baltimore: Genealogical Publishing Co., 1977.

Wells, Robert V. *The Population of the British Colonies in America before 1776: A Survey of Census Data*. Princeton, NJ: Princeton University Press, 1975.

Weslager, C. A. *The Stamp Act Congress: With an Exact Copy of the Complete Journal*. Newark: University of Delaware Press, 1976.

Westcott, Thompson. *A History of Philadelphia, from the Time of the First Settlements on the Delaware to the Consolidation of the City and Districts in 1854*. Excerpts from the *Philadelphia Sunday Dispatch*. 3 vols. Philadelphia: mounted and bound by Pawson and Nicholson for Brinton Coxe, 1886.

Wharton, Thomas. "Selections from the Letter-Books of Thomas Wharton of Philadelphia, 1773–1783." *PMHB* 33, nos. 3–4 (July and October 1909): 319–39, 432–53; 34, no. 1 (January 1910): 41–61.

White, Morton, and Lucia White. *The Intellectual Versus the City, from Thomas Jefferson to Frank Lloyd Wright*. Cambridge, MA: Harvard University Press and MIT Press, 1962.

White, Shane. *Somewhat More Independent: The End of Slavery in New York City, 1770–1810*. Athens: University of Georgia Press, 1991.

White, Shane, and Graham White. "Slave Clothing and African-American Culture in the Eighteenth and Nineteenth Centuries." *Past and Present* 148 (August 1995): 149–86.

Whitehill, Walter Muir. *Boston: A Topographical History*. Cambridge, MA: Harvard University Press, Belknap Press, 1959. Also 2nd ed. Cambridge, MA: Harvard University Press, Belknap Press, 1968.

Wilder, Craig Steven. *In the Company of Black Men: The African Influence on African American Culture in New York City*. New York: New York University Press, 2001.

Wilentz, Sean. *Chants Democratic: New York City and the Rise of the American Working Class, 1788–1850*. New York: Oxford University Press, 1984.

Wilkinson, Eliza. *Letters of Eliza Wilkinson*. Edited by Caroline Gilman. New York: Samuel Colman, 1839. Reprint, New York: Arno Press, 1969.

Willard, Carla. "Wheatley's Turns of Praise: Heroic Entrapment and the Paradox of Revolution." *American Literature* 67, no. 2 (June 1995): 233–56.

"Willem Johonas Von Dore Manadus." *To the Freeholders and Freemen of the City and County of New-York*. New York, February 19, 1768. Evans #11040.

Willett, Albert J., Jr., comp. *The Willett Families of North America*. Vol. 1. Easley, SC: Southern Historical Press, 1985.

Willett, William M. *A Narrative of the Military Actions of Colonel Marinus Willett, Taken Chiefly from His Own Manuscript*. New York: G. and C. and H. Carvill, 1831. Reprint, New York: New York Times and Arno Press, 1969.

Williams, George W. *St. Michael's, Charleston, 1751–1951*. Columbia: University of South Carolina Press, 1951.

Williams, Oscar R. "The Regimentation of Blacks on the Urban Frontier in Colonial Albany, New York City, and Philadelphia." *Journal of Negro History* 63, no. 4 (October 1978): 329–38.

Wilson, Kathleen. *The Sense of the People; Politics, Culture and Imperialism in England, 1715–1785*. Cambridge: Cambridge University Press, 1995.

Withey, Lynne. *Urban Growth in Colonial Rhode Island: Newport and Providence in the Eighteenth Century*. Albany: State University of New York Press, 1984.

Wokeck, Marianne S. *Trade in Strangers: The Beginnings of Mass Migration to North America*. University Park: Pennsylvania State University Press, 1999.

Wolkins, George Gregerson, ed. "The Boston Customs District in 1768." *Proceedings of the Massachusetts Historical Society* 58 (1924–25): 418–43.

——, ed. "Daniel Malcolm and Writs of Assistance." *Proceedings of the Massachusetts Historical Society* 58 (1924–25): 5–84.

——, ed. "The Seizure of John Hancock's Sloop *Liberty*." *Proceedings of the Massachusetts Historical Society* 55 (1921–22): 239–84.

Wood, Gordon S. *The Creation of the American Republic, 1776–1787*. Chapel Hill: University of North Carolina Press, 1969. Reprint, New York: W. W. Norton and Co., 1972.

——. *The Radicalism of the American Revolution*. New York: Alfred A. Knopf, 1992.

Wood, Peter H. *Black Majority: Negroes in Colonial South Carolina from 1670 through the Stono Rebellion*. New York: Alfred A. Knopf, 1974.

——. "'Liberty is Sweet': African-American Freedom Struggles in the Years before White Independence." In Young, *Beyond the American Revolution*, 149–84.

Woodmason, Charles. *The Carolina Backcountry on the Eve of the Revolution: The Journal and Other Writings of Charles Woodmason, Anglican Itinerant*. Edited by Richard J. Hooker. Chapel Hill: University of North Carolina Press, 1953.

Worrall, Arthur J. *Quakers in the Colonial Northeast*. Hanover, NH: University Press of New England, 1980.

Writers Program of the Works Progress Administration. *Boston Looks Seaward: The Story of the Port, 1630–1940*. Boston: Bruce Humphries, 1941.

Wroth, L. Kinvin. "The Massachusetts Vice-Admiralty Court." In *Law and Authority in Colonial America*, edited by George Athan Billias, 32–73. Barre, MA: Barre Publishers, 1965.

Wulf, Karin. *Not All Wives: Women of Colonial Philadelphia*. Philadelphia: University of Pennsylvania Press, 2000.

Young, Alfred F. *Beyond the American Revolution: Explorations in the History of American Radicalism*. DeKalb: Northern Illinois University Press, 1993.

———. *Democratic Republicans of New York: The Origins, 1763–1797*. Chapel Hill: University of North Carolina Press, 1967.

———. "English Plebeian Culture and Eighteenth-Century American Radicalism." In *The Origins of American Radicalism*, edited by Margaret Jacob and James Jacob, 185–212. London: George Allen and Unwin, 1984.

———. "George Robert Twelves Hewes (1742–1840): A Boston Shoemaker and the Memory of the American Revolution." *WMQ*, 3rd ser., 38, no. 4 (October 1981): 561–623.

———. "Liberty Tree: Made in America, Lost in America." In *Liberty Tree: Ordinary People and the American Revolution*, 325–94. New York: New York University Press, 2006.

———. "The Mechanics and the Jeffersonians: New York, 1789–1801." *Labor History* 5, no. 3 (fall 1964): 247–76.

———. *The Shoemaker and the Tea Party: Memory and the American Revolution*. Boston: Beacon Press, 1999.

———. "The Women of Boston: 'Persons of Consequence' in the Making of the American Revolution, 1765–76." In *Women and Politics in the Age of the Democratic Revolution*, edited by Harriet B. Applewhite and Darline G. Levy, 181–226. Ann Arbor: University of Michigan Press, 1990.

Zabin, Serena R. "Places of Exchange: New York City, 1700–1763." Ph.D. diss., Rutgers, 2000.

Zagarri, Rosemarie. *The Politics of Size: Representation in the United States, 1776–1850*. Ithaca, NY: Cornell University Press, 1987.

———. "Representation and the Removal of State Capitals, 1776–1812." *JAH* 74, no. 4 (March 1988): 1239–56.

———. "Women and Party Conflict in the Early Republic." In Pasley, Robertson, and Waldstreicher, *Beyond the Founders*, 107–28.

Zaret, David. *Origins of Democratic Culture: Printing, Petitions, and the Public Sphere in Early-Modern England*. Princeton, NJ: Princeton University Press, 2000.

Zierden, Martha A., and Bernard L. Herman. "Charleston Townhouses: Archaeology, Architecture, and the Urban Landscape, 1750–1850." In *Landscape Archaeology: Reading and Interpreting the American Historical Landscape*, edited by Rebecca Yamin and Karen Bescherer Metheny, 193–227. Knoxville: University of Tennessee Press, 1996.

Zobel, Hiller B. *The Boston Massacre*. New York: W. W. Norton and Co., 1970.

Zuckerman, Michael. *Peaceable Kingdoms: New England Towns in the Eighteenth Century*. New York: Alfred A. Knopf, 1970.

INDEX

Oyster Club, 72
  political orientation of, 75
  satire on, 76
  Social Club (N.Y.), 77, 97
  Society for the Promotion of Useful
    Knowledge, 75
  Society for the Reformation of
    Manners, 76, 93
  types of, 72
  women in, 70
Coalitions, 5–6
  in Newport, 118
  Patriot, 5–6
  urban, 14, 222
Coercion, 166, 171
Coercive Acts, 18, 60, 213. *See also*
    Intolerable Acts
Colden, Cadwallader, 81–82, 85, 93
Collectivism, 29
Collins, John, 114, 126, 129–30, 132
Colonial laws, 20
Colonies, 3, 64, 85, 95–96, 98
  as self-governing, 10
Colville, Alexander, 39–40
Commemorations, 223–24
Committee of Forty-Three, 199
Committee of Nineteen, 197–98
Committees of Correspondence, 57,
    199
Common Sense (Paine), 95, 204–5
Communication. *See also* Newspapers
  Atlantic web of, 67
  on Boston waterfront, 27–28
  in cities, 8–9, 12
  in clubs, 77
  in households, 144
  informal networks of, 55
  intercolonial, through taverns, 85,
    95–96, 98
  network of Charleston, 150
  networks, 57
  in New York City, 66
  political mobilization and, 67
  transatlantic networks, 123–24
Community, 3
  of Boston waterfront, 14, 25, 27–28
  response, 57
  weakening control over, 71
Conflict, 35, 39
  on Boston waterfront, 61
Congregation Yeshuat Israel, 118

Congregationalists, 104, 106. *See also*
    First Congregational Church
    (Newport); Second Congregational
    Church (Newport)
  Baptists v., 120, 125–29, 258n111
  "infant baptism" and, 258n111
  opposed to Great Britain, 123
  opposition to, 129–30
  in Philadelphia, 126
Consumption, 20
  by blacks, 157
  in Charleston households, 149–50,
    155–56
  by whites, 157
  by women, 158
Continental Army, 214–15
Continental Congress (1774), 12, 21,
    60, 162
  adjournment of, 202
  at Carpenter's Hall, 201
  delegates to, 198, 199, 200
  Philadelphia meeting, 172
  secrecy of, 201
Continental Congress (1775), 203
Conversion, 114
  among blacks, 137–38, 260n146
Cooper, Myles, 95
Cooper, Samuel, 61
Coreligionists, 100, 114, 124
Corruption, 117
Countermobilization, 8, 13, 16–17, 51,
    63, 93, 94, 122, 127, 144, 208,
    213, 221
  at Trinity Church (Newport), 104,
    131
Court House (Philadelphia), 174–77,
    175f, 176f, 185f, 211
  1742 election riot at, 177
  as inaccessible, 179
  satire aimed at, 184
  as unprotected, 193
Crèvecoeur, J. Hector St. John de, 73,
    78, 156
Crowd action, 14–15, 40, 44, 53, 84,
    93, 170–71, 221
  boat burning as, 55
  against British government, 38
  in Newport, 41
  tarring and feathering as, 55
  Whig, 95
Cruger, John, 88

Franklin, Benjamin, 29, 123, 182,
    188–90, 194
  as agent, 186, 188–89
  on cities, 216
  satire about, 189
Fraunces (or Francis), Samuel, 65, 83
Fraunces' Tavern, 66f
Free Negroes, 166
"Free thinking," 116
French Revolution, 220
Friendly Society of House Carpenters,
    76

Gadsden, Christopher, 152, 158, 162,
    167, 219
Gage, Thomas, 22, 88, 213, 217
Gailer, George, 53, 55
Galloway, Joseph, 183, 186–90, 198,
    201, 202, 211
Geneva Club, 69
George III, 22, 33, 60, 197, 202
Glen, James, 146, 156
Glorious Revolution (1688), 207
Goddard, William, 95, 96
Gold, Robert, 40
Golden Hill riot, 91, 92
Goodwin, Benjamin, 45, 46
Gordon, William, 64
Governmental oppression, 37
Gray, Samuel, 53
Graydon, Alexander, 65, 71, 72, 73,
    89, 179
Great Britain. See also British Empire;
    British troops; Imperial crisis;
    Imperial encroachment; Imperial
    policies; Parliament
  Congregationalists opposing, 123
  declaring independence from, 204
  as matriarchal, 154
  radical resistance to, 61
Greene, Nathanael, 129–30
Greenleaf, Stephen, 90
Greenough, John, 30
Grenville, George, 39
Grogshops, 64, 88
  illegal, 65, 166

Halifax (George Montagu-Dunk), 2nd
    Earl of, 10
Hallowell, Benjamin, 29, 41
Hambright, John, 183

Hamilton, Alexander (Dr.), 64, 70, 94
  on drinking, 73
  on New Yorkers, 72
  on Newport, 112
Hamilton, Alexander (treasury
    secretary), 218, 220
Hamilton, James, 4
Hammond, Pollipus, 139
Hancock, John, 23, 29, 31, 57
  as Boston's greatest patron, 45
  defiance by, 46–47
  economic power of, 33
  influence of, 30
Harrison, Joseph, 44, 46
Harrison, Peter, 110
Hart, Casper, 89
Hart, Oliver, 163
Hatch, Jabez, 32
Hays, Moses, 132
Hazard, Ebenezer, 156
Henshaw, Joshua, 30
Henshaw, Joshua, Jr., 46
Hewes, George R. T., 28, 31, 53, 57
Hewes, Samuel, 31
"Hillsborough paint," 50
An Historical Essay on the English
    Constitution (Hulme), 204
Honyman, James, 119, 136
Honyman, Robert, 96, 97
Hood, Zacharias, 81
Hooton, John, Jr., 57
Hopkins, Caleb, 45, 46
Hopkins, Samuel, 105–6, 117, 134,
    135–36, 138–40
Hopkins, Stephen, 131
Households. See also Charleston
    households
  as basic social unit, 144–45
  communication in, 144
Howard, Martin, Jr., 41, 122
Howard, Samuel, 57
Howard, William, 85, 86
Howe, Edward C., 57
Huger, Isaac, 166
Hughes, Hugh, 85
Hughes, John, 189–90, 194
Hughson, John, 69
Hulme, Obadiah, 204
Hulton, Ann, 47
Hulton, Henry, 44, 53
Hume, David, 77, 200

Lexington and Concord, battles of, 22, 60, 96, 202–3, 214
Liberty, 95, 106. *See also* Sons of Liberty
   of conscience, 117
   impressment and, 47
   public, 120
Liberty Pole, 90*f*, 223, 252*n*138
   in New York City, 89–90, 92
Liberty riot (1768), 18, 46–47
   aftermath of, 49
Liberty Tree, 60, 213, 220, 252*n*138
   in Boston, 44
Lilly, Theophilus, 52
Livingston, Peter R., 91
Livingston, Philip, 80
Livingston, Robert R., 81
Livingston, William, 75–76, 78–79, 93
Lloyd, Caleb, 43
London, 6, 9, 66, 106, 123–24, 188–89
Long Wharf (Boston), 23, 52
   British troops landing on, 24*f*
   proprietors of, 31
Lopez, Aaron, 118, 121, 132
Lords of Treasury, 25
Lovell, James, 215
Loyal Nine, 41
Loyalists, 16–17, 22, 62, 63, 94, 130, 164, 170, 214, 218
Lush, John, 67
Lyndon, Phyllis, 137

"Macaronis," 82
Macaulay, Catherine, 123
Mackay, William, 32, 45
Mackraby, Alexander, 64
Maier, Pauline, 83
Malcolm, John, 53, 55
Malcom, Daniel, 44–46
Manigault, Anne, 161
Manigault, Gabriel, 161
Manning, James, 126
Marchant, Henry, 123–24, 130
Marginal groups, 15, 142
Mariners
   of Boston waterfront, 27, 31–32
   New York Marine Society, 76
   resistance by, 29, 40
   tavernkeepers and, 67
Marshall, Christopher, 197, 203
Matchet, John, 45, 46, 52

Matlack, Timothy, 98, 210
Maxson, John, 130
Mayhew, Jonathan, 105, 114
McDougall, Alexander, 62–63, 80, 93
   imprisonment of, 91–92
McKean, Thomas, 205, 210
McMasters, Patrick, 53
Mechanics, 7
   Boston, 30, 51
   Charleston, 163–64, 168
   Philadelphia, 197–98, 199
Meetinghouses, 19, 104. *See also* Churches
   Baptist, 106
   Moravian, 109–10, 134
   Quaker, 106–7
   size/members of, 228
Mein, John, 51
Mellen, Mary, 114
Memory, of political mobilization, 223–24. *See also* Commemorations
Merchant Coffee House, 84
Merchants
   of Boston waterfront, 27–31, 38, 49–52
   business of, 50
   Charleston, 143
   in cities, 7
   in colonial courts, 39
   resistance by, 40, 51
   at State House (Pennsylvania), 192–93
Meserve, George, 43
Military mobilization
   political mobilization and, 97
   in State House Yard, 203
Military occupation
   of Boston, 23, 58, 60, 126, 214
   of Charleston, 214
   in cities, 8, 213–14
   impact of, 217
   of New York City, 214
   of Newport, 131, 214
   of Philadelphia, 214, 217
Minott, George, 30
Mobilization, 33. *See also* Countermobilization; Political mobilization
   of Charleston women, 158
   ecumenical, 140

Noble, James, 31
Nonimportation movements, 5, 16, 42, 44, 50–51, 154–60, 191–93
    associations, 57
    of Charleston women, 159–61
    Sons of Liberty and, 57
    of women, 134
North Enders (Boston), 41, 45
"Nothingarians," 115, 116, 141

"Old Colonial System," 35
Old Lights, 115
Oliver, Andrew, 41
Oliver, Peter, 19, 134
O'Neal, Catherine, 70
Osborn, Sarah, 104, 137
    female society of, 135
    on "Yoke of Bondage," 136
Otis, James, 39
Otis, Jonathan, 115
Out of doors politics
    Adams, John, on, 203
    in Boston, 191
    defined, 173
    discouraged in cities, 222
    as dominant force, 198
    in New York City, 191
    orderly, 196
    in Philadelphia, 172–212
    political mobilization by, 174
    protests, 184
    as representative, 174
    in State House Yard, 211, 223
Oyster Club, 72

Pacifism, 131
Packet boats, 66
Pain, Benjamin, 67
Paine, Thomas, 95, 169, 172, 204–5, 206, 215
Pamphlets, 184, 191, 200
Parliament, 6, 10–11, 17, 186, 188–89, 194, 195
    cities and, 11
    questioning authority of, 156, 173, 198
    rejection of, 172
Paterson, Robert, 52
Patriarchy, 157, 161
Patriots, 62. *See also* Radicals; Whigs
    ideology, 17

leaders, 18
    mobilization, 131
Patronage, 33
Paxton, Charles, 41, 44
Paxton uprising, 184
Peck, Samuel, 57
Peckom, Timothy, 115
Pemberton, John, 109, 126, 127–28
Penn, John, 184, 197
Penn, Thomas, 186
Pennsylvania Assembly
    broadside protest against, 208
    delegates to, 205–6
    elected representatives of, 200
    frustration with, 183
    indoor politics of, 188
    oligarchic nature of, 172, 183, 195, 205
    open debates in, 194–95, 210
    power of, 200, 209
    Quaker dominated, 177, 182–83
    radicals in, 206
Pennsylvania Chronicle, 191
Pennsylvania constitutional convention, 210–11
Pennsylvania Gazette, 183
Pennsylvania Packet, 196
"Perfect anarchy," 83
Pettit, Charles, 188
Philadelphia, 4, 6–7, 9, 219
    committee movement, 202, 203
    Congregationalists in, 126
    Continental Congress in, 172
    Declaration of Independence in, 209
    elections, 10, 177, 182
    during imperial crisis, 201
    against imperial policies, 190–91
    imperial policies in, 189
    independence in, 205, 206–7, 209
    mechanics, 197–98, 199
    military occupation of, 214, 217
    mutiny in, 218
    out of doors politics in, 172–212
    political gatherings in, 14, 21
    Quakers, 185*f*
    radicals, satire about, 191–92, 202
    1742 election riot in, 10, 177
    Stamp Act riots in, 189–90
    town meetings, 172, 190, 195–96, 198, 207
Philipse, Adolphe, 79

Philosophical Society Hall
(Philadelphia), 203
Pinckney, Eiliza Lucas, 158
Pitt, William (1st Earl of Chatham),
88, 252n138
Pitts, James, 30, 57
Pitts, Lendall, 57
Planters, 143, 169, 171
slaves and, 156–57
social patterns of, 145
Pluralism, 114, 126, 131, 208
of Newport, 99, 114, 126, 208
rebellion and, 118
urban, 80
Political mobilization, 5–6, 14, 15, 17,
20, 22, 87, 187
alcohol and, 78
on Boston waterfront, 25
challenges to, 13–18, 49, 121, 128,
208
in churches, 133
in cities, 221
city dwellers as minority in, 213
communication and, 67
face-to-face persuasion and, 127
Laurens, Henry, and, 143
memory of, 223–24
military mobilization and, 97
nature of, 6
in Newport, 124
by out of doors politics, 174
religious zeal and, 100
taverns for, 99
tools for, 14, 93, 94, 127, 203, 210,
212, 221
waterfront for, 8, 99
by women, 134, 161
Political participation, 5, 14–15, 19,
49, 194–95, 222
Political power
in cities, 7
in State House (Pennsylvania),
182
Politics. *See also* Indoor politics; Out of
doors politics
religion and, 118, 222
urban, 219
Popular tyranny, 162
Popular Whigs, 79, 80
Populations, 3–5, 25, 225
Presbyterians, 8, 19, 119, 125, 184

Press gangs, 36–37, 39, 46
Adams, Samuel, on, 37
animosity towards, 40
"Pretense of Zeal," 122
Privateering, 67
Proctor, Edward, 52, 56
Propertied white men, 16
Providence Gazette, 120
Provincial Whigs, 79, 80, 83
Public good, 14, 51, 77, 117–18
Public houses. *See* Taverns
"Public liberty," 120
Puritans, 64, 120
Purkitt, Henry, 57
Putnam, Rufus, 215

Quaker Meeting House (Newport),
106–7, 108f, 109
Quakers, 8, 43, 64, 101, 106–7, 142
antislavery cause of, 140–41
Callender as, 114
meetinghouses, 106–7, 174, 178
as pacifists, 131
in Pennsylvania Assembly, 177,
182–83
of Philadelphia, 19, 185f
Stiles and, 127–28, 131
women, 109, 134
Quartering Acts, 12, 88
Quebec Act, 127
Quincy, Josiah, Jr., 150, 163, 166, 170,
195

Racism, 117
Radicals, 199, 202. *See also* Patriots;
Whigs
meeting in State House Yard, 193
in Pennsylvania Assembly, 206
resisting Great Britain, 61
Ramsay, David, 156, 159
Rattray Green (Charleston), 147–50,
149f, 151f, 155–56, 262n20
Regan, John, 32
Rebellion
pluralism and, 118
spirit of, 40
Redwood Library (Newport), 118–19
Reed, Joseph, 195, 196, 201, 205
Refinement, of Charleston households,
149–50
Regulators, 162

military mobilization in, 203
out of doors politics in, 211, 223
radicals meeting in, 193
wall around, 180–82
Stephens, Zingo, 137
Stiles, Ezra, 105–6, 111, 114, 115,
119–20, 134
black parishioners of, 137–38
on cities, 216
as "Doctor Propheticus," 120
as Enlightenment thinker, 123
as key resister, 123–25
preaching of, 116, 260n141
Quakers and, 127–28, 131
satire about, 129
Stillman, Samuel, 130
Story, William, 41
Stranger, John, 86
Strikes, 222
Sugar Act, 11, 39, 67
Swift, Henry, 41
Synagogues, 110

Tarbox, Jonathan, 28, 37
Tarring and feathering, 53, 54f, 57, 164
as Boston waterfront justice, 54–55,
244n92
as crowd action, 55
transmission of, 55
Tavernkeepers, 65, 92
mariners and, 67
women, 68
Taverns. See also New York City taverns
for amusement, 64
on Boston waterfront, 32
class stratification of, 67, 73, 75,
222, 245n2
for political mobilization, 99, 245n2
as popular gathering places, 62
for public business, 64
Tax Taking and Rate Books (Boston
1790), 27
Taxation, 27, 49, 58, 67, 68, 196
Taxation without representation, 68
Tea. See also Boston Tea Party (1773)
protests, 5
tables, 159–61
Tea Act (1773), 11–12, 55, 93, 159,
160f, 195
Temple, John, 44
Tennent, William, 159, 163

Test Act, 132
Thomson, Charles, 190, 192, 193, 201
Thurston, Gardner, 106, 130, 139
Tilghman, James, 209
Toasts
bumper, 3, 73, 76
rituals, 72, 73
Todd, Robert, 70, 73
Tories. See Loyalists
Touro Synagogue, 108, 110–111, 116
Town meetings
Boston, 21, 50, 56, 213
Newport, 21, 126
Philadelphia, 172, 190, 195–96, 198,
207
Townshend Acts, 11, 90, 124, 154–55,
192
levy of, 43
repeal of, 51
resistance to, 44–45
Townshend, Charles, 11
Trade
in cities, 6–7, 38
"Illicit Traders," 36, 40
slave, 116, 139, 165, 170
sociability and, 145
Transatlantic networks, 123–24
Treaty of Paris (1783), 218
Trinity Church (Newport), 101–2,
103f, 104, 111, 113f, 114
blacks in, 137, 139
countermobilization at, 131
women of, 134
Tryon, William, 97
Tucker, Josiah, 9
Tully, Alan, 79
Tyranny
Jews against, 259n118
legislative, 204
popular, 162
royal, 162

Upham, Edward, 117
Urann, Thomas, 57
Urban coalitions, 14, 222
Urban environment, 13
of Boston waterfront, 28–29
of Charleston, 145
Charleston households as, 145–46
of Newport, 117, 141
Urban pluralism, 80